Psychology for Social Workers

Martin Herbert

First published 1981 by THE BRITISH PSYCHOLOGICAL SOCIETY and THE MACMILLAN PRESS LTD.

Reprinted 1982.

Distributed by The Macmillan Press Ltd, London and Basingstoke. Associated companies and representatives throughout the world.

ISBN 0 333 31866 8 (hard cover)
ISBN 0 333 31878 1 (paper cover)

Printed in Great Britain by A. Wheaton & Co. Ltd.

Note: throughout these texts, the masculine pronouns have been used for succinctness and are intended to refer to both females and males.

The conclusions drawn and opinions expressed are those of the authors. They should not be taken to represent the views of the publishers.

Contents

Foreword

This book is one of a series, the principal aims of which are to illustrate how psychology can be applied in particular professional contexts, how it can improve the skills of practitioners, and how it can increase the practitioners' and students' understanding of themselves.

Psychology is taught to many groups of students and is now integrated within prescribed syllabuses for an increasing number of professions. The existing texts which teachers have been obliged to recommend are typically designed for broad and disparate purposes, and consequently they fail to reflect the special needs of students in professional training. The starting point for the series was the systematic distillation of views expressed in professional journals by those psychologists whose teaching specialisms relate to the applications of psychology. It soon became apparent that many fundamental topics were common to a number of syllabuses and courses; yet in general introductory textbooks these topics tend to be embedded amongst much superfluous material. Therefore, from within the British Psychological Society, we invited experienced teachers and authorities in their field to write review chapters on key topics. Forty-seven chapters covering 23 topics were then available for selection by the series' Volume Editors. The Volume Editors are also psychologists and they have had many years of involvement with their respective professions. In preparing their books, they have consulted formally with colleagues in those professions. Each of their books has its own combination of the specially-prepared chapters, set in the context of the specific professional practice.

Because psychology is only one component of the various training curricula, and because students generally have limited access to learned journals and specialist texts, our contributors to the series have restricted their use of references, while at the same time providing short lists of annotated readings. In addition, they have provided review questions to help students organize their learning and prepare for examinations. Further teaching materials, in the form of additional references, projects, exercises and class notes, are available in Tutor Manuals prepared for each book. A comprehensive tutorial text ('Psychology and People'), prepared by the Series Editors, combines in a single volume all the key topics, together with their associated teaching materials.

It is intended that new titles will be added to the series and that existing titles will be revised in the light of changing requirements. Evaluative and constructive comments, bearing on any aspect of the series, are most welcome and should be addressed to us at the BPS in Leicester.

In devising and developing the series we have had the good fortune to benefit from the advice and support of Dr Halla Beloff, Professor Philip Levy, Mr Allan Sakne and Mr John Winckler. A great burden has been borne by Mrs Gail Sheffield, who with skill, tact and courtesy, has managed the production of the series: to her and her colleagues at the BPS headquarters and at the Macmillan Press, we express our thanks.

Antony J. Chapman
UWIST, Cardiff

Anthony Gale
University of Southampton

May 1981

Introduction
Martin Herbert

The central theme running through the many definitions of
the social work task, no matter what the school of thought,
is a statement about a genuine, humanely motivated attempt
to assist people to cope with the troubles and crises of
everyday life in a way which does not diminish their worth
or dignity as human beings.

Pincus and Minahan (1973), authors of a highly influential textbook, list among among the purposes of social work:
(i) enhancing the problem-solving and coping capacities of
people; (ii) linking people with systems and providing them
with resources, services and opportunities; (iii) promoting
the effective and humane operation of these systems, and
(iv) contributing to the development and improvement of
social policy. With a remit as broadly conceived as this, it
is not surprising that social workers feel confused about
the nature of their contemporary social work task and the
overinclusive knowledge it seems to imply. The knowledge
base of social work, after all, has to encompass the facts
and theories, skills and attitudes, necessary for effective
and efficient practice. That practice might have the social
worker acting variously (and at different times) as therapist, mediator, resource-mobilizer, resource-generator,
social broker, advocate, co-ordinator, teacher and friend
(see Yelloly, 1975). All this calls for a remarkable
flexibility of response and conceptual sophistication.

The social worker's role involves even further diversification in that interventions are directed towards individuals, groups, communities and organizations. Whatever
else is required, social work theory and practice obviously
call for a significant input on the psychological principles
affecting both individuals and groups.

As knowledge in the psychological disciplines increases,
it is important that social work practitioners are aware of
new (as well as tried) theories and technologies; they
should be able to evaluate them in terms of their usefulness
in furthering social work goals. A familiarity with (and
ability to evaluate) new inputs of psychological knowledge
is not enough. The practitioner should be able to identify
and clarify different ideological positions, so as to
liberate himself from undue reliance on any particular
stance which could deflect him from evolving novel solutions

or flexible ways of working in the light of specific demands of the tasks which face him.

Psychology is an inordinately untidy and many-sided subject. The psychologist himself is likely to be wondering how it is possible to keep up to date with, let alone evaluate and integrate, the theoretical and factual outpouring from his discipline. The knowledge is often fragmented and the psychologist is presented with the difficult task of achieving a 'working synthesis': a 'map' to chart his thinking and actions. If he has not done this for himself then he cannot expect his students - adrift in a sea of strange and apparently disparate concepts - to 'get it together'. This in turn makes the task of connecting psychological theory and social work practice highly problematic.

And therein lies a painful dilemma for the inexperienced lecturer. I can only speak as a teacher of psychology, but I imagine that most social scientists who are serious about teaching social work students (a commitment requiring a serious study of the complexities of the social work task) suffer from déjà vu: a disconcerting sense of failure at the end of the umpteenth revision of their course. The hapless lecturer has probably tried the role of courier, the Grand Tour of Psychology approach. It parallels the 'Guided Tour of Europe' experience: 'I know this is Pisa because it's Wednesday'. Like those passengers 'doing' Europe in three weeks, his charges disembark feeling exhausted, amnesic and none the wiser. So he changes direction (and the metaphor) and tries the gourmet approach: he introduces his customers to a few choice morsels, allowing them time to savour the rich fare; he intends (inductively) to educate their palates. But still the consumers complain; so many significant items are absent from the menu, and, in any event, what has such a selective diet got to do with ordinary everyday eating? It is a Catch-22 situation!

After many false starts, I would see my task as a psychology teacher (and as editor of this volume) as providing a 'map' of psychology, and its possible application in social work assessment and intervention. It is impossible to teach everything, but I would hope, by way of my own introductory section, and the more elaborate and detailed specialist contributions, to introduce social workers to 'map-reading' skills: in other words, the symbols, language, and relevant principles of psychology. Such an approach also gives them personal access to the wider psychological literature. It is, in general, a relatively small-scale map that I give in Part I; a guide on which I draw fairly broad features to give a picture of that part of psychology which throws into relief the problems that social workers meet. In the specialist contributions written by professional psychologists (Part II), the authors have provided the sharper focus of an 'ordinance survey map', putting in finer and important points in detail.

My aim in planning this psychology volume for social workers is to provide them with the wherewithal to carry out

'psychologically informed' social work. I wish to encourage
social work practitioners and students to identify and
understand ('internalize') a relatively small number of
general and operational psychological principles and skills
which are necessary for effective practice in a variety of
situations and changing circumstances. By internalization I
mean the assimilation of psychological ideas into the
'organic' construing system of the practitioner, so that his
psychological thinking is not simply 'tacked on' as an
afterthought. Such a desideratum poses a daunting problem
in terms of methods and imaginative styles of teaching and
learning. Psychology deserves to be part of the core curriculum of a social work course. Whether it attains this
status or is pushed into an ancillary role chiefly depends
on the skill and commitment with which it is taught.

Despite the plethora of social work tasks described
above, the social worker is still viewed primarily as
someone who works directly with individual clients. Rightly
or wrongly, the modern social worker tends to view casework
as a psycho-therapeutic treatment process, in which the
major emphasis is on the casework relationship and direct
counselling or therapeutic work with the client. It has been
argued (Yelloly, 1980) that social work's commitment to a
therapeutic person-orientated ideology, especially psychodynamic psychology, may have inhibited its study of, and
involvement in, those social and situational factors which
themselves create or contribute to personal distress.
Perhaps the relative lack of development of theory related
to these aspects bears this out.

How is it possible to keep up to date with, let alone
evaluate and integrate, the many theories and facts? Lewis
(1972) states that ultimately the test of the value of the
knowledge used will be its effectiveness in practice: the
results achieved in relation to the original goals as
evaluated by the practitioner and client. He insists that if
what we do is based on what we claim to know and value and
is intended to achieve preferred ends, then the results of
our professional actions should test our claims and show us
how to improve our efforts. Sadly, there has been only too
often a cavalier attitude towards (not to mention ignorance
of) the evidence for competing claims. The discussion of
scientific method (chapter 1) is a reminder of the need for
empirical confirmation of theories. Having said that, it is
necessary to add that competence involves not only the
skilled use of particular methods, but also the ability to
employ theoretical knowledge in various practical settings
in an imaginative fashion. I would link the word imaginative
to the concept of intuition.

The arts as well as the sciences are the progenitors (in
social work) of practice and theory. Some of the students
who come from an arts background feel themselves to be at
a disadvantage compared with those from a science training.
I would deny this! Henry Maas (1978) reminds us that: 'In
large measure, our Social Work practice - whether policy
development or direct work at the community level - is a

craft.' Each art has its technical side; the most fruitful
communication of those who work primarily with symbols (the
artists) and those who work primarily with sensed data (the
scientists) occurs in some of the crafts. I would deprecate
the tendency of some social workers and social work educators to argue as if the values, language and perspectives of
one part of social work are so radically different from the
other, so mutually exclusive, that they must alienate the
tender-minded (the intuitive 'artists') from the tough-
minded (the 'scientists'). Both the arts and the sciences
'involve intellect, intense creativity and passionate
commitment to purpose and to the means for its attainment'
(Maas, 1978).

The eminent personality theorist, Gordon Allport,
insisted on a marriage of the 'nomothetic' and 'idiographic'
approaches for a true understanding of the person and his
situation (Allport, 1937). The nomothetic disciplines seek
general laws and employ only those procedures admitted by
the exact sciences. Scientists can be overbearing in their
arrogant assumption that the only path to truth lies through
scientific method. Notcutt (1953) railed against 'scien-
tism', the pharisaical insistence on the letter rather than
the spirit of scientific method. Although there are many
routes to truth, psychology has been very dependent on
scientific method (as we shall see) to lift it out of the
rather unprofitable realm of 'armchair philosophy'.

I have emphasized the individual orientation of psychology so far. However, a person's behaviour is influenced by
the surrounding environment. The truth of this statement
must have struck home on many occasions for the social
worker who spends so much of his time visiting clients in
institutions. It does not take much sensitivity to see the
enormous effects on, say, children or the aged, brought
about by living in a caring and thoughtfully-run institution
as opposed to an indifferent or neglectful one (see Orford's
chapter 16 on institutional climates). Small group and
organization theory have a considerable contribution to make
to social work practice. For example, social psychology
offers information about the small group situation, where
individuals influence each other through face-to-face
interaction. The experimental study of social influence in
this kind of situation has been stimulated, on the one hand,
by the fact that in society a great deal of work and
decision making occur in a group setting, and on the other,
by the supposition that within a group, factors are at work
determining individual behaviour which are unique to that
setting.

Mary Barker (in press) makes the point that social work
students have been shown to be high in sensitivity and
concern for others but low in logical thinking and intellectual discrimination. They have needed - in situations of
great difficulty and complexity - to develop responsiveness
to feelings, flexibility and resourcefulness in finding
resources which fit the individual, not the system. Barker

comments that these are not the attitudes of a good 'organization man'. Probably the preferred work setting for such social workers would be a 'service organization' in which they have autonomy to work with their own case-load, drawing on the agency for salary, expenses, and the right to prescribe the resources their clients require. The actuality is that social workers work mainly in fewer, larger departments; they increasingly work to defined priorities, which clarify the 'rationing' element in their task. They have more structured and controlled roles towards many fellow employees, ranging from Assistant Directors to home-helps; their work is subjected to a degree of formalization and routine procedures, common in large organizations. Chapter 15, by Payne, describes the nature of organizations, and why they are the way they are. External and internal influences affect the structure of organizations and, in turn, the roles and behaviour of their members and management. These, and the nature of professional roles, are described.

This volume ranges from the microlevel of analysis (Herbert, chapter 3, on sensory psychology) to the macrolevel (Frude, chapter 10, on the family, and Payne on organizations); and from an introduction to that most individually-orientated skill, interviewing (Wicks in chapter 20), to those important group and socially-related skills (Argyle in chapter 14). It is hoped that this coverage - emphasizing the links between theory and practice - will help the social workers in their onerous but essential social work task.

References

Allport, G.W. (1937)
Personality: A psychological interpretation. New York: Holt, Rinehart & Winston.

Barker, M. (in press)
Organization theory. In P. Hardiker and M. Barker (eds), Theories of Practice in Social Work. London: Academic Press.

Lewis, H. (1972)
Developing a programme responsive to new knowledge and values. In E.J. Mullen and J.R. Dumpson (eds), Evaluation of Social Intervention. San Francisco: Jossey-Bass.

Maas, H. (1980)
Research and the knowledge base. In Discovery and Development in Social Work Education. Vienna: International Association of Schools of Social Work Publications.

Notcutt B. (1953)
The Psychology of Personality. New York: Philosophical Library.

Pincus, A. and Minahan, A. (1973)
Social Work Practice: Model and method. Itasca, Ill.: Peacock Publications.

Yelloly, M.A. (1975)
Ideologies in British social work. Unpublished PhD Thesis, School of Social Work, University of Leicester.

Yelloly, M.A. (1980)
Social Work Theory and Psychoanalysis. London: Van Nostrand Reinhold.

Part one

Concepts and Concerns of Psychology

1

What is Psychology?
Martin Herbert

'The age of anxiety' is an expression commonly applied to
the turbulent times in which we live. This somewhat melo-
dramatic label for our day and age does contain a grain of
truth. In a period of rapid change and great technological
sophistication, many people feel that they are not in
control of their own lives, that they are not really in
touch with other people. Somehow the person - the individual
- has become lost in what seems to be a vast, impersonal and
somewhat meaningless world. And here is the first attraction
of the discipline of psychology: psychology is basically
about the individual person!

Social workers know only too well how many persons
(especially women) are on tranquillizers or anti-depressant
drugs in order simply 'to keep going', for twentieth-century
man finds himself at the centre of a paradox. In a period
when he knows so much about the laws of the physical universe, he knows relatively little about the workings of his
mental world. There seems to be a frightening discrepancy
between man's understanding and mastery of his material
environment and his knowledge and control of himself. His
psychological awareness is still rudimentary. Nevertheless,
psychology (for all its limitations and immaturity) has much
to offer in the way of answers to serious human conflicts.
More and more institutions (clinics, educational centres,
industries and governmental agencies) are turning to
psychology for solutions to problems that beset individuals
in their home life, at school, at work, and in their social
and political existence.

We have said that psychology is an immature discipline.
But why should this be? Man has always been interested in
himself. It has long been said that the proper study of
mankind is man! So why do we not know more about the
psychological universe that exists within man? This is a
crucial question. To answer it we have to realize that
certain ways (or methods) of answering psychological questions are more fruitful than others. Lewis' text (1960)
explains how progress towards understanding man has been
enhanced by empirical enquiry and scientific method.

To appreciate this point we must begin at the beginning
and look at psychology:

* in terms of its past and present definitions;
* in terms of its changing subject matter.

It has been said of psychology that it has a short history but a long past. What this means becomes clear when we look at one of the contemporary definitions of psychology: 'Psychology is the scientific study of mind and behaviour.' Two of these terms (study and mind) belong to psychology's ancient past; the other two (scientific and behaviour) are part of its recent history. We have to go back in time to find the origins of this discipline. The word 'psychology' is made up of two Greek words:

* 'psyche' which means soul or mind;
* 'logos', meaning word or study.

PSYCHE: from time immemorial man has been preoccupied with the world of spirit and mind, fascinated and frightened by his nightmares, emotions, thoughts and fantasies. In other words he has tried to understand, in a personal and informal sense, those of his experiences which can be properly categorized as 'psychological events'. And for thousands of years men have been asking and trying to answer questions - in a more formal way, in treatises and books - about human and animal nature. These can be described appropriately as 'psychological questions'.

LOGOS: it is less than a century ago that psychology emerged as a separate discipline: that is, as a distinct area of study (logos), and the first real psychologists appeared as a 'profession', separate from the many academics and other groups who had speculated about things of the mind. Philosophers ('lovers of wisdom'), theologians, writers and artists have always sought to unravel man's understanding and mastery of his material environment and his knowledge and control of himself. The new enquirers were not simply interested in psychological reflection from the vantage point of an armchair. Their place was in the laboratory; their methods of study were systematic and scientific.

Although psychology's graduation as a science is so recent, its beginnings as a topic of serious study go back, like so many other subjects (notably education, philosophy, architecture, politics and history), to Ancient Greece. Science itself started there. The Greeks were fascinated by the problem of causation. The early philosophers searched for a material or physical cause of the world. The four elements, earth, air, fire and water - separately or in combination - were given this honour. One school of thought, the cosmologists, postulated an atomic theory of the universe. They were reductionists in the sense that they tried to reduce the physical universe into the irreducible elements of which they believed it to be made. Psychologists, many centuries later, were to apply an atomistic reductionist analysis to behaviour as we see later.

These early beginnings of the physical sciences were the first steps in a triumphant journey towards the present-day exploration of the physical universe in space itself. Somehow man's exploration of the mental world was left far behind. Although the Ancient Greeks began the process of asking psychological questions about the nature of such things as knowledge, happiness and justice, during the centuries which followed scholars did not evolve a scientific way of looking at these problems as had been the case for the physical universe.

The subject matter of psychology

This delay means that we are still asking the same sorts of questions as the ancients. A founder-figure of modern psychology - the American theorist Edward L. Thorndike (1911, 1932) - reduced psychological questions to four topics:

* the nature of the different kinds of thoughts and feelings;
* the purposes which they serve in life;
* the laws which govern their behaviour and that of the bodily states and acts connected with them;
* the ways in which they are related to the actions of the brain.

These questions contain certain assumptions about mental life and the mind and body.

The nature of mental life (mind and body)

In trying to understand himself and others, man has evolved a psychological vocabulary which helps him to make sense of his world, and one of the objectives of this introductory section is to provide the reader with the more important terms and concepts in that vocabulary. This he does by ordering and classifying his experiences. He experiences, thinks, desires, regrets and remembers. These 'events' he classifies as being of one kind (mental events). He feels pain, sensuous pleasure, cold and heat; he sometimes gets breathless, exhausted and ill. These 'events' are conceptualized as being of another kind (bodily events).

The point must be stressed that human behaviour is a complex combination of acts, feelings, thoughts and motives. The distinctions we make between body and mind and the further sub-divisions of mental life we make use of, such as emotion, intellect, drives (motives) and so on, are artificial and matters of convenience. These physical and mental processes are essentially indivisible, interacting and interdependent. We have to isolate them so as to study them and talk about them.

This point of view was not always accepted. There were endless, and somewhat futile, debates about the precise nature and relationship of body and mind. The extreme theory that mind and body are quite separate (called Cartesian dualism after the philosopher who formulated it: René Descartes, 1596-1650), is summed up in the jingle: 'What is mind? No matter. What is matter? Never mind.' Descartes gave the soul a place in the body - which was likened to a machine - but he did not think of it as a 'thing'. This notion of what might be called a 'ghost in the machine' led psychological inquiry up a long-lasting cul-de-sac of inconclusive speculation. Because the idea lingered on that the psyche (mind/soul) is a non-material substance, it was assumed that the methods of the natural sciences - observation and laboratory experimentation - could only be applied to man's bodily processes, and were inappropriate for studying his mind.

Public versus private events

The distinction of body and mind has important implications. As we saw earlier on, contemporary psychology is committed today to the scientific approach to knowledge. And the knowledge of our bodily activities including speech are, so to speak, visible to others and therefore public. But knowledge of our mental functions, our plans, ideas, and wishes, are hidden from others. They remain invisible to others and private, unless we wish to tell others about them.

Introspection - looking inwards on one's own thoughts - was thought to be the proper method of studying these private events and came to be known as 'armchair psychology'. Although the method provided some useful information, and adaptations of the technique are still in use today, as a major technique of a major school of psychology, it proved a blind alley. Such highly individual and subjective methods of study are unreliable and wide generalizations about human behaviour are not possible. Mental life, in any event, is incapable of analysis on such a restricted basis.

The really crucial milestone in the history of psychology came with the rejection of a clear-cut distinction between mental and bodily events. Psychologists began to focus the powerful spotlight of science on the bodily manifestations of man's psychological existence. They adapted the general methods of science to investigate (in particular) his public psychological acts: that is, his behaviour. This is reflected in a definition of psychology which some psychologists would prefer to the one we referred to earlier. They would define psychology quite simply as the scientific study of behaviour. The word mind is left out!

The absence of the word 'mind' may come as a surprise to you. Most of us still think of psychology as the study of 'mind'. Surely this modern technical definition of psychology is no more than semantic juggling? It should become clear why the word 'mind' is inappropriate in the context of modern psychology when we look at each of the terms in our definition: 'scientific' and 'behaviour'. Behaviour is what a person does and says, and it can therefore be seen and heard. Contemporary psychology is, as we shall see, not only a social science, but also one of the biological sciences. Just as the physiologist and zoologist study the form and function of all the members of the animal kingdom, the psychologist investigates the behaviour of animals as well as humans. Man is regarded as a social animal (see Argyle, chapter 14). There are many points in common between human and animal behaviour. Animals show, in elementary forms, some of the processes which make up human behaviour; however, it is misleading to extrapolate too much from animal to human behaviour. The point about our concentration on behaviour is that we can obtain appropriate conditions for the application of scientific methods.

The nature of science

What do we mean when we characterize a discipline as a science?

Science is empirical

This means that it is based upon observations rather than on opinion, belief, prejudice or argument. And it is not simply casual observations which make a science empirical; observations must be reliable which means they must be repeatable and carried out according to a strict set of rules (Popper, 1949). Empirical knowledge, then, is the agreement in reports of repeated observations made by two or more individuals under rigorously specified (controlled) conditions.

Science emphasizes measurement

The history of every scientific discipline is signposted by its attempts to measure with ever greater precision.

Science is systematic

Although data (observations) are the lifeblood of a science, by themselves they are of little value. They have to be put into some order or 'system' so as to make sense of the world.

Can there be a science of mind?

Having described the essential criteria of the scientific approach, can they be applied to 'mind' as such? Can we observe mental processes or measure them?

The problem of mental life

I said earlier that knowledge of our mental functions - our experiences, thoughts, plans, ideas, and wishes - are hidden from others. They remain unknowable to others. Our 'minds' are not entities in the sense that they have a location, and identifiable boundaries. It is not even theoretically possible that with new techniques we shall one day be able to observe the mind. For this reason mind cannot be studied empirically. The same applies to 'mental processes' such as thoughts! Scientists are unable to investigate anything that is outside the range of their senses, or which cannot be brought within this range by means of instruments such as microscopes, cameras, amplifiers, and so on.

The American psychologist, Donald Lewis (1960), predicts (probably quite accurately) that by this time you will be saying 'I think. And I have ideas too. And no psychologist is ever going to convince me of anything different.' Lewis replies, as would other psychologists: 'Of course you think. And so do your neighbours. But the point is that nobody else under any condition whatever, knows what you are thinking, or even if you are thinking, unless you tell him. And if you tell him, right away it is your verbal behavior that is being observed, not your ideas. Again, all we can ever observe directly is behavior.' All this is not to suggest that psychologists ignore what is known as conscious experiences (see Bannister, chapter 9). Private (subjective) processes, such as ideas, constructs, decisions and other aspects of thinking, can only be dealt with scientifically by trying to objectify them (i.e. by looking at their external public manifestations).

The nature of behaviour

Behaviour, as we saw earlier, is what a person does and says (verbal behaviour) and it can therefore be seen and heard, recorded and quantified. Behaviour is not just a series of unco-ordinated, discrete activities. It is a continuing process. Mental processes can only be inferred; they cannot be directly observed. Nevertheless, 'models' of mental processes can be deduced from their effects on behaviour. For example, the nature of intelligence - a highly mentalistic notion - has been deduced from the ways that thousands of individuals perform on tests which are assumed to measure ability. The same kind of analysis has been applied to the concept of personality. We now have, in the definition of behaviour given above, the appropriate conditions for the application of scientific methods.

Psychology as a science

What do we mean when we characterize modern psychology as a science?

Psychology is empirical

This means that it is based upon observations and experimentation rather than on opinion and belief. An example of empirical knowledge in psychology is the repeatedly observed fact that the unspecialized type of intellectual ability (known as 'fluid ability') reaches its maximum at adolescence, whereas a specialized ability (known as 'crystallized ability') may continue to develop throughout adult life.

Psychology emphasizes measurement

Psychology falls far short of the physical sciences in this ideal: nevertheless, it has struggled to quantify the elusive facets of behaviour. In everyday situations we make judgements of people, characteristics, and events in terms of qualities or kinds (e.g. good versus bad, cruel versus kind, intelligent versus unintelligent, strong versus weak and so on). These are:

* qualitative judgements: psychologists also use qualitative categories to describe behaviour, but these are crude judgements and it is not possible to do justice to the richness and complexity of human characteristics by putting them in these pigeon-holes. So they prefer to move on to:
* quantitative description: psychological characteristics also vary in degree (e.g. the IQ - intelligence quotient - is a measure of the degree of intellectual ability). Modern psychology offers many opportunities for the application of mathematics and a training in mathematics (and statistics) is an important component of the psychologist's skills.

Psychology is systematic

Psychology involves making systematic rather than aimless observations. They have to be put into some order or 'system' so as to make sense. They should tell a coherent 'story' about behaviour. The construction of large-scale general systems (or theories) of behaviour has gone out of favour among modern psychologists; nevertheless, they do create limited and precise theories in order to systematize the observations within specific areas of psychology.

Why study psychology?

We look in more detail at some of the terms used in relation to 'scientific method' in the following chapter. What we must now ask is the question: 'What is the objective of studying behaviour?'

Understanding

The questions 'what', 'why', and 'how' are the ones children ask when they wish to understand the world in which they live. These are also the questions psychologists ask in their quest for an understanding of behaviour and, indeed, the questions social workers ask in their attempt to assess and remedy social problems. This is all very well, but you might ask: what is wrong with our everyday answers to questions, our common-sense understanding? Are not we all psychologists in the sense that psychology is simply the application of common sense?

This common lore is a hodge-podge of notions about people. It is made up of some facts, many fallacies and even more misconceptions. These opinions, beliefs and values vary from person to person, but individuals in groups such as families, communities and nations share many of them in common. Because we are brought up with these aphorisms (e.g. 'spare the rod and spoil the child'; 'a woman's place is in the home', etc.) ringing in our ears, we tend to think they are axiomatic (self-evident).

Of course, we must not denigrate common-sense 'theories' too much. A common-sense view of what the world is like, and how people are likely to react to us, serves most of us fairly well in our day-to-day transactions with life. But it is important to remember that there are different levels of understanding (and of explanation) when it comes to investigating behaviour.

And as Harry Kay, President of the Central Council of Education and Training of Social Workers, and incidentally a psychologist, says:

> I am a great believer in commonsense, in relying on the good sense of mankind to 'get it right'. It generally does in the end. But the fact that commonsense may have had it wrong for a few preceding millennia does mean that we need to be on our guard and not be too hasty over the certainty of any answers. For example, at one time everybody knew we lived on a flat world; it was self-evident until someone went to the edge and did not fall off. About the same time, everyone knew that the sun charioted around the earth each day, whilst the earth was the centre of the universe, and so on. As we have come to accept, blood has to be spilt before commonsense accepts change, but eventually it does and yesterday's heresy becomes today's credo, whilst commonsense forgets that it was ever otherwise (Kay, 1978).

A psychologist would usually wish to understand the processes which precede certain behavioural outcomes to the extent that he is able to make accurate predictions on the basis of such knowledge. This is a more precise and technical level of explanation than the 'Aha! Now I've got it' level of understanding most of us are satisfied with in everyday life. Gordon Allport is clear about this. The objective of studying behaviour psychologically (that is to say, scientifically) is to produce 'understanding, prediction, and control above the levels achieved by unaided commonsense' (Allport, 1937).

Science is always in a state of flux; there are no ultimate answers. Principles are continually being defined, tested, reformulated, tested again, and so on. There is always a need for further investigations and extended principles and themes. In this painstaking manner, the frontiers of psychological knowedge are slowly pushed outwards. Although the scientific method is a very valuable way of acquiring new knowledge it does not yield absolute or eternal truth; rather one can say that it reduces uncertainty.

References

Allport, G.W. (1937)
Personality: A psychological interpretation. New York: Holt, Rinehart & Winston.

Kay, H. (1978)

Preface. In J. Radford and D. Rose (eds), The Teaching of Psychology. London: John Wiley.

Lewis, D. (1960)

Quantitative Methods in Psychology. New York: McGraw-Hill.

Popper, K. (1949)

In A. Pap (ed.), Elements of Analytic Philosophy. New York: Macmillan.

Thorndike, E.L. (1911)

Animal Intelligence. New York: Macmillan.

Thorndike, E.L. (1932)

The Fundamentals of Learning. Columbia University, New York: Teachers College.

2

Analysing Behaviour: Basic Components

Martin Herbert

**Introduction: S-R
units and S-R laws**

Before psychologists can apply themselves to any analysis of
behaviour, they need to know what to look for, and how to
look for it. This is the all-important matter of observation. The scientific way of looking at things is to begin
with the most basic units of phenomena. The 'atoms' of the
physical sciences have their equivalent in the so-called S-R
(stimulus-response) units; the atomic laws have their
figurative counterpart in the S-R laws.

Looking for lawfulness in human behaviour

Behaviour is lawful. If it were not so, society would collapse into anarchy. We can rely on most car drivers to
respond to the stimulus of a red traffic light by stopping.
If we could not, chaos would ensue. We can depend on the
vast majority of parents to respond to the stimulus of
a crying child by caring for his needs, otherwise children
would not survive.

  The words 'most' and 'majority' in these statements
about the lawfulness of human behaviour point to a problem
in the study of psychological causation which we shall take
up later.

  In chapter 1, psychology was described as a science that
studies the causes of behaviour in order to achieve understanding, prediction and control. This is the same thing as
saying that psychologists are trying to discover laws of
behaviour. Laws are statements about the regularities, the
order to be found in the world. As such, a law is a statement which describes the relationship between two or more
events.

Basic components of behaviour

In all, there are four particularly vital components which
the social worker needs to identify in order to understand
and analyse behaviour. Any situation in which behaviour
occurs can be analysed fruitfully with the aid of these
components, which are in fact psychological concepts.
Psychological laws often take the form of statements about
the relationship between events called STIMULI (on the one
hand) and RESPONSES (on the other). These are called
stimulus (S)-response (R) laws: for example, 'Given stimulus
Y one would expect response Z', or more economically: 'If Y,
then Z.'

* a STIMULUS (S) is anything (e.g. an event or happening, physical or psychological) that initiates or influences behaviour or arouses a state of conscious awareness; any event, in other words, that activates actions and/or thoughts and/or feelings.
* a RESPONSE (R) is a reaction of (for example) a muscle, gland or (on a larger scale) it may comprise a complex series of actions, elicited by stimulation. Some examples of stimulus-response (S-R) sequences are: (i) I click my fingers suddenly in front of your eyes (physical stimulus); you blink (physical response) and probably say: 'Why did you do that?' (verbal response); (ii) someone smiles (social stimulus) and says 'Hello' (verbal stimulus); you probably respond by smiling back (social response) and replying 'Hello' (verbal response).

There are two more important terms you need for a behaviour analysis:

* drive/motive: anything within or outside the person that created a desire or need. O is the symbol for events such as 'drives' occurring within the organism.
* reinforcement consequences: reinforcers (positive). When certain stimuli closely follow a certain behaviour they increase the probability of that behaviour occurring again in the future. Stimuli that serve this function are called 'positive reinforcers'.

    Reinforcers (negative). Other stimuli (aversive/ punitive events) increase the probability of behaviour occurring again when their removal closely follows that behaviour. These stimuli are called 'negative reinforcers'.

If you wish to understand the behaviour of another person the first thing you should do is try to identify each of the four aspects of the behavioural situation described above.

Analysing responses

Overt behaviour can be studied in terms of responses to various stimuli. Nearly all psychological functions can be described as responses because they are involved in the business of adjusting (adapting) to the environment.

Psychologists put the relationships between Ss, and Rs and Os as follows: $S \rightarrow O \rightarrow R$

$$R = f(O, S)$$
i.e. R is a function of O and S
or R depends on O and S

When we want to influence behaviour, we manipulate (vary) O or S or both.

Man is a creature of habit. This means that he relies on learning (a change in behaviour resulting from experience)

19

rather than instinct (complex, rigid and inborn patterns of behaviour universal to a species and not reliant for their appearance on experience).

The higher we go up the evolutionary scale, the less dependent are species on stereotyped inherited instinctive responses. At the summit is man, the most flexible of all creatures, who has reached this pinnacle because of his adjustive equipment, notably his brain. He has a tremendous capacity to learn and to change, and then to adapt to novel situations. Here is a crucial source of man's great variety: his susceptibility to many different types of environment. (An environment is defined as all the forces, physical, social, psychological and so on, to which the individual is exposed.)

The flexible (adaptable) and healthy person is much better placed to cope with these changes because his ability to learn - his openness to new ideas, his acceptance of reality - is efficient and always in a state of readiness. Not all people attain this flexibility.

Many different theories have been advanced regarding the most significant periods in human development. Some scientists believe that the first few months of life are crucial for the establishment of a stable personality. Others consider that in these months the nervous system is not sufficiently developed for a baby to be significantly affected by environmental stimuli. Despite the fact that the resilience of children to adapt to new situations has not been disputed and despite the fact that some of the notions that early trauma (e.g. separation from the mother) result in permanent damage have proved invalid, there is still substantial agreement that the first five to seven years of childhood are influential in forming the personality and establishing future behaviour patterns. Along with very rapid physical growth in the early years, there is also very rapid mental growth. A young child is open to learning in all its forms: the development of habits and traits, and ways of perceiving and dealing with the world, and the absorption of a vast amount of knowlege and new material.

Learning can be one of the most rewarding and mind-expanding experiences. By learning we enhance our consciousness of the world we inhabit. We also develop as individuals; becoming better at managing our lives and getting on with and understanding our fellow men and women. François Mauriac believed that we are moulded and remoulded by those who have loved us; and though the love may pass, we are nevertheless their work, for good or ill. Psychological thinkers tend to confirm this point of view. Erik Erikson (1965), for example, claims that the period of infancy is the time in which the baby learns whether the world is a good and satisfying place to live in or a source of pain, misery, frustration and uncertainty. He called those contrasting points of view 'basic trust' and 'basic mistrust', and they are very like our adult attitudes of optimism and pessimism. This is our cue to look more closely at the human infant.

It also introduces the reader to a branch of psychology called 'developmental psychology' (see Herbert and Schaffer in chapters 5 and 8 respectively). The study of child development involves a special and crucial way of looking at the human changes, events, characteristics and behaviours studied by general psychology. The developmental theorist looks at these psychological happenings and events, which are separated in time, as being lawfully and meaningfully associated with each other in a process of progressive change over time; a movement called 'development'. Development thus refers to the multiple forces and processes which are responsible for shaping each individual's personality.

There is no doubt, as McWhirter (1978) observes, 'that developmental psychology has the basic concepts, information and methodology for the observation, analyses and understanding of people of different ages, and also of the psychological changes within individuals with age', but she warns that, by itself, it lacks a basis for the understanding of problems encountered in social work.

References

Erikson, E.H. (1965)
Childhood and Society (rev. edn). Harmondsworth: Penguin.
McWhirter, E.P. (1978)
The social work context. In J. Radford and D. Rose (eds), The Teaching of Psychology. London: John Wiley.

3

Infancy: Basic Principles
Martin Herbert

Integrated behaviour begins with the reception of information (stimuli) from both the external and internal environment. Information from the external environment is processed
by the brain and translated into actions. After a discussion
of some of these aspects of human psychology, we move from
the so far rather abstract look at behaviour to the new
human being - a human baby - as a means of illustrating some
basic psychological principles.

Helpless (but not quite as helpless or as incompetent as
people once thought), the mother's young baby lies in her
arms and explores his surroundings with his eyes. What does
he make of his world; indeed, what can he make of it? If
the infant seems totally dependent, capable of little save
eating, sleeping and crying, then the casual eye is de-
ceived. He is, in fact, a surprisingly well-equipped creature, more able than many developmental theorists ever
suspected in their most speculative musings.

If the infant is to grow and flourish, then the priority
of the day is simply to stay alive. The baby has several
'ready made' reflexes which serve this purpose. Reflex
actions are controlled by the central nervous system - the
brain and the spinal cord - and are inborn and automatic
responses to an outside stimulus. A reflex action is a very
simple form of behaviour and it is usually a protective
device. If a finger accidentally comes into contact with a
hot radiator, it is automatically withdrawn before it gets
burnt further. The action is so quick that the rest of the
body is not really aware of what has happened.

New-born babies react to an ouside stimulus in the same
way; for instance if a baby is suddenly moved he is likely
to show the 'Moro', or startle, reflex. His arms suddenly
lift themselves from the sides of his body, his hands open,
and then the arms come back to the body.

**Perception: how we know
our world**

It is fascinating to speculate about what goes on beyond the
reflex level in the baby's mind. Can he (for example)
differentiate among distinctive forms or is his world
lacking in order; no more, as the eminent psychologist
William James expressed it at the turn of the century, than
a 'blooming, buzzing confusion'? Is his world ordered in any

way? The information or messages that we receive and act on (in order to adapt to the environment) begin at the level of sensation. All our knowledge of the world comes through our senses initially. Information from the external environment enters the body by the stimulation of receptor nerves; it is processed by the brain and translated into actions via the effector nerves. The messages we receive about our environment are integrated and organized into perceptions. What we respond to are changes in physical energy. A bell is rung; the energy of the hammer hitting the bell is transformed into physical energy. A light switch is clicked, and electricity is changed into radiant energy. Certain nerve cells (the so-called receptors) in the body are sensitive to various kinds of energy changes.

The physical energy to which such a cell is sensitive is called a stimulus. When a receptor detects the presence of a stimulus, it is said to respond to the stimulus and this causes an impulse (a message about the environment) to travel along the nerve until it reaches the brain. The nerve cells which make up the various parts of the brain perform different functions; these differences are reflected to some extent in the anatomy of the brain. For example, some parts of the brain are known to receive impulses from particular sense organs; the visual area (in the occipital lobe) receives those from the eyes through the optic nerve. The auditory area is connected to the ear, and so on. The basic elements of the system are many millions of nerve cells (neurons) which sense, store and transmit information. They function like minute live relays for scores of years, day in and day out.

Nervous transmission
The activity of the brain is mainly electrical. The brain performs its tasks by sending and receiving electrical currents from its own nerve cells to and from other nerve cells in various parts of the body. The nerve impulses which allow us to sense, perceive, think, feel and act, travel at speeds ranging from two to 200 miles an hour, and are transmitted from nerve cell to nerve cell (some having fibres several feet long). They have to cross over a gap, the 'synapse', of about one-millionth of an inch wide. They do this by means of chemicals released to the cell endings.

The body contains millions of neurons which penetrate every corner of the body and are connected into a huge network like a giant telephone system (to use a favourite metaphor). The spinal cord is the main cable which carries the bulk of the messages to and from the brain. Every neuron in the body has a minute electrical charge associated with it, even when it is not being stimulated. The charge is produced by the chemical difference between the inside of the nerve cell and the tissue which surrounds it. The cells themselves consist of chemical compounds. The nerve impulses are essentially electro-chemical events.

All this means that a study of the biochemistry of the brain (as well as its anatomy and physiology) is crucial for understanding mental functions like learning. Neurologists have pointed out that the brain of the infant is different from the adult's; the cells are smaller and the connections between them poorly insulated. Although immature, the baby's brain (as we shall see) functions efficiently enough to serve some remarkable perceptual abilities.

The brain must always be on the alert. Each and every second of waking life more than 100 million electrical impulses flow into the brain. Even when asleep more than 50 million neuronal 'messages' are being related every second to and from the brain and different parts of the body. Every neuron is 'all-or-none' in its action; just as an electric light is 'on' or 'off', a neuron either generates an impulse or it remains inactive.

Coding information

A single impulse arriving at the brain, say, a neuron in the retina of the eye, is indistinguishable from an impulse generated by a pain receptor in the sole of the foot. Yet a complex pattern of 'on' and 'off' retinal messages will enable the brain to perceive a face, and a comparable series from the foot will produce the feeling of pain. The 'on' and 'off' messages which the brain receives every second are like a code. How the brain decodes a message into meaningful terms or how it makes decisions has yet to be fathomed.

All in all, the brain carries out simultaneously a staggering array of tasks which control the machinery of the body and mind:

* it exercises choice over how and when to react to particular situations;
* it integrates and organizes information from the senses into perceptions;
* it regulates countless adjustments - physical and psychological - required by the person in his interaction with the environment;
* it stores and integrates vast amounts of information;
* it attends selectively to what is crucial in the individual's ever-changing environment.

The senses

With regard to the last point, adults can locate sounds to right and left with great precision, although there is no right and left within the auditory system. Perception of position of a sound source is elaborated from differences in the time of arrival and in intensity between the two ears, as well as patterns of vibration set up in the outer ear. It has been demonstrated that within seconds of birth infants can use this information, turning their eyes correctly towards a sound source. This shows not only auditory localization but also a simple form of intersensory (auditory-visual) co-ordination, an expectation that there will be something to be looked at: a source for the sound.

Vision itself has ...
the other senses, re...
functioning. Susta...
tary form within ...
ing of a moving ...
at about five ...
movements a...
cites evider ...
distance e...

An ...
that if a ...
and prefers ...
more often at th...
his mother) are of ...
tify members of his sp...
between them. The patte... c-
tive feature of a person and ... of
distinguishing and identifying pe... may
therefore be a specially powerful k... for a
baby and one to which he might be exp... give special
attention. In some experiments babies have ...en shown to
select it above all other patterns.

Bower describes how observations made of mothers feeding
their young babies reveal something of the way in which an
infant uses his eyes during the first few months of life.
For the first few days babies have their eyes shut for most
of the time. If their eyes are open they tend to shut them
when given the bottle or breast. Towards the end of the
second week a change occurs. Babies tend to have their eyes
open when given the bottle or breast, and to close them only
when they are coming to the end of the feed. At the same
time the baby tends to fix his eyes in the direction of the
mother's face for a large part of the feeding period. By
three or four weeks most infants have their eyes open for
most of the feeding time and they tend to direct their gaze
directly at the mother's face. Not all infants display this
pattern, but most do.

This behaviour may have several purposes. It ensures
that the infant has experience of a complex visual stimulus,
and it may well help the development of his visual system
and of those parts of the nervous system concerned with
processing visual information. In addition, this 'looking at
mother' may be one important aspect of the infant's first
social relationship, a matter which is dealt with by
Schaffer in chapter 8. Although it is not strictly possible
to compare his vision with an adult's, young infants have
vision as good as adults.

I have dealt with only a few findings with regard to
infantile perception. Bower makes the interesting observation that we could not make many inferences about the
newborn's knowledge of the world from watching the spontaneous behaviour of babies in western culture. They have
very few behaviours, and those that they have are not given
much chance to appear in standard western baby-care conditions. He explains that although newborns have some quite

precise head and eye movements and hand and arm movements
in their repertoire, when the baby is laid on his back (a
standard examination position) these behaviours virtually
disappear. They disappear because the baby, in this position, must use his head and arms to hold himself in a stable
position. If he picks up one arm to reach for something, he
will roll in that direction. Even a head movement can result
in a loss of postural equilibrium. Bower comments that the
problem is compounded if the baby is wearing a large wad
of nappies which tilt his weight up towards his head. It
follows that if the scientists wish to utilize these head
and eye and arm and hand behaviours to measure the baby's
knowledge of the world, the baby must be propped up in a
position that allows him to move head and arms freely.

**The stimulus control
of behaviour**

Having looked briefly at the way in which the infant receives stimulus information, it is important to recognize
that stimuli are vital simply as stimuli and also because
they direct our behaviour. Put another way, stimulation is
a vital component of our psychological existence because
it is a 'basic raw material' that we need in various forms,
and because it has a controlling function over our
behaviour.

There is evidence that all individuals need a certain
minimum level of stimulation. We all indulge in a certain
amount of self-stimulation when the environment is mono-
tonous; we hum or whistle, tap our fingers, touch our hair,
and so on. Just as muscles thrive on exercise, so human
brains thrive on a steady diet of varied and meaningful
stimulation. There is also (incidentally) evidence that
those who use their intellects (i.e. stimulate them) are the
ones who tend to remain alert and intellectually undimi-
nished in old age. Why these things should be so is not yet
understood. But it does seem as though messages from the
outside world act like a fuel for the brain. When they are
not present in sufficient quantity, the brain no longer
functions normally.

Deprivation of stimulation (sensory isolation)

At Princeton University, psychologists devised an apparatus
called the 'Black Room' which is a small cubicle suspended
inside a lightproof, soundproof room. Paid volunteers were
asked to lie on a bed within the cubicle without moving or
making a noise. This sort of isolation - the deprivation of
normal levels of stimulation - resulted in the experimental
subjects seeing things that were not there.

In a similar sort of experiment carried out at McGill
University, 86 per cent of the student volunteers experienced vivid and sometimes alarming hallucinations. These
occurred anywhere after between 20 minutes to 70 hours of
confinement. Typically the hallucinations progressed from
simple flashes of light to complex moving pictures. One
person saw rabbits with knapsacks on their backs marching

across a field. Another saw a tiny space ship firing pellets
and felt them strike his arm. Many people experienced
peculiar visual disturbances after leaving the isolation
experiment. Walls appeared to move in and out. Objects
changed their size and shape. Lights seemed brighter, and
colours more intense. Some subjects left the laboratories in
a state of panic saying that nothing would get them back
there again.

Brainwashing

A spell in isolation can also make a person more susceptible
to suggestion. Interrogators and 'brainwashers' know this
only too well!

After 20 hours of deprivation, a group of students were
exposed to a recorded propaganda message arguing for a
belief in ghosts, telepathy and so on. Their attitudes to
the supernatural were measured before and after the isolation, as were those of a control group who were not
isolated. Both groups showed a greater tendency to believe
in the supernatural after hearing the talk, but the isolated
subjects were much more fervent in their new-found beliefs
than the controls.

Of course, we can never be totally deprived of sensation. But then we do not need to be for the effects of
isolation to be felt. Simply a lack of sensory variety is
sufficient to produce dramatic disturbances in the way you
think, feel and see things. The reports of explorers, ship-
wrecked sailors, and prisoners in solitary confinement
confirm this.

There is evidence that infants who are deprived of a
continuing and varied supply of visual, auditory and social
stimulation (particularly in the first year of life) fail to
acquire certain crucial adaptive behaviours. Their ability
to learn, to make emotional relationships, and to perform
certain skills can all be adversly affected. Why the exposure to appropriate stimulation is so vital is our next
topic.

The stimulus-response equation and behaviour

The basic elements of a stimulus-response (stimulus control)
theory of behaviour include the assumption that most behaviour in the case of humans is learned. When two different
stimuli appear together repeatedly, the responses to one of
them are gradually transferred to the other. If a response
to a stimulus is followed by reinforcement, this reward
increases the probability of the response following that
stimulus on future occasions.

Let us consider the equation: $S \rightarrow O \rightarrow R$. In this
equation the stimulus component (S) specifies those aspects
of the environment that are related functionally to the
behaviour - the responses - of the individual (e.g. the
traffic light regulates the driver's behaviour). It has
specific consequences (C). The full equation becomes
$S \rightarrow O \rightarrow R \rightarrow C$.

Of the countless thousands of stimuli which impinge on the individual from the external and internal environments, only the particular components that influence some property of the persons's on-going behaviour are of relevance to our analysis.

Our analysis of how stimuli come to control behaviour can be illustrated in down-to-earth terms. There is a little story told by Lope de Vega (see Bousefield, 1955):

> Saint Ildefonso used to scold me and punish me lots of times. He would sit me down on the bare floor and make me eat with the cats of the monastery. These cats were such rascals that they took advantage of my penitence. They drove me mad stealing my choicest morsels. It did no good to chase them away. But I found a way of coping with the beasts in order to enjoy my meals when I was being punished. I put them all in a sack, and on a pitch black night took them out under an arch. First I would cough and then immediately whale the daylights out of the cats. They whined and shrieked like an infernal pipe organ. I would pause for a while and repeat the operation - first a cough, and then a thrashing. I finally noticed that even without beating them the beasts moaned and yelped like the very devil whenever I coughed. I then let them loose. Thereafter, whenever I had to eat off the floor, I would cast a look around. If an animal approached my food, all I had to do was to cough, and how that cat would scat!

This is an example of the 'stimulus control' of behaviour. A cough (S) regulates the avoidance behaviour (R) of the cats.

The development of stimulus functions

To understand the development of stimulus control we must start with the new-born child. Large aspects of his environment are essentially neutral in their effect on him; that is, they exert no influence on his behaviour.

As the infant grows older he acquires behaviour. He learns to crawl, walk, talk, sit at table, co-operate, read, and so on. Aspects of his environment begin to assume special properties for the child as a result of the quality of his experience of them. Some of them have pleasurable consequences, others have painful ones. He comes to associate his mother with warmth, comfort, stimulation and many other pleasant feelings. He tries to approach her or in some way ensure her proximity.

Some avoidance reactions to stimuli occur at an automatic level. If a child touches a hot stove the pain will cause him to withdraw it quickly. It will not take long for him to learn to associate pain and stoves and to avoid touching them.

Theorists state that the child's behaviour has come to be regulated by 'antecedent stimulus events'; and they call such learning the acquisition of 'stimulus functions'. In other words, he has learned to respond appropriately to particular situations. His survival would soon be in jeopardy if he did not acquire these functions.

Over time the person builds up habits of behaving and thinking.

Classical (respondent) conditioning

Some responses become functionally attached to stimuli by a process of association (or contiguity). This process, called 'classical conditioning', provides one explanation of how our behaviours come to be elicited by such a wide variety of stimuli. Some of them do not always have an obvious connection with the stimulus situation, nor do they always serve a useful purpose. A conditioned response is formed when a neutral stimulus comes to evoke a response which is normally elicited by another stimulus. You would not be surprised if a dog responded to an electric shock applied to his leg by lifting it, and thus withdrawing it. The withdrawal of the leg is called a respondent: it is an example of an innate behaviour (withdrawal) regularly elicited by a specific stimulus (shock). You would be surprised if he responded in this way to the sound of a bell.

However, if an experimenter arranges things so that a dog regularly hears a bell, just prior to receiving a slight shock to his leg, he does just that. After several pairings of bell and shock, the animal will give this response (lifting his leg) to the bell alone! This would be an example of classical or respondent conditioning. Ivan Pavlov, the Russian psychologist, is the scientist whose genius led to the exploration of this form of learning (1927). He believed that all learning is built up from basic units called conditioned reflexes (or responses).

Human beings also form conditioned responses. The mere thought of some event may produce an involuntary response. You may blush to think of some embarrassing incident. This is called mediation. Here is an example of classical conditioning.

Each morning for several weeks, a child steps through a green shower curtain and shudders as he is confronted with a cold shower bath. Eventually the sight of the green shower curtain evokes a shudder response. Still later, the thought of the green shower curtain is sufficient to elicit a shudder response.

Each phrase in column I is matched with the correct concept in column II:

Column I	Column II
1. The cold water	Unconditioned stimulus
2. Shuddering in the cold water	Unconditioned response
3. Shuddering at the sight of the green curtain	Conditioned response

4. The green curtain	Conditioned stimulus
5. Shuddering in response to the thought of green curtain	Mediation
6. The total learning experience	Classical conditioning

There then is another term ('reinforcement') that you need to know for this volume: a reinforcer is any event, any stimulus in the environment, which affects the rate of a given operant. Reinforcers can be:

* POSITIVE when the operant - some voluntary action - becomes more frequent following the occurrence of a stimulus;
* NEGATIVE when the disappearance of the stimulus (called an 'aversive stimulus') results in the increased probability of the operant's occurrence.

Instrumental conditioning
The phenomenon called operant or instrumental conditioning can be illustrated by an experiment which is the basis for educational and therapeutic work. The principle has been used, in fact, to aid the training of all sorts of humans and animals. Let us take a human experiment which illustrates the principle.

Yvonne Brackbill (1958) conducted an experiment on smiling in eight normal infants ranging in age from $3\frac{1}{2}$-$4\frac{1}{2}$ months. She studied her experimental subjects for two or three sessions a day for several days. After securing a base level of smiling in her infant subjects, that is, after she had measured the amount of smiling normally shown by the infants, she carried out the conditioning sessions. During these sessions she stood motionless and expressionless 15 inches above the subject. As soon as the baby (S) smiled, the experimenter (E) smiled in return, began to speak softly and picked it up. After holding, jiggling, patting, and talking to S for 30 seconds, E put it back in its crib. Brackbill put one group of four subjects on a schedule of regular reinforcement and the other group of four on intermittent reinforcement. Then she stopped the reinforcement altogether to extinguish the smiling response. The so-called extinction 'phase' was conducted in the same manner as the baseline period.

Brackbill measured the frequency of smiling throughout, plotting on a graph the child's acquisition of smiling responses. The resultant cumulative curve showed a steep rate of acquisition for the infants subjected to conditioning. By contrast, a 'cumulative' curve plotted for a control subject, which was run, but without reinforcement, for 19 conditioning periods or three times longer than the experimental subjects, showed no acquisition. In other words, the smiling response of eight normal infants between $3\frac{1}{2}$ and $4\frac{1}{2}$ months was brought under control. Infants 'can be taught' to increase the frequency of their smiling.

In the experiment just described, what we notice about instrumental conditioning is that the individual CHANGES his environment in some way to produce a reward instead of merely anticipating events in his environment as in classical conditioning. It has been found that there is a positive relationship between the number of reinforced (rewarded) trials an animal (or human) has had during the 'acquisition phase' of the experiment and the number of responses made during the 'extinction phase' when one is trying to extinguish the response. The greater the number of reinforcements during acquisition the greater the number of responses made during the extinction phase. Let us translate this situation into 'down-to-earth' terms.

A down-to-earth example
Suppose a child cries when he is made to go to bed and that the mother, who cannot bear to see his tears, gives in and lets him stay up late. After several similar scenes with the same outcome - mum giving in - she finally appreciates that she has been encouraging or reinforcing an undesirable habit. She decides to stand firm and be impervious to his tears. So she makes the child go upstairs to bed no matter how long or heart-rendingly he cries. How long will it take to extinguish the crying habit? The child has discovered, of course, that crying is instrumental in obtaining his reward: that is, staying up late. The difficulty the mother will have in extinguishing the crying tantrum will depend in large part on how often she has previously let him have his own way. We can see from this example how 'bad habits' may be reinforced.

Reinforcement consequences
Certain of a person's responses (behaviours) are strengthened when they occur in particular environmental situations; by making the appropriate responses to certain stimuli the person's actions are generally 'reinforced' by positive (rewarding) consequences. They can also be strengthened by the avoidance/removal of punishing consequences. The child's resolve to do his homework is strengthened by the thought of the teacher's punishment if he does not do it.

Responses can also be weakened in the context of particular situations. Inappropriate responses usually result in negative (painful, punishing) consequences. They can also be weakened by the removal of rewarding consequences.

Imitation
There is another type of social learning which takes place through the child's imitation of the people, real and imagined, whom he observes and hears about. Imitated behaviour is often rewarded by praise and encouragement and approval - in other words social rewards - from the 'model'. Such modelling, particularly on the parents, is important for the development of conforming patterns of social behaviour. This form of learning has also been called

'observational learning'; what the child does is to 'model' his behaviour on the basis of what he observes others to be doing.

Modelling effects have been demonstrated in a series of experiments by Bandura (1977) and his associates. They exposed one group of nursery-school children to aggressive adult models and a second group to models who displayed inhibited and non-aggressive behaviour. For the aggressive-model group the model exhibited unusual forms of physical and verbal aggression towards a large inflated plastic doll. In contrast, the non-aggressive-model group observed an adult who sat very quietly, totally ignoring the doll and the instruments of aggression that had been placed in the room. The children who observed aggressive models manifested similar patterns of behaviour, while those who were exposed to models who were not aggressive failed to show aggressive behaviour.

The family environment

The role of the family
The family is particularly significant in the moulding of the child because it is the first and most frequent agent determining which social stimuli will be presented to the child, what he will be taught, which behaviour patterns will be rewarded and consolidated and which will be punished and inhibited.

So much is determined by the intimate contacts, the complex learning and the emotional attachments of the formative years within the family, that psychiatrists and social workers trying to unravel the causes of mental and social breakdown in adult life try to obtain a 'case history' of the patient's early years of development. They hope to find in the story of his childhood and family upbringing clues to his present difficulties.

Differential reinforcement
Experiences tend to reinforce particular personality traits, and the more often these experiences are repeated the more enduring the traits become. Through a system of reward and punishment, patterns of behaviour are often effectively formed. A child subjected to repeated and violent beatings early in life may learn that, by complete submission, the painful experience may be avoided. Subsequently, he may develop a generally submissive manner in dealing with all other people. As a result of similar experiences an individual with a different combination of environmental influences and genetic constitution may believe that beating is the only way to produce a desired behaviour in others, and so he may become a strongly aggressive character.

The initial stage of learning patterns of behaviour and of developing personality characteristics is followed by a second period of development, the latency period, in which previous learning and experience is consolidated. In the third phase, adolescence, as the secondary sex characteristics begin to develop, there is an advance in learning and in processing emotional experience. This moulds the basic aspects of personality into the more permanent form they will assume in adult years. During adolescence there can be dramatic changes in behaviour.

References

Bandura, A. (1977)
Social Learning Theory. Englewood Cliffs, NJ: Prentice-Hall.

Bousefield, W.A. (1955)
Lope de Vega on early conditioning. American Psychologist, 10, 828.

Bower, T. (1975)
Competent newborns. In R. Lewin (ed.), Child Alive. London: Temple Smith.

Brackbill, Y. (1958)
Extinction of the smiling response in infants as a function of reinforcement. Child Development, 29, 115-124.

Fantz, R. L. (1963)
Pattern vision in newborn infants. Science, 140, 296-297.

Pavlov, I.P. (1927)
Conditional Reflexes. (Transl. G.V. Anrep.) Oxford: Clarendon Press.

4

The Child and the Family
Martin Herbert

Introduction

This chapter introduces the reader to some of the psycho-logical information available for a psycho-social life span study: a matter of concern to the social worker who finds his clients in all age groups, and is required to know about the life-tasks (developmental tasks) and the potential crises associated with childhood, adolescence, maturity and old age. These so-called 'developmental crises' are described in chapters 8, 11, and 17. The purpose of the present chapter is to introduce you to an area of study on which social work places considerable emphasis; viz. 'The child and the family'. When social workers arrange substitute care (foster home, day nursery, child minding) there is concern for the quality of such provision. However, this concern may be undermined by vaguely conceived (and even less rigorously assessed) parent-child attitudes and relationships. A critical examination of the literature (Herbert, 1974) indicates how many inconsistencies, even contradictions, there are.

The promise of effective preventive work by social workers, or better mental health through more enlightened psychological child care, remains a fond hope in professional circles, though still unfulfilled. Marian Radke Yarrow and her co-authors of the book 'Child Rearing' (1968) reflect sadly, from their own investigations and their extensive review of available evidence, that we are still searching for the specific conditions in the child's cumulative experience with his parents that evoke, strengthen, or modify his behaviour. Yet parent 'therapy' and education are still based on an assumption that there is a body of knowledge about the best techniques of child care. It follows that these can be taught to parents, foster parents and residential care staff. Much has been made (particularly in the psychoanalytic literature) of the allegedly disruptive effects on infant adjustment of different child-care practices, notably feeding, weaning and toilet-training procedures. The social worker should be familiar with the evidence (see chapters 8 and 10). We look at four areas in this volume:

* the family heritage: some sources of individual differences are described;

* the child as a developing organism: this concerns the foundational influences of early experience; reference is made to the range, direction and potency of subsequent development;
* the family as a social system: this sub-section is concerned with the dynamic inter-relatedness of a child's earliest encounter between self and others;
* the interior of the family: here we consider the unique experience of each family as a complex and dynamic psycho-social system.

The family heritage

It is a mind-boggling thought that in a world containing some four million million inhabitants, each one of us is quite unique. Nowhere could we find an exact replica of ourselves; no, not even when we have a so-called 'identical twin'. Mind you, this is the closest we get to a perfect likeness. This is because our individuality begins with the 'lottery' in which we received those units of life called genes. These ultramicroscopic bits of matter translate our family heritage into action. Identical twins inherit the same set of genes. What makes them different as persons is the unique effect the environment has in moulding each one of us as a personality.

Genetics, the science of heredity, is devoted to finding out about the way in which the hereditary factors are handed down from parents to their children by literally reproducing themselves. Every time someone assures a mother that her infant has his father's eyes or his granny's mouth, they are stating a fact of human heredity. All sorts of character-istics run in families. A tendency to freckles, for example, is hereditary; so are hair, skin and eye colour and the shape of face and features. There are hereditary diseases like haemophilia and inherited conditions such as colour blindness. Then again, important psychological attributes like intelligence and personality have a major genetic ingredient. Genetics as a science is concerned with the way in which the genes make their presence felt during a child's growth and development by producing the substances which influence the behaviour and development of the entire cell: the unit of living matter. It is also concerned with the way in which the action of genes is modified by the environment.

The environment
Environmental influences determine whether an individual achieves all his genetic potential. A youngster who is well endowed genetically with intellectual potential will fail to achieve it if he is deprived of opportunities to learn.

Height is another example of how heredity and environ-ment can interact. Let us take two children who are un-usually small. One is short because he has inherited a gene by which a body chemical essential to growth is absent. (The internal environment of his body can be changed by supplying

him with the missing chemical, and he will grow.) Another
child possesses the genes which would allow him to reach
average height, but he is shorter than normal because he is
under-nourished. (Increasing this child's daily intake of
food will change the way in which his genes are expressed.
This, too, is a change of environment.)

The differences in the hereditary contents of the germ
cells - the ones we transmit to our offspring - are not produced by any physical, spiritual or moral improvements we
bring about in ourselves as would-be parents. No amount of
body-building, yoga, spiritual commitment or leading the
good life in the father or mother will make any difference
to the genes transmitted to the new being. The child will
have to spend years acquiring and developing his own
intellectual, physical, spiritual and moral 'muscle'.

Mechanisms of heredity
All the genetic material a human child inherits comes from
his parents and is housed in two cells, the sperm and the
ovum (egg), which fuse when the sperm from the father
enters the egg produced by the mother. The resulting cell -
a barely visible particle of matter - is called a zygote.
Each and every individual sets out in life in this way. The
genes in this original cell turn up in all the estimated ten
million million cells that eventually constitute the adult
human person. From the moment of conception, every individual carries in his cells the information which determines
the genetic aspects of his development. This information is
borne by the genes, which are made of DNA, a chemical with
a regular structure which enables the genes to be accurately
interpreted and reproduced. The genes are strung together on
compact microscopic structures called chromosomes, themselves small bodies within the nucleus of every cell of the
body.

Environment and heredity interact
From the moment of fertilization, the environment (including the womb or uterus) in which he lives and all the
genetic capacities he possesses, interact to produce a
complete and unique human being. Although he is born with
inbuilt characteristics that shape him, at the same time his
society, his parents, brothers and sisters and other people
in his world, influence him. Man is a creature of habit. He
learns about life and acquires modes of behaviour and
strategies of adjusting to its difficulties. He is not
dependent like other animals on stereotyped, inbuilt
(instinctive) patterns of responding.

**The child as a
developing organism**

Environmental influences can determine, as we have seen,
whether an individual achieves all his genetic potential.
Thus a child who is well endowed genetically with intellectual potential will fail to achieve it if he is deprived
of opportunites to learn. The opposite is true too: an

unusually strong environment may lend assistance to limited genetic potential. A normal set of genes and an appropriate environment are each needed for satisfactory development and behaviour.

Characteristics influenced by environment
The vast majority of characteristics are influenced to a greater or lesser degree by the environment; for example

* height
* weight
* intelligence
* personality
* various physical illnesses
* mental illness

When development goes wrong
Sadly, not all babies are born perfect. One in a hundred is born with an abnormality: perhaps a minor defect like a birthmark or hare lip, or a major abnormality, such as spina bifida, that can cause death or tragic disability. Such conditions, present at birth, are known as congenital abnormalities; they occur because the orderly development of the unborn child breaks down. The blue-prints a child inherits may be faulty or the defences provided by the womb can fail. In either case it is quite likely that the resultant defective embryo will not go on to full development; there may be a spontaneous abortion or miscarriage.

Pre-natal influences
The nine months between conception and birth present more risks to the developing individual than any similar span up to the ninth decade. It is, of course, a period of rapid growth and development. For example, three weeks after fertilization, the whole sac containing the unborn child (the embryo) is only the size of a cherry, and the baby itself is about one-fifth of an inch long. Two weeks later, however, the embryo has DOUBLED in size. This is a quite fantastic achievement which will never be repeated in its life. The child-to-be faces trials which begin with fertilization and implantation; they continue with the development of the organs of the body and the establishment of the mechanisms required for the regulation of the internal environment; they come to an end with the birth process. The time scale for each physiological transition is finely prescribed, and failure to make the change at the correct time and in the correct manner is dangerous and can result in death or permanent damage to the organism. The concept of a 'critical period', so popular in social work accounts of early infant-mother attachment, comes from the study of embryology.

The first trimester of pregnancy is the most crucial in the child's development. The major organs and basic tissues are being laid down and developed during the first eight weeks after conception and these are therefore the ones during which disturbances in the child's first environment - the uterus - can produce major effects on growth. After this phase it is difficult, if not impossible, to affect the morphology of the organism in any fundamental manner; the embryo has all the important external and internal features of a human being.

Schaffer, in chapter 8, makes the point that it is apparent that children do not start life as psychological nonentities. From the beginning they already have an individuality that influences the adults around them. Thus a mother's initial task is not to create something out of nothing; it is rather to dovetail her behaviour to that of the child. He describes some of the forms this takes.

Temperamental individuality
Any nurse who has had the care of a nursery of newly born babies, or any mother who has had several children so as to be able to compare her babies, knows that they differ markedly in temperament right from the word 'go'. A group of research workers and clinicians, Stella Chess, Alexander Thomas and Herbert Birch (1968), have demonstrated just how important these inborn or constitutional aspects of personality - the temperamental qualities of the child - can be in the development of normal behaviour and emotional problems (see chapter 6).

Family inheritance is one source of this temperamental variety. The fertilized zygote brings together various combinations and permutations of parental chromosomes and in this way different genes are given to each child of the same parents. Ashley Montagu, in his book 'Human Heredity', estimates that in a single mating the possible combinations between the 23 chromosomes of the female and those of the male are 8,388,608 and the chance of any one such combination being repeated more than once is one in approximately 70 trillion. There can be wide variations within a family group, but nevertheless a child is somewhat more similar to his blood relations than to anyone else.

Implications for the development of individuality
In the wake of thinkers like Freud, Pavlov and Watson, almost exclusive emphasis was placed on environmental influences in the development of behaviour. And parents, being the major feature of the child's early environment, received all the blame when things went wrong. The possession of certain combinations of the temperamental qualities mentioned above can make a child exceedingly 'difficult' no matter how skilled the parents are. John B. Watson, a psychologist at Johns Hopkins University during the first decades of the century, believed that planned habit training could mould the child in any desired direction. This is how he expressed it:

> Give me a dozen healthy infants, well formed, and my own specified world to bring them up in, and I'll

guarantee to take any one at random and train him to become any type of specialist I might select - doctor, lawyer, artist, merchant chief, and yes, even beggar-man and thief, regardless of his talents, penchants, tendencies, abilities, vocations and race of his ancestors (1928).

He failed to take into account the potent proactive influence of differences in children's individual capacities, and their often unpredictable interpretations of, and reactions to, their environment. Environment (as we shall see) is vital in determining individual differences, but it is not the 'whole story' as some people assume.

The family as a social system

The family - a group of people closely related by birth or marriage - is one of the oldest social structures known to man. It is a basic unit in a variety of societies, ranging from the most 'primitive' to the most 'sophisticated'; indeed, it is a universal institution but one which varies in the precise pattern or form with which it manifests itself. For example, the father may take little part in the upbringing of the children, some other member of the extended family (such as the maternal uncle) being the dominant male influence. Children may not be the special responsibility of their parents at all in some societies; they may be reared by all the members of a group living together under one roof or in a small compact housing unit. The family name, wealth and land may be handed down from generation to generation through the mother's side and not the father's. After marriage the man may go to live with his wife's kin in their family residence. Or it may be the other way around.

Howells (1969) found that in a random sample of families in an English town, approximately 70 per cent followed the pattern of a nuclear family. Twenty per cent had an extended pattern, that is to say a joint family made up of two or more nuclear families. Ten per cent had an anomalous pattern: a variety of unusual combinations such as father and children alone; mother, grandmother and children; polygamy, and others. The contemporary western nuclear family (as part of a larger kinship network which, in turn, is a component of the larger social structure) introduces the child first of all to his kin and then to his wider community and society. In the family the child, as a member, has a role to play, responsibilities to assume and is called upon to give and receive attention. The family provides the individual with a sense of identity in terms of his family name and a feeling of belonging and being loved and needed. This is a significant achievement (if successful) given the tendency of our complex modern society - vast in scale and impersonal in attitude - to subvert the citizen's sense of importance, worth and meaning. At least the family does not make the child feel like a small (and replaceable) cog in a massive machine. (And this sense of special-ness is what the child without a family feels in all but the best-run and more intimate family-model care institutions.)

The family appears to have evolved earlier in human prehistory and occurred more ubiquitously than any other persistent social grouping by which man organizes his social relationships and activities, including church and state. This most enduring of human institutions has long engaged the attention of social psychologists. After all, if 'the proper study of man is man', then a key to the understanding of his ways must lie in the social grouping - the family - that he has evolved, no matter what part of the world or in what circumstances he has found himself.

Marriage is an important institution in the history of the family. The reason why there are rules, regulations and laws in all societies to institutionalize marriage is that they provide a reasonably secure framework within which to nurture and socialize children. They also define who has rights and duties towards the child, and responsibilities for his care. It has fallen to the woman in most societies to carry the main responsibility for rearing the offspring. In less advanced but more close-knit societies than our own, child care is often a group effort which reinforces a child's sense of community. Life is obviously more frag-mented in an urban environment. A youngster is given specialist care by a bewildering variety of experts: doctors, dentists, teachers, psychologists and social workers. Modern women are frequently inexperienced at child care. They may be unaccustomed to small children because they have been brought up in small families and not given responsibilities for caring for the young ones as older sisters of yesteryear (or in contemporary primitive societies) had to do. This is only remedied when they have children themselves. They need to learn mothering skills very quickly since they have not, unlike mothers of earlier generations, acquired these in the normal course of their own childhood. Social workers know well the potentially explosive situation of a socially isolated, inexperienced single parent, and a persistently difficult, screaming baby. This and other aspects of stress in family life are dealt with by Frude in chapter 10.

Many anthropologists and social psychologists claim that the family functions to satisfy certain universal needs which persist among all persons in all times. It is stated that the family is a universal phenomenon because it so accurately reflects and accommodates human beings' biolo-gical and psychological make-up; it permits their survival by enhancing their inborn capacities for adaptation. It fulfils their need to establish a socially approved struc-ture for gratifying the sexual drive, the need to reproduce and the necessity to provide a stable environment in which to raise children. It provides a shelter for its members within the society and against the remainder of society. It satisfies the child's biological and psychological needs, but at the same time restrains his early antisocial tenden-cies and prepares him for social living. The fact is that no completely workable substitutes for the family has been discovered, although some compromises (e.g. the kibbutz) have been tried.

What the family does achieve is nothing less than the transformation of a biological organism into a social creature. Nothing could be more basic than this to social life. This transformation process is usually called 'socialization'. From birth, a child is protected and trained by the family. This training includes not only physical skills, among them walking and feeding, but cultural skills, too, from good manners to a love of music. It encourages the need to achieve. One of the most important cultural skills a child learns is language, the tool which is central to all further learning processes. Language enables man to develop and transmit values, norms and moral judgements.

The patterns of co-operation and conflict which a child learns through family relationships teach him how to relate to groups outside the family; initially neighbours and schoolfriends, but later to wider groups. From his earliest years in the family a child is shown what is right, praiseworthy and acceptable, and what is wrong, ridiculed, punished. The family, then, is the primary transmitter of social skills and values; it acts as a mediator between the individual and society.

Another family function is that of social control. There are many agents of social control in society, but none has the continuous power of the family over its members. This is why the breakdown in family life is so often blamed for the dramatic rise in juvenile crime and violence. The family is in the best position to influence, cajole, threaten, and use all the positive and negative sanctions that come from intimacy to get the individual to conform to family norms. Social control is reinforced by the related family function whereby the child receives a status in society and a set of social roles from his family at birth. He may sometimes alter this 'ascribed' placement by his own achievements, but it often remains the basis of other people's view of his social standing.

This point leads us on to a further family function, its role as an economic unit. Even in industrial societies, although the family does not work as a team, as does the peasant farmer's family, the household is still an economic unit which does much of its budgeting collectively. A significant degree of family continuity in certain employments persists among doctors, printers and dockers in Britain, for instance.

In all societies there are specialized roles within the family. The child learns these in the home. As well as the division by sex there is a specialization of function according to one's role and status within the family; the expected behaviour of 'mother', 'father', 'grandfather', 'paternal-uncle', 'elder son', etc., is defined more or less closely by all societies. There is an immense variety of definitions of roles, however, and it would be unwise to assume that current western ones are valid elsewhere. This is crucial for the social worker to remember as he comes into contact with different ethnic groups. The ethnocentric social worker is likely to be a menace!

The interior of the family

The family adapts itself to changing conditions. The nuclear family which, as we observed, is the most common unit to be found in western nations is, in large part, the product of industrialization. Before the age of technology the family was frequently a working unit and children were important not for their own sake but for their potential as workers. Today, among the lower-income groups in our society, the children are still looked upon as having an essential role in financing the household. But this tendency is disappearing with the increase in affluence; the children are valued for their own sake and not as economic providers.

The role of husband and wife within the family has also changed in the last two or three decades. Increasing educational opportunities for women and better career prospects have given them a higher status in the home; the nuclear family with both husband and wife in professional jobs is no longer the exception. Coupled with this is the growing authority of the mother and the lessening of the father's authority within the home, particularly in decisions on education and discipline of the children. The child experiences difficulty when parents do not provide a united front so as to provide him with an emotionally secure and consistent learning environment (Herbert, 1980a). Marital schism and skew are terms applied to excesses of parental disharmony.

The duties and responsibilities of the nuclear family have been lessened by the taking over by the state of many functions, education being an obvious example. In the past the family has always had a responsibility for the care of its elderly members, but this too is sometimes being abrogated to the state as mobility increases and the nuclear family becomes more isolated. The elderly have become the major clients of the health and social services, an issue elaborated by Coleman in chapter 17. For all these changes, there is little evidence that the family as an institution is seriously threatened. Persistent notices of its demise are premature.

The parental role: mothering

'Mothering' is regarded in our society as the most appropriate term to describe the tender loving care of children. Significantly it is a feminine word and reflects the matricentric nature and connotation of child care. This connotation - mother - implies, in turn, that the woman is a housewife and that her role is minding home, husband and children. Biology and social convention have foisted these duties on her. For many women these roles are a joy and are

sufficient to fulfil her; for others they are not enough.
Social workers need to be alerted to some of the facile
rhetoric in the literature about motherhood. Myths and
erroneous beliefs which have attained wide acceptance due
to misunderstandings and publicity surrounding and following
the work of Bowlby and others (and it must be emphasized
that a lot of good was achieved for social work theory and
practice with regard to child care) have done a great
disservice to the confidence and spontaneity of women. Among
them is a concept of 'motherhood' which has raised it to a
position of unprecedented importance. Many would say that
an intolerable burden of anxiety and guilt was placed on
parents; the idea of a critical period implies that parents
are all-powerful, all-responsible 'and must assume the role
of playing preventive Fate for their children' (Bruch,
1954). The clinical and social work literature on child and
adult psychopathology over many years was replete with 'bad
mothers': schizophrenogenic mothers, asthmagenic mothers,
mothers accused of suffocating their offspring with
'smother' love, or in some other way overprotecting,
rejecting or double-binding them into abnormality. Chess
(1964) refers to this phenomenon as 'mal de mère'.

Maternal behaviour in animals is more closely governed
by basic instincts than is the case in humans. Nevertheless,
there are 'bad' mothers in the animal world as there are
among humans. Harry Harlow (1960) demonstrated how rhesus
monkeys, deprived during infancy of their mother or of
social contact generally, grow up to be incompetent, rejecting and even vicious mothers. The human species would soon
be extinct if people carried on with the same carelessness
as fish, which spawn eggs and then pass on, or turtles,
which come together at random and abandon their fertilized
eggs to the tender mercies of the environment.

Marriage and parenthood are the two central institutional elements of the family. Marriage, as we saw, is a
formalized way of regulating parenthood. By trying to insist
that parenthood be confined within the family, society
provides attention and care for both mother and child. There
is usually a differentiation of role between the sexes,
certain tasks and privileges being regarded as feminine and
others as masculine.

The mother, in our society - despite the feminist
movement - bears a special responsibility for the care of
the children. Whatever the lip-service paid to changes of
attitude by men, this is still the reality. Our society is
markedly matricentric in this aspect of life. When there is
a showdown it is the mother who is expected to stay (and
usually does) with the children. She is made aware by the
mass media, the books she reads and the experts she con-
sults, that the child's growth, contentment, and even
survival depends to a significant extent on her skill at
being a stimulating and tender parent. The father is often
out at work so that a child in western society may spend the
first crucial years of his life in the almost exclusive

company of his mother. From a historical and cross-cultural perspective, this is a unique situation. It is only since, approximately, the beginning of this century that western society has seen such an intense preoccupation with the needs of children. This concern has done a lot to enlarge the mother's duties towards the child.

Motherhood may mean many sacrifices, hard work and pain to women, but it is still rare (although not as rare as it used to be) to hear women say that they do not enjoy their role, for all its irritations and frustrations, or to find others who repudiate the role of mother. In part this is due to a deep-seated biological awareness of their capacity to create new life, and in the younger woman, the reminder - in the form of menstruation - of the ovum. The potentiality for life which might have been fertilized is shed each month. But much of the undoubted need of women to have children is built in to their expectations by the manner in which little girls are encouraged to play with dolls, and to take the part of the 'little mother'. All in all, today's mothers bear much more responsibility in the child's early years than their predecessors and their counterparts in earlier societies.

Being a mother in western society requires considerable adjustments. The modern mother is quite likely to be a woman who is educated, and perhaps highly trained in some skill. She has usually been employed for a number of years. Marrying in her twenties she will have her children before she is 30, and during this time usually remains at home with them. Many young women making the first adjustment to motherhood find their economic dependence on their husbands frustrating. They may also find that one important loss, due to the initial move from a working environment to full-time housework at home, is the loss of the social contacts which were enjoyed at work. Similarly, a woman in her forties making the adjustment back again to the world outside the home may find her capacity for forming new social relationships inhibited by the years of full-time domesticity. The most demanding change in the life of today's mother has been introduced by the appearance of the nuclear family unit. New opportunites take families away from their familiar surroundings and set them down among strangers in a strange town. This is an inevitable result of the increasing 'upward social mobility' that is disrupting traditional working-class social structures by providing individuals with the opportunity to improve their standard of living, but often at the cost of resettlement. Environmentally the modern western family tends to be very much an isolated unit: the husband and wife in their own home, living perhaps miles away from even their closest relations.

Housewives used to experience a sense of community in living amongst parents, brothers, sisters and cousins, all setting up home within reach of one another. The housewife in such a community did not suffer the problem of loneliness. She had a firmly established background that provided

a reassuring certainty to everyday life. It might be said
that the malaise of today's housewives is loneliness; a new
condition with the attendant symptoms of nagging boredom and
an acute sense of wasting oneself, of unfulfilment. The
woman who is today's housewife may find herself on her own
for hours on end, day after day, month after month, especially as one or more of her children reach the age when
they go away to school. Lack of a feeling of belonging and
community can do great harm to mothers' sense of purpose or
well-being. Depression, a sense of being trapped and helpless, are the 'symptoms' with which such women fill social
workers' case-notes; also other ill-defined feelings of
anxiety and discontent. Without suitable outlets, these
vague feelings can build up into a strong sense of alienation and of not being in charge of their own lives and
destinies.

The consequence of our modern definition of the mother's
role is that children receive much better care physically
and emotionally than they did a century ago, or than they
do in 'primitive' societies today. But at another level this
highly focussed relationship has allowed children to become
much more vulnerable. The strains and tensions in modern
family life come not so much from its economic or socializing functions but rather from the fact that it is to such
an extent the source of emotional support in the contemporary world. Where marriage is contracted, not by arrangement, but in romantic love, and where many of modern man's
social relationships are fleeting and superficial, he relies
more and more on the family for his deepest emotional satisfactions. In fact, with the decline in its other functions,
rather too much emphasis is placed on the emotional rewards
provided by the family and inevitably in some cases disap-
pointments and a certain amount of disillusionment result.
It is a heavy burden for the family to carry. Margaret Mead
(1935), the eminent anthropologist, has observed that the
Samoan child, brought up in a household of between 10 and
20 people, is much less likely to be hurt by the death of
his parents, or by a poor relationship with either of them,
than the child reared exclusively by the mother in a nuclear
family setting. In the intimacy of the modern mother-child
relationship a child can prosper, but he can also suffer.
The mother too is much more vulnerable. She has been made
to feel even more vulnerable by the long-standing debate on
maternal deprivation.

Maternal deprivation
The debate over the 'maternal deprivation' theory, generated
by Bowlby's (1951) report to the World Health Organization,
focussed attention on the possible importance for his future
development of the child's first interpersonal relationships. Research relevant to this debate suggested that lack
of opportunity for the child to form, in the first years of
life, a specific relationship with his caretaker or other
adult may have been responsible for the later difficulties

in personal relationships experienced by children who had
spent their early years in the older type of institutional
care.

This lack of a specific tie may - in addition to the
deficiency of environmental stimulation - contribute to the
retarded intellectual and educational development found in
many of these children. Controversy over the so-called
critical or sensitive period in childhood is described in
the excellent text by Michael Rutter, 'Maternal Deprivation
Reassessed'.

Freud put forward a somewhat similar 'sensitive period'
theory regarding the early and long-term antecedents of
attributes such as optimism, pessimism and narcissism. He
described certain character traits which are thought to be
associated with either too great frustration or overly
indulged gratification at each of three psychosexual stages
of development: the oral, anal and phallic stages. (We look
at these in the following chapter.) Sadly, the concept of
maternal separation (or maternal deprivation) has been a
great 'thought-stopper' for some practitioners. So, in more
recent times, has been the concept of 'emotional bonding'.
It is fairly common practice, especially in social work,
psychiatric and paediatric settings, to hear the term
'bonding' used in an explanatory and diagnostic sense. For
example, one is quite likely to hear at case conferences (or
see in case reports) the dichotomous classification 'successful versus unsuccessful' bonding invoked in cases of
child battering or other allegedly pathological instances of
mother-child interaction. The term bonding is referred to in
both a cause and effect sense. Where early, relatively brief
- or longer - periods of separation between mother and baby
can be identified, the failure of bonding is seen as a
consequence; this failure, in turn, might be inculpated in
the causation of the particular child abuse incident which
is being examined.

The notion of a critical or optimal period for the
development of attachments (bonds), extended now from the
infant-to-mother side of the equation to the mother-to-
child, purports to be an ethological explanation. It seems
to suggest that bonding behaviour is species specific and
relatively uninfluenced by the previous experience and state
of the mother or her expectations and cultural values. The
evidence (see Herbert, Sluckin and Sluckin, in press) is
dubious.

In any event, assuming that one can identify a failure
of bonding, for instance of mother-child attachment, with
the appropriate degree of reliability and validity, how much
would it contribute to making a diagnosis? The value of a
diagnostic term lies in its descriptive functions, and its
implications for aetiology, treatment and prognosis. A label
without implication would be pointless. How appropriate then
is the concept of a maternal bonding as a descriptive term
for maternal behaviour? There is no general agreement about
what are the most desirable attributes of maternal

behaviour, and there is little available information
(Herbert, 1980b) to indicate which aspects of parental
behaviour foster particular traits - good or bad - in their
offspring, or which make for optimal conditions in mother-
child interactions. Nevertheless, bonding is generally
valued as a necessary and desirable condition, and its
absence as putting the child at risk. But does it describe a
consistent set of attitudes or actions? The fact is that we
cannot assume the simplicity or the unidimensionality of
mother-infant attachment behaviour. Whiten (1977) has
demonstrated, in his study of the effects of perinatal
events, that it is extremely difficult to arrive at a
sensitive and objective description of those features of
mother-infant interaction which are important in terms of
their developmental significance or prominence in the
everyday life of the mother and baby.

It is the present author's experience that particular
weight is given to the influence of these periods of separation while the consideration of the influence of other
potentially important variables, such as the parity of the
mother, the sex and temperament of the infant, state variables in the mother and family social class are neglected
(see Herbert, Sluckin and Sluckin, in press, for a full
review of the evidence). There is space here to mention only
one study. Robson and Kumar (1980), in a prospective study
of (inter alia) 119 primaparae and 41 multiparae, found that
approximately 40 per cent of primiparous women and 25 per
cent of multiparae recalled that their predominant reactions
when holding their babies for the very first time had been
one of emotional indifference. For most women these feelings
of indifference dissipated within a few days.

The following variables seemed to be associated with a
delayed onset of maternal affection: separation from own
father before the age of 11 years; 'masculine' score on a
projective test; lack of prior experience of looking after
babies; higher negative self-reports about being pregnant
and about somatic symptoms; not perceiving the foetus as a
person by 36 weeks ante-natally; having an amniotomy (mem-
branes ruptured artificially) and reporting pain in labour
as worse than expected and/or having more than 125 mg of
pethidine.

At three months post-natally there was a trend between
early reported maternal feelings and the way a mother now
said she felt about her baby. There was also a significant
association between initial indifference and negative
reports on an 'attitude to baby scale' throughout the whole
of the first postpartum year. There appeared to be no
association, however, between initial maternal feeling for
the neonate and later breastfeeding problems, maternal post-
natal depression or reported maternal aggression towards the
babies.

When factors such as the ones enumerated above are known
to be important determinants of the mother's attitudes and
actions, the emphasis on a sensitive period in mother-infant

contact as the sole independent variable producing 'bonding' or, beyond that, symptoms of a pathological mother-child relationship, is seen to be unacceptable. In any event, there are several implications of this sort of emphasis, which need to be thought through. The belief in the primacy of the neonatal period in the establishment of appropriate attachment between a mother and her infant would surely put a question mark over the whole institution of adoption; yet adoptive parents tend to do very well as parents (Tizard, 1977).

Like so many other would-be explanatory concepts in social work, 'maternal deprivation' and 'bonding' are over-inclusive and too imprecise to be of any predictive value. They have been used as if they described unitary phenomena. In fact, as the evidence suggests, there are many moderating influences which determine the seriousness of the consequences for the child (Rutter, 1972).

Fathering

The contemporary young middle-class husband, as he fulfils his paternal role, is quite likely to assist with the feeding or bathing of the baby for his working wife. Such notions of fathering are alien to earlier times and other species. Throughout the animal kingdom, males play little or no part in the care and nurture of their offspring. Students of human societies believe that men learnt to develop a relationship with their children as a result of setting up long-term living arrangements with one or more women. The human male established a family unit whereas most male and female animals come together for mating purposes and then part. In fact, humanity took a long time to discover what fatherhood was. The 40 weeks of pregnancy dividing the moment of conception from the birth of a baby prevented our ancestors from connecting the two events.

Henry Biller (1971) has examined the father's contribution to family life and concludes that any new father should be encouraged to spend as much time as possible with his wife and child. The earlier he can feel involved with the child, the more likely is a strong relationship to develop between them. He believes that having a child should be a careful decision for both father and mother, and before the child is conceived the prospective parents ought to feel a joint commitment to their future family. This mutual interest should carry on through pregnancy, though it is easy for the father to begin feeling left out at this stage. Too often all the attention is focussed on the expectant mother and the expectant father is left out in the cold. Biller found that it helped for husbands to be involved in pre-natal visits to the doctor and then, if the hospital allows it, they can be with their wives during labour and in the delivery room where they can be of enormous support. A father can be very important to his child's development even in the first year of life.

Western society is becoming increasingly compartmentalized as specialized social groups become larger and people's social contacts increase. For instance, a man's role in the work situation may have nothing to do with his role as a father and husband, or as a member of the local sports club or political party. The most frequent barrier between father and child is the father's work schedule. Many fathers, because of long-term goals, sacrifice time with their families only to find that they have lost their children, at least psychologically, in the process. They may end up with financial security but a very empty family. In some cases, modifications in the daily work routine may be possible to ensure his fuller participation in family life, but all too often work is used as an excuse for avoiding family responsibilities. Many fathers who are competent and active at work feel totally inexperienced and ineffectual when at home with their children.

Where previously mothers were inculpated in the psychopathology of childhood, almost to the exclusion of fathers, we now see the return of the father to share the 'blame' as well as the glory. His absence from the family is associated (inter alia) with the development of depression in his offspring (Brown, 1966).

The child is father to the man

It is probably true to say that among the many factors that determine what an individual becomes - of the forces that shape his abilities, interests, motives, goals, desires, personality characteristics and social attitudes - none will be as influential as the family into which he is born. It is a popular saying that 'the child is father to the man'; those who make a scientific study of behaviour agree that the early experiences of infancy and childhood have a profound influence on adult behaviour.

But how profound and irreversible are these early influences? It is assumed that the child's personality traits are 'fixed' in the family mould during earliest childhood and that all that happens subsequently is that they continue to grow, emerging in recognizable but more elaborate form (i.e. in full bloom) at maturity. Some do. But there are difficulties in predicting adult personality from traits observed in early childhood.

Studies that follow up children over long periods of time show that there is only a modest correspondence between many specific traits seen during earliest childhood and adult life although overall trends enable one to identify some fairly gross stabilities or continuities in personality. The characteristic which is most stable (that is to say, unchanging) is achievement-orientation. Most other traits are very poor predictors of adult personality development. These findings are somewhat out of keeping with the ideas held by many theologians, philosophers and psychoanalysts, that the learning experiences of the first five to seven years of a child's life are all-important in determining the sort of person he is to be; that what happens to an individual after that is merely a ripple on the surface of his already 'set' character structure!

Early learning

What is the evidence - rather than the folk-lore - about these issues of early learning and their consequences? Clarke and Clarke (1976), British psychologists, have painstakingly reviewed the available evidence. Their conclusions are as follows.

* At the moment valid scientific knowledge is sadly lacking. Indeed, dogmatism about either the long-term effects or non-effects of early experience is at the present time entirely misplaced. Nevertheless, it is possible to identify certain consistencies in the data.

* There is little reason to suppose that infant learning is acquired more easily than later learning. Nor is there any indication that it is better retained or more resistant to extinction. Experiments in fact suggest that infants and young children are strikingly inferior to adults in many dimensions of learning.

* The long-term effects of short-traumatic incidents seems to be negligible both in animals and young human beings. Only when early learning is continually reinforced do long-term effects appear, and these may well be the result of the later reinforcement rather than of the original learning as such.

* With human infants the specific effects of experiences before seven months of age appear to be of very short duration. Indeed, it is experiences after the first year of life which appear to have a longer-term effect, and even so, extinction occurs unless there is reinforcement.

* It is unwarranted to assume that all psychological processes are affected to an equal extent by early experiences. Different functions appear to show different degrees of recovery following early adversity with the motor processes being the most resilient and emotional functions least so.

* There seem to be large individual differences in vulnerability to early adverse experiences, and in resilience thereafter. This may be due to genetic factors, or to minimal brain injury which could be very common.

* The rigidity of personality structuring during infancy appears to have been exaggerated by some authorities and early learning experiences appear not to set for the child a necessarily fixed and invariable path. After all, the newly born and young infant is an immature creature who can be said to be culturally neutral and psychologically uncommitted. It can only slowly, and with much parental effort and the gradual maturation of its faculties, be socialized.

* The view commonly held by workers in the field of mental health that early characteristics remain relatively unchanged seems to be true only of a specially vulnerable section of the population.

* Evidence suggests that early learning is of importance mainly for its foundational character. Development proceeds at different rates through a sequence of well-marked stages. Each stage depends on the integrity of previous stages. It seems appropriate to talk of optimal periods of learning in human beings. Deficits arising from early environmental handicaps can, to varying extents, be made good.

The Clarkes emphasize the point that the child should not be viewed as a passive organism whose character is moulded solely by the impact of environment upon genetic predispositions.

The child himself acts indirectly as a reinforcer of his own behaviour. For example, the mother-child pair (dyad) is a feedback system (see Lee, Wright and Herbert, 1972), and the degree to which the child's actions have the power to change the mother's behaviour increases with development. The child is not the passive reactor to events he has often been assumed to be. This notion of an essentially passive and reactive infant on whom the environment made its mark led to the corollary that his early environment should receive all the 'blame' when things went wrong. Children labelled 'at risk' have often been regarded in the social work literature as passive victims of external forces. The victims have often been deliberately excluded from study because their roles have been presumed to be irrelevant. Because much of the research on child neglect and abuse has been prompted by concerns with prevention and remediation, attention has been focussed on those aspects of the problem which have been thought to be more easily changed. The parents and their child-rearing practices (again), rather than the children themselves, have been most frequently nominated for this role. For a long time in psychology the infant was misleadingly viewed as a 'tabula rasa' - a blank sheet - passively reacting to the environment, and thus the research literature on such fraught problems as the battered child or the child who fails to thrive has generally adopted the 'mal de mère' approach to the study of developmental failures.

Theorists failed to take into account the influence of the child's individual capacities and his active manipulations of, as well as reactions to, his environment. He 'reaches out', using his magnificent repertoire of grasping, smiles, cries, baby talk and the like, to shape his parent's behaviour. He is himself an agent of socialization and in Rheingold's telling phrase: 'of men and women he makes fathers and mothers' (1963). His temperament, age, sex and state, his cuddliness and his individual demandingness all influence the mother. The possession of certain combinations of temperamental qualities can make a child exceedingly 'difficult', no matter how skilled the parents are. It is just such idiosyncratic features which cause her to change her methods from one of her babies to the next, or to adapt her style of mothering away from preconceived plans and theories she might have had about child-rearing. For, despite his apparent helplessness, even the new-born infant (as we saw earlier) has considerable physical powers.

The emotional 'bond'

In any discussion of the development and rearing of infants, with social workers and social work students, the child's attachment to his parents and others (and how it comes about) constitutes a major theme. There is a strange paradox, in a sense, about a child becoming a person in his own right. In order first of all to become a person he must become attached to his mother by that all-important bond of love, as she will shape his early encounters with his 'world' which give him social awareness. For it would only be correct to speak of a child as a person when he becomes aware of other persons and of himself as a separate individual: in other words, a social being. Then, in order to become a person in his own right, he must later detach himself, at least partially, from her protective cocoon, and develop a point of view of his own. The child must move out of safe orbit around mother and strike out to find his own place in the world.

It is the child's early yearnings for love and relatedness which are among the most important driving forces in the shaping of his personality. There is fairly general agreement among experts that the infant's first human relationship is the foundation stone of his personality, and as the child's first tie of love is usually to his mother, a great deal of research effort has been put into studying this 'attachment' between the child and his mother (see Schaffer, chapter 8).

Loss and bereavement in the family

The spectre of the death of a loved person - someone in the family - plays a central role in the life of every individual. We have all known, or will come to know, death, grief and mourning. A continuing challenge for the social worker is meeting the needs of clients who are bereaved, not only by death but by the loss caused by separation or the sense of loss and pity engendered by the birth of a mentally handicapped child.

Western society reacts to a death by providing varying amounts of solace for the bereaved. The relief of guilt may be simply informal words of comfort and exculpation, as in reassurances like 'nobody could have done more for him than you did'. Some communities have more formal procedures. Maori tribes, for example, had a complex and magical procedure: they used professional mourners who symbolically accepted the sorrows and grief of the bereaved and in their turn were treated as outcasts by the rest of the tribe. It is surprising how often the prescribed rituals lasted between 9 and 12 months, the time which psychologists accept a normal person needs to come to terms with his grief, although some would say it takes longer.

As it is used in everyday conversation grief usually refers to an extreme degree of sorrow associated with loss or separation. We grieve the departure of a dear friend to another country; the child grieves when his mother leaves him in hospital; we feel grief when we lose a loved one's love or when we lose our illusions about him or her. Psychoanalysts have emphasized that the identification of the bereaved person with the deceased is the main process involved in mourning: part of himself, an extension of his ego, has died. Let us look more closely at these processes.

Bowlby (1969) formulates a theory of mourning which distinguishes three main phases. During the first phase, the individual's attachments are still focussed on the lost object, but because of the deceased's absence they cannot be resolved. As a result, the bereaved individual experiences repeated disappointment, the anxiety of persistent separation and, insofar as he accepts reality, grief. So long as the affections and dependencies are focussed on the deceased, there are strenuous and often angry efforts to recover him.

In the second stage, before the final resolution, there is a disorganization of the personality accompanied by pain and despair. In the first two stages, feelings often fluctuate between an angry demand for, or an expectancy of, the loved one's return, to a despair expressed in subdued pining, to total lack of any expression. Though hope and despair may alternate for a long time, there evolves, at last, a degree of emotional detachment from the deceased.

During the third stage, the function of mourning is complete, and a new and different state has come about: a reorganization of attitudes and feelings, partly in relation to the image of the lost person, partly in connection with a new object or objects. Children show this pattern of mourning when separated early in life from their mothers. The consequences can be serious if adequate substitute care is not provided.

Bowlby claims that the pattern of mourning behaviour in higher animals is similar to that of humans. He concludes that the evidence, fragmentary though it is, makes it fairly certain that each of the main behavioural features alleged to be characteristic of human mourning is essentially shared by man with lower animals. Members of animal species protest at the loss of a loved object and do all in their power to seek and recover it. Externally directed hostility is frequent; withdrawal, rejection of a potential new object, apathy and restlessness are the rule. And, given time and opportunity, a reorganization of behaviour in connection with a new object, as well as recovery, often follows.

This theory has received support from the zoologist Konrad Lorenz in his studies of jackdaws, geese, dogs, orang-outangs, and chimpanzees (1961, 1966). A greylag goose which had lost its mate at first began a frantic searching and calling. Then, in the phase of depression, there was a lack of energy, movements were slow, eyes seemed smaller, feathers were loose and slightly fluffed, head and neck were less erect, and there was a noticeably decreased readiness to fly. These deserted, solitary geese also exhibit a disinclination for social contacts: they are generally ignored by other geese, and 'grief-stricken widows of this type are hardly ever courted by males, even if a quite considerable shortage of females prevails in the goose society ... The general picture of grief is just as clearly marked in a widowed goose as it is in a dog.'

A chimpanzee reacting to the death of his mate made repeated efforts to arouse her; he manifested yells of rage and expressed his anger by snatching the short hairs of his head, subsequently giving way to crying and moaning. Later he tended to become more attached to his keeper than he had been before the death and would become angry when the keeper left him.

All this does not mean that there are not features of mourning which are specific to humans; there obviously are uniquely human responses. Perhaps the most significant of these is the intimate relationship between grief and the intense emotional anxiety caused by separation. There is evidence that suggests that when the infant or young child loses his mother he habitually shows responses comparable to a process of mourning in the adult. This observation is also based on studies of healthy children undergoing limited separation experiences in residential nurseries or hospital wards. A predictable sequence of behaviour appeared in the separated child; again we see the three-stage response. At first, with tears and anger the child demands the return of his mother and seems hopeful he will succeed in getting her. This phase of protest may last several days. In the subsequent periods of despair he becomes quieter but it is clear that he still remains preoccupied with his absent mother and still yearns for her return; his hopes, nonetheless, have faded.

Often the first two phases alternate: hope turns to despair and despair to renewed hope. Eventually, however, a greater change occurs. He seems to forget his mother and when she does come back to him, he remains curiously uninterested in her, perhaps not even recognizing her. This is the phase of detachment. In each of these phases the child is prone to tantrums and episodes of destructive behaviour, often of a disquietingly violent kind. Bowlby maintains that there is good reason to think that the sequence of responses described - protest, despair, and detachment - is, in one variant or another, characteristic of all forms of mourning. (This formulation has not escaped criticism and the observation that these patterns are not invariable.) For example, the prediction that if the loss of a loved one is experienced in early childhood, decisive changes in the personality structure often follow, requires a qualification. What is critical is the way the matter of the death is handled and what substitute care (in the case of maternal death) of a loving and continuous kind is available. The emotional scars from such traumatic occurrences appear to be more profound the younger the age of the be-reaved (not counting the earliest months), but they are not necessarily irreversible (see Rutter, 1977).

Many parents tend to avoid the unpleasant subject of death. They say, 'There's plenty of time to worry about that later'. But all children who lose a parent or a brother or sister or a beloved relative or playmate can be spared unnecessary or serious emotional repercussions later if they are encouraged to express their feelings at the time, if they are helped to mourn the loss and thus eventually come to accept the death.

In chapter 18, Carr deals with not only the reactions to death, but also the dying.

References

Biller, H.B. (1971)
Father, Child and Sex Role. Lexington, Ky: Heath Lexington Books.

Bowlby, J. (1951)
Maternal Care and Mental Health. Geneva: WHO.

Bowlby, J. (1969)
Attachment and Loss, Volume 1. London: Hogarth Press.

Brown, F. (1966)
Childhood bereavement and subsequent psychiatric dis-order. British Journal of Psychiatry, 112, 1035-1041.

Bruch, H. (1954)
Parent education or the illusion of omnipotence.
American Journal of Orthopsychiatry, 24, 723-732.

Chess, S. (1964)
Editorial, in American Journal of Orthopsychiatry, 34, 613-614.

Clarke, A. and Clarke A.D.B. (1976)
Early Experience: Myth and reality. London: Open Books.

Harlow, H.F. (1960)
Primary affection patterns in primates. American Journal of Orthopsychiatry, 30, 676-684.

Herbert, M. (1974)
Emotional Problems of Development in Children. London: Academic Press.

Herbert, M. (1980a)
Behavioural social work in families. In D. S. Freeman (ed.), Perspectives on Family Therapy. Western Canada: Butterworths.

Herbert, M. (1980b)
Socialization for problem resistance. In P. Feldman and J. Orford (eds), The Social Context. Chichester: Wiley.

Herbert, M., Sluckin, W.S. and Sluckin, A. (in press)
Mother to infant 'bonding'. Journal of Child Psychology and Psychiatry.

Howells, J.G. (1969)
Fathering. In J.G. Howells (ed.), Modern Perspectives in International Child Psychiatry. Edinburgh: Oliver & Boyd.

Lee, S.G.M., Wright, D.S. and Herbert, M. (1972)
Aspects of the development of social responsiveness in children. Unpublished report to the Social Science Research Council, Psychology Department, University of Leicester.

Lorenz, K. (1961)
Imprinting. In R.C. Birney and R.C. Teevan (eds), Instinct. London: Van Nostrand.

Lorenz, K. (1966)
On Aggression. New York: Harcourt, Brace & World.

Mead, M. (1935)
Sex and Temperament in Three Primitive Societies. London: Routledge & Kegan Paul.

Montagu, M.F.A. (1962)
Prenatal Influences. Springfield, Ill.: Thomas.

Rheingold, H.L. (ed.) (1963)
Maternal Behaviour in Mammals. Chichester: Wiley.

Robson, K.M. and Kumar, R. (1980)
Delayed onset of maternal affection after childbirth. British Journal of Psychiatry, 136, 347,-353.

Rutter, M. (1972)
Maternal Deprivation Reassessed. Harmondsworth: Penguin Books.

Rutter, M. (1977)
Other family influences. In M. Rutter and L. Hersov (eds), Child Psychiatry: Modern approaches. Oxford:: Blackwell Scientific Publications.

Thomas, A., Chess, S. and Birch, H.G. (1968)
Temperament and Behaviour Disorder in Children. London: University of London Press.

Tizard, B. (1977)
Adoption: A second chance. London: Open Books.

Watson, J.B. and Watson, R.R. (1928)
Psychological Care of Infant and Child. New York: Norton.

Whiten, A. (1977)
Assessing the effects of perinatal events on the success of the mother-infant relationship. In H.R. Schaffer (ed.), Studies in Mother-Infant Interaction. London: Academic Press.

Yarrow, M.R., Campbell, J.D. and Burton, R.V. (1968)
Child Rearing: An inquiry into research and methods. San Francisco: Jossey-Bass.

5

Stages of Development and Life-Tasks
Martin Herbert

Man has always entertained theories about the nature of development. One of the ancient notions was called 'preformationism'; man's tendencies and attributes were thought to exist preformed at birth. The 'homunculus' view of human development was an elaboration of preformationism; this theory proposed that the sperm contains a fully formed, miniature man, who simply develops, once conception has taken place, in an incremental way, until maturity is reached. These things have their modern and more sophisticated (but also dubious) counterparts in concepts such as human instincts and innate ideas.

Theologians and philosophers speculated about man's nature and motives. Some of the explanations of the mainsprings of man's actions were profoundly optimistic views, while others involved extremely pessimistic ideas; some suggest that man is self-centred and driven by what is good for himself and for his ego. This is the theory of 'egoism'. In this tradition Thomas Hobbes, the seventeenth-century philosopher, believed that man is basically selfish and (incidentally) brutish and destructive. Freudian psychology contains elements of the pessimistic view as can be seen in the emphasis on instincts which have to be repressed. Freud argued in 'Civilization and its Discontents' that every advance of civilization is bought at the cost of a communal (and therefore individual) renunciation of instinctual gratification. Some theorists believe man always chooses to do what is basically pleasurable: the theory of 'hedonism'. Freud made a great deal of this motive which he called the 'pleasure principle'. It also shows itself in modern learning theories.

Others again (like the seventeenth-century philosopher John Locke) feel that man is not basically selfish. He is driven by a fundamental inclination to co-operate peacefully with his fellow-men. This theory of 'altruism' (formulated, among others, by Rousseau) maintains that nature knows best. The child is like the noble savage pure and unspoilt until he is corrupted by society interfering with natural processes.

One of the controversies in developmental psychology concerns the concept of 'stage', and its importance in describing the development of psychological processes such as thinking and personality. Mussen, Conger and Kagan (1979) illustrate the problem by contrasting the growth of a butterfly with that of a leaf. Once a leaf has grown from its form as a seed, it never changes its basic shape or organization while it grows larger; growth seems to be continuous, with no transformations in shape. By contrast, the butterfly passes through several dramatically different forms - or stages - before it reaches its adult organization. The theorists point out that the mature form of a maple leaf can be predicted easily from an early version, but it would be difficult to guess that the caterpillar and the butterfly are part of the life history of the same creature. Psychologists debate which psychological systems grow continuously without marked transformations, and which pass through different stages in growing toward maturity.

Psychosexual stages of development

Sigmund Freud (1932) believed that the development of a normal sex life involves the successful traversing of various psycho-sexual stages. The basic drives, according to Freud, remain the same throughout life. What changes is the manner of the expression of our motives. There are shifts in the zones of the body (and the associated psychological attitudes) through which gratification is sought and obtained, and in the objects which satisfy our needs. Freud noted that three sensitive areas of the body - the mouth, anus and genitals - are particularly associated with sexual or libidinous gratification. He described certain character traits which are associated with either too great frustration or overly indulged gratification at each of these stages. Certain children, according to the theory, become fixated at one or other of these developmental stages, and the residues of this fixation show themselves in the adult personality.

The development of cognitive functions

Another proponent of stages of development - this time with regard to the growth of cognitive functions - is Jean Piaget. On the basis of his observations and questioning of his own and other children he delineated several successive stages in the development of intelligent behaviour in infancy. Piaget's basic orientation is biological. He proposed that intelligence is an aspect of adapting to the environment; in other words, adaptation is the cognitive striving of the thinking child to find an equilibrium between himself and his milieu.

Adaptation depends upon two interrelated processes which Piaget calls assimilation and accommodation (1932). Assimilation involves a person's adaptation of the environment to himself, and represents the individual's use of his environment as he perceives it. Accommodation is the converse of assimilation and involves the impact on the individual of the actual environment itself. To accommodate is to perceive and to incorporate the experience provided by the environment as it actually is.

The whole span of development from birth to maturity is classified into major stages which can be related to approximate age ranges. Although there are qualitative differences between the stages, the movement from one to the next is continuous. Piaget would claim that the order is fixed.

The complexity of the child's schematic structure – which reflects the development of his intelligence – depends upon the variety of the environmental objects which are available for the child to assimilate and which simultaneously induce accommodation. The Piagetian description of cognitive development in terms of an interplay of accommodatory and assimilatory processes is analogous (according to Danziger, 1971) to the interplay of EGO and ALTER in personality development: namely, the achievement of a balance between the poles of recognizing and adapting to the needs of others and imposing self-centred demands on the social environment. An extreme lack of balance in reciprocity between self and others in either direction gives rise to unsatisfactory social relationships. Children (for example) demand parental support and they try to limit the restraints parents put upon their pleasures. The balance, therefore, is about a compromise between sometimes incompatible mutual demands, and about a style of life which maximizes the mutually rewarding possibilities of the parent-child relationship.

Developmental discontinuity

The periods in which qualitatively new and discontinuous (inter-stage) changes in personality organization are being formulated are described by Ausubel and Sullivan (1970) as transitional phases or developmental crises. During these transitional periods the individual is in the marginal position of having lost an established and accustomed status, and of not yet having acquired the new status towards which the factors impelling developmental change are driving him. Knowledge of 'sensitive periods' in the person's development could alert the social worker to the developmental tasks which put a heavy burden on his adjustive capacities. Each stage of development corresponds to a particular form of social demand: the person must deal with and master a central problem, a potential crisis. At each of eight stages a conflict (as Erikson, 1965, sees it) between opposite poles in a pattern of reciprocity between self and others, has to be resolved.

From birth to about four years of age, to illustrate one of the developmental tasks described by Erik Erikson, the child needs to develop a sense of trust and, later, a growing independence. A lasting sense of trust, security, confidence or optimism (as opposed to distrust, insecurity, inadequacy or pessimism) is thought to be based upon affection, a degree of continuity of care-giving and the reasonably prompt satisfaction of the infant's needs. The major hazards to the development of a perception of a benign, trustworthy and predictable world in which the child initiates his independence-seeking, are neglect, abuse, indifference, extreme inconsistency and other conditions - social and physical - which interfere with the child's sense of personal adequacy or which hinder his acquisition of skills.

Life tasks: attachment

In becoming 'civilized' the child, who is basically 'self-centred' (being concerned only with the immediate gratification of his own needs and desires), must give up much. He must accept many restraints in order to fit into society; the wishes of others have to be taken into account. The love of a child for his parents (in large part) is what makes many of these sacrifices possible. The psychoanalyst Otto Fenichel (1945) believes that the small child loses self-esteem when he loses love and attains it when he regains love. That is what makes children educable. They need supplies of affection so badly that they are ready to renounce other satisfactions if rewards of affection are promised or if withdrawal of love is threatened. What, then, is the source of this bond of love, of social 'attachment', as psychologists refer to it?

The first year of life is the critical one to look at, because within 12 months of birth almost all babies have developed a strong attachment to the mother or a mother-figure. And it is fortunate that this is so! The long period of helpless infancy of the human species entails serious risks, so looked at from an evolutionary point of view it is of crucial importance for the survival of the human species that the child and its parent should become attached to one another for the protection of the young. An interesting theory with regard to early human infant attachment behaviour is offered by Schaffer (chapter 8). The author suggests that the infant demonstrates a primary need (not so much for proximity to other people) but for stimulation. At first the infant seeks optimal arousal from all aspects of the environment. In time he learns that humans are a particularly satisfying source of stimulation and that they are also often sources of non-social stimulation. A need for proximity to other people develops when the infant has learned about their particular characteristics. Eventually, a narrowing down occurs and attachments are formed to specific people.

Other theorists have postulated that an infant is born with a primary 'need' or 'drive' for social contact. Not all would accept this idea of an instinctual response. According to social learning theorists, it is the mother's function to provide the child with positive reinforcing stimuli (i.e. stimuli such as food, water, warmth and many others which meet primary motivations and needs); they follow upon and strengthen the responses of the infant. General characteristics of the mother, such as her attention, her affection and her proximity to the infant, which often precede or are presented at the same time as such reinforcing stimuli, acquire positive reinforcing value.

Here then are the concepts of drive and motivation. What happens, according to some theorists, is the development of a fundamental need for the mother - a dependency - which becomes more compelling than such physical needs as hunger and thirst. The child's early love, in other words, is a form of 'cupboard love', which it learns. More recently, John Bowlby in Britain and Mary Salter Ainsworth (1973) in the USA and other research workers, have rejected this as an oversimplified picture of early social responsiveness. The child is not just a passive recipient of love and stimulation.

Researchers have remarked on the way children often seem to dictate their parents' behaviour by the insistency of their demands. Infants do not wait passively for things to be done to them; they reach out actively to their surroundings for stimulation and social contact. Early on the baby smiles, laughs, reaches out and coos at his mother. Later, when he is able to, he greets and approaches her and does delightful things which ensure that she will continue to do the things he likes, such as making funny noises at him, tickling him, and so on. The mother has a powerful influence on her child's behaviour, and by encouraging some activities and discouraging others she 'shapes' his personality. But in all sorts of subtle ways her behaviour is also shaped by the child. There is a two-way traffic in the relationship between mother and child in the crucial business of his becoming a person.

This observation has meant that psychologists have found it useful to conceive of the mother and child as a single 'attachment system' while they are interacting with each other. We cannot describe attachment (or dependency) in the child without describing the attributes and behaviour of his mother. Psychologists have observed and analysed the attachment system in the laboratory and the natural setting of the youngster's home. What evidence we have - and it is still incomplete - has been interpreted by Bowlby, the author of 'Attachment and Loss' (1969), as supporting the view that the child's attachment can occur (as it does in animal species) without the rewards of food, warmth and the like. It is suggested that the child is 'programmed' by its heredity so that it is sensitive to certain types of stimulation in its surroundings. The human face in movement, for example, is one of the most dependable 'triggers' of a smile in young babies. And as all mothers know, her baby's smile binds her to him with a deep feeling of joy and love (Schaffer, 1971, 1977, reviews some of these events).

Failure to master previous developmental tasks is thought to hinder the individual in the next social endeavour. All these formulations are difficult to prove or disprove, although they are articles of faith for many psychologists.

We have referred to the interplay of ego and alter in personality development: the balance between a self-centred and altruistic point of view in social interactions. The family, like other socializing agents of society, uses various techniques to teach and control the child in its care, and not least to encourage the 'alter' component of personality. Among those used are material and psychological rewards, praise, reproof, corporal and psychological punishment, examples, giving or withholding love, approval and explanation of rules.

One may say that all children in all societies are socialized in numerous behaviours by many agents, using a wide variety of techniques and practices. The emphasis on particular social behaviour patterns and the means for developing them often varies from culture to culture, but certain systems of behaviour are universally brought under social control: eating, elimination, dependency and aggression. In the Tarongan child, from the Philippines, co-operativeness is a culturally desirable characteristic. Manifestations of this quality are rewarded even during the child's earliest years. Rewards are predominantly verbal or edible. Sharing toys or food with other children is highly approved, as is helping another child who needs assistance. Either will gain lavish praise for the child, and perhaps a biscuit or a bit of fruit.

References

Ainsworth, M.D. (1973)
The development of infant-mother attachment. In B.M. and H.N. Ricciuti (eds), Review of Child Development Research. Chicago: University of Chicago Press.

Ausubel, D.P. and Sullivan, E.V. (1970)
Theory and Problems of Child Development (2nd edn). London: Grune & Stratton.

Bowlby, J. (1969)
Attachment and Loss, Volume 1. London: Hogarth Press.

Danziger, K. (1971)
Socialization. Harmondsworth: Penguin.

Erikson, E.H. (1965)
Childhood and Society (rev. edn). Harmondsworth: Penguin.

Fenichel, O. (1945)
The Psychoanalytic Theory of Neurosis. London: Routledge & Kegan Paul.

Freud, S. (1932)
New Introductory Lectures on Psychoanalysis. London: Hogarth Press.

Mussen, P.H., Conger, J.L. and Kagan, J. (1979)
Child Development and Personality. New York: Harper & Row.

Piaget, J. (1932)
The Moral Judgement of the Child. New York: Harcourt Brace.

Schaffer, H.R. (1971)
The Growth of Sociability. Harmondsworth: Penguin.

Schaffer, H.R. (1977)
Mothering. London: Fontana/Open Books.

6

Personality, Emotion, Motivation and Intellect
Martin Herbert

In trying to understand differences in the characteristic
but varied responses individuals make to life situations,
psychologists have developed theories of personality.
Margaret Mead's work (1935) among the South Sea Islanders
showed the huge variation in patterns of adjustment which
can be produced in humans by different styles of upbringing.
The Arapesh of New Guinea are gentle, peace-loving people,
among whom self-assertion is so rare as to be regarded as
abnormal. For their periodic celebrations they persuade some
of their members, much against their will, into the role of
organizers. Passivity and selflessness form an essential
part of the nurture and education of each individual. From
birth, the child is exposed to traits like these in the
behaviour of those about them; in the course of development,
he assimilates many of them into his own personality.

Another island group, the Mundugumor, in complete
contrast, fosters aggression from infancy. If a suckling
baby does not take a firm grip on his mother's breast she
will pull the nipple away and the infant will go hungry. As
a child grows up his early experience is shaped by training
in warlike pursuits.

Cultural influences
The cultural milieu into which a child is born is highly
significant in determining many aspects of the life style
and characteristics the individual will adopt. The process
of socialization is a sometimes pleasurable, sometimes
painful route, which the child travels in his own unique
way, acquiring those minimal social and personality attributes regarded as desirable by the community. Of course, he
does not become an exact replica of his fellow group members. As we saw in chapter 4, many influences operate to
make each individual quite unique; Kluckhohn and Murray
(1953) put it in this way: 'every man is in certain respects
like all other men, like some other men, like no other man'.
Even identical twins - sharing precisely the same genetic
endowment - can be socialized in different ways to become
very different persons.

Personality represents the enduring properties of individuals which tend to separate them from other individuals.
It expresses consistency and regularity. Personality

includes both structure and dynamics, in the sense that it is characterized both by parts and by relationships among the parts. In this sense it can be viewed as a system. Indeed Allport (1937), in a classical text, defined personality as a dynamic organization within the individual of those psycho-physical systems which determine his unique adjustments to his environment.

This rather technical-sounding definition emphasizes certain important features of personality. It stresses the changing (dynamic) nature of personality. Personality is less a finished product than a transitive process. It has some stable features; at the same time, it is continually undergoing change. Allport (1955) described this course of change, or 'individuation', as a process of 'becoming'. It is one of the paradoxes of social case work that social workers spend much of their time delving into the client's past, whereas the person himself is preoccupied with the present and in projecting his life towards the future.

The definition also stresses the inter-relatedness (organization) of different personal traits. In other words, man is not simply a static aggregation of qualities. Allport emphasizes the psychological and physical bases (psycho-physical systems) of human attitudes, habits, values, emotions, beliefs, motives and sentiments. These in turn determine the unique adjustments each person will make to any situation (family, school, work or community) in which he finds himself. They, in turn, are shaped by the environment, so there is a continuing transaction between an individual and his environment.

A transactional model stresses the changing character of the environment and of the organism as an active participant in its own development. The child's response to events, for example, is thought to be more than a simple reaction to his environment. He is thought to be actively engaged in attempts to organize and structure his world. He is not a 'tabula rasa' passively accepting the etchings of experience. The infant is already something of an individual at birth, reaching out in his own way to 'shape' his environment. Among the idiosyncracies which have been demonstrated in early infancy are autonomic response patterns, social responsiveness (cuddliness), regularity of sleeping, feeding and other biological patterns, and perceptual responses (Thomas et al, 1968).

Temperament

There are others to take account of, in particular the 'temperamental' factors related to the child's general level of activity, sensory threshold, intensity of response and the general affective tone of his transactions with the environment. Emphasis is on the 'how' rather than the 'why' or 'what' of behaviour. Any social worker who has worked on the maternity ward of a hospital so as to be able to contrast babies knows that they differ markedly in temperament. This term is essentially applied to the inherited (or innate) aspects of personality and is used to describe the person's characteristic behavioural style independently of the content of his specific behaviour.

Historically, the psychological notion of temperament originated with Galen, the Greek physician of the second century AD, who developed it from an earlier theory based on the assumption of four basic fluids (humours) which were supposed to produce four types of temperament: the warm and pleasant (sanguine), slow-moving (apathetic), sad and depressed (melancholic) and the hot-tempered and quick to react (choleric). His theory was one of the first of many attempts to classify people into types.

Personality types

Among the many factors which are thought to predispose a client to one sort of problem rather than another are the basic combinations of such personality attributes as extraversion-introversion and neuroticism (also known as emotionality or instability). The psychologist Hans Eysenck (1963), among others, has systematically studied the traits making up these personality types. He described the typical extravert as sociable, a person who likes parties, needs to have people to talk to and does not like reading or studying by himself. He tends to crave excitement, takes chances, is impulsive, sticks his neck out, and behaves on the spur of the moment. He is carefree, easy-going, fond of practical jokes, likes change, and always has a ready answer. He tends to be optimistic, laughs a lot and prefers to keep on the move. He is inclined to be aggressive and loses his temper rather swiftly.

Eysenck's characterization of the typical introvert encompasses a very different sort of person. He tends to be shy, quiet and retiring, introspective and more attracted to books than people at large. He tends to plan ahead, being cautious rather than impulsive. He avoids excitement, takes matters of everyday life with some seriousness and prefers a well-ordered style of life. He keeps his feelings under tight control, is not aggressive and not hot-tempered. He is more reliable than the extravert, and more pessimistic. He places a lot of emphasis on ethical issues.

These descriptions are, of course, profiles of 'pure' types and do not necessarily fit people who tend to be extraverted or introverted in only some respects. It is a matter of degree. The term 'personality dimension' has been introduced to represent the fact that people can be assigned a position (depending on a personality test score) somewhere along a scale, such as extraversion-introversion.

These personality dimensions are thought to arise from genetic and environmental causes. There are thought to be differences in certain nervous processes in the brain which determine some of the characteristic behaviour patterns and traits of the extravert and introvert. Because of their hereditary make-up, some individuals have more sensitive or reactive central nervous systems than others. Experimental studies and comparisons of identical and fraternal twins provide the evidence for this claim. Although it is commonly said that a person is a 'born' extravert or 'born' introvert, early family and other environmental experiences also have their effect. Happy social experiences encourage the child to want to repeat them. By comparison, too many miserable social experiences tend to reinforce negative attitudes towards social experiences and towards other people. Children are particularly impressionable during their formative years and can therefore be influenced in the direction of being sociable, unsociable or antisocial more easily in early childhood than later on.

The nomothetic approach

Here is a theory that was derived from the study of large numbers of subjects (people and their test results). The approach emphasizes common principles of functioning across individuals. Such a theory involves the systematic recording of responses and is usually associated with structured, objective tests (see Pervin, 1970, who provides a detailed account of how psychologists assess individual differences in personality, temperament, mood, motivation, aptitude, interests, intelligence and perception of people). Raymond Cattell (1946) also presents this kind of theory formulation. Both Cattell and Eysenck emphasize the structural elements of personality based on a statistical (factorial) analysis of test results. The basic element for Cattell is the trait. Traits are distinguishable along the traditional lines in psychology of emotion (temperament), motivation (dynamic) and cognition (ability).

Three other theories of personality social workers should be acquainted with might be called clinical theories; they are derived to a great extent from observations of individuals in treatment. The theorists, Sigmund Freud (1932), Carl Rogers (1951, 1959, 1961; see Hopson, chapter 13), and George Kelly (1955: see Bannister, chapter 9), share an emphasis on individual differences and on the total, holistic functioning of the organism. All are valuable (along with others described by Hopson) in the social worker's vital role as a counsellor. The psychologist Lawrence A. Pervin provides an excellent text relating personality theory to practice in his book, 'Personality: Theory, assessment and research' (1970).

Emotionality

What of that dimension of personality referred to earlier, known as neuroticism? The client who has a high degree of this attribute is often referred to as being 'nervous', 'timid', 'emotional', or 'highly-strung', because his emotions seem to be so labile, so volatile. It has been demonstrated by experimental investigation that the emotional person displays a variety of related traits. He tends to be anxious, worried, unhappy, ego-centric and quickly and easily aroused. Such traits set him apart from the 'calm' individual. But we must remember that it is all a matter of degree, not an absolute distinction. The calm person tends to be persistent, steadfast, carefree, hopeful and contented. The client who shows intense emotionality and anxiety is susceptible to neurotic breakdown. Such a vulnerability implies a low tolerance for stress, whether it be physical, as in painful situations, or psychological, as in conflict or frustration situations. There is some evidence that highly-strung over-reactive attributes are in part the consequences of inherited factors.

The issue of emotion is an important one to social workers; they ascribe great significance to 'feelings': that is, the affective tone and content of their clients.

Emotion

The word 'emotion' comes from the Latin word 'movere', meaning 'to move'. Children and adults alike often feel that they are driven or moved by their feelings and, in fact, the study of emotion is closely linked to the investigation of 'motivation', a subject discussed in detail by Allport (1937, 1955). Scientists have investigated different aspects of emotion. Some define it in terms of the feelings experienced by the person, others define it in terms of the bodily changes which always accompany these feelings. Most emphasize the reaction as the main aspect of emotion, but others stress the way in which people perceive situations that arouse emotion or the effect that emotion has on ordinary behaviour.

The term emotion has now become rather vague and there are many feelings and reactions to which the label 'emotion' is given. Some are predominantly negative states such as rage, horror, fear, agony, anxiety, disgust, embarrassment, boredom or grief. Others are more positive; love, joy, pleasure, amusement, ecstasy and so on. It has been theorized that there are eight basic emotional reactions: anticipation, anger, joy, acceptance, surprise, fear, sorrow and disgust. There are patterned bodily reactions and it is thought that the primitive prototypes for these can be found in animals.

In a classic book, 'The Expression of the Emotions in Animals and Man', written in 1872, Charles Darwin proposed three principles for interpreting emotional manifestations: among them was the utility of the behaviour which appears during emotional excitement. He gave the example of the hostile animal baring the canine teeth in preparation for biting; when an angry man curls his lip and shows the canine teeth he does not intend to bite but the expression is a vestige of a biologically useful act. Walter Cannon (1932) elaborated this principle of utility to include internal bodily changes that occur during the so-called 'emergency emotions': rage, fear, excitement and pain. Cannon demonstrated that during a crisis the physical changes mobilize the energies of an individual in preparation for a vigorous fight or a flight for one's life. These issues are taken up again in a section on stress in chapters 11 and 19.

Emotional development

There is an important link between social and emotional development. The sorts of emotions called delight, love, anger and jealousy depend upon social awareness: a consciousness of 'me' and 'mine' and 'other people'. The newborn infant gradually learns to perceive himself as a separate individual, and to distinguish 'things out there' from internal impressions or feelings. We have been referring to emotion (in the form of a noun) as if it were an entity. This is the reification fallacy. Emotion is no more a thing than is intelligence, or mind. It is a complete set of psycho-physiological processes, partly learned, partly inherited. What do seem to be inherited are certain physiological structures which enable a child to react with a particular degree of sensitivity to stimulating events in his environment, and to act with a particular level of intensity of emotion. This 'emotional tone' means that some children live at a relatively high and consistent level of activity and passivity, elation and depression. Neonates (new-borns) - as we have seen - differ quite markedly in their senstivity, susceptibility and responsiveness to all kinds of stimulation.

In this volume, as is the practice of many psychologists, we started with behaviour. As Murray puts it in 'Explorations in Personality': 'upon behaviour and its results depends everything which is generally regarded as important: physical wellbeing and survival, development and achievement, happiness and the perpetuation of the species' (Murray, 1938). However, as was made clear in chapter 1, we are not interested in overt behaviour to the complete exclusion of such psychological phenomena as feelings, fantasies, inner conflicts, emotions, attitudes, beliefs, needs and motives. The analysis of an individual's motives helps the psychologist to understand his behaviour by clarifying what is reinforcing to him. It helps him to predict how the person may act in future situations.

Motivation

Motivation has three aspects:

* motivating states (called needs, drives or motives);
* motivated behaviour;
* the conditions that satisfy or alleviate the motivating conditions.

The American psychologist Robert Woodworth introduced the term 'drive' in 1918 to describe the energy which impels an animal into some action as opposed to the habits that guide its behaviour in one direction or another. The term 'drive' came to be used to describe specific urges such as sex, hunger, and so on.

Biologically-based 'drives' are motives which originate in some organic or tissue need. They are best described as 'homeostatic needs'. What does this mean? The term 'homeostasis' (steady state) is used for a situation in which internal environment fluctuations are held within certain tolerable limits; the body has to maintain a steady internal environment because man is exposed to widely fluctuating external conditions. If the blood-sugar concentration increases above its normal level, homeostatic mechanisms (functioning like thermostats) cause it to decrease. Body temperature, too, must not be too high or too low. In any homeostatic system (think of the thermostat in the central heating boiler) a response is fed back into the system as a stimulus for homeostasis: that is, the reaching of a certain temperature is the stimulus for a reverse in the direction of change. Such systems are called 'feedback systems'; these concepts have found their way into contemporary social work jargon in relation to systems theory and family therapy.

As we saw, physiological mechanisms take care of many of the problems of maintaining a homeostatic equilibrium, but the body also makes use of what is called 'regulatory behaviour'. It motivates the regulatory behaviour that is instrumental in satisfying the physiological needs. Since homeostasis is necessary for life and since a primary goal of behaviour is to maintain life at an optimal level, it is scarcely surprising that a secondary goal of behaviour is the maintenance of what might be called 'psychological homeostasis': a form of tension reduction. To give an example, a man with a reputation as an up-and-coming executive reacts to the arrival of a highly experienced newcomer in the firm by extra endeavour in order to maintain his status. His behaviour might be described as analogous to a homeostatic mechanism, and is designed to restore his mental equilibrium. Biological needs and psychological (or social) needs are accompanied by feelings of tension or disequilibrium. Much of our psychological adjustive behaviour can be thought of as reducing tension.

Social motives
There are many social motives (or needs). To mention but a few:

* security;
* approval;
* power;
* affiliation (companionship);
* sympathy;
* self-actualization (self-fulfilment).

These secondary motives, as they are called, are learned as a result of the unique experiences of the individual in various environments. There are several theories which try to explain social/psychological motives as derivatives of more basic physiological ones, hence terms such as secondary or acquired motives/drives. None are totally convincing.

Needs

This is a familiar term in the social worker's vocabulary;
for example, the 'needs' of the child have to be considered
in adoption or care proceeding decisions. A social need is
usually defined as a state of disequilibrium, for instance,
a need for love and affection, which drives the individual
in a direction which will restore his equilibrium (e.g.
looking for a marital partner). Although some psychologists
have rejected the directional (that is, motivational)
aspects of living processes, most sciences have accepted
such tendencies.

Needs and motives usually manifest themselves in
relation to particular kinds of stimulus situations. The
stimulus situation is that part of the total environment to
which the individual attends and reacts. The environment as
it appears in a psychological description occurs not most
often as a physical or chemical agent impinging on the body
or sense organs, but in terms of its meaning for the individual. Notcutt (1953) states that the same stimulus may
have many different meanings, and many different stimuli
may have the same meaning. It is the meanings that are
important and not the stimulus in its own nature as a
physical or chemical process. This notion of 'meaning' -
mediating stimulus and response - takes us to the cognitive
aspects of personality.

Cognitive learning

According to Albert Bandura and many other theorists, the
processes that govern human adjustment (and maladjustment)
are cognitive in nature. Bandura (1977) points out that if
human behaviour could be fully explained in terms of external stimulus conditions, there would be no need to
postulate any additional regulating mechanisms. Reviews of
the evidence on operant and classical conditioning in adult
humans seem to indicate that awareness (a cognitive process)
mediates the so-called conditioning processes. Behaviour is
not always predictable from external sources of influence;
cognitive factors, in part, determine what we observe, feel,
and do at any particular point in time.

Cognitive learning is a generic term for learning about
the world by the use of reasoning, judgement, imagination,
and various perceptual and conceptual abilities. Such
learning makes use of images, symbols, concepts and rules.
Cognitive processes involved in cognitive learning include
attentional processes, the encoding of information, the
storage and retrieval of information in memory, the posi-
ting of hypotheses, their evaluation, and inductive and
deductive reasoning. These are some of the attributes which
are measured in estimates of a person's intelligence.

Intelligence

There is no definitive statement to be made about the nature
of intelligence. To begin with, it is a multi-faceted
phenomenon; intellectual activity takes many forms.

Psychologists have found the term useful to summarize many
mental activities which underlie behaviour we choose to call
'intelligent' or 'unintelligent' in everyday life. We talk
of verbal intelligence (a facility with words and verbal
problems) and spatial intelligence (a facility with spatial
relationships) and so on.

Intelligence matures rapidly during childhood until
about 12. The rate of growth slows down until, for the
majority of the population, maximum intellectual capacity in
the biological sense is reached somewhere between the ages
of 15 and 25. Early investigations of intellectual changes
associated with ageing suggested (as we saw) that full
intellectual capacity is reached by the early twenties,
followed by a more or less static period (a plateau) and
then by a slow, long decline. Early studies were concerned
with different age cross-sections of the population which
meant that older groups were not always as well-educated,
quick or highly motivated and confident to do intelligence
tests as younger groups. Consequently, the early reports
were in error in significant ways. More recent studies have
been of the longitudinal kind, which is to say that the same
individuals are followed up and re-tested over long periods
of time. The first longitudinal reports that showed continuing intellectual gains in older adults were from investigations of gifted individuals, and as a result continued
gains were thought to be characteristic only of people of
superior intelligence. Later studies included individuals of
more average abilities and even in these circumstances,
gains in adult intellectual activity have been observed.

Theoreticians have divided intelligence into an un-
specified type of intellectual ability (Type A), also
referred to as 'fluid ability', or 'g' (general ability),
which involves abstract thinking, capacity for perceiving
and discriminating between things, discerning relationships
and groupings and working out implications. It reveals
itself in new situations where successful adaptation cannot
rely on the person's existing repertoire of intellectual
skills. This ability reaches its maximum growth at the same
time as general biological maturity, at adolescence. The
subsequent decline is not noticeable until after the age of
about 25. Another type of intellectual ability is postulated. This is Type B, a specialized ability sometimes
referred to as 'crystallized ability' or 'verbal and
educational ability'. It consists of cognitive skills and
conceptual categories which allow the individual to assimilate and learn from new experiences. Crystallized intelligence reveals itself in those tests which require learned
habits or thinking. This ability may continue to develop
(particularly in the individual who uses his mind) throughout adult life. The psychologist Dennis Bromley makes the
point that during maturity and old age, intellectual activity is concerned mainly with the application of acquired
techniques and the assimilation of experience to established
frames of reference. The wisdom of the older person is the

wisdom of experience because, as unspecialized mental ability declines with age, the older person relies more on what
he has learned. The wisdom of the younger person is the
wisdom of insight because, as specialized mental ability is
lacking for want of experience, the younger person must
think things out from first principles (Bromley, 1968).

Personality also changes and develops. It is the executive processes of personality which come to prominence in
middle age: self-awareness, selectivity, manipulation and
control of the environment, mastery, competence, and a wide
array of strategies for coping with life. The middle-aged
individual places more importance on, above all, the restructuring of experience: that is, the processing of new
information in the light of past experience. Forty year olds
often seem to see the environment as one that rewards
boldness and the taking of risks, and they perceive themselves as having the energy to deal with the opportunities
they see around them.

There is another important component of mind to
consider: the self-concept.

The self-concept

Common sense would seem to demand concepts such as 'self'
to account for, and unify, the complex elements which make
up personality. It seems, on the face of it, essential to
postulate the self as the integrating core of the individual's personality, the reference point around which his
thinking and feeling about matters, his attitudes, experiences and reactions are organized. Could there be any
alternative way of explaining the apparent coherence, unity
and purposiveness of personality?

In fact, for several decades, many psychologists attempted to study personality without resorting to these
allegedly circular and question-begging terms. The objection
of the early experimental psychologists to the term self is
seen in their appeal for 'a psychology without a soul'. They
saw clearly the scientific dangers of invoking a convenient
'homunculus', or ghost in the machine (labelled 'ego' or
'self') to explain away awkward or discrepant facts about
personality, or to produce consistencies where there were
none. Since the 1950s many psychologists have embraced the
'heresy' of yesteryear. Allport (1955) believes that the
primary requirement of an adequate psychological approach to
the person are matters of fact to him; between what he feels
to be significant, vital and central in becoming a person
and what belongs to the periphery of his being. He suggests
that use of the term 'proprium' for those aspects of personality, those areas of life, that have powerful personal
relevance and which we regard as peculiarly ours.

The description 'propriate' certainly applies to our
term 'self-image' (see Bannister, chapter 9). The self-image
is a crucial propriate function, and is referred to by some
writers as the phenomenal self. Allport describes two aspects of the self-image: the way the individual perceives

his present abilities, status and roles and what he would like to become, his aspirations for himself: his idealized self-image. Various researchers have marshalled evidence from various sources to demonstrate that even very young babies exhibit a need to be competent, to master or deal effectively with their own environment. This need is referred to as 'effectance motivation' and is thought to be related to such motives as mastery, curiosity and achievement.

Martin Seligman (1975) suggests that what produces self-esteem and a sense of competence in a child (two crucial attributes for positive mental health) and what immunizes him against depression and helplessness, is (in part) the actual quality of his experience. But what is also crucial is the child's perception that his own actions controlled the experience. Seligman states that to the degree that uncontrollable events occur, either traumatic or positive, depression will be predisposed and ego strength undermined.

The love and affection of parents for a child and their unfolding attitudes toward him as he grows up are of continuing importance in the more and more sophisticated evolution of his self-image. But beyond the early years of childhood, many other persons outside the family assume an increasingly important role in forming the self-concept: teachers, classmates, playmates and friends. In adult years, his work associates, spouse and children contribute to this process. It is the process of identification which is important in incorporating aspects of other persons into the self. Once a person (consciously or unconsciously) is chosen for this significance, the individual not only models his overt behaviour after him, but also takes on his thoughts and feelings and ways of looking at things; in other words, takes on the attitude of the other.

References

Allport, G.W. (1937)
   Personality: A psychological interpretation. New York: Holt, Rinehart & Winston.
Allport, G. (1955)
   Becoming. New Haven, Conn.: Yale University Press.
Bandura, A. (1977)
   Social Learning Theory. Englewood Cliffs, NJ: Prentice-Hall.
Bromley, D.B. (1968)
   The Psychology of Human Ageing. Harmondsworth: Penguin.
Cannon, W.B. (1932)
   The Wisdom of the Body. New York: Norton.
Cattell, R.B. (1946)
   The Description and Measurement of Personality. Yonkers, NY: World Book Co.
Darwin, C. (1872)
   The Expression of the Emotions in Animals and Man. New York: John Murray.

Eysenck, H.J. (1963)
Uses and Abuses of Psychology. Harmondsworth: Penguin.
Freud, S. (1932)
New Introductory Lectures on Psychoanalysis. London:
Hogarth Press.
Kelly, G.A. (1955)
The Psychology of Personal Constructs. New York: Van
Nostrand Reinhold.
Kluckhohn, C. and Murray, H.A. (eds) (1953)
Personality in Nature, Society and Culture. New York:
Knopf.
Mead, M. (1935)
Sex and Temperament in Three Primitive Societies.
London: Routledge & Kegan Paul.
Murray, H.A. (1938)
Explorations in Personality. New York: Oxford University
Press.
Notcutt B. (1953)
The Psychology of Personality. New York: Philosophical
Library.
Pervin, L.A. (1970)
Personality: Theory, assessment and research. New York:
Wiley.
Rogers, C.R. (1951)
Client-Centered Therapy. Boston: Houghton-Mifflin.
Rogers, C.R. (1959)
A theory of therapy, personality and interpersonal
relationships, as developed in the client-centred
framework. In S. Koch (ed.), Psychology: The study of
a science, 3. New York: McGraw-Hill.
Rogers, C.R. (1961)
On Becoming a Person: A therapist's view of
psychotherapy. Boston: Houghton-Mifflin.
Seligman, M.E.P. (1975)
Helplessness. San Francisco: Freeman.
Thomas, A., Chess, S. and Birch, H.G. (1968)
Temperament and Behaviour Disorder in Children. London:
University of London Press.
Woodworth, R.S. (1918)
Dynamic Psychology. Milford, USA: Jesup Lectures,
1916-1917.

7

Psychology: Models of Causation and Change
Martin Herbert

Psychopathology is the study of 'diseases of the mind' (see Shapiro, chapter 19). Man has always suffered from mental illness. Studies carried out in this century indicate that the members of primitive, pastoral societies suffered from all the mental diseases that are known in modern industrial nations, even though the manifestations and treatment were sometimes different. For centuries the bizarre behaviour of the mentally ill aroused the cruel hostility and prejudice of ignorance.

Very early in the development of medicine societies devised ways to treat mental disorders. Skulls have been found with holes cut carefully in them - an operation carried out while their owners were alive - showing that trepanning, as this procedure is called, was used by far-flung cultures. More recently, patients were made to walk along dark corridors with trap-doors, through which they fell into ice-cold water below, to shock them back to normality.

In the twentieth century increasing numbers of people have suffered from various forms of mental illness; now-adays, with the improvement in standards of physical health, their problems have received greater attention.

Definitions

The terms 'insanity' and 'madness' are the colloquial expressions often applied to psychological disturbance in adults. In the very old Hollywood films, the scheming villain tried to drive his heiress wife crazy by a series of nefarious tricks, like her counterpart, the heroine from even earlier movies, who teetered on the edge of a precipice while the dastardly villain tried to push her over. The victim, nearly 'terrified out of her wits', or 'driven out of her senses', teeters on the edge of the chasm of insanity. For the authors of these melodramas and the fascinated audiences who watched them, the issue was quite simple: there was a clear-cut dividing line between sanity and insanity. The popular view, even today, is that there is a breaking point - a fairly precise point - at which some overwhelming emotion, or profound physical illness, or excessive fatigue might lead to 'a nervous breakdown'. It is, in fact, much more complicated than this. How does one recognize that a change - which would be labelled insanity (or to use the correct psychiatric term, psychosis) - has actually taken place? As far as the public are concerned, they can tolerate a great deal of peculiar behaviour, eccentric ideas and strange manners and speech, as long as the individual does not threaten or attempt to do anything which threatens his own or other people's safety. It is basically the loss of self-control which is the distinguishing mark of what the public regards as insanity, and it is very much the same for the individual. It is at that point when he has to admit, 'I have lost my self-control, I am no longer master of my own mind' that the person doubts his own sanity. To establish the insanity of a person in a court of law it must be demonstrated that the person does not know the difference between right and wrong, or that he is unable to exercise that control over his actions generally expected and observed in the average individual.

Psychiatrists have moved away from legal definitions and would tend to diagnose mental illness by the presence of 'symptoms'. The individual's mental functions are so profoundly disturbed that he is incapacitated from participating in everyday activities. He usually shows signs of thought disorder, including delusions and hallucinations and disturbed motor behaviour, all of which give the bizarre, irrational colouring to his behaviour. Essentially, there is an alteration of that central aspect of his personality: his ego, or self. Sometimes it is the disintegration or fragmentation of the various aspects of self which usually work harmoniously together. But there are many mentally ill patients who do not show such extreme symptoms. Here is one of the most trying problems of deciding upon the presence or absence of mental abnormality; the symptoms of mental illness are so often only the exaggeration of traits occurring in normal people. When does a sense of injustice or resentment or suspicion become paranoid: that is to say, a delusion of persecution? When does shyness and solitariness or imaginative introspection become schizoid? These are not easy questions to answer. Certainly the issue of mental health and mental ill-health are not simple matters and straight opposites like black and white.

Every society has certain patterns of behaviour which it expects from its members. The eminent psychiatrist Karl Menninger (1963) defined normality of behaviour as the adjustment of human beings to the world and to each other with a maximum of effectiveness and happiness. A reading of popular literature shows that wisdom - that pinnacle of our social ideals - is perceived as adapting oneself to nature or to one's environment, an effort after harmony, a striving for self-control. It is not surprising that society should expect a 'wise man' to be a balanced person, a man in harmony with his world, a man with self-possession.

What is this concept of 'adjustment' or 'adaptation' which psychologists are so fond of using?

The nature of adjustment

Living creatures can exist only within rather narrow limits of pressure and temperature and under a limited variety of chemical conditions. Adjustment is biologically and psychologically fundamental to life. As beings that consume energy, they must adjust their input of energy to their output at all times. This effort, with its particular and often precise demands, is termed adaptation. Adaptation is a concept which is central to Charles Darwin's theory of evolution. Over countless thousands of years, new species appeared and flourished because genetic mutations allowed some forms of life to adapt better than others to their often harsh circumstances.

The fascinating subject, of course, is man who, because of the complexity and flexibility of his adjustive equipment (complex brain, flexible fingers, upright position, etc.), has attained his pre-eminent position on earth. Human living is a matter of give-and-take, a continuous transaction between the individual and his surroundings, one which takes place on the physical and psychological level. Throughout his life the individual is required to adjust to a never-ending stream of changing events, situations and people. Many of the physical adaptations are reflex in nature, mediated by inherited physical processes; but the majority of the psychological strategies for coping with life-situations are learned, many of them during childhood.

There are great difficulties in defining effective adjustment. If adjustment is efficient, that is, favourable in its consequences, psychologists tend to call it normal. The word normal comes from the Latin 'norma' meaning a 'standard' or 'rule'. A norm is a standard prescribed by society, in the case of social norms. The word normal is usually taken to mean three things: that behaviour is understandable, predictable and controllable. Thus the child who does bizarre things, who is inconsistent - being one way one day and another way the next - and whose behaviour is difficult to control, would seem abnormal and cause a parent to worry. The majority of human problems are a matter of degree. All people are aggressive to some extent, all individuals are fearful to some degree, all of us show relatively bizarre, difficult behaviour at certain times. Many ordinary citizens have problems like phobias, nightmares, obsessions and compulsions. Generally the expert will apply the following criteria to answer questions about a person's mental health. What are the consequences - favourable or unfavourable - of this individual's patterns of traits and ways of behaving? Does the person's general style of life and his mode of adjusting to situations, or his particular tensions and conflicts, prevent him from leading a happy life in which he is able to enjoy social and loving relationships, and work (and play or relax) effectively?

Even in the psychological realm the slogan might be 'adapt or perish'. Those whose adjustive mechanisms are defective (e.g. the severely subnormal or the mentally ill) have to be taken care of in special institutions because they cannot survive in the outside world. Many, who cannot make the necessary adjustments to life, opt out of it by committing suicide.

Recent advances in the treatment of the mentally ill have virtually all been in the realm of physical methods. Physical treatment, mainly by electro-convulsive therapy and drugs, has radically changed the whole outlook over the range of psychiatric disorders. Many people with mental illnesses can be treated as out-patients and for those who have to be admitted to hospital, the length of stay is now usually measured in weeks rather than in months or years, as used to be the case.

Life problems

There are countless other persons who survive, but whose survival is so restricted and in some cases marginal that they can only be said to be existing. Feeling as they do - alienated, unloved, unreal and aimless - they cannot be said to be living life to the full. Some of these people would be diagnosed as suffering from a psychoneurosis (or neurosis). Neurosis is a shorthand term for something as pervasive as emotional disturbance or life problems; it can be applied to a set of attitudes (Horney, 1947); and it can also be defined narrowly and technically (see Fenichel, 1945; Wolpe, 1973). The neurotic person is invariably a suffering person.

The generic term 'neurosis' can encompass:

* feelings of unhappiness, distress, misery;
* vague feelings that life is not being lived as meaningfully, effectively or joyfully as it should be;
* a feeling of having lost control;
* a loss of the ability to make decisions;
* a loss of the ability to make choices;
* a loss of the feeling of being real, vital, committed to or enthusiastic about life;
* a sense of conflict, apathy, aimlessness;
* a sense of alienation (with self and/or society);
* a sense of being compelled to do things against one's will;
* an avoidance of situations/people/objects one should not have to avoid;
* a sense of emotional turmoil (anger, fear, anxiety, dread, guilt, depression, disgust);
* a feeling of helplessness, of not being fully in control of one's life.

Many of these problems afflict (for a variety of reasons) the clients of social workers and they rank among the alleviating tasks (helping, healing) social work sets itself. The theories about the nature of neurosis have ranged from the neurological ('nerves'), through the intrapsychic (Freud), to the social-cultural (Mead).

78

Transition and change are common themes in social workers' problem caseloads. It is important that they should understand how people react during periods of transition and how to recognize the symptoms of transitional stress. This knowledge of coping techniques could offer invaluable assistance to clients in time of need. Crisis intervention is concerned with the short-term treatment of individual clients or families who are undergoing some form of crisis - perhaps an illness, loss, or the birth of a handicapped child - which precipitates a state of emotional disruption and in which the customary repertoire of problem-solving or coping mechanisms fails to suffice. An introduction to various ideas about psychotherapy, counselling and other forms of helping is provided by Hopson in chapter 13.

Stress theory

The form of brief social work treatment known as crisis intervention depends for its maximum effectiveness upon an amalgam of psychological theories, stress theory, crisis theory, behavioural and cognitive learning theories.

The term 'stress' belonged to the field of engineering until the 1940s when psychologists and psychiatrists (in military work) began to use it. They had to cope with men who, under the strain of war, presented extreme psychological problems. Research into the stresses and strains of civilian life has continued and produced very interesting and useful information. The term covers any state of overload when the human being is being pushed to his limits, that is, when he is beset by powerful pressures which tax his capacities to cope (adjust). It can refer to physical factors like injuries, infections or excessive cold, or to psychological situations involving frustration, threat or conflict.

There are many sources of stress in our modern affluent societies and in the deprived parts of society in which social workers spend so much of their time. All forms of stress are commonly accompanied by negative emotional reactions such as anger, depression and especially anxiety. To take the last as an example, anxiety is usually inferred from three kinds of responses:

* subjective feelings of apprehension, worry, uneasiness or fear;
* motor reactions such as restlessness, jumpiness or the physical avoidance of stressful situations;
* physiological changes in respiration, heart rate, muscular tension, pupil size, gastro-intestinal secretions and blood pressure. These are by-products of the release into the bloodstream of hormones under control of the autonomic nervous system and the endocrine glands.

Fear can be viewed as a natural response to events which are threatening to an individual's personal security. In its

79

positive role, it mobilizes physical energy to overcome obstacles and alerts the individual mentally to unexpected and unexplained changes in the environment. If the newly perceived situation or object turns out to be dangerous or threatening there are three basic types of self-protective responses available: attack, flight and submission.

Some strategies are designed to deal directly and actively with a problem. Attack and aggression are the most basic animal and human methods for removing or surmounting obstacles which stand in the way of the satisfaction of their needs. Extrapunitiveness is the psychological expression (blaming others, criticizing) of this strategy. Another basic method of coping with life is strategic withdrawal, or (not to put too fine a point on it) flight. It may not necessarily be physical withdrawal; it can take the form of psychological retreat such as avoidance behaviour, inhibition or emotional isolation ('being switched off'). Some people characteristically take the blame on themselves when circumstances are frustrating. They are referred to as being intropunitve.

Psychosomatic responses
Some psychosomatic illnesses may arise from prolonged emotional reactions to stress producing permanent tissue changes, for example:

*   an unduly prolonged rise in blood pressure might contribute to hypertension, or
*   persistent gastro-intestinal changes may lead to the formation of gastric ulcers.

Stress inoculation
Behavioural methods (behaviour modification/therapy) offer remediation of, or 'inoculation' against, those destroyers of spontaneous social life: the helplessness associated with depression and the avoidance behaviour associated with fear (see chapter 12 by Beech). Stress inoculation and coping-skills training may involve (inter alia) self-instruction or cognitive restructuring, behaviour rehearsal, role-playing or desensitization. The aim is to convert learned helplessness into learned resourcefulness.

There is evidence that all human beings need to perceive themselves in at least a moderately favourable light. There are wide ranges of variation in the ways this need manifests itself, particularly in the case of the neurotic person. Nevertheless, the desire for an acceptable self-image, as a general characteristic of the development of the healthy child, appears to be a critical and significant motivating factor in his behaviour. Children discover and make use of complex defensive reactions designed to protect and enhance the gradually evolving self-image.

It is important for the individual's self-esteem that he should perceive how other persons see him, and that he should be able to compare his self-image with the expectations he believes others have concerning what he should be like. The individual's perception of his appearance to a particular group of other persons, or a significant other individual, has been termed his 'subjective public identity'. A person may have as many such identities as there are groups of significant other persons whom he believes perceive him in a distinctive way. People differ markedly in the degree of permanence and stability with which the self is organized. The self of some individuals is a very loosely organized pattern of different selves with only a small core of elements common to all. Such a person is described as poorly integrated. His self consists of the various roles that he characteristically plays. Those individuals who lack the stabilizing direction of a well-integrated self and a coherent self-concept tend to display different characteristics with different groups of people and are therefore called 'outer-' or 'other-directed'. People who are more 'self-' or 'inner-directed' (and it is always a matter of degree) have a large core of personal traits and tendencies which are consistent factors in their lives.

Social workers often have to deal with alienated, unhappy, unfulfilled clients. The psychologist Charlotte Buhler (1935), who has tried to fathom what constitutes a sense of meaning, unity and fulfilment in the course of human life, identified four groups of individuals with different attitudes to their failure or success in reaching life goals: first, those who felt they had done their life's work and wanted to rest and relax and were content to do so; second, those who felt that their active life was never finished and who continued striving to the end; third, those who, though not satisfied with their lives and accomplishments, but lacking strength, ability or willpower to go on struggling, find an unhappy sort of resignation; and fourth, those who led thoughtless and meaningless lives, and are now not only frustrated but bothered by guilt and regret. Buhler concluded that, in the later years of life, the most critical factor in adjustment or maladjustment was the person's self-assessment as to whether he had fulfilled his promise, rather than any feeling of insecurity or physical decline.

The author of the chapter on transitions, Hopson, could be addressing himself particularly to social workers when he says:

> Today, more than any other time in our history, people
> have to cope with an often bewildering variety of
> transitions: from home to school; from school to work;
> from being single to being married and - increasingly -
> divorced; from job to job; from place to place and
> friend to friend; to parenthood and then to children
> leaving home; and finally to bereavements and death.
> Alongside these and other major life events people are
> happy to learn to cope with the passage from one stage
> of personal development to another - adolescence, early
> adulthood, stabilization, mid-life transition, old age.

The personality adjustments - physical, social and psychological - of adolescents (Schaffer) and of the elderly (Coleman) are detailed in chapters 8 and 17 respectively.

Treatment

During several decades, British social work has incorporated components from various psychotherapy and counselling approaches which have added depth to the person-orientated individual service which has always been its raison d'être. Whatever forms social work may take in the future, any knowledge from the psychotherapeutic literature which helps social workers to respond sensitively to people and which can inform their counselling role (they tend not to do psychotherapy) must form an important part of social work education.

Psychoanalysis

Psychoanalysis is a motivationally (instinct) based theory which assumes determinism in all human behaviour, the existence and significant influence of unconscious mental processes, and the centrality of psychological conflict, anxiety and defence mechanisms in both normal personality development and in the evolution of psychopathology (e.g. neuroses). Sigmund Freud (1856-1939), the founder of psychoanalysis, set up models of underlying entities and mechanisms, the former exemplified by his division of the personality into id, ego and super-ego. He wished to account for the whole of human mentation at the psychological level of explanation. While he did not deny the possibility - indeed, probability - of physiological accompaniments for all mental phenomena, he did not concern himself with these in any detail. He was concerned with the experience of the neurotic patient and with the meaning of his symptoms (in a semantic sense). He was not concerned (despite his eminence as a neurologist) with the functioning of the patient's cells or nerves.

Most of Freud's thinking was inductive in character. He was not an experimentalist and did not use, formally, the hypothetico-deductive method in this work. Steadily, through a long life, he added further findings and theoretical formulations to the huge body of psychoanalytic statements. This accounts partly for the contradictions and changes of mind in the writing of Freud. While it is a tribute to his flexibility of mind that he was able to modify his ideas over so long a time, this makes the task of the social worker even harder, in that he has to spend time trying to pin down a Freudian dictum to its definitive form before he can even begin to try to verify its truth. For the experimentalist, there is an additional difficulty in that Freud did not specifically set out his formulations in the form of specific, experimentally testable hypotheses (see Farrell, in Lee and Herbert, 1970).

Freud was essentially a proponent of 'verstehende' or 'understanding' psychology; he wished to answer the 'whys' of human conduct. It is impossible to do more than hint at the discoveries Freud made about the human psyche. Many people have misinterpreted him; a generation of children was brought up on a permissive basis because of a failure to understand what Freud meant by inhibitions and repression.

* Psychoanalysis is first a system of human psychology: a theory which describes and interprets human development, memory, thought processes, creativity, social behaviour, religious belief, humour and grief. A characteristic of psychoanalytic theory which has a bearing on its viability as a scientific theory is that it is not a unified theory but a collection of parts. Even if certain psychoanalytic hypotheses are shown to be false, it does not refute the entire system.
* Psychoanalysis is also a therapeutic discipline concerned with the treatment of certain kinds of human suffering. It is, in this context, a collection of procedures used by those trained in it to treat patients/clients who come to them for help (for a detailed account of the method see Glover, 1955). That vaguest of terms - psychodynamic approach - beloved of therapeutically-minded social workers, is based upon an attentuated form of psychoanalysis and its offshoots.
* It is more than these things; it is also an implied philosophy (weltanschauung), a general view of man's place in nature. That it does imply a philosophical attitude, which has had a widespread influence, is demonstrated by a number of writers who have felt it necessary to take up their pens to attack it as a philosophy of exculpation: one which undermines society's view that its 'normal' citizens are fully responsible for their actions.

Freudian psychoanalysis (proper)
The basic goal is very broad: the basic restructuring of the total personality (as opposed to psychotherapy based on behavioural principles, where the goal is more to do with presenting problems). The basic treatment rationale is to make the unconscious conscious; to 'know thyself' and to remove the underlying basis of neurotic behaviour, viz., repressed unconscious material based upon infantile, instinctive desires.

Most of the major casework approaches owe a considerable debt to the psychoanalytic or (as it is more often referred to) the psychodynamic model. However, it should not be forgotten that non-psychoanalytic perspectives (behaviour modification, communication theory, systems theory, role theory, etc.) have also informed casework since the 1960s.

Status of psychoanalysis
Psychoanalysis has been called many things: there is no consensus in our culture about the position of psycho-

analytic theory on our map of knowledge and belief (see Yelloly, 1980). There is a little doubt that psychoanalysis is not in favour amongst 'scientific' psychologists. It is often assumed that only the physical sciences are intellectually respectable! Both psychiatry and psychology have suffered an inferiority complex in relation to their ancestry and status. Social work has inherited this burden.

A lot hinges on what is meant by science; some argue that unless the word 'science' is understood in a very rigid and narrow sense it is perfectly possible for psychoanalytic investigations to be scientific. Others are of the opinion that unless the scientific canons are to be so flexible as to become valueless, psychoanalysis cannot be termed a science. To imply that psychoanalytic theory is a myth as some do is to state that it is a closed system. Although parts of it may be closed to the sort of testing characteristic of science, it is open to the influences and control of fact: experimental, clinical and sociological. The theories in fields such as economics, jurisprudence, history and sociology are (typically) not scientific narratives, but they are (typically) rational ones. The domain of the rational is wider than that of the scientific. The accusations of irrationality and myth-making do not square very easily with the early history of the development of psychoanalytic theory. It was empirical fact (brilliant clinical observation) that led to Freud's views which, indeed, he changed when he came up against discrepant facts. It may be true that in later years the distinction between observation and interpretation became somewhat blurred. Most critics admit to Freud's genius, and many to his insights.

Lee and Herbert (1970), introducing an account of Freud's work, had this to say:

> Three thinkers, probably more than any others, have contributed to the dethronement of Man's confidence in himself as being of unique importance in the Universe. In physical and cosmological terms, Copernicus displaced him from the central place in that Universe. Charles Darwin showed clearly that he had much in common with 'lower' animals and that he did not owe his existence as a species to an act of special creation by an omniscient deity, but that the pressures to selective evolution had been brought to bear, through millenniums, on him as on others. Freud, against a background of the surge of 'progress' and technical development in the nineteenth century sowed grave doubts about the rationality of man and about his ability to solve his problems - particularly individual ones - by conscious ratiocination alone.

The best introduction to Freud is to read Freud himself, in the original. A surprising number of people who have strong opinions about Freud and psychoanalysis depend upon secondary sources - someone else's exegesis of Freudian psychology - for their criticisms. However, a fine account of the evolution of his thinking is provided by Wollheim, (1971; see also Shapiro, chapter 19).

Neo-Freudians

Several eminent psychoanalysts broke away from Freudian orthodoxy because of different kinds of dissatisfaction with theory, or with the Freudian coterie. Common themes in the repudiation of parts of the Freudian doctrine were the rejection of the emphasis on id forces, or biological instinctual drives (libido theory), and a desire to focus on cultural influences and interpersonal relationships (i.e. the social context). It was felt necessary to emphasize the conscious aspects of personality, self or ego (self-evaluation, self-esteem, the need for security, etc.), and modifications made in therapeutic practice to reflect this change in orientation. Among the names of such theorists are Jung, Adler, Fromm, Horney and Sullivan, to mention but a few.

The psychoanalytic movement has evolved over the years and there is now a recognized school of 'ego psychology'. The ego psychologists postulate an autonomous ego which is a rational institution responsible for intellectual and social achievements, and whose functioning is not solely dependent on the wishes of the id. Among the concepts of ego psychology which have particular relevance for social work practice are the defences and coping strategies: the ways in which the ego characteristically deals with threat, pain and loss by mobilizing anger, denial, displacement, emotional insulation and so on. British contributions to ego psychology are to be found, most particularly, in the work of Melanie Klein and W. Ronald Fairbairn. They have elaborated an object-relations theory of personality (see Fairbairn, 1954; Klein, 1954). These works have thrown much light on the characteristic ways in which people adapt to, and cope with, the normal as well as the more traumatic crises of living (Garrett, 1958).

Psychodynamic psychotherapy

Coinciding with these developments within psychoanalysis, psychoanalytic principles were applied more and more to other forms of psychotherapy, and referred to by the portmanteau term 'psychodynamic' psychotherapy. Some claim that there are fundamental differences between psychodynamic psychotherapy and psychoanalysis, in form and technique and the therapeutic processes that occur. Others say the differences only concern intensiveness and thoroughness of application.

Commentary

Many of Freud's insights (radical and even revolutionary findings at the time) are statements of the obvious today! It is difficult to sort out precisely how psychoanalysis informs social work. The profession does not adhere to any single theoretical model when dealing with, say, family relationships or individual psychological problems. Most of the major casework approaches owe a considerable debt to the psychodynamic model. Freud saw his work as psychology (Lee and Herbert, 1970). Psychodynamic social casework thus tends, like other clinical approaches, to be psychology and individual orientated. The treatment, or clinical, model of social work (still powerful in Canada, the USA and elsewhere) has been subject to considerable criticism from within the profession itself because it tends to emphasize certain aspects of professional activity while playing down others: notably community and policy interventions. And if social casework is thought to be over-identified with a therapeutic-cum-psychodynamic orientation (Yelloly, 1980), it should not be forgotten that, in addition, psychoanalytic perspectives on personality and child development and rearing have been most influential in social work.

The humanistic approach

Ego psychology has generated a multitude of diverse therapeutic - 'human potential' and 'training' - movements. The offspring range from the academically respectable and serious to the rather dubious and raffish. Some of the more cultish groups are decidedly bizarre and esoteric.

Among the most thoughtful and well-researched and productive 'therapies' is the client-centred approach developed by Carl Rogers (1951, 1959, 1961). The goal of therapy is to intervene in such a way as to increase positive self-regard and self-direction.

Rogers comes from an academic background in counselling and is less influenced by psychoanalytic thinking than most others in the humanist/existential traditions of ego psychology.

Framework for therapy

Rogers has a clear notion of the wholeness of the self; the basic assumptions about the nature of man are not pessimistic like Freud's.

Man is essentially good, rational, realistic, social and forward-looking; however, he may need help with his basic impulse to grow. Rogers states that it has been his experience that individuals have a basically positive direction: that is, constructive, moving towards self-actualization, growing towards maturity and evolving towards socialization.

Therapy is akin to good education and, essentially, to the basic process of socialization. The therapist is encouraged to feel warm and positive toward the client, accepting him, experiencing what the client is experiencing (empathy) and manifesting 'unconditional positive regard'. The necessary and sufficient conditions for therapeutic change in Rogers' opinion are: empathic understanding, positive regard, genuineness, acceptance and non-possessive warmth.

The human relationship factor

These qualities in the therapist are associated with

'healing' properties. Whether a trained professional has special access to these qualities (or some unique development of them) is thrown into doubt (surely even for those who give most weight to the relationship factor in therapy) by the absence of substantive differences in the results of professional as opposed to non- or para-professional 'therapists' (Durlak, 1979). Attempts have been made - and they are highly speculative - to apportion the relative influence of 'personal/relationship' factors as opposed to technical input in the favourable outcome to therapy. It has been argued (Fischer, 1978) that the former account for a substantial proportion of the variance in the change process, sufficient to warrant special training in the so-called core conditions.

Bergin (1978) asserts that the technical claims of the diverse therapeutic schools have never been adequately vindicated. Comparative studies, in his view (one which is hotly contested), show little difference in the outcomes of diverse approaches even though each therapy, by itself, can be shown to have significant effects when compared to no treatment at all. It is just such an assumption which leads Jerome Frank in his book, 'Persuasion and Healing' (1961), to argue that the effective factors are the same for all therapies and they can be identified with the common components of all types of influence and healing (warmth, respect, kindness, hope, understanding, provision of 'explanations'). Psychoanalysis and behaviour therapy are instrumentally (i.e. technique) orientated, whereas in the client-centred, humanistic and existential psychotherapies, much emphasis is given to the therapist's personal attributes. Client-centred therapy and humanistic therapy parallel some varieties or social work in their rejection of soft-pedalling of the instrumental aspects of the therapist's work. Instead, they highlight his values, beliefs, attitudes and human qualities.

The evidence presented by Murray and Jacobson (1978) strongly suggests that both traditional and behavioural psychology achieve their results as a function of critical parameters and processes for which there is little place in the theoretical systems of these therapies. In general, Murray has found that the current state of theory in both traditional and behavioural therapy is inadequate. The explanation of traditional therapy in terms of personal growth and personality reorganization does not take sufficient account of social learning and social influence processes; the explanations of behavioural therapies do not yet adequately recognize the importance of cognitive and emotional response systems operating within interpersonal relationships.

The arguments and counter-arguments about the effectiveness of competing therapies are confounded by their reliance on a very unrefined, broad and abstract (global) definition of problems and outcomes. The outcome of therapy is not a unitary variable. It differs according to the perspective of the client, relatives, therapist, work colleagues or others. Another source of obfuscation is the definition of neurosis to which so much of the time of psychotherapists is devoted. The criteria of an effective outcome in the treatment of a neurotic phobia might be very different as between the psychoanalyst and behaviour therapist (neurosis is one of those infuriating portmanteau terms in psychopathology).

Sadly, there is yet another problem. We started with an assumption that psychotherapy is effective. Not everyone accepts this. Psychotherapy has been challenged (see Rachman, 1971) with regard to its impact (or lack of one) with adults and children. Criticism of the nomothetic scientific research methods used to evaluate psychotherapy casework or counselling is one way of reconciling the apparently contradictory findings. It is argued (by the critics of psychotherapy) that it does no better than the spontaneous remission effect (the improvement of the client over a period of time without the aid of any therapeutic intervention). Bergin (1978) argues that when improved and unimproved cases are all lumped together in an experimental group, they cancel each out to some extent and the overall yield in terms of improvement is no greater than the change occurring in a control group. And although reports and studies show little difference in the average amount of change occurring after treatment, a significant increase in the variability of criterion scores appears at post-testing in the treatment groups. This spread of criterion scores, Bergin concludes, implies that treatment has a beneficial effect on some clients and an unfavourable effect on others. It is being said, then, that some therapists have a benign effect on their clients' problems while others have a deleterious effect.

Superordinate concepts in psychotherapy

There have been attempts to bring about a conceptual integration of the methods used in traditional and behavioural psychotherapy within a framework of modern social learning theory. Some dynamic theorists (Alexander, 1963; Wachtel, 1977) have come to accept the idea of a rapprochement between psychodynamic psychotherapy and learning theory approaches to therapy. Others disagree entirely.

The evaluation of casework

Fischer (1973) aimed a broadside at social casework with a review that demonstrated (in nine out of eleven controlled studies) that the professional caseworkers were unable to bring about any positive, significant, measurable changes in their clients beyond those that could have occurred without the specific interventive programme, or that could have been evidenced by non-professionals dealing with similar clients, often with less intensive service programmes.

Behavioural social work

What is most poignant (not to say paradoxical) about the particular points of criticism of social casework raised by

Joel Fischer (1973, 1978), is that they precisely indicate areas of relative strength of behaviour modification. It is this fact that makes so bewildering the profession's failure to embrace behavioural social work with even half-open arms. There is little evidence that social workers and social work educators have enquired seriously (i.e. critically) into its potential value as one social work method among others. Here are some of the points made by Fischer (1978) about casework:

* it is inefficient, even where successful, in terms of the professional time invested;
* it is not orientated (in the sense of having a relevant knowledge base) toward social-environmental change;
* it does not make adequate use of people in the client's natural environment;
* it gives disproportionate attention to diagnosis and assessment while paying insufficient attention to intervention, this situation being encouraged by a lack of techniques for changing behaviour and a low correlation between the assessment and choice of treatment techniques;
* a reliance on talking (interview) therapies is misplaced as the outcomes are doubtful (most clients being treated in the same way whatever the problem);
* a focus on a revelatory approach, that is, client self-understanding, rather than on changes in his social functioning, seldom changes the disruptive environmental patterns which instigate and maintain the problems;
* clients are minimally involved in any active sense in the change process, and there is a neglect of presenting complaints in favour of more remote, internal inferred disorders. The paradox here is that the vast majority of clients describe their problems in terms of maladaptive social functioning;
* high drop-out rates are wasteful of resources. These are exacerbated by disagreements between the social workers and clients over what has to be accomplished during contacts, and ignorance about what the process is about;
* most damning of all is the claim that social work research on traditional approaches reveals, at best, questionable results.

It should be a source of concern that at this relatively late date and despite the availability of such excellent texts as those of Jehu (1967, 1972), Fischer and Gochros (1975) and Gambrill (1977), so many social workers and social work educators hold ideas about behaviour modification and behavioural theories that go back to the 1930s or, at best, the 1950s! Some cover their ignorance of behavioural theory and practice by a dismissive comment (usually couched in humanistic terminology) about not being interested in the field because it is dehumanizing, mechanistic, and so on.

What is behaviour modification?

We need to begin by clarifying the nature of behaviour modification; it has grown and diversified considerably since its formal beginnings in the late 1950s and early 1960s. Kazdin (1978) observes that behaviour modification has become so variegated in its conceptualizations of behaviour, research methods and techniques that no unifying scheme or set of assumptions about behaviour can incorporate all extant techniques.

Nevertheless, there are certain distinguishing features of behaviour modification and these are succinctly listed by O'Leary and Wilson (1975):

* behaviour modification is based on a model in which abnormal behaviour is viewed not as symptomatic of some kind of underlying quasi-disease process but as the way a person has learned to cope with the stress and difficulties of living in a changing and increasingly more complex physical and social environment;
* since abnornmal behaviour is learned and maintained in the same manner as normal behaviour, as opposed to being a manifestation of hypothetical intrapsychic conflicts, it can be treated directly through the application of social learning principles rather than indirectly by 'working through' presumed underlying personality conflicts;
* behaviour modification entails the rejection of psycho-dynamic and personality trait labels to describe people and their behaviour. It is assumed that the individual is best described and understood by determining what he thinks, feels and does in particular life situations;
* behaviour modification emphasizes the principles of classical and operant conditioning but is not restricted to them; it draws upon principles from other branches of experimental psychology such as social and developmental psychology. The importance of 'private events' or the cognitive mediation of behaviour is recognized, and a major role is attributed to vicarious and symbolic learning process, for example modelling;
* reliance upon basic research in psychology as a source of hypothesis about treatment and specific therapy techniques;
* specificity in defining, treating, and measuring the target problems in therapy;
* the goal of behaviour modification is eventually to help an individual to control his own behaviour and achieve self-selected goals.

Behaviour modification represents an optimistic ideology

The higher species, as we saw earlier, are less dependent than lower forms on stereotyped, inherited, instinctive responses. At the summit are humans, with their vast capacity to learn how to solve problems, to change, and to adapt to novel situations. Here is a crucial source of human variety: the susceptibility of people to many different types of environment. It is this human flexibility, the potential to learn afresh new ways of living or to unlearn self-defeating behaviours, that should allow behaviour modification to command the attention of social workers. Certainly it is the cautious conclusion of Briar and Miller (1971) that principles of behaviour modification lend themselves to flexible application to a large array of problems in a variety of settings; and there is reason to believe that these principles will prove useful in casework practice generally.

Behavioural casework

One variant of behaviour modification, the behavioural casework approach (Herbert and O'Driscoll, 1978; Herbert and Iwaniec, 1979, 1981 in press; Herbert, 1980a and b, 1981), is anchored in the natural environment: the community. The triadic model, as it is called, is crucial to the social work task, be it in residential settings (Child Treatment Research Unit Reports 1-7) or natural home settings (Herbert, 1978). Indeed, there is growing evidence that effective assessment and treatment of many emotional and behavioural disorders requires observation and intervention in the natural environment. Furthermore, the systematic and successful involvement of parents, and particularly mothers, in the work with children has increased considerably (O'Dell, 1974).

Where else can behaviour modification help?

The areas are too many to enumerate in detail (however, see Gambrill, 1977). They include:

* anxiety reduction;
* conflict resolution;
* antisocial behaviour;
* addictive behaviour and substance abuse;
* juvenile delinquency;
* poor self-esteem and related problems;
* social skill deficits;
* stress inoculation;
* development.

Over recent years methods such as family therapy, crisis intervention, task-centred casework, contract work and systems theory have all been incorporated into casework practice. These are all ways of approaching particular problems and can be adapted for use with whichever theoretical model one adheres to, be it sociological, psychodynamic or behavioural. Behavioural theory is particularly congruent with, and nourishing of, these ideas.

References

Alexander, F. (1963)
    The dynamics of psychotherapy in the light of learning theory. American Journal of Psychiatry, 120, 440-448.

Bergin, E.J. (1978)
The evaluation of therapeutic outcomes. In S.L.
Garfield and A.E. Bergin (eds), Handbook of
Psychotherapy and Behaviour Change: An empirical
analysis (2nd edn). Chichester: Wiley.

Briar, S. and Miller, H. (1971)
Problems and Issues in Social Casework. New York:
Columbia University Press.

Buhler, C. (1935)
From Birth to Maturity. London: Routledge & Kegan
Paul/Trench Trubner & Co.

Child Treatment Research Unit (undated)
Reports 1-7. Available from The School of Social Work,
University of Leicester.

Durlak, J.A. (1979)
Comparative effectiveness of paraprofessional and
professional helpers. Psychological Bulletin, 86, 80-
92.

Fairbairn, W.R. (1954)
An Object-relations Theory of Personality. New York:
Basic Books.

Fenichel, O. (1945)
The Psychoanalytic Theory of Neurosis. London: Routledge
& Kegan Paul.

Fischer, J. (1973)
Is casework effective? A review. Social Work (US), 18,
5-20.

Fischer, J. (1978)
Effective Casework Practice: An eclectic approach. New
York: McGraw-Hill.

Fischer, J. and Gochros, H.L. (1975)
Planned Behaviour Change: Behaviour modification in
social work. London: Collier Macmillan.

Frank, J.D. (1961)
Persuasion and Healing. London: Oxford University Press.

Gambrill, E. (1977)
Behaviour Modification: Handbook of assessments,
intervention and evaluation. San Francisco: Jossey-
Bass.

Garrett, H. (1958)
Modern Casework: The contribution of ego psychology.
In H. Parad (ed.), Ego Psychology and Dynamic
Casework. New York: Family Service Association of
America.

Glover, E. (1955)
The Technique of Psycho-analysis. London: Baillière,
Tindall & Cox.

Herbert, M. (1978)
Conduct Disorders of Childhood and Adolescence: A
behavioural approach to assessment and treatment.
Chichester: Wiley.

Herbert, M. (1980a)
Behavioural social work in families. In D.S. Freeman
(ed.), Perspectives on Family Therapy. Western Canada:
Butterworths.

Herbert, M. (1980b)

Socialization for problem resistance. In P. Feldman and J. Orford (eds), The Social Context. Chichester: Wiley.

Herbert, M. (1981)

Behavioural Treatment of Problem Children: A practice manual. London: Academic Press; New York: Grune & Stratton.

Herbert, M. and Iwaniec, D. (1979)

Managing children's behavioural problems. Social Work Today, 10, 12-14.

Herbert, M. and Iwaniec, D. (1981: in press)

Behavioural psychotherapy in natural homesettings: an empirical study applied to conduct disordered and incontinent children. Behavioural Psychotherapy.

Herbert, M. and O'Driscoll, B. (1978)

Behavioural casework - a social work method for family settings. Australian Child and Family Welfare, 3, 2, 14-25.

Horney, K. (1947)

The Neurotic Personality of Our Time. London: Routledge & Kegan Paul.

Jehu, D. (1967)

Learning Theory and Social Work. New York: Humanities Press.

Jehu, D. (1972)

Behaviour Modification in Social Work. Chichester: Wiley.

Kazdin, A.E. (1978)

History of Behavior Modification. Baltimore: University Park Press.

Klein, M. (1954)

Psychoanalysis of Children. London: Hogarth Press.

Lee, S.G.M. and Herbert, M. (eds) (1970)

Freud and Psychology. Harmondsworth: Penguin.

Menninger, K. (1963)

The Vital Balance: The life process in mental health and illness. New York: The Viking Press.

Murray, E.J. and Jacobson, L.I. (1978)

Cognition and learning in traditional and behavioural psychotherapy. In S.L. Garfield and A.E. Bergin (eds), Handbook of Psychotherapy and Behaviour Change: An empirical analysis (2nd edn). Chichester: Wiley.

O'Dell, S. (1974)

Training parents in behavior modification: a review. Psychological Bulletin, 81, 7, 418-433.

O'Leary, K.D. and Wilson, G.T. (1975)

Behaviour Therapy: Application and outcome. London: Prentice-Hall.

Rachman, S. (1971)

The Effects of Psychotherapy. Oxford: Pergamon Press.

Rogers, C.R. (1951)

Client-Centered Therapy. Boston: Houghton-Mifflin.

Rogers, C.R. (1959)

A theory of therapy, personality and interpersonal relationships, as developed in the client-centred framework. In S. Koch (ed.), Psychology: The study of a science, 3. New York: McGraw-Hill.

Rogers, C.R. (1961)
On Becoming a Person: A therapist's view of psychotherapy. Boston: Houghton-Mifflin.

Wachtel, P.L. (1977)
Psychoanalysis and Behaviour Therapy: Toward an integration. New York: Basic Books.

Wollheim, R. (1971)
Freud. London: Fontana.

Wolpe, J. (1973)
The Practice of Behaviour Therapy (2nd edn). Oxford: Pergamon Press.

Yelloly, M.A. (1980)
Social Work Theory and Psychoanalysis. London: Van Nostrand Reinhold.

Further reading

Adler, A. (1924)
The Theory and Practice of Individual Psychology. New York: Harcourt, Brace & World.

Caldwell, B.M. (1964)
The effects of infant care. In L.W. Hoffman (ed.), Review of Child Development Research. New York: Russell Sage Foundation.

Fromm, E. (1955)
The Sane Society. London: Holt, Rinehart & Winston.

Herbert, M. (1975)
Problems of Childhood: A guide for all concerned. London: Pan Books.

Horney, K. (1945)
Our Inner Conflicts. New York: Norton.

Jung, C.G. (1961)
Modern Man in Search of a Soul. London: Routledge & Kegan Paul.

Maslow, A.H. (1954)
Motivation and Personality. New York: Harper & Row.

Rycroft, C. (1966)
Causes and meaning. In C. Rycroft (ed.), Psychoanalysis Observed. London: Constable.

Part two

Psychological Theory for Social Work Practice

8

Social Development in Early Childhood
H. R. Schaffer

Psychologists study children for two main reasons. First, they want to find out how a helpless, naïve and totally dependent baby manages in due course to become a competent, knowledgeable adult. They are interested therefore in studying the process of development. The second reason stems from the many social problems associated with childhood. Should we protect children from viewing violence on television? Are children of mothers who go out to work more likely to become delinquent? Does hospitalization in the early years produce later difficulties? How can one mitigate the effects of divorce on children? Why do some parents become baby batterers? Increasingly the psychologist is asked to examine such problems and produce answers useful to society. It is primarily to this aspect of child psychology that we shall pay attention here.

How a child develops depends very much on the people around him. From them he learns the skills and values needed for social living, from the use of knives and forks to knowing the difference between right and wrong. Other people are always around the child, influencing him by means of example and command, and none more so at first than the members of his own family. On them depend the initial stages of his socialization.

Disadvantaged children and their families
It is, of course, only too apparent that not every family carries out its socializing task with equal effectiveness. By way of illustration, let us look at the way in which the child's intellectual development is shaped by his social environment.

At one time it was thought that intelligence is entirely determined by an individual's inborn endowment. There are few who now believe this: it seems rather that the environment in which a child is reared can have a powerful effect on his development.

The issue has been much debated in relation to the poor educational achievement of 'disadvantaged' children. These are children who come from the economically and socially most deprived sectors of the community and who so often appear to be at a severe disadvantage when first starting school, because (as it has been put) 'they have learnt not to learn'. Their failure in the education system, in other words, is ascribed not so much to some genetic inferiority as to factors operating in the home, which result in an inability to make use of whatever intellectual capacities they have.

A great many schemes have been launched to counter this situation, especially in the USA. Some of the earlier efforts, designed to give children some extra training in basic cognitive skills before school entry, were clearly inadequate and produced no lasting benefits. This is partly because the schemes were too brief, partly because they came too late in the child's life, but partly also because they left untouched the home situation. Given a conflict of values about education between home and school it is highly likely that the home will always win. It is there that the child has already lived and learned for several years before ever starting school, and it is therefore significant that more recent efforts have attempted to involve the parents as well as the child or even to work solely through the parents.

There is now little doubt that parents can enhance or suppress the child's educational potential. One way in which they apparently do this is by the extent to which they foster the development of language: a function so necessary for the expression of intelligence. There are pronounced social class differences in the style of language mothers use to communicate with their children; in addition, however, it has also been shown that mothers from disadvantaged homes engage in face-to-face talking with their infants less frequently than middle-class mothers. The poorer child often lives in much noisier surroundings than the middle-class child in his quiet suburban home, but to profit from stimulation the young child must be exposed to it under the personalized conditions that only the to-and-fro reciprocity of a face-to-face situation provides. It is in this respect that many lower-class 'socially deprived children' are at a disadvantage.

Child effects on adults

Let us not now jump to the conclusion that children's development is totally a matter of what parents do to them. A child is never just a passive being that one can mould into whatever shape the adult desires. Even the youngest baby can already exert an influence on his caretakers and so help to determine how they behave towards him.

Take an obvious example: babies cry and thereby draw attention to themselves. It is a sound that can have a most compelling effect on the adult: we have all heard of the mother who can sleep through a thunderstorm, but is immediately awoken by her child's whimper in the next room. The baby, by this powerful signal, can initiate the interaction:

he can thereby influence both the amount and the timing of attention which others provide.

Babies come into the world as individuals. Some are active and restless, others quiet and content; some are highly sensitive, others are emotionally robust and easy-going. The kind of care provided for one is therefore inappropriate for another, and any sensitive mother will therefore find herself compelled to adopt practices suitable for her individual child. A good example is provided by babies' differences in 'cuddliness'. Not all babies love being held and cuddled: some positively hate it and resist such contact by struggling and, unless released, by crying. It has been found that these 'non-cuddlers' tend to be more active and restless generally, and to be intolerant of all types of physical restraint (as seen when they are being dressed or tucked into bed). The mother is accordingly forced to treat her child in a manner that takes into account his 'peculiarity': when frightened or unwell these children cannot be comforted by being held close but have to be offered other forms of stimulation such as bottles, biscuits or soothing voices. Each mother must therefore show considerable flexibility in adjusting to the specific requirements of her child.

There is one further, and perhaps unexpected, example one can quote of the way in which parents are influenced by their children. It concerns the phenomenon of baby battering, which has attracted so much attention in recent years. It is by no means a new phenomenon; historically speaking, it is probably as old as the family itself. What is new is public concern that such a thing can happen, and this in turn has given rise to the need for research into such cases. As a result of various investigations it is now widely agreed that violence results from a combination of several factors: the presence of financial, occupational and housing problems facing the family; the parents' emotional immaturity which makes it difficult for them to deal with such problems; their social isolation from potential sources of help such as relatives and neighbours; and, finally, some characteristic of the battered child that singles him out as a likely victim.

It is the last factor that is particularly relevant to us, for it illustrates once again that the way in which parents treat their children is influenced by the children themselves. There is evidence that children most likely to be battered are 'difficult': they are more likely to be sickly, or to have been born prematurely, or to have feeding and sleeping problems. Being more difficult to rear, they make extra demands that the parents are just not able to meet. The child's condition acts on the parent's inadequacy, and so the child, unwittingly, contributes to his own fate.

Mother–child mutuality
It is apparent that children do not start life as

99

psychological nonentities. From the beginning they already have an individuality that influences the adults around them. Thus a mother's initial task is not to create something out of nothing; it is rather to dovetail her behaviour to that of the child.

Such dovetailing takes many forms. Take our previous example of the non-cuddlers. If the mother herself has a preference for close physical contact with the baby which he then rejects, some mutual readjustment will need to take place. Fortunately, most mothers quickly adjust and find other ways of relating to the child. It is only when they are too inflexible, or interpret the baby's behaviour as rejection, that trouble can arise from a mismatch.

Mutual adjustment is the hallmark of all interpersonal behaviour; it can be found in even the earliest social interactions. The feeding situation provides a good example. Should babies be fed by demand or by a rigid, pre-determined schedule? Advice by doctors and nurses has swung fashion-wise, sometimes stressing the importance of exerting discipline from the very beginning and of not 'giving in', at other times pointing to the free and easy methods of primitive tribes as the 'natural way'. In actual fact each mother and baby, however they may start off, sooner or later work out a pattern which satisfies both partners. On the one hand, there are few mothers who can bear to listen for long to a bawling infant unable as yet to tell the time; on the other hand, one should not under-estimate the ability of even very young babies to adjust to the demands of their environment. An example is provided by an experiment, carried out many years ago, in which two groups of babies were fed during the first ten days of life according to a three-hour and four-hour schedule respectively. Within just a few days after birth each baby had already developed a peak of restlessness just before the accustomed feeding time, and this became particularly obvious when the three-hour group was shifted to a four-hour schedule and so had to wait an extra hour for their feed. In time, however, these babies too became accustomed to the new timetable and showed the restlessness peak at four-hourly intervals. We can see here a form of adaptation to social demands that must represent one of the earliest forms of learning.

Not surprisingly, the major responsibility for mutual adjustment lies initially with the adult. The degree of flexibility one can expect from the very young children is limited. Yet the very fact that they are involved in social interactions from the very beginning of life means that they have the opportunity of gradually acquiring the skills necessary to become full partners in such exchanges. Observations of give-and-take games with babies at the end of the first year have made this point. Initially the baby knows only how to take: he has not learned that his behaviour is just one part of a sequence, that he needs to take turns with the other person, and that the roles of the two participants are interchangeable (one being a giver, the other a taker). Such and other rules of behaviour he will learn in time; they form the basis for much of social intercourse, and it is through social intercourse that the child acquires them in the first place.

Socialization is sometimes portrayed as a long drawn-out battle, as a confrontation between wilful young children and irritated parents that must at all cost be resolved in favour of the latter. Goodness knows such battles occur, yet they are far from telling us everything about the process of socialization. There is a basic mutuality between parent and child without which interaction would not be possible. The sight of the mother's face automatically elicits a smile from the baby; that produces a feeling of delight in the mother and causes her in turn to smile back and to talk or tickle or pick up, in this way calling forth further responses from the baby. A whole chain of interaction is thus started, not infrequently initiated by the baby. Mother and child learn about each other in the course of these interactions, and more often than not mutual adjustment is brought about by a kind of negotiation process in which both partners show some degree of flexibility. On the mother's part, this calls for sensitivity to the particular needs and requirements of her child, an ingredient of parenthood that we return to subsequently; on the child's part, it refers to one of the most essential aspects of social living that he must learn early on.

Some conditions that foster development

If we are to promote the mental health and social integration of children, it is necessary to identify the factors that further, or on the contrary hinder, such an aim. We all have our favourite theories as to why some children do not develop in what we regard as a desirable manner: not enough parental discipline, too much violence on television, the declining influence of religion, the social isolation of today's family, and so on. It is much more difficult, however, to substantiate through objective research that any one factor does play a part. Nevertheless, there are some conclusions to which we can point.

The blood-bond: myth or reality?
Is it essential, or at least desirable, that children should be brought up by their natural parents? Is a woman who conceived and bore a child by that very fact more fitted to care for this child than an unrelated individual?

This is no academic question. Children have been removed by courts of law from the foster parents with whom they had lived nearly all their lives and to whom they had formed deep attachments, in order to restore them to their biological mother from whom they may have been apart since the early days of life, and all because of the 'blood-bond'. Yet such a thing is a complete myth. There is nothing at all to suggest that firm attachments cannot grow between children and unrelated adults who have taken over the parental role.

The notion that the biological mother, by virtue of being
the biological mother, is uniquely capable of caring for her
child is without foundation.

Were it otherwise, the whole institution of adoption
would be in jeopardy. Yet there is nothing to suggest that
adoptive parents are in any way inferior to natural parents. In a study by Barbara Tizard (to which we shall refer
again), children who had been in care throughout their early
years were followed up on leaving care. One group of children was adopted, another returned to their own families. It
was found that the latter did less well than the adopted
children, both in the initial stages of settling in and in
their subsequent progress. The reason lay primarily in the
attitudes of the two sets of parents: the adoptive group
worked harder at being parents, possibly just because the
child was not their own. There have been a good many studies
which have examined the effects of adoption, and virtually
all stress the high proportion of successful cases to be
found. And this despite the difficulties such children may
have had to face, such as problems in the pre-adoption phase
and the knowledge gained later on of the fact of their
adoption. Successful parenting is a matter of particular
personality characteristics that need to be identified, not
of 'blood'.

Fathers as parents: more myths?
Do children have to be cared for primarily by women? Is
there something about females that makes them more suitable
for this task than males? What part should fathers play in
the child's upbringing?

The answer is simple. There is no 'should' or 'should
not'. It is a matter of what each society and each family
decides about the division of roles between the parents.
There have in fact been marked changes over the last few
decades in the extent to which fathers participate in child
care. They now do so to a far greater extent than they used
to, and this trend is continuing. For instance, with
increasing unemployment it is no longer uncommon to find
families in which a complete role reversal has taken place:
mother, having found a job, goes out to work, leaving her
unemployed husband in charge of home and children. Fortunately, there is no evidence to indicate that the biological
make-up of men makes them unfit for this task or even
necessarily inferior to women in this respect. Parenting is
unisex; the reasons for the traditional division of labour
(such as the need to breast-feed the child and the importance of using men's greater physical strength for hunting
and tilling the fields) are no longer applicable.

Children brought up without a father are more likely to
encounter difficulties than those in a complete family.
There are various reasons for this. One is that in any
single-parent family the remaining parent must cope with a
great multiplicity of stresses - financial, occupational, or
emotional - and the strain felt by him or (more often) her

is very likely to have repercussions for the child too.
Again, a fatherless boy has no model to imitate, and the
developmental tasks of acquiring sex-appropriate behaviour
may be more difficult. And, finally, the child isolated with
his mother and caught up in one all-encompassing relationship does not have the same chance of learning from the
beginning about some of the complexities of the social
world: having two parents helps him to learn at once that
not all people are alike and that he must adapt his own
behaviour according to their different characteristics and
different demands.

Parenthood: full-time or part-time?

Until fairly recently there was a widespread belief among
parents and professional workers that children in the pre-
school period required full-time mothering, and that it was
the duty of mothers to stay with the child night and day,
24 hours on end. Otherwise, it was feared, children's mental
health would suffer.

We can look at this situation from both the mother's and
the child's point of view. As far as mothers are concerned,
a crucial consideration is the recent finding of an extremely high incidence of depression among house-bound
women. With no outlet such as a job, tied to the house by
the presence of several dependant children, a large proportion of mothers (especially among the working class) become
isolated and hence depressed. Mothers, on the other hand,
who do go out to work are far less likely to suffer from
depression, anxiety and feelings of low self-esteem.

As far as the children are concerned, comparisons of
those with mothers at work and those with mothers at home
have not found any differences between them. Far from being
adversely affected, the former may even stand to gain both
intellectually and socially. The intellectual effects stem
from the extra stimulation and extra provision of play
materials that most children in day care obtain: a point of
particular significance for those from disadvantaged backgrounds. And, socially, not only is there no evidence that
the child's attachment to the mother is in some way 'dilu-
ted' by a daily period of being apart, but also the child in
day care has the enormous advantage of coming into contact
with other children. The benefit of such experience for
social development has until quite recently been overlooked;
yet other children, even in the early years, can exercise a
considerable socializing influence, and in addition may
further the child's diversification of social behaviour.
After all, the more a child is encouraged to adapt to a
variety of other individuals the more his repertoires of
social skills will grow.

Thus a daily period away from mother may produce good
rather than harm. There is, however, one important proviso,
and this concerns the quality of the substitute care which
the child receives. For one thing, there is a need for consistency: a young child continually being left with

different people is likely to become bewildered and upset. And for another, we have the enormous problem of illegal child-minders, looking after an estimated 100,000 children in Britain. According to recent findings, the quality of care provided by such childminders is only too frequently of an unsatisfactory nature, being marked by ignorance and neglect that in some cases can be quite appalling. It is only in the officially provided facilities, such as nursery schools, that the care given by trained staff is such that the social and intellectual benefits can be felt.

Sensitive and insensitive parents

A child's development does not take place in a vacuum; it occurs because the people responsible for his care carefully and sensitively provide him with the kind of environment that will foster his growth. They do so not only by such conscious decisions as to what toys to buy him for Christmas or which nursery school to send him to, but also quite unconsciously by the manner in which they relate to him.

Take the language which adults use in talking to a child. This is in many ways strikingly different from the language used to address another adult: it has a much more restricted vocabulary, a considerably simplified grammar, and a great deal of repetition. In addition, it is charac-terized by a slowing down in the rate of speech, a high pitch of voice, and the use of special intonation patterns. Not only mothers but most adults will quite unconsciously adopt this style when confronted by a young child. What is more, the younger the child the more marked is the simpli-fication, repetition, slowing down and all the other charac-teristics listed. It is as though the adult is making allow-ance for the child's limited ability to absorb whatever one tells him, thereby showing sensitivity to the abilities and requirements of that particular child.

Such examples of (usually quite unconscious) sensitivity in relating to children are numerous. Watch how a mother hands her baby a rattle to grasp: how carefully she adjusts the manner and speed with which she offers the toy to the still uncertain reaching skills of the child. She shows thereby that she is able to see things from the child's point of view, that she is aware of his requirements and can respond to these appropriately. Sensitivity is an essential part of helping a child to develop. Children brought up in institutions, in which they are all treated the same and where care is never personalized, become developmentally retarded. While most adults show sensitivity to children quite naturally, some parents are unfortunately devoid of this vital part of parenting. Why this is so we still do not know for certain; it does seem, however, that parents who themselves had a deprived childhood and did not themselves experience sensitive care are more likely to show the same attitude to their own children.

Are the early years special?

There is a widespread belief that experience in childhood, and particularly so in the earliest years, has a crucial formulative influence on later personality. Thus the early years are said to be the most important, and special care therefore needs to be taken to protect the child during this period against harmful experiences that might mark him for life. Let us look at the evidence for this belief.

The influence of child-rearing practices

According to Freud, a child's development is marked by a series of phases (oral, anal, genital) during which he is especially sensitive to certain kinds of experience. During the oral phase, for example, the baby is mainly concerned with activities like sucking, chewing, swallowing and biting, and the experiences that matter to him most thus include the manner of his feeding (breast or bottle), the timing of feeding (schedule or demand), the age when he is weaned, and so on. When these experiences are congenial to the child he passes on to the next developmental phase without difficulty; when they are frustrating and stressful, however, he remains 'fixated' at this stage in the sense that, even as an adult, he continues to show characteristics such as dependence and passivity in his personality make-up that distinguish babies at the oral stage. In this way Freud's theory suggests that there are definite links between particular kinds of infantile experiences on the one hand, and adult personality characteristics on the other.

However, this theory has not been borne out. A large number of investigations have compared breast-feeding with bottle-feeding, self-demand with rigidly scheduled regimes, early with later weaning, and other aspects of the child's early experience that could be expected to produce lasting after-effects. No such effects have been found. The sum total of these investigations adds up to the conclusion that specific infant care practices do not produce unvarying traces that may unfailingly be picked up in later life. Whatever their impact at the time, there is no reason to believe that these early experiences mark the child for good or ill for the rest of his life.

And just as well! Were it otherwise we would all be at the mercy of some single event, some specific parental aberration, that we happened to have experienced at some long-distant point in our past. Freud's theory made little allowance for the ameliorating influence of later experience, yet the more we study human development the more apparent it becomes that children, given the opportunity, are able to recuperate from many an early misfortune. Let us consider some other examples that make this point.

Maternal deprivation

In 1951 a report was published by John Bowlby, a British child psychiatrist, pointing to the psychological ill-effects of being deprived of maternal care during the early years. The evidence, Bowlby believed, indicated that a child

105

must be with his mother during the crucial period of the first two or three years if he is to develop the ability to form relationships with other people. Deprived of a relationship with a permanent mother-figure at that time, such an ability will never develop. Thus children in institutions and long-term hospitals, where they are deprived of this necessity, become 'affectionless characters': that is, they are unable ever to form a deep, emotionally meaningful relationship with another person. Having missed out on a vital experience, namely being mothered, the child is mentally crippled for life. And that experience has to happen at a particular time, namely in the first years. No amount of good mothering subsequently can remedy the situation.

There is no doubt about the tremendous influence on the practice of caring for children that Bowlby's ideas have had. And no wonder, for so many children are thereby implicated. Many thousands of children every year are taken into the care of local authorities; many thousands are admitted to hospital. Anything that can be done to improve the lot of so many children is therefore worth considering, and there is no doubt that in the last two decades a great deal has been done in the UK. Children's institutions have become less impersonal with the introduction of family group systems; there is greater emphasis on fostering children with ordinary families and, most important, far more stress is placed on prevention and keeping children with their own parents. Similarly, the psychological care of children in hospitals has improved greatly during this period. Visiting by parents is nowhere near as restricted as it was at one time; mother-baby units make it possible for parents to stay with their children; and again the emphasis on prevention means that rather more thought is now given to the need to admit the child in the first place.

Anyone who has ever seen a young child separated from his mother and admitted, say, to a strange hospital ward, where he is looked after by strangers and may be subjected to unpleasant procedures like injections, knows the extreme distress that one then finds. It is perhaps difficult for an adult to appreciate the depth of a child's panic when he has just lost his mother: a panic that may continue for days and only be succeeded by a depressive-like picture when the child withdraws into himself from a too painful world. Parents also know only too well about the insecurity which the child shows subsequently on return home, even after quite brief absences, when he dare not let the mother out of sight. There is no doubt about these dramatic short-term effects, and for their sake alone the steps taken to humanize procedures have been well worth while.

Far more problematic, however, is the question of long-term effects: that is, the suggestion that periods of prolonged maternal deprivation in the early years impair the child's capacity to form interpersonal relationships. What evidence we have here suggests that things are not as cut and dried as Bowlby indicated, and to make this point we can do no better than to turn to the report by Barbara Tizard to which we have already referred.

Tizard examined adopted children who had spent all their early lives in institutions, with no opportunity to form any stable attachments to any adult during that period. One might have expected them to be so marked by this experience as to be incapable of forming any emotional relationship to their adoptive parents and to show all the signs of the affectionless character. Yet this proved not to be the case. Nearly all these children developed deep attachments to their adoptive parents, and this included even a child placed as late as seven years of age. They did show some deviant symptoms, such as poor concentration and over-friendliness to strangers, but there was no indication that the inevitable outcome of their earlier upbringing was the 'affectionless character'. We must conclude that children's recuperative powers should not be under-estimated: given a new environment in which they receive very much improved treatment, the outlook can be good. There is no reason to believe that they will be marked for life by earlier misfortunes, just because these occurred early on.

Birth abnormalities and social class
When misfortune takes a 'physical' form, such as some abnormality of the birth process, the outcome is again not necessarily a poor one. Once more, it all depends on the child's subsequent experience.

Take such birth complications as anoxia (the severe shortage of oxygen in the brain) or prematurity. Follow-up studies of children who arrive in the world in such a precarious condition show that, on the basis of the child's condition at birth, it is impossible to predict his subsequent development. Two children coming into the world with the identical kind of pathology may develop along quite different lines. In one case, the child's condition at birth may give rise to a whole sequence of problems that continue and even mount up throughout his life; in the other, the difficulty is surmounted and the child functions normally.

The answer to this paradox lies in the different kinds of social environment in which the children develop. Where these are favourable the effects of the initial handicap may be minimized and in due course be overcome altogether. Where they are unfavourable the deficits remain and may even be amplified. The outcome, that is, depends not so much on the adverse circumstances of the child's birth as on the way in which his family then copes with the problem. And this, it has been found, is very much related to the social class to which the family belongs.

Social class is in many respects a nebulous concept. Nevertheless, it does refer to a set of factors (concerned with education, housing, health and so forth) that usually exert a continuing influence on the child throughout his formative years, and it is therefore not surprising that social and economic status turn out to have a much stronger influence on the course of development than some specific event at birth.

Thus even organic damage, just as the other aspects of a child's early experience, cannot in and of itself account for the particular course which that child's development takes. The irreversible effects of early experience have no doubt been greatly overrated. To believe in such effects is indeed dangerous for two reasons: first, because of the suggestion that during the first few years children are so vulnerable that they are beyond help if they do encounter some unfortunate experience; second, because it leads one to conclude that the latter years of childhood are not as important as the earlier years. All the evidence indicates that neither proposition is true: the effects of early experiences are reversible if need be, and older children may be just as affected by unfortunate circumstances (though possibly different ones) as younger children.

Conclusions

A child's development always occurs in a social context. Right from the beginning he is a member of a particular society, and the hopes and beliefs and expectations of those around him will have a crucial bearing on his psychological growth.

There is still a tremendous amount to be learned about the nature of the child's development and the way that it is affected by particular features of the environment. But in the meantime we can at least make one negative statement with some very positive implications: development can never be explained in terms of single causes. Thus we have seen that isolated events, however traumatic at the time, do not preclude later influences; that the one relationship with the mother does not account for everything. For that matter, development is not simply a matter of the environment acting on the child, for the child too can act on his environment. Not surprisingly, when confronted with a specific problem such as child abuse, we invariably find that a combination of circumstances needs to be considered if one is to explain it. Simple-minded explanations of the kind, 'juvenile delinquency is due to poverty (or heredity or lack of discipline)' never do justice to such a complex process as a child's development. And, similarly, action taken to prevent or treat which focusses on only single factors is most unlikely to succeed.

Questions

1. What are the principal controversial issues that have been raised by the study of maternal deprivation?
2. In what way can a child's social experience affect his intellectual development?
3. Can and should children be studied scientifically?
4. What advice would you give to the mother of a three year old who is considering taking up employment?
5. Why are the effects of early experience not necessarily

permanent? Describe the circumstances under which you do find them to be long-lasting.

6. What is known about the reasons for baby battering? What effects on the child would you expect such treatment to have?

7. Discuss the pros and cons of parent education schemes. On what principles would you organize such a scheme?

8. What is the role of the father in the family?

9. How can one mitigate the effects of social disadvantage on the young child's intellectual development?

10. The parent-child relationship is said to be 'reciprocal'. Explain what is meant and provide examples.

11. Discuss the role of language in intellectual development, and examine the suggestion that there are class differences in language use.

12. Socialization - conflict or mutual adjustment?

13. What principles ought to guide a child's adoption?

14. Should education begin during the pre-school years? Explain what you mean by 'education' and discuss the settings in which it could take place.

15. Describe some of the social skills that children generally acquire during the early years, and the conditions that foster their development.

16. Explain what is meant by 'sensitivity' in a parent, and describe the likely effects on a child of its absence.

17. In what way is a family's social class likely to affect a child's development?

18. How do relationships with other children affect development during the pre-school years?

19. What implications does our knowledge of social development in the early years have for the upbringing of handicapped children?

20. What psychological principles should be taken into account in looking after children in residential care?

Annotated reading

Booth, T. (1975) Growing up in Society. London: Methuen (Essential Psychology Series).

A general account of the influences that determine the way in which people grow up together. It takes into account not only the contribution of psychology but of such other social sciences as sociology, anthropology and social history. Its main value lies in the way child development is seen as occurring within the social context of each particular culture.

Bowlby, J. (1965) Child Care and the Growth of Love. Harmondsworth: Penguin.

A more widely available version of Bowlby's classic report, first published in 1951, concerning the link between maternal deprivation and mental pathology. It should be read in conjunction with Rutter's book (see below).

Clarke, A.M. and Clarke, A.D.B. (1976) Early Experience: Myth and evidence. London: Open Books.
   A collection of contributions by different authors, all concerned with the question of whether early experience exerts a disproportionate influence on later development. A wide range of research studies are reviewed, and the consensus is against seeing the early years as in some sense more important than later stages of development.

Dunn, J. (1977) Distress and Comfort. London: Fontana/Open Books.
   Discusses some of the issues that concern parents during the early stages of the child's life, with particular reference to the causes and alleviation of distress, but places these issues in the wider context of the parent-child relationship and its cultural significance.

Kempe, R.S. and Kempe, H. (1978) Child Abuse. London: Fontana/Open Books.
   An account by the foremost experts on child abuse of the state of knowledge regarding all aspects of this vexed area: causation, treatment and prevention.

Lewin, R. (1975) Child Alive. London: Temple-Smith.
   Various researchers summarize in brief and popularized form what we have learned about child development in recent years. Most contributions deal with young children, and the book as a whole emphasizes how psychologically sophisticated even babies already are.

Rutter, M. (1972) Maternal Deprivation Reassessed. Harmondsworth: Penguin.
   A systematic review of the evidence on this controversial topic that has accumulated since Bowlby highlighted its importance. Discusses the various studies that have been carried out on the effects, both short- and long-term, of early deprivation of maternal care.

Schaffer, H.R. (1971) The Growth of Sociability. Harmondsworth: Penguin.
   A description of work on the earliest stages of social development. It shows how sociability in the early years has been studied, and reviews what we have learned about the way in which a child's first social relationships are formed.

Schaffer, H.R. (1977) Mothering. London: Fontana/Open Books.
   An account of what is involved in being a parent. Brings together the evidence from recent studies of the mother-child relationship, and examines different conceptions of the parent's task. Gives special emphasis to the theme of mutuality in the relationship.

Tizard, B. (1977) Adoption: A second chance. London: Open Books.

An account of an important research study on children in residential care who were subsequently adopted. Raises some crucial issues regarding the effects of early experience and the public care of young children.

9

Knowledge of Self
D. Bannister

What is self?

Definition is a social undertaking. As a community we
negotiate the meaning of words. This makes 'self' a
peculiarly difficult term to define, since much of the
meaning we attach to it derives from essentially private
experiences of a kind which are difficult to communicate
about and agree upon. Nevertheless, we can try to abstract
from our private experience of self qualities which can
constitute a working definition. Such an attempt was made
by Bannister and Fransella (1980) in the following terms.

**Each of us entertains a notion of our own separateness from
others and relies on the essential privacy of our own
consciousness**
Consider differences between the way in which you communicate with yourself and the way in which you communicate with
others. To communicate with others involves externalizing
(and thereby blurring) your experience into forms of speech,
arm waving, gift giving, sulking, writing and so on. Yet
communicating with yourself is so easy that it seems not to
merit the word communication: it is more like instant recognition. Additionally, communicating with specific others
involves the risk of being overheard, spied upon or having
your messages intercepted and this contrasts with our
internal communications which are secret and safeguarded.
Most importantly, we experience our internal communications
as the origin and starting point of things. We believe that
it is out of them that we construct communications with
others. We know this when we tell a lie because we are aware
of the difference between our experienced internal communications and the special distortions given it before transmission.

**We entertain a notion of the integrity and completeness of
our own experience in that we believe all parts of it to be
relatable because we are, in some vital sense, the
experience itself**
We extend the notion of me into notion of my world. We think
of events as more or less relevant to us. We distinguish
between what concerns and what does not concern us. In this
way we can use the phrase 'my situation' to indicate the
boundaries of our important experience and the ways in which
the various parts of it relate to make up a personal world.

We entertain the notion of our own continuity over time; we possess our biography and we live in relation to it

We live along a time line. We believe that we are essentially the 'same' person now that we were five minutes ago or five years ago. We accept that our circumstances may have changed in this or that respect, but we have a feeling of continuity, we possess a 'life'. We extend this to imagine a continuing future life. We can see our history in a variety of ways, but how we see it, the way in which we interpret it, is a central part of our character.

We entertain a notion of ourselves as causes, we have purposes, we intend, we accept a partial responsibility for the consequences of our actions

Just as we believe that we possess our life, so we think of ourselves as making 'choices' and as being identified by our choices. Even those psychologists who (in their professional writing) describe humankind as wholly determined, and persons as entirely the products of their environments, talk personally in terms of their own intentions and purposive acts and are prepared to accept responsibility, when challenged, for the choices they have made.

We work towards a notion of other persons by analogy with ourselves; we assume a comparability of subjective experience

If we accept for the moment the personal construct theory argument (Kelly, 1955, 1969) and think not simply of 'self' but of the bipolar construct of self versus others, then this draws our attention to the way in which we can only define self by distinguishing it from and comparing it to others. Yet this distinction between self and others also implies that others can be seen in the same terms, as 'persons' or as 'selves'. Our working assumption is that the rest of humankind have experiences which are somehow comparable with, although not the same as, our own and thereby we reasonably assume that they experience themselves as 'selves'.

We reflect, we are conscious, we are aware of self

Everything that has been said so far is by way of reflecting, standing back and viewing self. We both experience and reflect upon our experience, summarize it, comment on it and analyse it. This capacity to reflect is both the source of our commentary on self and a central part of the experience of being a 'self'. Psychologists sometimes, rather quaintly, talk of 'consciousness' as a problem. They see consciousness as a mystery which might best be dealt with by ignoring it and regarding people as mechanisms without awareness. This seems curious when we reflect that, were it not for this problematical consciousness, there would be no psychology to have problems to argue about. Psychology itself is a direct expression of consciousness. Mead (1925) elaborated this point in terms of the difference between 'I' and 'me', referring to the 'I' who acts and the 'me' who reflects upon the action and can go on to reflect upon the 'me' reflecting on the action.

Do we or do we not know ourselves?

The question 'do you know yourself?' seems to call forth a categorical 'yes' by way of answer. We know, in complete and sometimes painful detail, what has happened to us, what we have to contend with and what our thoughts and feelings are. We can reasonably claim to sit inside ourselves and know what is going on.

Yet we all have kinds of experience which cast doubt on the idea that we completely know ourselves. A basic test (in science and personal life) of whether you understand someone is your ability to predict accurately what they will do in a given situation. Yet most of us come across situations where we fail to predict our own behaviour; we find ourselves surprised by it and see ourselves behaving in a way we would not have expected to behave if we were the sort of person we thought we were.

We also sense that not all aspects of ourselves are equally accessible to us. There is nothing very mysterious in the notion of a hidden storehouse. We can confirm it very simply by reference to what we can readily draw from it. If I ask you to think about what kind of clothes you wore when you were around 14 years old you can probably bring some kind of image to mind. That raises the obvious question: where was that knowledge of yourself a minute ago, before I asked you the question? We are accustomed to having a vast knowledge of ourselves which is not consciously in front of us all the time. It is stored. It is not a great step to add to that picture the possibility that some parts of the 'store' of your past may not be so easily brought to the surface. We can then go one stage further and argue that although parts of your past are not easily brought to the surface they may nevertheless influence the present ways in which you feel and behave.

The best known picture of this kind of process is the Freudian portrait of the unconscious. Freud portrayed the self as divided. He saw it as made up of an id, the source of our primitive sexual and aggressive drives; a super-ego, our learned morality, our inhibitions; and an ego, our conscious self, struggling to maintain some kind of balance between the driving force of the id and the controlling force of the super-ego. Freud argued that the id is entirely unconscious and a great deal of the super-ego is also unconscious, and that only very special strategies such as those used in psychoanalytic therapy can give access to the contents of these unconscious areas of self. We do not have to accept Freud's particular thesis in order to accept the idea of different levels of awareness, but it may well be that the enormous popularity of Freudian theory is due to the fact that it depicts what most of us feel is a 'probable' state of affairs; namely, that we have much more going on in us that we can readily be aware of or name.

Indeed, if we examine our everyday experience then we may well conclude that we are continually becoming aware of aspects of ourselves previously hidden from us.

A great deal of psychotherapy, education and personal and interpersonal soul-searching is dedicated to bringing to the surface hitherto unrecognized consistencies in our lives.

How do we know ourselves?

There is evidence that getting to know ourselves is a developmental process: it is something we learn in the same way that we learn to walk, talk and relate to others. In one study (Bannister and Agnew, 1977), groups of children were tape-recorded answering a variety of questions about their school, home, favourite games and so forth. These tape-recordings were transcribed and re-recorded in different voices so as to exclude circumstantial clues (names, occupations of parents and so forth) as to the identity of the children. Four months after the original recording the same children were asked to identify their own statements, to point out which statements were definitely not theirs and to give reasons for their choice. The children's ability to recognize their own statements increased steadily with age, and the strategies they used to pick out their own answers changed and became more complex. Thus, at the age of five, children relied heavily on their (often inaccurate) memory or used simple clues such as whether they themselves undertook the kinds of activity mentioned in the statement; 'That boy says he plays football and I play football so I must have said that'. By the age of nine, they were using more psychologically complex methods to identify which statements they had made and which statements they had not made. For example, one boy picked out the statement 'I want to be a soldier when I grow up' as definitely not his because 'I don't think I could ever kill a human being so I wouldn't say I wanted to be a soldier'. This is clearly a psychological inference of a fairly elaborate kind.

Underlying our notions about ourselves and other people are personal psychological theories which roughly parallel those put forward in formal psychology.

A common kind of theory is what would be called in formal psychology a 'trait theory'. Trait theories hinge on the argument that there are, in each of us, enduring characteristics which differentiate us from others, who have more or less of these characteristics. The notion that we or someone else is 'bad-tempered' is closely akin to the notion in formal psychology that some people are constitutionally 'introverted' or 'authoritarian' and so forth. The problem with trait descriptions is that they are not explanatory. They are a kind of tautology which says that a person behaves in a bad-tempered way because he is a bad-tempered kind of person. Such approaches tend to distract our attention from what is going on between us and other people by firmly lodging 'causes' in either us or the other person. If

115

I say that I am angry with you because I am 'a bad-tempered person' that relieves me of the need to understand what is going on specifically between you and me that is making me angry.

Environmental and learning theories in psychology have their equivalents in our everyday arguments about our own nature. The fundamental assertion of stimulus-response psychology, that a person can be seen as reacting to his environment in terms of previously learned patterns of response, is mirrored in our own talk when we offer as grounds for our actions that it is all 'due to the way I was brought up' or 'there was nothing else I could do in the circumstances'. Those theories and approaches in formal psychology which treat the person as a mechanism echo the kinds of explanation which we offer for our own behaviour when we are most eager to excuse it, to deny our responsibility for it and to argue that we cannot be expected to change.

Any theory or attempt to explain how we come to be what we are and how we change involves us in the question of what kind of evidence we use. Kelly (1955) argued that we derive our picture of ourselves through the picture which we have of other people's picture of us. He was arguing here that the central evidence we use in understanding ourselves is other people's reactions to us, both what they say of us and the implications of their behaviour towards us. He was not saying that we simply take other people's views of us as gospel. Obviously this would be impossible because people have very varying and often very disparate reactions to us. He argued that we filter others' views of us through our view of them. If someone you consider excessively rash and impulsive says that you are a conventional mouse, you might be inclined to dismiss their estimate on the grounds that they see everyone who is not perpetually swinging from the chandelier as being a conventional mouse. However, if someone you consider very docile and timid says that you are a conventional mouse, then this has quite different implications. You do not come to understand yourself simply by contemplating your own navel or even by analysing your own history. You build up a continuous and changing picture of yourself out of your interaction with other people.

Do we change ourselves?

That we change in small ways seems obvious enough. Looking at ourselves or others we readily notice changes in preferred style of dress, taste in films or food, changes in interests and hobbies, the gaining of new skills and the rusting of old and so forth.

Whether we change in large ways as well as small involves us in the question of how we define 'large' and 'small' change. Kelly (1955) hypothesized that each of us has a 'theory' about ourselves, about other people, and about the nature of the world, a theory which he referred to as our personal construct system. Constructs are our ways of discriminating our world. For many of them we have overt labels such as nice-nasty, ugly-beautiful, cheap-expensive, north-south, trustworthy-untrustworthy and so forth. He also distinguished between superordinate and subordinate constructs. Superordinate constructs are those which govern large areas of our life and which refer to matters of central concern to us, while subordinate constructs govern the minor detail of our lives.

If we take constructs about 'change in dress' at a subordinate level then we refer simply to our tendency to switch from sober to bright colours, from wide lapels to narrow lapels and so forth. If we look at such changes superordinately then we can make more far-reaching distinctions. For example, we might see ourselves as having made many subordinate changes in dress while not changing superordinately because we have always 'followed fashion'. Thus at this level of abstraction there is no change because the multitude of our minor changes are always governed and controlled by our refusal to make a major change, that is, to dress independently of fashion.

Psychologists differ greatly in their view of how much change takes place in people and how it takes place. Trait psychologists tend to set up the notion of fixed personality characteristics which remain with people all their lives, which are measurable and which will predict their behaviour to a fair degree in any given situation. The evidence for this view has been much attacked (e.g. Mischel, 1968). Direct examination of personal experience suggests that Kelly (1955) may have been right in referring to 'man as a form of motion and not a static object that is occasionally kicked into movement'.

Psychological measurement, to date, suggests that people change their character, if only slowly, and have complex natures so that behaviour is not easily predictable from one situation to another. Psychologists have also tended to argue that where change takes place it is often unconscious and unchosen by the person. The issue of whether we choose change or whether change is something that happens to us is clearly complex. One way of viewing it might be to argue that we can and do choose to change ourselves, but that often we are less aware of the direction which chosen change may eventually take.

A person in a semi-skilled job may decide to go to night-school classes or undertake other forms of training in order to qualify themselves for what they regard as more challenging kinds of work. They might be successful in gaining qualifications and entering a new field. Up to this point they can reasonably claim to have chosen their direction of personal change and to have carried through that change in terms of their original proposal. However, the long-term effect may be that they acquire new kinds of responsibility, contacts with different kinds of people, new values and a life style which, in total, will involve personal changes not clearly envisaged at the time they went to their first evening class.

On the issue of how we go about changing ourselves,
Radley (1974) speculated that change, particularly self-
chosen change, may have three stages to it. Initially, if we
are going to change, we must be able to envisage some goal;
we must have a kind of picture of what we will be like when
we have changed. He argued that if we have only a vague
picture or no picture at all then we cannot change; we need
to be able to 'see' the changed us in the distance. He went
on to argue that when we have the picture then we can enact
the role of a person like that. That is to say, we do not at
heart believe that we are such a person but we can behave
as if we were such a person, rather like an actor playing a
role on stage or someone trying out a new style. (This may
relate to the old adage that adolescence is the time when we
'try out' personalities to see which is a good fit.) He
argued that if we enact in a committed and vigorous way for
long enough then, at some mysterious point, we become what
we are enacting and it is much more true to say that we are
that person than that we are our former selves. This is very
much a psychological explanation, in that it is about what
is psychologically true, rather than what is formally and
officially true. Thus the student who qualifies and becomes
a teacher may officially, in terms of pay packet and title,
be 'a teacher'. Yet, in Radley's terms, the person may still
psychologically be 'a student' who is enacting the role of
teacher, who is putting on a teaching style and carrying out
the duties of a teacher but who still, in his heart of
hearts, sees himself as a student. Later, there may come a
point at which he becomes, in the psychological sense, a
teacher.

However, we are also aware that there is much that is
problematic and threatening about change. The set expectations of others about us may have an imprisoning effect
and restrict our capacity to change. People have a picture
of us and may attempt to enforce that picture. They may
resist change in us because it seems to them unnatural, and
it would make us less predictable. Phrases such as 'you are
acting out of character', or 'that is not the true you', or
'those are not really your ideas' all reflect the difficulty
people find and the resistance they manifest to change in
us. Often the pressure of others' expectations is so great
that we can only achieve change by keeping it secret until
the change has gone so far that we can confront the dismay
of others.

This is not to argue that we are simply moulded and
brainwashed by our society and our family so that we are
merely puppets dancing to tunes played by others. We are
clearly influenced by others and everything, the language we
speak, the clothes we wear, our values, ideas and feelings,
is derived from and elaborated in terms of our relationships
with other people and our society. But the more conscious
we become of how this happens, the more likely we are to
become critical of and the less likely automatically to
accept what we are taught (formally and informally), and

the more we may independently explore what we wish to make of ourselves as persons.

Equally, when we attempt to change we may find the process personally threatening. We may lose sight of the fact that change is inevitably a form of evolution: that is to say, we change from something to something and thereby there is continuity as well as change. If we lose faith in our own continuity we may be overwhelmed by a fear of some kind of catastrophic break, a fear of becoming something unpredictable to ourselves, of falling into chaos. Whether or not we are entirely happy with ourselves, at least we are something we are familiar with, and quite often we stay as we are because we would sooner suffer the devil we know than the unknown devil of a changed us. Fransella (1972) explored the way in which stutterers who seem to be on the verge of being cured of their stutter often suddenly relapse. She argued that stutterers know full well how to live as 'stutterers'; they understand how people react and relate to them as 'stutterers'. Nearing cure they are overwhelmed with the fear of the unknown, the strangeness of being 'a fluent speaker'.

Monitoring of self

One of the marked features of our culture is that it does not demand (or even suggest) that we formally monitor our lives or that we record our personal history in the way in which a society records its history. True, a few keep diaries and practices such as re-reading old letters from other people give us glimpses into our past attitudes and feelings. For the most part, our understanding of our past is based on our often erratic memory of it. Moreover, our memory is likely to be erratic, not just because we forget past incidents and ideas but because we may actively 're-write' our history so as to emphasize our consistency and make our past compatible with our present.

Psychologists have tended to ignore the importance of personal history. The vast majority of psychological tests designed to assess the person cut in at a given point in time; they are essentially cross-sectional and pay little heed to the evolution of the person. It would be a very unusual psychology course that used biography or autobiography as material for its students to ponder. There are exceptions to this here-and-now preoccupation. In child psychology great emphasis is laid on the notion of 'development' and a great deal of the research and argument in child psychology is about how children acquire skills over a period, how they are gradually influenced by social customs and how life within the family, over a period of years, affects a child's valuing of himself. Additionally, clinical psychologists involved in psychotherapy and counselling very often find themselves engaged in a joint search with their clients through the immediate and distant past in order to understand present problems and concerns. This does not necessarily argue that a person is simply the end product of their past. We need to understand and acknowledge our past, not in order to repeat it but in order either to use it or to be free of it. As Kelly (1969) put it, 'you are not the victim of your autobiography but you may become the victim of the way you interpret your autobiography'.

Obstacles to self-knowledge and self-change

To try and understand oneself is not simply an interesting pastime, it is a necessity of life. In order to plan our future and to make choices we have to be able to anticipate our behaviour in future situations. This makes self-knowledge a practical guide, not a self-indulgence. Sometimes the situations with which we are confronted are of a defined and clear kind so that we can anticipate and predict our behaviour with reasonable certainty. If someone asks you if you can undertake task X (keep a set of accounts, drive a car, translate a letter from German and so forth) then it is not difficult to assess your skills and experience and work out whether you can undertake the task or not. Often the choice or the undertaking is of a more complex and less defined nature. Can you stand up in conflict with a powerful authority figure? Can you make a success of your marriage to this or that person? Can you live by yourself when you have been used to living with a family? The stranger the country we are entering the more threatening the prospect becomes; the more we realize that some degree of self-change may be involved, the more we must rely upon our understanding of our own character and potential.

In such circumstances we are acutely aware of the dangers of change and may take refuge in a rigid and inflexible notion of what we are. Kelly (1955, 1969) referred to this tendency as 'hostility'. He defined hostility as 'the continued effort to extort validational evidence in favour of a type of social prediction which has already been recognized as a failure'. We cannot lightly abandon our theory of what we are, since the abandonment of such a theory may plunge us into chaos. Thus we see someone destroy a close relationship in order to 'prove' that they are independent or we see teachers 'proving' that their pupils are stupid in order to verify that they themselves are clever.

Closely connected to this definition of hostility is Kelly's definition of guilt as 'the awareness of dislodgement of self from one's core role structure'. Core constructs are those which govern a person's maintenance processes; they are those constructs in terms of which identity is established and the self is pictured and understood. Your core role structure is what you understand yourself to be.

It is in a situation in which you fail to anticipate your own behaviour that you experience guilt. Defined in this way guilt comes not from a violation of some social code but from a violation of your own personal picture of what you are.

There are traditional ways of exploring the issue of 'what am I like?' We can meditate upon ourselves, ask others how they see us, or review our history. Psychologists have devised numerous tests for assessing 'personality', though insofar as these are of any use they seem to be designed to give the psychologist ideas about the other person rather than to give the people ideas about themselves. Two relatively recent attempts to provide people with ways of exploring their own 'personality' are offered by McFall (in Bannister and Fransella, 1980) and Mair (1970).

McFall offers a simple elaboration on the idea of talking to oneself. His work indicated that if people associate freely into a tape-recorder and listen to their own free flow then, given that they erase it afterwards so that there is no possible audience other than themselves at that time, they may learn something of the themes, conflicts and issues that concern them; themes that are 'edited out' of most conversation and which are only fleetingly glimpsed in our thinking. Mair experimented with formalized, written conversation. Chosen partners wrote psychological descriptions of each other (and predictions of the other's description) and then compared and discussed the meaning and the evidence underlying their written impressions.

Although we have formal ways of exploring how we see and how we are seen by others (the encounter group), and informal ways (the party), it can be argued that there is something of a taboo in our society on direct expression of our views of each other. It may be that we fear to criticize lest we be criticized, or it may be that we are embarrassed by the whole idea of the kind of confrontation involved in telling each other about impressions which are being created. Certainly if you contemplate how much you know about the way you are seen by others, you may be struck by the limitations of your knowledge, even on quite simple issues. How clear are you as to how your voice tone is experienced by other people? How often do you try and convey to someone your feelings and thoughts about them in such an oblique and roundabout way that there is a fair chance that they will not grasp the import of what you are saying?

Psychologists are only very slowly seeing it as any part of their task to offer WAYS to people in which they may explore themselves and explore the effect they have on others.

Role and person

Social psychologists have made much use of the concept of 'role'. Just as an actor plays a particular role in a drama it can be argued that each of us has a number of roles in our family, in work groups, in our society. We have consistent ways of speaking, dressing and behaving which reflect our response to the expectations of the group around us. Thus within a family or small social group we may have inherited and developed the role of 'clown' or 'hardheaded practical person' or 'sympathizer'. Jobs often carry implicit role specifications with them so that we perceive different psychological requirements in the role of teacher from the role of student or the role of manager from the role of worker. We are surprised by the randy parson, the sensitive soldier, the shy showbusiness person. Society also prescribes very broad and pervasive roles for us as men or women, young or old, working-class or middle-class and so forth. It is not that every word of our scripts is pre-written for us, but the broad boundaries and characteristics of behaviour appropriate to each role are fairly well understood. These social roles can and do conflict with personal inclinations and one way of defining maturity would be to look on it as the process whereby we give increasing expression to what we personally are, even where this conflicts with standard social expectations.

Kelly chose to define role in a more strictly personal sense in his sociality corollary which reads: 'to the extent that one person construes the construction processes of another he may play a role in a social process involving the other person'. He is here emphasizing the degree to which, when we relate to another person, we relate in terms of our picture of the other person's picture of us. Role then becomes not a life style worked out by our culture and waiting for us to step into, but the on-going process whereby we try to imagine and understand how other people see the world and continuously to relate our own conception to theirs.

The paradox of self-knowing

We reasonably assume that our knowledge of something does not alter the 'thing' itself. If I come to know that Guatemala produces zinc or that the angle of incidence of a light ray equals its angle of reflection, then this new knowledge of mine does not, of itself, affect Guatemala or light. However, it alters me in that I have become 'knowing' and not 'ignorant' of these things. More pointedly, if I come to know something of myself then I am changed, to a greater or lesser degree, by that knowledge. Any realization by a person of the motives and attitudes underlying their behaviour has the potential to alter that behaviour.

Put another way, a person is the sum of their under-standing of their world and themselves. Changes in what we know of ourselves and the way in which we come to know it are changes in the kind of person we are.

This paradox of self-knowledge presents a perpetual problem to psychologists. An experimental psychologist may condition a person to blink their eye when a buzzer is pressed, simply by pairing the buzzer sound with a puff of air to the person's eyelid until the blink becomes a res-ponse to the sound of the buzzer on its own. But if the person becomes aware of the nature of the conditioning process and resents being its 'victim' then he may not condition at all, or at least take much longer to condition. The person's knowledge of what is going on within him and between him and the psychologist has altered the person and invalidated the psychologist's predictions. Experimental psychologists seek to evade the consequences of this state of affairs by striving to keep the subject in ignorance of the nature of the experimental process or by using what they assume to be naturally ignorant subjects: for example, rats. But relying on a precariously maintained ignorance in the experimental subject creates only a mythical certainty in science. Psychotherapists, on the other hand, generally work on the basis that the more the person (subject, patient, client) comes to know of themselves, the nearer they will come to solving, at least in part, their personal problems.

This self-changing property of self knowledge may be a pitfall for a simple-minded science of psychology. It may also be the very basis of living, for us as persons.

References

Bannister, D. and Agnew, J. (1977)
The Child's Construing of Self. In A.W. Landfield (ed.), Nebraska Symposium on Motivation 1976. Nebraska: University of Nebraska Press.

Bannister, D. and Fransella, F. (1980)
Inquiring Man (2nd edn). Harmondsworth: Penguin.

Fransella, F. (1972)
Personal Change and Reconstruction. London: Academic Press.

Kelly, G.A. (1955)
The Psychology of Personal Constructs, Volumes I and II. New York: Norton.

Kelly, G.A. (1969)
Clinical Psychology and Personality: The selected papers of George Kelly (ed. B.A. Maher). New York: Wiley.

Mair, J.M.M. (1970)
Experimenting with individuals. British Journal of Medical Psychology, 43, 245-256.

Mead, G.H. (1925)
The genesis of the self and social control. International Journal of Ethics, 35, 251-273.

Mischel, W. (1968)
Personality and Assessment. New York: Wiley.

Radley, A.R. (1974)
The effect of role enactment on construct alternatives. British Journal of Medical Psychology, 47, 313-320.

Questions

1. Discuss the problem of defining 'self'.
2. Examine the way in which a person's idea of 'self' is affected by the nature of their work.
3. Discuss the nature of sex differences in ideas about 'self'.
4. How can we 'keep track' of ourselves?
5. What does Kelly mean by 'hostility'? Give examples.
6. Outline one theory of 'self' you have read about.

7. Describe some way in which you have increased knowledge of self.
8. Comment on Radley's idea of change through role enactment.
9. Outline Freud's picture of self as made up of id, ego and super-ego.
10. How would you go about teaching a course in 'self-knowledge'?
11. How do parents influence their children's ideas about 'self'?
12. To what extent is our picture of our self influenced by our physical state and appearance?
13. Some institutions require their staff to meet regularly and formally to discuss how their personal differences affect their work. Is this a good idea?
14. We come to understand ourselves through our relationship with others. Discuss.
15. Examine the way in which social customs inhibit our revealing of 'self'.
16. Self is just a product of our environment. Discuss.
17. People are born with a fixed character which they cannot alter. Discuss.
18. Adolescence is the time when we experiment with self. Discuss.
19. Write an essay on 'roles'.
20. Can psychologists measure personality?
21. What, in your view, are the main hindrances of self-knowledge?
22. Write an essay on 'guilt'.
23. 'He is not himself today.' What triggers off this kind of comment, and does it say more about the speaker than the person of whom it is said?
24. How can we go about changing ourselves?
25. What idea about 'self', proposed by anyone (psychologist, poet, friend or whatever) has impressed you most? Why?
26. Your family teaches you what to think of yourself. Discuss.
27. Your job enables you to express yourself. Your job prevents you being yourself. Discuss.

Annotated reading

Axline, Virginia M. (1971) Dibs: In search of self. Harmondsworth: Penguin.
    A finely written description of a withdrawn and disturbed child who in the process of psychotherapy comes vividly to life. It casts light on our early struggles to achieve the idea of being a 'self'.

Bannister, D. and Fransella, F. (1980) Inquiring Man: The psychology of personal constructs. Harmondsworth: Penguin.
    The second edition of a book which sets out the way George Kelly sees each of us as developing a complex personal view of our world. The book describes two

decades of psychological research based on the theory
and relates it to problems such as psychological
breakdown, prejudice, child development and personal
relationships.

Bott, M. and Bowskill, D. (1980) The Do-It-Yourself Mind
Book. London: Wildwood House.
A lightly written but shrewd book by a psychiatrist on
the ways in which we can tackle serious personal and
emotional problems without recourse to formal
psychiatry.

Fransella, F. (1975) Need to Change? London: Methuen.
A brief description of the formal and informal ways in
which 'self' is explored and change attempted.

Rogers, C.R. (1961) On Becoming a Person. Boston: Houghton-
Mifflin.
Sets out the idea of 'self-actualization' and describes
the ways in which we might avoid either limiting
ourselves or being socially limited and come to be what
Rogers calls a fully functioning person.

10

The Family
N. Frude

Psychology and the family

The psychologist may regard the family as a background against which to view the individual, asking perhaps how the parents influence the development of a child or how families of alcoholics may help the individual to overcome his or her difficulties, or alternatively the family itself may be the unit of study. The family is a small group and we can observe the patterns of communication within it, the process of mutual decision making, and so forth. It is a system, with individuals as sub-units or elements within. Typically, psychologists have focussed their interests on the biological and social nature of the individual, but they are now becoming increasingly concerned not only with individuals or even 'individuals in relationships' but with the relationships themselves.

Clinical and educational psychologists, for example, are increasingly working within the family context and some problems which were initially identified as 'belonging' to the individual adult or child are now seen, more appropriately, as problems of the 'family system'. Also, psychologists working, for example, with handicapped children have come to recognize that the powerful influence and involvement of the parents means that they can be harnessed as highly potent sources of training, and such clinicians are increasingly using these strategies to establish a far more effective educational programme than they themselves could possibly provide. But the needs of parents, and the stresses which such a high level of involvement may place upon them, are also recognized and so the psychologists may well regard themselves as involved with the problems of the family as a whole.

So there are vital problems in the area and there are some impressive results. Let us look at some of these, choosing some of those areas which relate to major social problems and some innovations which suggest methods for their alleviation.

Family planning

Current surveys of the plans of young married couples for families have shown a high level of conscious control and active planning, a reflection of the wide availability of highly effective contraceptive techniques. The number and spacing of children are controlled with varying degrees of skill and success. The number of couples who opt for voluntary childlessness seems to be increasing. In about half of such cases the couple have planned from the start not to have children, while the other half postpone pregnancy and eventually decide to remain childless.

Contraceptive use varies greatly. Despite the numerous methods available, none is perfect, for various reasons. Some men find that the sheath reduces pleasurable sensation, the pill may have side effects on health or mood, and a number of women find methods such as the cap bothersome and distasteful. The coil may involve a painful initial fitting and an extensive gynaecological involvement which some find embarrassing and disturbing. Sterilization or vasectomy may be advisable for the older and highly stable couple, but a number of people who have undergone such surgery later change their partners. They may then request reversal surgery and in many cases successful reversal will not be possible. The solution to the contraception problem is thus by no means always simple and family planning counselling, and the tailoring of recommendations to the particular needs and life stage of the couple, is a task requiring considerable skill and insight as well as knowledge of the technical features of the particular methods.

Different couples have different 'ideal family structures', often specifying not only the number of children but also their spacing and sex. There is still some preference, overall, for boys and current research makes it likely that in the near future couples will be able, with some accuracy, to determine the sex of their baby. Many will prefer to 'leave it to nature' but others will choose one option or the other. This is likely to result in a relative excess of boys, with longer-term social results which can only be guessed.

Reactions to pregnancy range from unqualified delight to profound despair. The option of abortion is now increasingly available. Reactions to this also vary from relief to regret and while, overall, the evidence is that there are rarely long-term negative consequences for the women, several studies have suggested the need for pre- and for post-termination counselling. A number of women miscarry, some repeatedly, and again this can be a very stressful experience requiring skilled intervention.

Birth and early interaction

The process of birth is biological, but the importance of social variables is also apparent. The pregnant woman may anticipate the sex and looks of her baby, but initial acceptance is by no means inevitable. Premature babies, for example, may look very unlike the baby-food advertisements which may have conditioned the mothers' expectations.

Fathers are now often present at the delivery and there is evidence that this helps the woman in the birth process itself and also helps the couple to feel that the baby is part of both of them. The demands which the baby makes may not have been fully anticipated and the initial period with the infant may call for a difficult process of adaptation and adjustment, just as the first period of the couple living together calls for give and take and the setting-up of new norms of interaction.

Not all babies are the same: they differ in their activity level, their crying and their patterns of sleep and wakefulness. Some are not easy to care for, and may be unresponsive and difficult to soothe. Baby-care makes great demands and the mother may be totally unprepared for the energy and level of skill required. Surveys show that many of them find the period of early childhood highly stressful. They may be tired and feel inadequate and, at times, very angry. If they fail to understand and control the baby their treatment of him may be poor and, sometimes, harsh.

The level of medical care in pregnancy and around the time of the birth may be high, but many mothers then feel isolated with the baby, unsure about such matters as feeding, toileting and weaning.

In assuming that a 'mother's instinct' will aid her in these tasks we may have seriously under-estimated the extent to which, in earlier times, the informal training opportunities offered to the young girl by larger family units and the close neighbourhood community helped her in her own parenting.

The developing child

In the early years interactions with parents form the major social background for the child. There is a good deal of informal teaching and the child learns by example. Guidance and discipline help the infant to establish a set of internal rules and encouragement and praise help to develop skills and intellectual abilities. Overhearing conversations between adults enables the child to learn about the structure of language and conversation and the rules of social interaction. Watching the parents' interactions and reactions enables children to develop their own emotional repertoire and social skills, and they will experiment and consciously imitate the behaviour of their parents. The child may identify strongly with a particular parent. Games of pretence enable youngsters to practice complex tasks and build a repertoire of interactive styles, and in collaboration with other young children they may rehearse a number of roles. In both competitive and co-operative play social interaction patterns are devised and perfected, children learn about rule-following and discover their strengths and weaknesses relative to their peers.

Different parents treat their children differently, and there are many styles of parenting. Some parents are warm and affectionate, others are more distant, and some are openly hostile. Some give the child a lot of freedom and exercise little control while others are very restrictive. Not surprisingly, the children reared in such atmospheres develop somewhat differently. The children of highly restrictive parents tend to be well-mannered but lack independence, the children of warm parents come to have a confident high regard for themselves, and the children of hostile parents tend to be aggressive. There are various ways in which such findings can be explained. Do the aggressive children of hostile parents, for example, behave in that way because they are reacting against the pressures which their parents put on them, are they simply imitating the behaviour of the adults around them and picking up their interactive styles, or is there perhaps some hereditary biological component which makes both parents and children hostile?

Probably, as in so many cases of such overall correlations, there is a combination of such factors. It is also possible, of course, that hostility originating in the children themselves causes a parental reaction. We must be wary of the conclusion that children simply respond to the atmosphere of their home. They also help to create that atmosphere and the relationship between parents' behaviour and the child's behaviour is a fully interactive one. Children are not shapeless psychological forms capable of being moulded totally in response to their social environment, but have dispositions and levels of potential of their own which they bring into the family.

Children have certain psychological needs which the family should be able to provide. They need a certain stability, they need guidance and a set of rules to follow and the feeling needs to be conveyed to them that they are 'prized' by their parents. In the traditional system with two parents there may be a certain safeguard for the constant provision of these needs by one or other of the parents, and for the prevention of total lack of interest or of rejection. But if the natural family with two parents is ideal in many ways as an arrangement in which to provide for the child's development, this is not to say that the child's best interests cannot also be met in alternative contexts. Most children in single-parent households fare well and develop happily. For the child living apart from the natural parents adoption seems a better option than does fostering (though long-term fostering seems to share many of the positive features of adoption) and fostering seems to be better for the child than a continued stay in an institution. Even this context, however, can provide reasonably well for the child's needs if there is stability, a high level of staffing, high intimacy between staff and children and the provision of high levels of verbal and other types of stimulation.

The family and stress

Just as the family is a principal source of a person's happiness and well-being, it can also be the most powerful source of stress. Research has now been done to try to establish inventories of the life stresses which people experience and in even a cursory glance through such a list it is difficult not to be struck by the extent to which the relationships within the family are bound up with personal change. Some of these events, like the birth of a handicapped child or the death of a child, happen to only a few people, but others, such as the older child leaving home, marital conflict, sexual problems, and the death of a parent happen to many or most. Stress precipitated by such life events has been shown to have a marked effect on both physical and mental health, and if illness is the result then this in turn will provide added hardship.

It is not only particular events which cause stress. The constant presence of ill-health, handicap or marital conflict can similarly take its toll over the years. On the other hand, the stability and comfort of the family setting and the constant presence of others seems to provide much that is beneficial. Marriage reduces the risk of alcoholism, suicide and many forms of psychological ill-health, and interviews with separated and widowed people reveal the elements which they feel they are now missing in their lives, and which in turn may help to explain why living in relative isolation tends to be associated with a greater risk of experiencing psychological problems. As well as providing the opportunity to discuss problems and providing stability, the presence of a spouse reduces loneliness. It also facilitates discussion of a variety of issues and so enables the partners to forge a consensus view of the world: it provides extra interest and social contact, the opportunity to give love and express concern, and provides constant feedback to the individuals about themselves, their value and their role. Practical tasks may be shared and the person may be aware of being prized by the other. This then fosters the sense of self-worth which has been found to be very important for overall well-being.

Of course, not all marital relationships are good and some may lead to far greater problems than those of living in isolation. Certainly recent family changes and conflict seem, in many cases, to be a trigger factor leading to subsequent admission to a psychiatric hospital. Overall, however, it seems that the emotional impact of an intimate relationship, in adult life as in childhood, is likely to involve many more gains for the individual than losses, that people value the protection which such relationships provide and that they often suffer when such support ends.

Schizophrenia, depression and the family

There is a popular notion that schizophrenic illness originates in family relationships, and that certain forms of family communication, in particular, may cause an adolescent or young adult to become schizophrenic. A considerable number of studies have now been carried out to establish whether or not there is a firm evidential basis for such an assumption and, at this point, it looks as if the decided lack of positive evidence should lead us to abandon the hypothesis that such relationship problems constitute the major cause of the illness. While no strong data to support the family interaction claim have been forthcoming, however, a great deal of evidence implicating the role of genetics in schizophrenia has been found and it now looks as if a predominantly biological explanation may eventually be given. But while there is no good evidence that family relationships are formative in schizophrenia, there is strong support for the notion that family inter-action markedly influences the course of a schizophrenic illness and the pattern of relapses and remission from symptoms over the years. It seems that the emotional climate in the home and particular family crisis events often trigger renewed episodes of schizophrenic breakdown.

On the other hand, it seems that depression often has its origin in severe life events and difficulties and that the family context provides many of these. In a recent study conducted in London, Brown and Harris (1978) found that depression was more common in those women in the community who had recently experienced a severe event or difficulty. Many of the events involved loss. Women with several young children were more vulnerable than others, as were the widowed, divorced and separated. Social contact seemed to provide a protective function against the effects of severe life events and the rate of depression was lower in those women who had a close intimate relationship with their husbands. Women without employment outside the home were found to be more vulnerable and the loss of a mother in childhood also seemed to have a similar effect. Brown and Harris suggest that such early loss through the death of a parent may change the way in which the person comes to view the world and attempts to cope with the problems that arise. The study provides clear evidence that family relationship factors may make a person more or less susceptible to clini-cal depression, and again illustrates how the contribution of family life to personal problems is two-sided. The family may be the source of much stress, but a close supportive marital relationship will enable the individual to cope with many problems without succumbing to the threat of clinical depression.

Sexual behaviour and sexual problems

Married couples vary greatly in the frequency of their sexual contact and in the style and variety of their sexual interaction. The rate of intercourse does not seem to be related to overall satisfaction with the marriage, except that where a marriage is failing for other reasons sexual contact may be low or absent. If there is a marked discre-pancy, however, between the expectations or needs of the partners then this may lead to conflict and dissatisfaction. Sex is also one of the factors which can cause problems in the early stages of adjustment to marriage.

Although several medical men and women wrote 'marriage manuals' during the nineteenth century and in the early part of this century, our knowledge of human sexuality was very limited before the studies of people such as Kinsey and Masters and Johnson. Using interviews, and later observational and physiological techniques, researchers have now provided us with extensive information about sexual practices. Masters and Johnson (1966, 1970), in particular, have supplied a thorough and detailed account of human sexual behaviour, and they have also provided insights into such questions as sexuality in the older person and sexual behaviour during pregnancy.

It has become clear that problems of sexual dysfunction affect a great many people at some stage in their marriage. Masters and Johnson have produced a range of therapies which has been shown to be highly effective, and many of these have now been adopted by other psychologists, psychiatrists and marriage counsellors. The couple, rather than the individual man or woman, is considered to be the most appropriate treatment unit, and discussion and detailed advice are followed up with 'homework assignments' which the partners carry out in the home. Anxiety about sexual performance can have a serious effect on behaviour and a vicious circle can easily form, for example, between anxiety and failure to achieve erection. Awareness of the female orgasm has increased considerably in recent years and it appears that the pattern of problems for which advice is sought has changed. Whereas the majority of sexual problems encountered by counsellors some decades ago involved a mismatch of sexual appetites, with the woman complaining about her husband's excessive demands, a dominant problem now seems to be that of the woman's dissatisfaction with her husband's ability to bring her to orgasm.

Opinions differ about how much the 'couple unit' is always the appropriate focus for treatment and how far deep-seated relationship difficulties, rather than specific sexual skills and attitudes, underlie the problems presented. It does appear that in about half of the cases seen there are other serious marital difficulties in addition to the sexual dysfunction and sex therapy which is aimed at improving other aspects of the relationship.

Family conflict and violence

There is open conflict at times in most families. Sometimes the focus of disagreements is easily apparent; it may centre, for example, on matters concerning money, sex or the handling of children, but at other times the row seems to reflect underlying resentments and difficulties in the relationship. Studies have been made of how arguments start, how they escalate and how they are resolved, and some research in this area has been successful in identifying patterns of conflict which seem to predict later marital breakdown. It appears that there are right ways and wrong ways to fight with other family members. In some marriages there may be constant conflict which, however, is successfully worked through and which does not endanger the basic relationship.

Inter-generational conflict is also common. In the early years the parents have the power and may use discipline to settle matters of disagreement. Again, the way in which this is done is important and it seems that parents should not use their power in such a way that the child feels rejected. Children should be made to feel that their behaviour, rather than their whole personality, is the target of the parents' disapproval. In the adolescent years, the child's struggle for power and independence is often the focus of conflict. Adolescence is frequently a period of stress and young people may have doubts about their status and future. It is also a time when peer-influence may conflict with that of the parents.

Marital conflict sometimes leads to physical assault and a number of wives have to receive medical attention for injuries inflicted by their husbands. Many such wives choose to return to the home after such an incident although some seek the haven of a women's refuge. Even where there is repeated violence, the wife often feels that her husband is not likely to treat her badly in the future; she may feel that drinking or stress triggered the assault, and such wives often report that the man is generally caring and responsible and that his violent outbursts are out of character. Jealousy and sexual failure or refusal are also associated with attacks on the wife, though it is also true that for some couples physical assault or restraint represents a modal response in conflict situations, and that in some marriages (and indeed in some sub-cultures) there are few inhibitions against the couple hitting one another.

Violence against children also occurs with alarming frequency in families, and it is estimated that about two children die each week in England and Wales as a result of injuries inflicted by their parents. The children involved are often very young, and it does not take much physical strength to seriously injure a small child or baby. Only a small proportion of the parents involved in these attacks have a known psychiatric history and, contrary to one popular image, they often provide well for the general needs of their children. Sadistic premeditated cases do occur but they are relatively rare. Generally the attack occurs when a child is crying or screaming or has committed some 'crime' in the eyes of the parent. The mother or father involved is often under considerable stress, and there are frequently severe marital difficulties. The parents involved are often young and may have little idea of how to cope with the crying child, and there is evidence that many abused children are themselves difficult to handle. They may be disturbed, over-active or unresponsive although, of course, many such problems may themselves be the result of longer-term difficulties in the family.

amily therapy

There has recently been a considerable growth of interest in 'family therapy'. This is practised in a variety of ways and with a number of alternative theoretical underpinnings but it claims, in all its forms, that when there is a psychological disturbance it is useful to work with the 'family system' rather than with the individual identified client. The view is often expressed that the symptom should properly be seen as an attribute not of the individual but of the family as a whole. By focussing on the structure of the group, on the emotional climate and on the pattern of relationships and communication, an attempt is made to bring about a fundamental change which will result in a well-functioning family and an alteration in the circumstances which have maintained the symptom.

Thus a child who is truanting from school may be presented as the only problem by a family who, in fact, have a number of difficulties. By focussing on or scapegoating the child in this way, the family system may preserve itself from serious conflict between other members or between the family group and another part of the wider social system. The child's problem with school is therefore in some way 'useful' to the family and any direct attempt to deal with the truanting may be directed at reducing the underlying conflict or at changing a disordered style of communication which has led to the family 'needing' the child's symptom.

In the therapeutic sessions family members are seen together. The focus is largely on the group processes operating and involves the observations of such interactional elements as coalitions, stratagems and avoidances. As these are further analysed, they may be revealed to the family or they may be simply 'corrected' by the direct authoritative action of the therapist. The periods intervening between treatment sessions are seen as being of primary importance for the family, who may then revert to original dysfunctional patterns or may continue in the direction of therapeutic change.

The role of the therapist is varied. Some therapists regard themselves primarily as analysts and concentrate on making the family aware of its interactional style, whereas some regard themselves as mediators or referees or may take sides with one or more family members to provide a necessary balance of power. If two or more therapists work as a team then they may present their own relationship as a model of open communication and in this way try, for example, to illustrate the constructive potential of conflict.

The professional background of family therapists is highly varied and their original training may be in psychology, social work or psychiatry. The theoretical concepts used similarly cover a wide range including psychoanalysis, communications theory and behavioural analysis. Concepts have also been borrowed freely from general system theory, which is predominantly a mathematical theory with applications in cybernetics and biology. In behavioural family therapy the focus is on the manipulation of the family consequences of individual behaviour and the attempt is made to analyse and modify social reinforcement patterns and observational learning.

Because family therapy involves a varied and often subtle set of procedures, it is very difficult to carry out satisfactory studies to measure its effectiveness. Many of the variables said to be involved are rather intangible and the processes underlying changes in social systems are highly complex. Preliminary evidence suggests that it is often useful but this can also be said of many other forms of therapy, and the 'cost-effectiveness' considerations which play a part in treatment choice sometimes make it difficult to support a strong case for the use of family therapy. Many critics would return a general verdict of 'not proven', but the level of interest by professionals is undoubtedly high and growing. One special difficulty has been the failure of those working in this area to provide an adequate means of identifying the cases which may be most appropriately treated in this way. Any attempt to treat all conditions with a uniform approach is unlikely to return a high overall rate of effectiveness. With a more limited set of identified problems this mode of treatment may in future prove to be the optimal means of effective intervention for a range of cases. At present, family therapy reflects just one aspect of the increasing awareness of the importance of understanding the social context when dealing with a presented psychological symptom.

The effects of marital breakdown

Divorce statistics represent a very conservative estimate of marital failure and a still more conservative estimate of marital unhappiness and disharmony, but the rates are high and increasing. There are various estimates of the likely divorce rate of currently made marriages but one in four is a frequently encountered figure. There are certain known predictors of marital breakdown. It is more frequent, for example, when the couple married at an early age, when they have few friends, when they have had relatively little education and when their life style is unconventional. The marital success or failure of their own parents also bears a direct statistical relationship to the couple's chances of breakdown.

Psychological studies have shown that certain measures of personality and social style are also predictors of failure. If the wife rates her husband as being emotionally immature, if the husband's self-image is lacking in coherence and stability, or if either of the partners is emotionally unstable then marital breakdown is more likely than if the reverse holds. Good communication, a high level of emotional support and the constructive handling of conflict situations are, not surprisingly, features of relationships which are associated with high levels of marital happiness and low rates of breakdown. In many of these studies it is, of course, difficult to disentangle cause and effect.

The process of adjustment to a marriage may be a long and difficult one, and some marriages never successfully 'take'. The highest rates of breakdown therefore occur in the first years, but many relationships are stable and satisfactory for a while and are then beset with difficulties at a later stage. Divorce is usually preceded by months or years of intense conflict and may eventually come as a relief, but the evidence suggests that generally the whole process is a very painful one for many members of the family involved, both adults and children.

Research with divorcees has revealed a high degree of stress and unhappiness which may last for a very long time. On the whole, it appears that the experiences of women in this situation result in rather more disturbance than those of men, but for both sexes the status of divorce is associated with higher risk of clinical depression, alcoholism and attempted suicide. The psychological effects of a marriage breakdown may stem largely from lack of social support, the absence of an intimate relationship and a loss of self-esteem, but there are often additional pressures relating to the loss of contact with the children or of having to bring them up alone. There is a high rate of remarriage among the divorced; and divorce itself, for all the apparent risks which it brings, is still often preferable to continuing in a marriage which has failed.

The 'broken home' is associated with increased aggressiveness and delinquency in children, but there seems to be only a weak association with neurotic and other psychiatric problems of childhood. While the rate of conduct problems in the children of divorce is considerably higher than that for children of stable marriages, there is apparently little increase in such antisocial behaviour for children whose homes have been broken by the death of a parent. This suggests that it is the discord in the home which produces the effect rather than the mere absence of one parent. This is supported by the finding that conduct problems also occur with increased frequency in homes with continual discord, even when there is no separation or divorce.

Single-parent families

Children are raised in single-parent families when the mother has not married, when there has been a divorce or separation, or when one parent has died. 'Illegitimacy' is a somewhat outmoded term and an increasing number of single women now feel that they want to rear their child on their own. Social attitudes against illegitimacy and single parenthood have softened over the years and this has encouraged more mothers to keep the baby rather than have it adopted.

Single parenthood appears to be more stressful for the remaining parent than sharing the responsibilities with a partner. Lack of emotional support and of adult company are some of the reasons for this but there are also likely to be increased financial hardships, and the homes of single parents have been shown to be overcrowded and often lack both luxuries and basic amenities. During times of parental illness there may be few additional social resources to call upon, and the single parent is less likely to be able to organize a social life for herself (about 90 per cent of single parents are women). A number of self-help organizations have now been formed to fulfil some of the special needs of the single parent.

One-parent families are viable alternatives to the more traditional nuclear families, and most of the children raised in such circumstances do not appear to show any signs of disturbance or impaired development. There have been suggestions that the boy without a father might tend to be more effeminate but it has been found that most boys brought up by their mothers are as masculine as the rest. If anything, they tend to make fewer sex-identity based assumptions about tasks and roles. We could say that they seem to be less 'sexist' than other boys. Similarly, the girl brought up with the father alone does not seem to lack feminine identity. These findings reflect a more general conclusion that children seem to base their own stereotypes on the wider world around them rather than on the conditions prevailing in their own immediate family.

The family life of old people

Old age is marked by declining health and mobility and by a process of disengagement from several life enterprises, notably employment. There may be low income and financial difficulties, contemporaries are likely to die, and the old person may find it difficult to replace such contacts with the result that they live in a shrinking social world. The high emphasis which some old people place on privacy may reduce the uptake of potential neighbourhood and community resources.

The major exception made to such concern with privacy is with the immediate family. Typically, contacts with children and grandchildren are highly prized and may be a major focus of interest in their lives. While there is likely to be an increase in dependency, however, this is often recognized by the old and they often respect the independence of the younger family and feel a crushing sense of obligation if they are forced through circumstance to accept aid from them. In some families there is an informal 'exchange of services' between generations with the older person, for example, looking after the grandchildren while parents are working or having a short holiday.

Recent social change has resulted in fewer three-generation households, but with increasing age and decreasing health, and perhaps the death of one of the parents, the younger couple may want to offer the surviving partner a place in their home. There may be doubts about how well this will work out and conflict may be initiated between the marital partners over how far feelings of duty should lead to changes which might disrupt the family. As the children become older the pressure on space may build up, and with increasing health difficulties the burden of the older person may become too great. Deafness may become an irritation, there may be restricted mobility and the elderly parent may become incontinent.

The increased strain on the family may lead to harsh feelings or even violence towards the old person as well as to a detrimental effect on the health of other members of the family. Eventually the pressure may become unmanageable and the old person may be forced to enter an institution. For many elderly people, living with a child is a halfway stage between having a home of their own and living in an old people's home. Both moves may involve their giving up possessions and pets. The quality of institutions varies greatly, but a frequent reaction is one of withdrawal, depression and depersonalization. Despite having many people around the old person may suffer from a deep sense of loneliness and isolation.

While it seems inevitable that old age will always bring unhappiness to some people, for many it is a time of contentment and fulfilment and in a number of cases the positive aspects centre on activities and memories of relationships within the family. Older women, for example, may play a major role in organizing family get-togethers and may act as a social secretary for members of the extended family, and grandmothers and grandfathers may gain great satisfaction from their relationships with their grand-children. Many of the recent social changes in housing organization and mobility, it is true, militate against a high level of interaction between the generations, and there seems as yet little awareness by policy-makers of the social costs which such changes entail.

The future of intimate life styles

Contact with intimates in the family group seems to provide the individual, overall, with considerable benefits. Significant relationships are highly potent and there may be dangers, but generally the benefits far outweigh the costs. A variety of psychological needs are very well fulfilled in the traditional family setting. The child growing in the caring and stable family setting can generally develop skills and abilities and achieve a potential for happiness better than in any other setting, and the adult can fulfil with the marital partner the needs of emotional support, freedom from loneliness, sex, stability, and the building of a mutually comfortable 'social reality'. When the basic family pattern is disturbed there can be grave consequences for each of the people involved.

There is no uniform change in western society to a single alternative life style arrangement but there is rather an increasing diversity. There are now fewer children in families, more single-parent families, more divorces and separations, and there is a high incidence of transitory relationships and less contact between generations. Several lines of evidence suggest that children are valued less than in the recent past; that women, in particular, are looking more outside the family for their role-orientation and their life satisfactions; that there is now less 'family feeling'; and that family duties and responsibilities impinge upon individual decision making less than was the case some decades ago.

We may expect this variety to increase further as ideas regarding the roles of men and women evolve, as changes in biological and 'hard' technology take place and as patterns of employment and leisure alter. It would be premature to forecast, at this stage, what effects such changes will bring to interpersonal relationships and personal life styles. What does seem certain, however, is that there will be important effects. To some extent these can be affected by direct social intervention and some undesirable effects may be prevented.

Family life, then, is a key variable in society and adverse changes may inflict an enormous social bill. For this reason the effects on individuals must be carefully monitored. Psychologists are just one of the groups which will be involved in this vitally important enterprise.

References

Brown, G.W. and Harris, T. (1978)
Social Origins of Depression. London: Tavistock Publications.
Masters, W. and Johnson, V. (1966)
Human Sexual Response. Boston: Little, Brown.
Masters, W. and Johnson, V. (1970)
Human Sexual Inadequacy. London: Churchill.

Questions

1. Write an essay on 'The family and psychology'.
2. Assess the importance of personal relationships in the lives of individuals, referring to psychological and other studies to support the analysis you present.
3. Consider some of the factors which might lead a couple to decide to remain childless.
4. Now that there are a number of highly effective contraceptive methods why do so many unwanted pregnancies occur, and how might this be changed?
5. How is a relationship between the mother and her baby likely to differ from that between the father and his baby? Why is this so?
6. Many mothers find looking after a young baby a difficult and stressful experience. Why is this?
7. Hospital births may be medically the safest, but are there likely to be psychological dangers in treating birth more as a biological than as a social and family process?
8. What are 'the needs of children' and how may they be met?
9. Critically assess the evidence relating to the effects of a mother's work outside the home on the children.
10. Write an essay on 'The family as a source of stress'.
11. Some people have maintained that schizophrenia arises as

a result of problems within the family. Critically assess the evidence relating to this issue.

12. Write an essay on 'The alcoholic in the family'.
13. Describe current approaches to the treatment of sexual dysfunction.
14. The family seems to be the context for a good deal of violence, particularly towards children and wives. Why should this be so?
15. Write an essay on 'The after-effects of divorce'.
16. Consider the special problems of the single-parent family.
17. 'The natural social setting for old people is with their younger family.' How true is this statement? Consider the problems which may arise in a three-generation household.
18. Is the family an institution worth preserving?
19. Are there 'experts' in child-rearing? Is this process too important to be left to parents?
20. Some authors have claimed that the family is oppressive and that people should be liberated from the limits that it places on them. How far do you share this view? Give reasons.

Annotated reading

Belliveau, F. and Richter, L. (1971) Understanding Human Sexual Inadequacy. London: Hodder & Stoughton.
    Non-technical report of the work of Masters and Johnson on sexual behaviour and sexual problems, including details of treatment methods.

Herbert, M. (1975) Problems of Childhood. London: Pan.
    A comprehensive account of the problems of the early years, their treatment and prevention.

Kellmer Pringle, M. (1980) The Needs of Children (2nd edn). London: Hutchinson.
    Important review of children's needs and how they may be met both inside and outside the family. Readable and authoritative book with important implications for social policy.

Kempe, R. and Kempe, E. (1978) Child Abuse. London: Fontana/Open Books.
    The nature of treatment of violence and sexual assault on children in the family, with an account of methods of treatment and prevention.

Rutter, M. (1976) Helping Troubled Children. Harmondsworth: Penguin.
    Leading British child psychiatrist examines the nature of the more severe problems of childhood. Provides good coverage of the importance of family factors and related methods of treatment.

11

Transition: Understanding and Managing Personal Change
Barrie Hopson

> In the ongoing flux of life, (the person) undergoes many
> changes. Arriving, departing, growing, declining,
> achieving, failing - every change involves a loss and a
> gain. The old environment must be given up, the new
> accepted. People come and go; one job is lost, another
> begun; territory and possessions are acquired or sold;
> new skills are learned, old abandoned; expectations are
> fulfilled or hopes dashed - in all these situations the
> individual is faced with the need to give up one mode of
> life and accept another (Parkes, 1972).

Today, more than at any other time in our history, people
have to cope with an often bewildering variety of transitions: from home to school; from school to work; from being
single to being married and - increasingly - divorced; from
job to job; from job to loss of employment; retraining and
re-education; from place to place and friend to friend; to
parenthood and then to children leaving home; and finally to
bereavements and death. Alongside these and other major life
events people are having to learn to cope with the passage
from one stage of personal development to another: adolescence, early adulthood, stabilization, mid-life transition
and restabilization.

What is a transition?
We define a transition as a discontinuity in a person's life
space (Adams, Hayes and Hopson, 1976). Sometimes the discontinuity is defined by social consensus as to what constitutes a discontinuity within the culture. Holmes and Rahe
(1967) provide evidence to show the extent of cultural
similarity in perceptions of what are important discon-
tinuities, in the research they conducted to produce their
social readjustment rating scale. The life changes represented here (see table 1), along with their weighted
scores, were found to be remarkably consistent from culture
to culture: Japan, Hawaii, Central America, Peru, Spain,
France, Belgium, Switzerland and Scandinavia. For example,
death of a spouse requires about twice as much change in
adjustment worldwide as marriage, and ten times as much as
a traffic violation. The correlation between the items
ranged from 0.65 to 0.98 across all the cultures.

Another way of defining a discontinuity is not by general consensus but by the person's own perception. These two may not always coincide: for example, adolescence is considered to be an important time of transition in most western cultures, whereas in other cultures like Samoa it was not considered to be a time of stressful identity crisis. Also, in a common culture some children experience adolescence as a transition while others do not. Consequently it cannot be assumed that everyone experiences a transitional event (e.g. a change of job) in the same way.

Table 1

The Holmes and Rahe social readjustment rating scale

LIFE EVENT	Mean value
1. Death of a spouse	100
2. Divorce	73
3. Marital separation from mate	65
4. Detention in jail or other institution	63
5. Death of a close family member	63
6. Major personal injury or illness	53
7. Marriage	50
8. Being fired at work	47
9. Marital reconciliation with mate	45
10. Retirement from work	45
11. Major change in the health or behaviour of a family member	44
12. Pregnancy	40
13. Sexual difficulties	39
14. Gaining a new family member (e.g. through birth, adoption, oldster moving in, etc.)	39
15. Major business readjustment (e.g. merger, reorganization, bankruptcy, etc.)	39

16. Major change in financial state
    (e.g. a lot worse off or
    a lot better off than usual)   38

17. Death of a close friend   37

18. Changing to a different line of work   36

19. Major changes in the number of arguments
    with spouse (e.g. either a lot more
    or a lot less than usual regarding
    childbearing, personal habits, etc.)   35

20. Taking on a mortgage greater than
    $10,000 (e.g. purchasing a home,
    business, etc.)   31

21. Foreclosure on a mortgage or loan   30

22. Major change in responsibilities
    at work (e.g. promotion,
    demotion, lateral transfer)   29

23. Son or daughter leaving home (e.g.
    marriage, attending college, etc.)   29

24. In-law troubles   29

25. Outstanding personal achievement   28

26. Wife beginning or ceasing work
    outside the home   26

27. Beginning or ceasing formal schooling   26

28. Major change in living conditions
    (e.g. building a new home, remodelling,
    deterioration of home or neighborhood)   25

29. Revision of personal habits (dress,
    manners, associations, etc.)   24

30. Trouble with the boss   23

31. Major change in working hours or
    conditions   20

32. Change in residence   20

33. Changing to a new school   20

34. Major change in usual type and/or
    amount of recreation   19

35. Major change in church activities (e.g.
    a lot more or a lot less than usual)   19

36. Major change in social activities (e.g.
    clubs, dancing, movies, visiting, etc.)   18

37. Taking on a mortgage or loan less than
    $10,000 (e.g. purchasing a car, TV,
    freezer, etc.)   17

38. Major change in sleeping habits (a lot
    more or a lot less sleep, or change
    in part of day when asleep)   16

39. Major change in number of family
    get-togethers (e.g. a lot more or a
    lot less than usual)   15

40. Major change in eating habits (a lot
    more or a lot less food intake, or
    very different meal hours or
    surroundings)   15

41. Vacation   13

42. Christmas   12

43. Minor violations of the law (e.g.
    traffic tickets, jaywalking,
    disturbing the peace, etc.)   11

For an experience to be classed as transitional there should be:

*   PERSONAL AWARENESS of a discontinuity in one's life space; and
*   NEW BEHAVIOURAL RESPONSES required because the situation is new, or the required behaviours are novel, or both.

A person can sometimes undergo a transitional experience without being aware of the extent of the discontinuity or that new behavioural responses are required. This at some point will probably cause the person or others adaptation problems. For example, following the death of her husband, the widow may not be experiencing strain - she might even be pleased that he is dead - but suddenly she becomes aware that no house repairs have been done, and a new dimension or loss becomes evident along with the awareness of new behavioural responses required.

Why is an understanding of transitional experience important?

Life in post-industrial society is likely to bring more and

more transitions for people in all arenas of living. Any transition will result in people being subjected to some degree of stress and strain. They will be more or less aware of this depending upon the novelty of the event and the demands it makes upon their behavioural repertoires. Thus, there is likely to be a rise in the number of people experiencing an increased amount of stress and strain in the course of their daily lives.

Many practitioners in the helping professions are dealing directly with clients who are in transition. It is vital for them to understand how people are likely to react during transition, and to recognize the symptoms of transitional stress. Professionals also need helping techniques to ensure that individuals cope more effectively with their transitions, and to make organizations and social groups more aware of what they can do to help people in transition.

Is there a general model of transitions?

As we began to discover other work on different transitions, increasingly a general picture began to emerge. It appeared that irrespective of the nature of the transition, an overall pattern seemed to exist. There were differences, of course, especially between those transitions that were usually experienced as being positive: for example, marriage and desired promotion, and those usually experienced negatively, like bereavement and divorce. But these differences appeared to reflect differences of emphasis rather than require a totally different model.

The major point to be made in understanding transitions is that whether a change in one's daily routine is an intentional change, a sudden surprise that gets thrust upon one, or a growing awareness that one is moving into a life stage characterized by increasing or decreasing stability, it will trigger a CYCLE of reactions and feelings that is predictable. The cycle has seven phases, and the identification of these seven phases has come about through content analysis of reports from over 100 people who have attended transition workshops for the purpose of understanding and learning to cope more effectively with transitions they were experiencing and through extending the findings reported above.

Immobilization

The first phase is a kind of immobilization or a sense of being overwhelmed; of being unable to make plans, unable to reason, and unable to understand. In other words, the initial phase of a transition is experienced by many people as a feeling of being frozen up. It appears that the intensity with which people experience this first phase is a function of the unfamiliarity of the transition state and of the negative expectations one holds. If the transition is not high in novelty and if the person holds positive expectations, the immobilization is felt less intensely or perhaps not at all. Marriage can be a good example of the latter.

Minimization

The way of getting out of this immobilization, essentially, is by movement to the second phase of the cycle, which is characterized by minimization of the change or disruption, even to trivialize it. Very often, the person will deny that the change even exists. Sometimes, too, the person projects a euphoric feeling. Those readers who recall seeing Alfred Hitchcock's film 'Psycho' will remember that Tony Perkins spent considerable time shrieking at his mother in the house on the hill. It is not until the end of the film that one learns the mother has been dead for some time, and it is her semi-mummified body with which he has been carrying on his 'dialogue'. That is an extreme example of denying or minimizing the reality of a major change in one's life. Denial can have a positive function. It is more often a necessary phase in the process of adjustment. 'Denial is a normal and necessary human reaction to a crisis which is too immediately overwhelming to face head-on. Denial provides time for a temporary retreat from reality while our internal forces regroup and regain the strength to comprehend the new life our loss has forced upon us' (Krantzler, 1973).

Depression

Eventually, for most people - though not for Tony Perkins in 'Psycho' - the realities of the change and of the resulting stresses begin to become apparent. As people become aware that they must make some changes in the way they are living, as they become aware of the realities involved, they sometimes begin to get depressed: the third phase of the transition cycle. Depression is usually the consequence of feelings of powerlessness, of aspects of life out of one's control. This is often made worse by the fear of loss of control over one's own emotions. The depression stage has occasional high energy periods often characterized by anger, before sliding back into a feeling of hopelessness. They become depressed because they are just beginning to face up to the fact that there has been a change. Even if they have voluntarily created this change themselves, there is likely to be this dip in feelings. They become frustrated because it becomes difficult to know how best to cope with the new life requirements, the ways of being, the new relationships that have been established or whatever other changes may be necessary.

Letting go

As people move further into becoming aware of reality, they can move into the fourth phase, which is accepting reality for what it is. Through the first three phases, there has been a kind of attachment, whether it has been conscious or not, to the past (pre-transition) situation. To move from phase three to phase four involves a process of unhooking from the past and of saying 'Well, here I am now; here is what I have; I know I can survive; I may not be sure of what I want yet but I will be OK; there is life out there waiting for me.' As this is accepted as the new reality, the person's feelings begin to rise once more, and optimism becomes possible. A clear 'letting go' is necessary.

Testing

This provides a bridge to phase five, where the person becomes much more active and starts testing himself vis-à-vis the new situation, trying out new behaviours, new life styles, and new ways of coping with the transition. There is a tendency also at this point for people to stereotype, to have categories and classifications of the ways things and people should or should not be relative to the new situation. There is much personal energy available during this phase and, as they begin to deal with the new reality, it is not unlikely that those in transition will easily become angry and irritable.

Search for meaning

Following this burst of activity and self-testing, there is a more gradual shifting towards becoming concerned with understanding and for seeking meanings for how things are different and why they are different. This sixth phase is a cognitive process in which people try to understand what all of the activity, anger, stereotyping and so on have meant. It is not until people can get out of the activity and withdraw somewhat from it that they can begin to understand deeply the meaning of the change in their lives.

Internalization

This conceptualizing, in turn, allows people to move into the final phase of internalizing these meanings and incorporating them into their behaviour. Overall, the seven transition phases represent a cycle of experiencing a disruption, gradually acknowledging its reality, testing oneself, understanding oneself, and incorporating changes in one's behaviour. The level of one's morale varies across these phases and appears to follow a predictable path. Identifying the seven phases along such a morale curve often gives one a better understanding of the nature of the transition cycle. This is shown in figure 1.

Interestingly, the Menninger Foundation's research on Peace Corps volunteers' reactions to entering and experiencing training (a transition for each person) produced a very similar curve. More recently, Elisabeth Kubler-Ross and those who joined her death and dying seminars have also charted a very similar curve of the reaction cycle people go through upon learning they are terminally ill, which is the ultimate transition.

Before proceeding, it is necessary to make it clear that seldom, if ever, does a person move neatly from phase to phase as has been described above. It can help someone in distress, however, to be made aware that what they are experiencing is not uncommon, that it will pass, and that they have a great deal they can do in determining how quickly it will pass.

Figure 3

Self–esteem changes during transitions

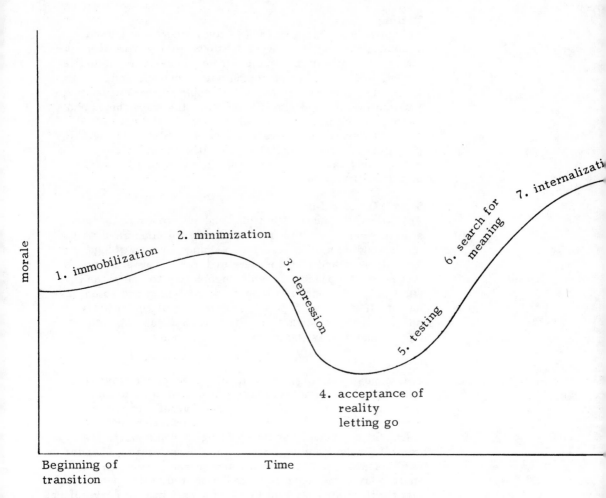

It is also important to point out that each person's experience is unique and that any given individual's progressions and regressions are unique to their unique circumstances. For example, one person may never get beyond denial or minimization. Another may end it all during depression. Yet another might experience a major failure just as things begin to look up, and slip back to a less active, more withdrawn posture.

What is important is the potential for growth arising from any major disruption or calamity. One realizes this potential and moves toward it when one lets go and fully accepts the situation for what it is; one dies a 'little death' to become larger.

What effects do transitions have on people?

It is important to note here that all transitions involve some stress, including those considered by society to be positive changes, such as being left large sums of money, parenthood or marriage (Holmes and Rahe, 1967). Our own studies investigating this relationship show the following results:

*   transitions are most stressful if they are unpre-
    dictable, involuntary, unfamiliar, of high magnitude
    (degree of change), and high intensity (rate of
    change);
*   the incidence of illness is positively correlated with
    the amount of life change one undergoes;
*   lack of feedback on the success of attempts to cope with
    strain-inducing events causes more severe stress-
    related diseases than when relevant feedback is present;
*   interpersonal warmth and support during stressful
    periods seems to reduce the impact of the stress;
*   viruses alone do not cause illnesses. The incidence of
    bad emotional experiences seems to upset the body and
    allow the viruses to take over;
*   hypertension occurs more often in environments charac-
    terized by high stressors and few ways of responding to
    those stressors;
*   the more major the life changes the higher the risk of
    coronary heart disease.

Every transition contains 'opportunity value' for the mover

However undesirable a particular transition may be for the mover, there is always opportunity for personal growth and development contained within it. If one takes a severe example such as death of a spouse, for the majority of those bereaved nothing will compensate for that loss. On the other hand, given that the loss is out of their control, what is under their control is what they decide to do with their lives from there on. There are opportunities for new relationships, travel, career change, new interests, etc. Obviously, during the grief process - which is essential - the opportunities are difficult and often obnoxious to contemplate but part of the 'letting go' stage involves doing exactly that. The Chinese have two symbols for the concept of 'crisis': one means 'danger' while the other signifies 'opportunity'.

What are the coping tasks relevant to all transitional events?

We believe that there are common elements in any transition, which enable us to talk generally about transitional beha-viour. We also assert that in dealing with any transitional event a person has two tasks to perform as he moves through the phases of the model:

*   MANAGEMENT OF STRAIN: to manage the degree of
    strain generated by the stress in such a way that the
    individual can engage with the external problems caused
    by the transition.

149

* COGNITIVE COPING TASKS: a transition will always necessitate adjustment. Any adjustment requires decisions to be made about the appropriateness of new and old behaviour patterns. The individual will be asking himself questions such as: (i) How can I accept this situation?; (ii) What behaviour is expected of me?; (iii) What do I want from this situation?

How successfully he manages these two tasks determines the speed with which he completes the transition.

What are the coping skills relevant to transitions?

At the Counselling and Career Development Unit at Leeds University we have been working for a number of years on developing training programmes to help adults in transition and to teach transition coping skills to young people in schools and colleges.

We have developed a questionnaire to be used to help people identify the transition coping skills they already possess and which simultaneously highlights the deficits in their coping repertory. Figure 2 reproduces the questionnaire designed for use with adults. People are asked to answer 'yes' or 'no' to all the questions. Each time they reply 'no', it suggests an area where they are lacking in some theoretical understanding of the nature of transitions, or deficient in cognitive or behavioural skills. Each of the items is dealt with briefly below, along with some teaching points we make to participants. In a workshop, this learning would take place experientially and participants would have an opportunity to develop and practise their skills. The language used is written to convey the flavour of the workshop approach. The following text should be read in conjunction with the questionnaire.

Figure 2

Coping skills questionnaire

1. KNOW YOURSELF

a. Would I have chosen for this to have happened?
b. Am I proactive in new situations: do I take initiatives, have a purpose as opposed to sitting back and waiting on events?
c. Do I know what I want from this new situation?
d. Do I know what I don't want from this new situation?
e. If I feel under stress do I know what I can do to help myself?
f. Do I know how to use my feelings as indicators of where I am?

2. KNOW YOUR NEW SITUATION

a. Can I describe the transition?
b. Do I know how I'm expected to behave?
c. Can I try out the new situation in advance?

3. KNOW OTHER PEOPLE WHO CAN HELP: do I have other people:

a. To depend on in a crisis?
b. To discuss concerns?
c. To feel close to - a friend?
d. Who can make me feel competent and valued?
e. Who can give me important information?
f. Who will challenge me to sit up and take a good look at myself?
g. With whom I can share good news and good feelings?
h. Who will give me constructive feedback?

4. LEARN FROM THE PAST

a. Is there anything similar that has happened to me?
b. Can I identify what I did which helped me get through that experience?
c. Can I identify what I would have done differently?

5. LOOK AFTER YOURSELF

a. Do I know how to use supportive self-talk?
b. Do I get regular exercise or have a personal fitness programme?
c. Am I eating regularly and wisely?
d. Do I know how to relax?
e. Am I keeping to a regular schedule?
f. Do I know my 'personal anchor points'?
g. Do I give myself 'treats' when under stress?
h. Do I have other people who will take care of me?
i. Can I survive?
j. Do I know when my low points are likely to be?

6. LET GO OF THE PAST

a. Do I easily let go of old situations?
b. Do I continuously feel that this should not happen to me?
c. Do I know how to vent my anger constructively?

7. SET GOALS AND MAKE ACTION PLANS

a. Do I know how to set goals?
b. Do I know what my goals are for this transition and for my life generally?
c. Do I know how to make and implement action plans?
d. Do I know how to set priorities?

    e. Do I know how to make effective decisions?

    f. Do I know how to generate alternatives, because there is always an alternative?

8. LOOK FOR THE GAINS YOU HAVE MADE

    a. Can I find one thing which is positive about this experience?

    b. Can I list a variety of new opportunities that did not exist before or that I would not have thought of previously?

    c. Have I learned something new about myself?

Know yourself

1. WOULD I HAVE CHOSEN FOR THIS TO HAVE HAPPENED? You may not have chosen this situation. This could make it more difficult for you to accept the transition. But it has happened. You now have three alternatives:

(A) accept it and put up with it

(B) refuse to accept

(C) accept it and try to benefit from it

(A) will help you to survive. (B) will bring you nothing but bad feelings and worse; you will be less able to cope with the tasks facing you in the new situation. (C) will help you to grow in addition to merely surviving.

    Given the inevitable, ask yourself the key question: 'What is the worst thing that could happen?' Having identified that, ask yourself if you can cope with that. Is it really so terrible?

    It is essential to remember that problematic situations constitute a normal aspect of living. It is also useful to recall the variety of transitions that you have encountered and survived up until now. Through having survived you will probably have developed some skills. If, on looking back, you feel dissatisfied with how you managed a transition, it is important to ask yourself whether you had all the skills needed to deal effectively with that situation. More than likely you did not. Do not berate yourself for not having these skills. Instead be glad that you have identified the need for additional skills, for that in itself is the first stage of skill development.

2. AM I PROACTIVE IN NEW SITUATIONS: DO I TAKE INITIATIVES, HAVE A PURPOSE, AS OPPOSED TO SITTING BACK AND WAITING ON EVENTS? To be proactive involves a certain sequence of behaviour:

* knowing what you want;
* knowing alternative ways of achieving this;
* choosing one alternative;
* evaluating the results against your original objective.

The essence of proactive behaviour is that there is a REASON
for it, even if the end result involves no action. The
reason, however, must stem from what Maslow (1968) calls
a 'growth' need as opposed to a 'deficiency' need. Deciding
not to give a public talk (objective), and knowing various
ways of avoiding this (knowing alternatives), choosing one,
and thereby achieving the objective at first glance seems to
fit the description of 'proactive behaviour'. However, if
the reason is based on fear of making a fool of oneself,
this would not be classed as proactive. If it were due to
over-commitment, or the feeling that you are not the best
equipped person to do it, that would be proactive.

3. DO I KNOW WHAT I WANT FROM THIS NEW SITUATION?

4. DO I KNOW WHAT I DO NOT WANT FROM THIS NEW
SITUATION? If you are unclear as to what you want or do
not want from a new situation this usually signifies a lack
of knowledge about your own values or about what the new
situation has to offer. There is an entire educational technology designed to help young people and adults to crystallize their needs and values. It has been developed in the
USA and is known generically as values clarification (Simon,
Howe and Kirschenbaum, 1972; Simon, 1974; Howe and Howe,
1975; Kirschenbaum, 1977). Obtaining more information about
the new situation is dealt with in the next section.

5. IF I FEEL UNDER STRESS DO I KNOW WHAT I CAN
DO TO HELP MYSELF? Avoid situations where you might over-
react. If you have recently separated from your spouse and
it is still painful, do not accept an invitation to an event
where you know you will encounter your spouse again. Make
as few decisions as possible as you will not be thinking
clearly enough. Do not make more than one transition at a
time. It is amazing how often people choose one transition
to be the stimulus for a host of others. If you have changed
your job, do not change your spouse, residence and/or life
style all at the same time. A new broom can sometimes sweep
you over!
    Look after yourself (see section on this below).
    Do not waste time blaming yourself (see below).
    Remember that time itself will not eliminate the stress
or heal you, it is what you do with that time. There are a
variety of cognitive shielding techniques that you can use
to minimize the strain. These all involve controlling the
amount of stimulation in the environment. Some examples are:

*   time management: making priorities;
*   making lists;
*   queuing: delaying decisions during a difficult period
    by queuing them up, dealing with them one at a time,
    and not thinking about future decisions until the time
    to make them arrives. Writing down a decision in a diary
    to be made at a future date is a good way of queuing.
*   temporary drop-out: refusing to resolve decisions until

after a recuperation period. This can appear initially as reactive; however, it is correctly termed proactive as the mover is deliberately opting out of the situation temporarily as part of a strategy to move in later and thereby more effectively.

There are now some excellent resources available for techniques of preventing and managing stress; for example, Sharpe and Lewis' 'Thrive on Stress' (1977), Lamott's 'Escape from Stress' (1975), and Forbes' 'Life Stress' (1979).

6. DO I KNOW HOW TO USE MY FEELINGS AS INDICATORS OF WHERE I AM? Many people, especially men, as a result of their upbringing are emotionally illiterate: that is, they have not developed the skills of 'reading' their own emotions. One's 'gut' feelings are the surest indicator of how one is coping at any particular time. The skill is in learning to recognize the changes in feelings when they occur and then having an emotional vocabulary to be able to label them correctly. Often when people are asked what they are feeling they will answer you in terms of only what they are thinking (see Hopson and Scally, 'Lifeskills Teaching Programmes no. 1 - How to manage negative emotions', 1980a; Johnson's 'Reaching Out', 1972).

Know your new situation
1. CAN I DESCRIBE THE TRANSITION? An essential prerequisite to successful transition coping is to know that you are in one. It is essential to be aware of when the transition began, where you are in relation to it and what are all the variables involved. For example, considering changing your job might involve geographical change, relationship changes, financial implications, holiday plans for this year, etc.

2. DO I KNOW HOW I AM EXPECTED TO BEHAVE? Transitions are naturally accompanied by stress even if they are desired. Anxiety certainly increases the less information you have about your new situation. Collect as much data as you can about what others expect of you, what society expects and how you are to behave. You may decide not to live up to or down to those expectations, but again you need the initial data before you can make that decision. You also need to know the consequences of any decision before you make it.

You can ask people who have made a similar transition or indeed are presently going through the same transition. A variety of self-help and special interest groups have developed in recent years to provide mutual support and information to people undergoing similar transitions: ante-natal classes, induction courses, orientation programmes, women's and men's 'rap' groups for people redefining their sex roles, widows' clubs, singles' clubs, one-parent family groups, etc.

It is important to remember that other people often forget, or in some cases are not even aware, that this is a new situation for you. They may need reminding. For example, one new day at the end of your first week at a new job constitutes 20 per cent of the time you have worked there. For someone who has been here for five years, one new day represents less than 0.4 per cent of the time he has been there. Consequently, his feelings about that day are likely to be quite different from your feelings about the same day.

3. CAN I TRY OUT THE NEW SITUATION IN ADVANCE?
Some transitions can be 'sampled' in advance, for example, starting a new job, moving to another country; even a divorce or death can sometimes be anticipated. Reading books about anticipated transitions can be valuable, as can talking to others who have experienced it, while remembering that no one will experience it just like you. Where appropriate you can visit places, meet people, watch films, etc., prior to your transition.

Knowing other people who can help
There is now considerable evidence to show the beneficial effects on stress reduction of talking problems through with people: friends, colleagues, even strangers.

We often make the mistake of expecting too few people, typically a spouse and children, to satisfy too great a proportion of our needs. Check the list in the questionnaire. How many categories of person do you have available to you in your life? Are there any gaps? How many different people make up your 'support' group? How dependent are you on one or two?

We are also better at developing some forms of support at the expense of others. For example, people are often better at developing friendships than relationships with people who challenge us. The challengers in most people's support systems are about as abrasive as a marshmallow. Yet sometimes challengers are exactly what we require to shift us out of stereotyped thinking. Who are the challengers in your support systems? Remember, you may not even like them.

Learn from the past
Our past is an important part of our present. Our past is the history of our successes and our failures and is thereby a record of our learning. As such, we can continue to learn from our past experiences. 'Mistakes' are another way of labelling 'opportunities for learning'. If we can identify times in the past when we have had similar feelings or experienced similar transitions, we have an opportunity to monitor those chapters of our history and evaluate our performances against the criteria of our own choosing. What did we do that really did not help the situation? What would we avoid if we were to have that experience again? Can we learn from that experience and generalize it to the new transition? A sense of one's own history is a prerequisite

to a fully functioning present and a portent for one's range of possible futures.

Look after yourself
1.   DO I KNOW HOW TO USE SUPPORTIVE SELF-TALK? Many of the problems we create for ourselves and much of the support that we give ourselves derives from the same source: our internal dialogue with ourselves. This dialogue continues throughout most of our waking hours. These 'cognitions' are vital to our survival and growth. They enable us to adapt to new situations, to learn, to feel and to enact cognitively a variety of scenarios without having to perform any of them. Ellis (1975), with his RATIONAL EMOTIVE THERAPY, for years has claimed that the way we think determines what we feel, with the corollary that if we can change how we think we can also change how we feel. His therapeutic method involves retraining people to talk internally to themselves to minimize the negative emotions which they otherwise would create. Ellis claims that most people carry a variety of 'irrational beliefs' in their heads unfounded in reality, but which result in their creating bad feelings for themselves as a result of 'shoulds' and 'oughts' which they believe are infallible. These beliefs usually belong to one of three categories, which Ellis calls the 'Irrational Trinity' on the road to 'mustabation':

*   A belief that I should be a certain sort of person, or a success, or perfect, or loved by everyone, and if I'm not, I'm a failure and worthless;
*   a belief that you, or other people, should do as I want them to do: love me, work for me, understand me, etc., and if they do not, it is terrible, and I deserve to be miserable or they should be made to suffer;
*   a belief that things should be different; there should not be racial hatred, this organization should run better, our parents should not have to die, etc., and if things are not as I want them to be it is awful and either I cannot cope and deserve to be miserable, or I have every right to be furious.

Since it takes years to develop our patterns of self-talk, changing them involves practice. There are a variety of programmes now available for helping people to restructure their self-talk into more supportive statements. Mahoney and Mahoney (1976) call this process 'cognitive ecology': cleaning up what you say to yourself.

2.   DO I GET REGULAR EXERCISE OR HAVE A PERSONAL FITNESS PROGRAMME? Physical fitness is related to one's ability to cope with stress. It has also been shown to be related to the ability to create effective interpersonal relationships (Aspy and Roebuck, 1977) which in turn is related to stress reduction.
     You need to be fit to cope effectively with transitions. Yet, of course it is often when we are most in need of

fitness that we are often least inclined to make time for it. There are a number of well-researched fitness programmes available (Health Education Council, 1976; Carruthers and Murray, 1977; Cooper, 1977; Royal Canadian Air Force, 1978).

3. AM I EATING REGULARLY AND WISELY? Now is not the time for a rash diet. Your body needs all the help it can get. People in transition often have neither the time nor inclination to eat wisely. There is sometimes a reliance on quick junk foods, take-away meals or eating out. Remember to eat something every day from the four major food groups: meat, fish, poultry; dairy products; fruits and vegetables; bread and cereals.

Do not replace food with alcohol or smoking. Obviously there are times when alcohol will help you get through a lonely evening. You need a holiday from self-work as much as from any other kind of work. The danger signs are when alcohol or a cigarette is used as a substitute for meals.

Be wary of developing a dependence on drugs at this time. Sleeping tablets can sometimes be helpful during a crisis, but get off them quickly. They can serve to prevent you from developing healthier coping strategies.

It is a good idea to acquire an easy to read book on diet but one that is critical of food fads. The Health Education Council's booklet, 'Look After Yourself' (1976), contains a simple introduction to good nutrition, and Breckon's 'You Are What You Eat' (1976) is a fascinating survey of dietary facts and fiction, arguing strongly against overdosing oneself with vitamins and dealing in a balanced way with the hysteria over additives.

4. DO I KNOW HOW TO RELAX? There are two ways of reducing stress. One is to organize your life to minimize the number of stressors working on you. The other concerns how to reduce the effect of stress WHEN it hits you. The latter is typically the biggest problem when coping with a transition. Unfortunately, the very people who are most prone to stress illnesses often exacerbate the problem by packing their lives with transitions.

There are numerous relaxation methods, each of which have their advocates. A brief guide follows.

*   Learn a relaxation technique. Progressive relaxation is simple and easy to learn. It is described in 'Exercises in Personal and Career Development' by Barrie Hopson and Patricia Hough (1973). It is described there as a classroom exercise. Transcendental meditation is now well researched and strong claims are made for it as a technique which directly affects the body's physiology. Most cities have a TM centre. You could also read 'The Transcendental Meditation Technique' by Peter Russel (1977). For those who do not enjoy the ritual cliquishness that accompanies TM, read Herbert Benson's 'The Relaxation Response' (1977).

* Direct body work to encourage relaxation: massage. The basics can be learned quickly on a course. If there is a Personal Growth centre near you, make contact as they might run courses. Read 'The Massage Book' by G. Downing (1972). You will need to keep an open mind regarding some of the sweeping generalizations made on behalf of some of these techniques.

5. AM I KEEPING TO A REGULAR SCHEDULE? If your internal world is in crisis, keep your external world in order. Keeping irregular hours, eating at strange times, going to lots of new places, meeting new people; all these can be disorientating.

6. DO I KNOW MY 'PERSONAL ANCHOR POINTS'? Toffler (1970) described this concept as one antidote to 'future shock'. When all around us things are changing we need an anchor point to hold on to. For some people it is their home, for others a relationship, children, a job, a daily routine, a favourite place or a hobby. Anchor points are plentiful, and it is vital to have at least one. In the midst of instability a stable base offers confirmation of identity, disengagement from the problem, and maybe even relaxation.

7. DO I GIVE MYSELF 'TREATS' WHEN UNDER STRESS? This list of tips has been packed with work. But play is vital too. If you are feeling low, or under stress, how about simply giving yourself a treat? It might even be a reward for accomplishing a difficult test or situation, but it does not have to be.

Draw up a list of treats. Try to become an expert on self-indulgence: a theatre trip, a massage, a book, see friends, make love, have a disgustingly 'bad for you' meal, take a holiday, or pamper yourself.

The only warning about treats is: do not spend so much time treating yourself that you use these as a diversion from coping directly with the transition.

8. DO I HAVE OTHER PEOPLE WHO WILL TAKE CARE OF ME? It is all right to be taken care of sometimes. Allow a friend, lover or colleague to look after you. If they do not offer, be proactive, ask them. Be brave enough to accept help from others. Recall what you feel when others close to you ask for help. There are pay-offs for helpers as well as those who receive help.

9. CAN I SURVIVE? Of course you can. You may doubt it at the moment. Perhaps it will help to remind yourself that what you are feeling now is normal for someone having experienced what you are experiencing. It is also necessary before you can move on to the next stage of finding out more about you and what this transition can do FOR you instead of TO you.

Do not worry about feelings of suicide. Sometimes
survival does not seem like such a good idea. If these
feelings really seem to be getting out of hand see a
counsellor, ring a Samaritan, or consult a doctor; you will
probably get more librium than counselling, but that can
take off the pressure until you have regrouped your
resources.

The feeling will pass. Talk to people, keep a regular
routine, treat yourself; at the end of each day recall one
good experience, then you can match it with a bad one, then
another good experience followed by a bad one, etc., or
contract with a friend to call you at certain times.

10. DO I KNOW WHEN MY LOW POINTS ARE LIKELY TO
BE? These can usually be predicted quite easily; after a
phone call to your children (in the case of a divorced
parent), seeing your ex-spouse with a new partner, just
seeing your ex-spouse, discovering a personal belonging of
your dead spouse, seeing an old workmate (redundancy,
retirement), etc.

Keep a diary or a journal. This will help you to clarify
your thoughts and feelings as well as to identify times,
places and people to avoid. If you are experiencing the loss
of a love it is usually advisable to fill your Sundays, bank
holidays and Saturday nights!

Let go of the past
1. DO I EASILY LET GO OF OLD SITUATIONS? Sometimes
people cannot let go because they try too hard to hold on.
It is permissible to grieve. Grief shows that you are alive.
Think about what you are missing, feel it. Ask people if you
can talk to them about it. They will often be too embarrassed to mention it or worry that it will 'upset' you. Cry,
rage, scream, recognize the loss, do not deny the pain.
Wounds hurt when you dress them, but you know that is the
first stage of the wound getting better. It is permissible
to feel anger too.

2. DO I CONTINUOUSLY FEEL THAT THIS SHOULD NOT
HAPPEN TO ME? Then you are guilty of making yourself
unhappy by hitting yourself over the head with 'shoulds' and
'oughts'. You need to look again at the section on supportive self-talk.

3. DO I KNOW HOW TO VENT MY ANGER CONSTRUC-
TIVELY? Allow yourself to feel the anger. If it is kept
inside it will only hurt you. Feel angry at the person who
left you, at the person who took something from you, at the
world that let you down or at friends who cannot be trusted.
Hit a pillow, scream aloud (in a closed car this is very
effective; just like an echo chamber) or play a hectic
sport. Do not hurt anyone, including yourself.

Anger is only a feeling. It cannot hurt anyone. Only
behaviour hurts. Once the anger is cleared away, you are
then freer to begin to evaluate, make plans and decide.

Set goals and make action plans

1. DO I KNOW HOW TO SET GOALS? Some people fail to manage their transitions effectively because they have not identified a desirable outcome. 'If you don't know where you're going, you'll probably end up somewhere else' (David Campbell, 1974).

It is essential to identify what you want to achieve in terms which are as behaviourally specific as possible, such as 'I want a new job worth £8,000 per annum where I have overall responsibility for financial operations of a medium-scale department.' 'In six months I want to be able to go out on my own, to visit friends by myself, and to have developed one new interest' (this was an objective of a recent widow in one of my workshops).

2. DO I KNOW WHAT MY GOALS ARE FOR THIS TRANS-ITION AND FOR MY LIFE GENERALLY? This requires the specific skill of knowing how to set, define, and refine objectives.

3. DO I KNOW HOW TO MAKE AND IMPLEMENT ACTION PLANS? Once the objectives are clear the action steps follow next. There are a variety of resources available with guidelines on making effective action plans. Carkhuff's two books, 'The Art of Problem Solving' (1974a) and 'How to Help Yourself' (1974b), are useful. An action plan needs to be behaviourally specific: 'I will make an appointment to see the solicitor tomorrow morning'. It needs to be in terms of 'what I will do now', not in terms of 'what I will do sometime', or 'what we will do eventually'. An action plan should read like a computer programme, with each step so clearly defined that someone else would know how to carry it out.

4. DO I KNOW HOW TO SET PRIORITIES? Having a variety of goals is one thing, having the time to achieve them all is another. Skills of time management are required along with a systematic way of measuring the desirability of one goal with another.

5. DO I KNOW HOW TO MAKE EFFECTIVE DECISIONS? Katz (1968) has talked about the importance, not so much of making wise decisions but of making decisions wisely. There are a variety of teaching programmes now available to help people become more proficient at making choices (Hopson and Hough, 1973; Watts and Elsom, 1975).

6. DO I KNOW HOW TO GENERATE ALTERNATIVES, BECAUSE THERE IS ALWAYS AN ALTERNATIVE? Often people do not make as good a decision as they might have simply because they have not generated enough alternatives. The techniques of 'brainstorming', 'morphological forced connections' and 'synectics' (all described in Adams, 1974) are all ways of doing this. The key quite often, however,

is the belief that no matter now hopeless the situation, how constrained one feels, there is always an alternative, no matter how unpalatable it may initially appear, and that you can choose. This is the central concept in the model of the 'self empowered person' described by Hopson and Scally (1980b).

Look for the gains you have made
If gains are not immediately apparent, review the section again under 'Know yourself'. Have you had to cope with something with which you have not had to cope before? If so, this will have shed light on a new facet of your personality. What is it? Do you like it? Can you use it to any advantage in the future?

Quick check-list on client's transition coping skills

1. DOES HE KNOW WHAT HE WANTS FROM THE NEW SITUATION? If not, you must help him to define what he wants; getting him to be as specific as possible. He may not be used to thinking in terms of objectives. You will have to teach him. Write down options on a blackboard, flip chart, or a note book. Help him to evaluate the costs and benefits of different alternatives. Give him homework on this to be discussed at a future session.

2. DOES HE TEND TO BE PROACTIVE IN NEW SITUATIONS OR TO SIT BACK AND WAIT FOR THINGS TO HAPPEN? If he appears to be proactive, check out that it really is proactivity and not just acting to minimize anxiety, for instance jumping into something to alleviate ambiguity. If he is reactive you will need to point out that this will minimize his chances of getting what he wants and you will need to give him a task which is small enough for him to complete successfully (e.g. doing some homework) in order to develop his confidence in the ability to make things happen. Give him a suitable book to read (see the section on self-help books) which is simultaneously instructive and a task to be completed.

3. DOES HE HAVE OTHER PEOPLE HE CAN RELY ON FOR HELP? Get him to specify who and what they can do for him. If he is deficient in help, steer him towards an appropriate self-help group.

4. HAS ANYTHING LIKE THIS HAPPENED TO HIM BEFORE? Look for links with previous experiences. Help him to discover what he did then which helped, and what in retrospect he would now choose to do differently.

5. HOW WELL CAN HE LOOK AFTER HIMSELF? Is he physically fit and eating sensibly? If not, advise him of the importance of this. Similarly, help him to discover the 'anchor points' in his life and persuade him to keep to a regular schedule. Encourage him to give himself a treat from

time to time. Help him to identify when the low points are likely to be and to plan to minimize the impact of these: for example, always have something planned for Sunday when you are newly divorced.

6. CAN HE LET GO OF THE PAST? If not, encourage him to experience the grief and the anger as a way of discharging it and accepting that these feelings are normal and acceptable. They only become a problem if we can never let go of them.

7. CAN HE SET GOALS AND MAKE ACTION PLANS? Persuade him to begin thinking about specific goals as outlined under point 1. Help him define priorities, generate alternatives, and weigh them up.

8. CAN HE SEE POSSIBLE GAINS FROM HIS NEW SITUATION? Gently pressure him to begin to look for gains. The timing of this is vital. If he has not sufficiently let go of the past your intervention can appear heartless. Empathy is essential, but also you are trying to get him to see that however much he may not have chosen for an event to happen, that there will be something to gain.

Is it possible to train people to cope more effectively with transitions?

This has had to be empirically tested. Our general hypothesis is that people experiencing transitions will have similar tasks to cope with, namely, managing strain and dealing with cognitive tasks presented by the transition. We are assuming that to a considerable extent people's reactions to being in transition are learned as opposed to being inherited. To the extent that individuals' reactions are learned, we should be able to develop preventive, educative and re-educative strategies to help them manage their affairs and relationships more effectively at lower psychological costs, and derive greater benefits from the opportunity values embedded in every major transition.

This means that training programmes could be generated to help develop more effective coping styles for a number of people either (i) experiencing different transitional events, or who are anticipating transitional events, or (ii) as general training for any presently unknown future transitions.

We have already conducted a variety of transitions workshops in the UK, the USA and Scandinavia with populations including managers, trade unionists, counsellors, organization development specialists, social workers, case workers, teachers and youth workers. These have been primarily designed for participants who in turn will have to deal with individuals in transition. We believe that it is only possible to do such work when one has a clear understanding not just of a theoretical orientation, a collection of coping skills and teaching techniques, but also of one's own transitional experiences, skills and deficits, joys, confusion and sadness.

The final question is always 'why'? Why spend the energy, use the time, deplete the resources, all of which could be directed to something else?

We can only give our answer. A transition simultaneously carries the seeds of our yesterdays, the hopes and fears of our futures, and the pressing sensations of the present which is our confirmation of being alive. There is danger and opportunity, ecstasy and despair, development and stagnation, but above all there is movement. Nothing and no one stays the same. Nature abhors vacuums and stability. A stable state is merely a stopping point on a journey from one place to another. Stop too long and your journey is ended. Stay and enjoy but with the realization that more is to come. You may not be able to stop the journey, but you can fly the plane.

References

Adams, J.L. (1974)
Conceptual Blockbusting. San Francisco: Freeman.
Adams, J.D., Hayes, J. and Hopson, B. (1976)
Transition: Understanding and managing personal change.
London: Martin Robertson.
Aspy, D.N. and Roebuck, F.N. (1977)
Kids Don't Learn From People They Don't Like. Amherst,
Mass.: Human Resource Development Press.
Benson, H. (1977)
The Relaxation Response. London: Fountain Well Press.
Breckon, W. (1976)
You Are What You Eat. London: BBC Publications.
Campbell, D. (1974)
If You Don't Know Where You're Going You'll Probably
End Up Somewhere Else. Hoddesdon, Herts: Argus
Publications.
Carkhuff, R.R. (1974a)
The Art of Problem Solving. Amherst, Mass.: Human
Resource Development Press.
Carkhuff, R.R. (1974b)
How To Help Yourself. Amherst, Mass.: Human Resource
Development Press.
Carruthers, M. and Murray, A. (1977)
F/40: Fitness on forty minutes a week. London: Futura.
Cooper, K. (1977)
The New Aerobics. New York: Bantam.
Downing, G. (1972)
The Massage Book. New York: Random House.
Ellis, A. and Harper, R. (1975)
A New Guide to Rational Living. Hollywood, Ca:
Wilshire Books.
Forbes, R. (1979)
Life Stress. New York: Doubleday.
Health Education Council (1976)
Look After Yourself. London: Health Education Council.
Holmes, T.H. and Rahe, R.H. (1967)
The social readjustment rating scale. Journal of
Psychosomatic Research, 11, 213-218.

Hopson, B. and Hough, P. (1973)
Exercises in Personal and Career Development. Cambridge: Hobsons Press.

Hopson, B. and Scally, M. (1980a)
How to cope with and gain from life transitions. In B. Hopson and M. Scally, Lifeskills Teaching Programmes No. 1. Leeds: Lifeskills Associates.

Hopson, B. and Scally, M. (1980b)
Lifeskills Teaching: Education for self-empowerment. London: McGraw-Hill.

Howe, L.W. and Howe, M.M. (1975)
Personalizing Education: Values clarification and beyond. New York: Hart.

Johnson. D.W. (1972)
Reaching Out. Englewood Cliffs, NJ: Prentice-Hall.

Katz, M.R. (1968)
Can computers make guidance decisions for students? College Board Review, No. 72.

Kirschenbaum, H. (1977)
Advanced Value Clarification. La Jolla, Ca: University Associates.

Krantzler, M. (1973)
Creative Divorce. New York: M. Evans.

Lamott, K. (1975)
Escape from Stress. New York: Berkley.

Mahoney, M.J. and Mahoney, J. (1976)
Permanent Weight Control. New York: W.W. Norton.

Maslow, A. (1968)
Towards a Psychology of Being (2nd edn). New York: Van Nostrand.

Parkes, C. Murray (1972)
Bereavement: Studies of grief in adult life. London: Tavistock.

Royal Canadian Air Force (1978)
Physical Fitness. Harmondsworth: Penguin.

Russel, P. (1977)
The Transcendental Meditation Technique. London: Routledge & Kegan Paul.

Sharpe, R. and Lewis, D. (1977)
Thrive on Stress. London: Souvenir Press.

Simon, S. (1974)
Meeting Yourself Halfway. Hoddesdon, Herts: Argus Publications.

Simon, S., Howe, L.W. and Kirschenbaum, H. (1972)
Value Clarification. New York: Hart.

Toffler, A. (1970)
Future Shock. New York: Random House.

Watts, A.G. and Elsom, D. (1975)
Deciding. Cambridge: Hobsons Press.

Questions

1. Why is an understanding of the psychological processes of level 1 transitions important to your profession?
2. What are the major types of transition and how are they related?

3. How would you set about rating the impact of life events on people?
4. Critically evaluate the Hopson-Adams model of transitions.
5. What effect do transitions have on people?
6. What are the coping tasks relevant to all transitions?
7. Describe the coping skills which are relevant to transitions.
8. Which will be the most important influence in ensuring a successful transition and why? Is it the coping skills of the mover or the structure and practices of the organization, institution or social norms?
9. Describe a life transition in terms of the stages the person might go through and what he could do to maximize the chances of coping with it effectively and gaining from the experience.
10. How effectively can we train people to improve their transition coping skills?

Annotated reading

Adams, J.D., Hayes, J. and Hopson, B. (1976) Transition: Understanding and managing personal change. London: Martin Robertson.
  This is the first attempt to provide a conceptual framework to describe the psychological sequence of a transition. It is primarily a theoretical book, although some guidelines for the practitioner are available.

Hopson, B. and Scally, M. (1980) How to cope with and gain from life transitions. In B. Hopson and M. Scally, Lifeskills Teaching Programmes No. 1. Leeds: Lifeskills Associates.
  This is for a classroom teacher of young people and consists of a series of carefully described group exercises to teach young people about transitions and how to cope more effectively with them.

Parkes, C. Murray (1975) Bereavement: Studies of grief in adult life. Harmondsworth: Penguin.
  This book is about more than bereavement, although it is discussed at great length. Parkes generalizes from bereavement to other aspects of separation and loss in people's lives.

12

Creating Change
H. R. Beech

Politicians and kings have perhaps made the most distinctive
and historically interesting attempts to change the behaviour of those they seek to control. Sometimes this has
involved extreme measures, such as torture and execution,
sometimes more subtle legal approaches to behaviour control,
but these attempts perversely - and to the bafflement of the
controller - have often failed to produce the desired
outcome. Somehow, it seems, human nature appears to be
resistant to change.

Psychologists are disposed to argue that such failures
are mainly attributable to two causes. First, until
recently, there was an obvious lack of the technology to
effect changes with any degree of reliability: the methods
which had been used before were both crude and unsystema-
tically applied. Second, sometimes the attempts to effect
change involved very fundamental aspects of human functioning and it might not be within the capacity of the
species to accomplish them. Indeed, the contention of the
behavioural psychologist these days might be that substantial changes can be wrought in carefully selected
behaviours where the appropriate techniques can be freely
applied. This is not to say, of course, that some psychologists fail to perceive in these strategies a means of
acquiring very substantial or near complete control over
human nature or, indeed, the means by which the very fabric
of society could be altered. Of course, it would be unwise
to allow psychologists (even if their techniques did permit
such achievements) also to determine the types of change to
be brought about. Psychologists are in no better position to
decide what kind of society we should live in than is any
other group.

For the most part, however, the aims and aspirations of
psychologists are generally less ambitious and merely
involve the deployment of strategies for change to areas
where help is needed and requested. But to understand the
origin of these strategies it is first useful to describe
the influence exerted by Freud and Pavlov.

Freud's theories (Munroe, 1955) were important because
they gave an entirely new interpretation to 'bad', 'wrong'
or 'unacceptable' behaviour. Rather than seeing these behaviours as the reflection of something defective in the very

166

substance of man, Freud argued that such conduct arose out of environmental experiences. Indeed, Freud is often thought of as a thoroughgoing psychic determinist, believing that all behaviour is determined by prior experience and, in a very real sense, is programmed to be just the way it is, free will and choice being merely illusory. In short, enormous importance is attached to the influence of the environment as a determinant of what we are.

Pavlov (1927) was also interested in how behaviour became modified (although primarily concerned with how the physiological systems of animals worked) and devised the method of classical conditioning to assist in this endeavour. The definitive experiment carried out in his laboratory was to show that, after training, the sound of a bell could produce salivation in dogs. Clearly the dog does not start life with this capacity and needs to learn this reaction, and it is the process by which such learning takes place that is called 'classical conditioning'. Briefly, the process involves presenting the new stimulus (bell) before the old stimulus (food) to the response (salivation). Repetitions of this arrangement, with only a brief (say half a second) interval between the sound of the bell and presentation of food leads to the new association being formed. Instead of requiring food before salivating, the dog now has come to salivate at the sound of the bell alone.

Perhaps not of itself a particularly compelling piece of learning, but to many psychologists this type of association appeared as one of the fundamental building blocks of learning; such learning could be seen as underpinning all human behaviour.

An early enthusiast of Pavlov's work, Watson, was said to have been so impressed by such demonstrations of conditioning that he declared that any American child might be turned into the President using these methods. Whether or not Watson accorded such power to classical conditioning, he was certainly enthusiastic to use it and has achieved an important place in psychological history through his Little Albert experiment (1920).

In this study Watson's aim was to investigate the acquisition of emotional responses, arguing that they are probably learned by the associative process called conditioning. For this demonstration he chose an 11-month-old boy called Albert and set out to create a learned emotional reaction in this child. Watson had observed Albert's fondness for a tame white rat and chose to reverse this feeling by arranging for a loud noise to be made (by crashing two metal plates together behind Albert's head) whenever the child reached out for this pet. After just a few trials of this kind, Albert's fear, occasioned by the sudden loud noise, was transferred to the white rat so that every time this animal appeared Little Albert would whimper and crawl away. Furthermore, it was noted that the new fear reaction had transferred to other objects with some similarity to the rat (e.g. a ball of cotton wool) and it appeared to be enduring over the period of observation.

This latter observation led Watson to speculate upon the fate of a more mature Albert, lying on the psychoanalyst's couch, and vainly trying to understand how he came to worry about white fluffy objects! But the conditioning process might well be the basis for all our irrational (neurotic) fears.

It is important to point out, however, that the environment is not the only contributing factor to learning since, from Pavlov on, it has been observed that not all learning opportunities are realized or, if they are, there are individual differences in the character of the learning which is affected.

The earliest experimental observations of such limitations of a purely environmentalist approach were made by Pavlov. He is said to have first formed this conclusion as a result of flood waters entering his laboratories in Leningrad, finding that this had made some of the animals very disturbed while others appeared to treat the matter with indifference. Later, experiments showed more conclusively that some animals appeared to be susceptible to disturbance and others more phlegmatic, these two types being labelled 'weak' and 'strong' nervous systems respectively. This differentiation has been repeatedly confirmed in the experimental work of other investigators and clearly shows that an opportunity to learn is not all that is involved: a major influence is the basic temperament of the organism which is doing the learning.

Another study which points to this conclusion was conducted by Rachman (1966). The problem posed by the investigator here was that of whether or not fetishistic behaviour (sexual arousal to unusual stimuli) could be acquired by a simple associative process. Briefly, three male volunteers were exposed to conditions in which pictures of boots were linked with pictures of an erotic nature to see if bonding occurred in such a way that the sight of boots alone would produce sexual excitement. Such was in fact found to be the case and establishes that fetishes can come about through associations of this kind. However, the point to be made here is that the subjects took varying numbers of trials to lose such reactions; in short, the disposition of the individual seems to be very much implicated in what we learn and how well such learning is preserved.

Generally these results are thought to reflect some permanent characteristics of the individuals concerned, but it is important to add that even temporary states of the organism can affect learning, a point which has been made by Beech and others (see Vila and Beech, 1978).

Clinical experience would tend to indicate that symptoms of distress (e.g. inability to go out of the house or to meet others socially without feeling anxious) often appear to be preceded by a period of general tension and emotional upset; it is as if such states prepare the ground for certain kinds of learning to take place: as if they put the organism on a defensive footing, ready to react adversely to relatively minor provocation. The kind of disturbance referred to here is quite commonly experienced by women in the few days prior to menstruation and has been given the name of pre-menstrual tension. If this condition is a good parallel to the situation in which abnormal fears can arise, then it should be possible to show a propensity for 'defensive' or adverse learning in pre-menstrual days which is not present at other times in the cycle. This is, in fact, what has been found. The evidence indicates that the state of the organism at the time when some noxious event is present not only determines the speed at which learning takes place but also any tendency for the learning to be preserved over time. One might be tempted to argue that this 'natural' disposition to acquire neurotic symptoms could explain why disproportionately large numbers of women complain of neurotic symptoms.

Another influence to be taken into account as limiting the scope of a purely environmentalist view of human behaviour is that of biological potential for learning. The argument here has been cogently presented by Seligman and Hager (1972), who conclude that all organisms appear to show a great readiness to acquire certain associations while other connections will be made only with difficulty or even not at all. Among the examples cited by Seligman and Hager is that of the dog which can very quickly associate the operation of a latch with its paw to escape from a box, but seems quite unable to learn to effect escape by wagging its tail. It is not that tail-wagging is a difficult action for the dog to perform or even that it is an uncommon reaction; rather it seems that the problem lies in making the connection itself. It is argued that the species has no biological propensity to make such a connection; the evolutionary history of the dog did not prepare the animal for this kind of learning.

It is not yet known to what extent humans are affected by preparedness, although it is obvious that certain connections appear to be 'natural' and made quite easily, while others are not. It has been suggested that a good example of preparedness is to be found in the prevalence of spider and snake phobia found in populations not at all at risk from these creatures. A more purely environmentalist approach might argue that one would need to be bitten by a spider or snake before a phobic reaction could be developed yet, obviously, there seems to be a great readiness in many people to display a wariness about spiders in a country such as England, while no such widespread fear is evoked by horses or hamsters. Somewhere in our evolutionary history, it can be argued, the species has acquired a readiness to respond with fear to potential dangers, including spiders and snakes. Perhaps this is why open spaces present a problem for many people; such 'exposure' was to be avoided in the interests of survival and this potential for acquiring a fear of open spaces is easily tapped.

The thoroughgoing environmentalist would want to argue that man is virtually a blank sheet, a complicated learning machine and, given the appropriate incentives and opportunities, can be moulded to any desired pattern. In the light of the limitations to learning which have been mentioned it is obviously appropriate to take a more moderate view and regard man as a creature highly susceptible to modification through learning, but far from infinitely so. As yet, we do not know quite how far the capacity to learn can take us. Can it, for example, so change human nature that one becomes entirely altruistic, greed, selfishness and other 'human failings' becoming totally alien? There are those, like Dawkins (1978) who would not think this possible but, on the other hand, Skinner (1953) and many others see almost limitless possibilities to behaviour modification with the psycho-technology currently available even now.

For Skinnerians the basic principle of change can be stated quite simply; the consequences of any piece of behaviour affects the future of that behaviour. If the consequence is rewarding then the behaviour is strengthened (i.e. rendered more likely to occur again); if it is punishing, then the same response tends to be weakened. Using this basic proposition, it is argued, far-reaching changes can be made to occur.

Of course, such a view is as profoundly hedonistic as Pavlov's or Freud's, the basic contention being that man is simply a pleasure-maximizing, pain-minimizing organism; this is as much part and parcel of his make-up as any other creature. Changing behaviour, according to this view, depends upon the nature, timing and other attributes of rewards and punishments rather than upon appeals to reason or religious precepts.

There is, understandably, considerable resistance to accepting such a stark view of man's nature; it appears to accord no place at all to free will and choice, nor does it allow man any special place in biological or other terms. Hedonism is the key mechanism in what we are; man can (and does) learn to do and to be anything, providing that the rewards and punishments are there to chart the way.

What we can now do is to examine the achievements to date; to see how far Pavlovian and Skinnerian principles of learning have been effective in producing change. It is anyone's guess how much further it is possible to go.

Aversive learning

Most of us subscribe to the validity of the adages that 'the burnt child dreads the fire' or 'once bitten, twice shy'. These sayings simply embody the importance of pain avoidance in our biological make-up. Clearly, deprived of such protection the species could hardly be expected to survive; we learn pretty quickly and thoroughly if the consequences of some actions are painful. Yet there appear to be some notable exceptions to such a compelling principle; martyrs and heroes often seem to subject themselves to avoidable pain while hard-bitten criminals may appear unaffected by the punishment society metes out to them. Obviously the problem is more complex than at first sight appears. Perhaps one should not be overly influenced by these exceptions, since the rule does seem to hold in general, but it is just as well to begin by recognizing that the results of punishment are unpredictable. For that matter, the outcome of rewarding behaviours shows much the same variability and such findings make fools of those who argue for simple solutions. For example, on the one hand there are those who want to create a better society by wreaking extreme retribution upon all who infringe rules while, on the other, the 'progressives' appear to think that the solution to crime is to remove all sources of discomfort and irritation. Both views, obviously, are patently absurd; crime has persisted in spite of great harshness in past years and, as is now well documented, the rate has risen dramatically as the number of social workers, leisure centres and social welfare has increased.

There are several arguments advanced to explain why punishment fails to achieve good effects in the context under discussion. In the first place it is said that its application is seldom timely: it works very well if immediate, but poorly or not at all if the crime and later court sentence are separated by lengthy intervals of time. Second, it is said that the rate of successful to unsuccessful crime is unfavourable to learning to resist temptation: numerous crimes may be rewarded before one act leads to punishment. A third argument is that the rate of criminal behaviour is inversely related to the strength of punishment, and that deterrents are not nearly strong enough to be effective. Yet another reason is said to be the temperament of the habitual criminal who, it is alleged, does not generate the kind of anxiety which most of us experience when 'wrong doing'. This last point refers to evidence that the nervous systems of individuals appear to extend over a range from the excessive 'jumpiness' of the chronically anxious at one end of the spectrum to those who appear to be 'psychopathically' resistant to showing disturbance to even strong stimulation.

There is probably something to be said for each of these points and, at least, all serve to indicate the complexities which may underlie the application of punishments.

To some extent it is possible to avoid a number of these problems when aversive consequences are part of a treatment programme; here, more of what takes place is under the control of the therapist or experimenter. Perhaps the best-known example of this is to be found in the treatment of alcoholism. With this, an attempt is made to ensure that drinking (and stimulus situations related to it) leads to aversive consequences; a convenient means of achieving this in practice has been to administer an emetic drug and, when this is beginning to take effect, the individual is permitted to sip the alcohol to which he is addicted. Unpleasant feelings of nausea and vomiting will, in this way, become associated with the particular sight, smell and taste involved (Voegtlin and Lemere, 1942).

Of course, it can be argued that simply punishing the 'wrong' response is hardly likely to lead to the adoption of a socially-acceptable reaction. What, for example, can the homosexual do with the sexual impulses he experiences after the usual way in which these are expended have been denied to him by punishment? Accordingly, more sophisticated attempts to help have included not only punishment but also opportunities to escape from punishment. In the context of treating homosexuals, for instance, the individual concerned has been allowed access to slides depicting homosexual activity only at the cost of receiving strong electric shocks, while the rejection of such slides and their substitution by heterosexual material can lead to the avoidance of punishment altogether.

A perennial problem of aversive training has been that of securing appropriate levels of co-operation and motivation and, no doubt, many failures are attributable to this difficulty. A simple example of this clarifies the point in practical terms. The investigation here was of a young boy whose habit of thumb-sucking was to be dealt with by capitalizing upon his enjoyment of cartoons. The therapist arranged for the boy to sit through protracted showings of cartoon films but these showings ceased abruptly if thumb-sucking occurred, and the film would only be continued when this behaviour stopped. It took a relatively short time for the boy to control his bad habit during the film shows but it was noted that the training had no effect upon what happened outside that situation! Indeed, one might reasonably argue that, in this case, the boy had learned how to control the behaviour of the psychologist, rather than the opposite!

Since aversion therapy is given only to those voluntarily submitting themselves to this form of training, one should be able to assume a reasonable level of motivation to change. However, as we all recognize from personal experience, our commitment to change can be quite ephemeral and today's resolution to give up smoking (or whatever) can disappear completely tomorrow. Perhaps this is only another way of saying that the aversive condition has not been applied sufficiently vigorously or intensively to inhibit the temptation: the associative bond between aversive feelings and the 'unwanted' action is insufficiently strongly made. Nevertheless, it is apparent that this problem is a major obstacle to the success of punishment as a means of control.

Systematic desensitization

Few doubt the power of anxiety to alter and disrupt ordinary behaviour patterns; anxiety can handicap our attempts to cope with a whole range of life's problems, it may prevent anything approaching an adjustment to quite ordinary events and it may totally ruin our enjoyment of relationships and circumstances which should be pleasurable. The capacity to deal with and eliminate anxiety can be regarded as of major importance to the effective control of our behaviour since, essentially, anxiety is a disruptive influence which erodes our capacity to control our own thought and action. In short, changing behaviour often seems to involve removing anxiety.

The behavioural strategy to resolve this problem appears to be surprisingly direct and simple. All that is needed is a gradual, step-by-step approach to the feared object or situation together with some means of inhibiting anxiety at each of these stages. The technique for accomplishing this was developed and refined by Wolpe (1969). More than 30 years earlier Mary Cover Jones (1924) had described essentially the same method in successfully eliminating the children's fears and, in a sense, there seems to be nothing particularly remarkable or novel in the method. Nevertheless, Wolpe's standardization of an effective technique for the analysis of anxiety and the application of a treatment strategy was enormously important from both practical and theoretical points of view.

The basic argument is that fear (or anxiety) has inadvertently, through a process of association, become a learned reaction to the presence of certain cues. For example, fear may be triggered by the presence of several people because, at some time in the past, the individual has been made anxious in a social setting; or anxiety is aroused by the sound of quarrelling voices because, at some time, the individual was threatened by the belligerence of others. The task of treatment, therefore, is to sever this connection: to detach anxiety from the innocuous cue.

Some years ago the author was asked for help in removing an extreme fear of spiders in a lady so incapacitated by this anxiety that she was unable to perform household chores. Any article of furniture moved or corner dusted might dislodge one of these alarming creatures and so occasion acute anxiety. Being outdoors clearly also presented problems to this lady, although she recognized that her fear was actually groundless in the sense that none of the spiders she encountered, indoors or out, could actually harm her.

Questioning revealed that the fear she experienced could be broken down into a number of separate components which, in various combinations, could evoke either more or less anxiety. Size, for example, was an important variable: the larger the spider the more fear would be experienced. Similarly, blackness, hairiness, degree of activity, and proximity all affected the amount of fear experienced. It was possible, therefore, to describe 'spider situations' which would produce little by way of upset, and others which would create a good deal. A small, light-coloured, apparently hairless spider, quite dead and at some distance away, would cause only mild apprehension, while an active, large, black and hairy spider, galloping across her body, would produce a sense of panic.

One must begin, in desensitization treatment, with the least anxiety-provoking situation and as each of these ceases to produce anxiety, so one moves on to the next step in the hierarchy. In the spider phobic case quoted, one can obviously begin with exhibiting a small, dead, pale-coloured, hairless spider in one corner of the room, while the patient sits in the opposite corner. When this condition ceases to produce anxiety, then the insect can be moved a little closer or, alternatively, some characteristic can be changed (e.g. substitution of a slightly larger specimen) so that we have moved one notch up the fear hierarchy.

What is notable here is that each step in the hierarchy appears to produce a smaller reaction than was anticipated before treatment; it is as if accomplishing each step has resulted in some small but discernible loss in the total anxiety now experienced. This kind of psychological arith-metic applies with every step taken, so that the total amount of anxiety to be eliminated becomes less and less.

So far so good, but systematic desensitization involves some means of INHIBITING anxiety at each stage, for only in this way can the anxiety connection be broken. Each hierarchical step, therefore, must be capable of producing some amount of fear, but this must be sufficiently small to be extinguished by some other feeling state, and the most convenient means of achieving this is to train the indivi-dual in muscle relaxation.

It is argued that muscle relaxation is in fact an ideal counter to anxiety feelings, since it is both easy to learn and very effective. In short, there is good evidence that one cannot be anxious and completely relaxed at the same time; relaxation effectively inhibits the experience of fear. Accordingly, such training precedes the hierarchical presentation of fear stimuli; the individual is instructed to remain as relaxed as possible each time the fear-stimulus is presented so that the experience of anxiety is con-trolled. In this way a new type of association is being learned: that in the presence of certain cues which previously occasioned fear, no such feelings are present.

Understandably, while this method may work quite well it is not one which is easily put into practice in all cases. The various spider specimens needed to form the hierarchy may be easily secured, but in the case of, say, a fear of flying, there are serious practical problems. One could not, for example, easily arrange that the aeroplane merely completes the dash down the runway (as one item on the hierarchy) without actually taking off (which may occupy a very different hierarchical level). The necessary control over the situation here, and in numerous other cases, simply could not be achieved.

This problem is solved by presenting such situations as imagined scenes instead of as real-life experiences. This obviously makes it very much easier to arrange for events to accord precisely with treatment requirements and allows all the refined control over circumstances that one would wish to have. The only question to ask about this solution is that of whether or not dealing with an imagined situation is as beneficial as dealing with the real one. The evidence indicates that it is, although all therapists like to include experience of the real event (the real spider, lift, aeroplane, etc.) as a way of consolidating and affirming the new found absence of fear. Merely learning not to experience anxiety in imagined examples of fear aspects or situations, using the little-by-little approach and suppressing any worry by preserving muscle relaxation, can produce important changes in behaviour.

This approach is widely used in the treatment of major and incapacitating phobias with considerable success, but it is worth pointing out that less extreme conditions, including those commonly found in young children, respond very well to sympathetic handling along these lines. Fear of school, of being left by mother, of playing with strange children, of insects, of the car, and many others respond well to the graduated approach described and, of course, the benefit to behaviour generally of shedding such fears makes the effort well worth while.

Cognitive learning

It will be apparent from the description of the behavioural approaches given so far that they seem to depend upon a rather mechanical conception of learning. Insight, explanation, logic and other ways in which we come to modify or correct our view of things appear to count for nothing: the assumption is that we simply cannot talk anyone out of being alcoholic or experiencing acute anxiety; they must be taught to do so by a painstaking and carefully conceived programme of training which avoids any appeal to the 'mind'. Yet we are aware that cognitive learning does occur since we can behave differently as a result of being told that this or that is the case, or by receiving instructions to do something in a particular way. Indeed, if everything about our behaviour had to be acquired by trial and error or successive approximations, then learning would be tedious, slow and in many cases inefficient.

The charge often levelled at the behavioural approach is that it ignores the conceptual thinking that is so peculiarly and importantly human. But this is to misunderstand the situation since it is apparent that the kind of learning process required to effect change appears to depend upon what it is about our behaviour that we are trying to modify. Furthermore, it has been argued that mental events (cognitions, thoughts) are also behaviours and amenable to the same laws and, to an extent, the same training methods.

A good example is the technique called 'thought stopping'. Essentially this represents the attempt to produce the disruption or inhibition of a mental process in much the same way as some more overt activity might be stopped. It is usual to begin (see Wolpe, 1969) with a demonstration by the therapist that a sudden, unexpected and loud noise (banging the table, for example) can interrupt a particular focus of attention. In the same way, it is pointed out, an unpleasant and persistent idea can be interrupted and, with practice, might become permanently inhibited. By stages, the control of the interruptive signal is transferrred from therapist to patient and then from an external signal (banging on the table) to an internal one (saying 'stop' to oneself).

It is readily apparent that this strategy is direct, simple, and treats ideas or cognitions in much the same way as any reflex or motor action. There is, in the application of this technique, nothing special about mental events: they are simply regarded as internal behaviours.

A rather less rigorous behaviour approach is to be found in Rational Emotive Therapy; indeed, many hard-nosed behaviourists would reject any claim that RET derives from learning or conditioning theories and deny that there is any identifiable trace of the behavioural tradition in RET. Nevertheless, this cognitive approach has features which are 'behavioural' in character; for example, the emphasis upon the here-and-now rather than the influence of early life experiences, the parsimonious theoretical formulations, the implicit and explicit dependence upon reinforcing experiences and the directness of attack upon a clearly-identified source of malfunctioning. The main thrust of the technique (Ellis, 1962) derives from the assumption that faulty thinking is revealed in what people say to themselves; such 'self-talk' influences overt behaviours, so changing the cognitions can influence the way we act and feel.

Part of the immediate appeal of this technique lies in the very obviousness that 'self-talk' is a major preoccupation of us all when we are beset by difficulties. As a simple example, when girl informs boy that their relationship is ended a positive torrent of internal conversations is likely to be triggered: 'I am in a terrible mess ... I can't believe it ... there's no hope ... what can I do, nothing matters any more ...' etc. Such self-talk is likely to be accompanied by observable behaviour such as weeping, not eating or sleeping, refusing to socialize, failing to deal adequately with work assignments, and so on.

RET concentrates attention upon those things which are objectively true (e.g. 'she no longer loves me') and those which are not ('no one cares ... life is over ... there'll never be anyone else for me ...'). It is contended that when one is forced to examine the illogicality of deducing certain conclusions from the premise 'she doesn't love me', then shifts toward more positive emotions and behaviours have to occur. Attention is, of course, directed to all faulty ideas which serve as props for disappointment and disillusion: many of these quite commonplace errors of thinking which we are better rid of. For example, that one must always appear competent and without sign of weakness, that one must always have evidence that one is loved, needed and approved of, or that any adverse comment means that no one is to be trusted.

There is no doubt that this kind of counselling approach can help us to gain a perspective on life's bumps and abrasions and so prevent exaggerated and damaging emotional reactions. Yet there are obviously important limitations to an approach which depends so heavily upon exposing the illogicality of much self-talk; the point about such states of mind, as about prejudices of all kinds, is that they tend to be rather resistant to a logical approach. There is, it often seems, a strong desire to bring ideas into line with the feelings being experienced.

Furthermore, a cognitive strategy tends to pay little attention to the internal alterations of state which can often prompt the appearance of faulty ideas. Anyone with experience of depression will recognize that talking someone out of such a state is not just a tall order but pretty well impossible. No doubt where the pattern of gloomy thoughts and ideas arise out of what may be a purely environmental circumstance - a lost job, a failed exam, a lost love - a logical analysis of thoughts and feelings can be beneficial, but perhaps such circumstances are less common than one might at first suppose. Perhaps in part these environmental traumas are not random events but, to a degree, are visited upon those of us who are already vulnerable to an extent.

A cognitive technique which translates rather better from the traditional areas of behavioural concern to mental events is covert sensitization (Cautela, 1966). Basically, this method represents the application of aversive control to thoughts (as opposed to 'actions' such as drinking alcohol or operating a fruit machine) and involves imagined scenes of the unwanted behaviour followed by imagined noxious consequences. For example, the overweight gluttonous lady may be asked to conjure up images of a table groaning under the weight of delicious food, stuffing herself to bursting with cream cake and other goodies and then to create the mental picture of being sick: vomit spilling out over the table, over her dress, on to the food, and so on. In short, it is hoped to create the cognitive equivalent of real events with the consequences of overeating being highly unpleasant and embarrassing.

Another example comes from Foa (1976), whose male client derived sexual gratification from dressing in woman's clothing. This had brought him to the courts, where he was then referred for treatment. Covert sensitization took the form of requiring the patient to imagine that he is driving along in his car when he sees a clothes line on which desirable articles of clothing are hanging; he stops, gets out and attempts to take these clothes, but as he does so, he is overcome by intense feelings of nausea. He is then required to imagine throwing the clothes away and feeling very much better.

It is worth pointing out that in this case, as in other examples of aversive training, the unwanted habit returned again following an initially successful outcome. Generally, the therapist takes account of the need to deal with this problem by arranging 'booster' courses of treatment as and when the need arises.

Operant training

It is apparent from the accounts given that the behavioural approach to change is strongly hedonistic; organisms learn when rewarded and 'unlearn' when punished. Perhaps more than in any other technique of learning, operant training exemplifies this dependence upon the manipulation of the consequences of behaviour: a consequence which is rewarding (positively reinforcing) will strengthen some reaction or response, while one which is punishing (negatively reinforcing) will weaken and discourage further behaviour of the same kind.

It was not until B. F. Skinner's 1953 publication that there was any systematic account of the circumstances under which rewards and punishments work best. Experimenting with small animals, often rats, Skinner was able to demonstrate convincingly that if some observable piece of behaviour (response) was followed consistently by reward, the chances of the same behaviour occurring in a similar situation on subsequent occasions would increase. Similarly, if a response was punished, it would become less likely to occur. Three very important aspects of the apparently simple relationship between response and consequences arose from these animal studies. First, it is imperative that the reinforcement applied to the subject really is rewarding or punishing for them. A puff at a cigarette is obviously pleasant and rewarding to some humans but would probably prove aversive to most rats, whereas the dry food pellets enjoyed by rats would be of little interest to most humans. The second point was that, at least initially, the reinforcement (reward or punishment) must follow immediately after the target response is performed. If we wish to increase the frequency with which a rat presses a lever, it is no use providing the reward half-an-hour after the response has occurred; the necessary association between lever-pressing and, say, food reward would simply not be made. Third, as well as being immediate, the reinforcement must be applied consistently. Under all but very extreme circumstances, the rat does not learn to press a lever as a result of a single reward for doing so but needs numerous rewarded trials until lever-pressing is acquired. It is best to reward every trial initially, for although learning can take place if rewards (or punishments) are more spread out, it is very much slower. However, once learned, a response may be maintained by occasional reinforcement.

Many psychologists have been attracted by Skinnerian research and have applied the rules to the modification of human behaviour. The degree of success which has been achieved has been surprising in view of the frequent criticisms of Skinner's approach as essentially simplistic and mechanistic. Perhaps the greatest changes that have been made in order to accommodate Skinner's system to work with humans have been in response to the obvious superiority of their thinking, memory and reasoning as well as their capacity to use and to understand language. These skills have had most effect on the second aspect of reinforcement described above. As long as a person realizes that reinforcement will be contingent upon his behaviour within a reasonable time, it may not be necessary for the reinforcement to be immediate. That individual will be able to think about or anticipate the delayed outcome. When working with children, however, some tangible reminder may be given of the reinforcement to come, such as a gold star immediately on completion of some school work as a token representing, say, extra playtime during the day.

The types of problems to which reinforcement procedures may be applied range from minor irritating habits to major disorders which threaten the well-being or even life of the sufferer. Many examples from the field of child-management may be cited to illustrate the least severe end of this scale.

Many young children go through 'phases' which are both worrying and irritating to their parents but usually not harmful in themselves. An example of this would be the temper tantrums fairly frequently observed in toddlers. In nearly all cases such episodes last a few weeks or at most months and then disappear of their own accord. In a few cases they persist much longer, or with greater severity, and perhaps begin to disrupt family life. Providing the cause is not due to some physical illness, one may attempt to modify the behaviour by applying appropriate reinforcements. Very often it is found that the child receives a great deal of attention when he has a tantrum, usually because it is alarming and upsetting to his parents. On the other hand, when he is occupied and behaving well, his parents, sighing with relief, turn their attention to other things, effectively ignoring good behaviour. Evidently the child is being rewarded for having a tantrum but is punished (as being ignored can be aversive) for being well behaved. With these contingencies it is no wonder that such behaviour becomes more frequent and good behaviour becomes rarer. Tantrums may be modified simply by reversing reward and punishment; his parents leave him to his own devices when he has a tantrum but take great care to play with him and talk to him when he is being good. Applied systematically, such a straightforward alteration of reinforcements can have amazingly rapid and beneficial effects.

Even relatively minor behaviour problems in children may have more serious effects on their eventual welfare. One form of difficulty that has been tackled fairly often in this way is disruptive classroom behaviour. A child who is frequently out of his seat, moving around and making a noise, usually benefits less from his schooling than his more appropriately behaved peers and is likely to fall behind with his work. In addition he may become unpopular with his companions as he upsets their work and interferes with their games. In a busy classroom, such a child is often reprimanded by the teacher when he is a nuisance but receives very little attention for being 'good' since this occurs infrequently and he rarely produces work of a high

enough standard to merit praise. Relatively mild chastise-
ments from the teacher may be more rewarding for the child
(being preferred to no attention at all) so the child is
rewarded for being disruptive and ignored for practically
everything else. As with the younger child, the task is to
reverse the contingencies. In this case it may not be possible for the teacher to ignore the bad behaviour entirely
but, usually, the amount of time and effort spent in the
reprimand can be reduced significantly so that the child
receives a minimum of attention for each disruptive act. At
the same time he is rewarded for appropriate behaviour and
an acceptable (although possibly lower than average) standard of work. If possible, the reward is given immediately
with attention and praise but may be supplemented by the use
of stars or marks for good conduct, and these tokens can be
exchanged for privileges at the end of the day. Usually the
co-operation of not only the teacher and pupil but also of
the entire class is required to make this procedure fully
effective.

The much-publicized condition of anorexia nervosa is an
example of a life-threatening state which may sometimes be
ameliorated by the use of reinforcement procedures. Patients
suffering from this disorder are most commonly girls in
their mid- to late-teens who have begun to diet excessively,
and now refuse to eat and sabotage attempts to feed them
by hiding the food or vomiting. Many lose so much weight
that they must be confined to bed. The main management
problem is to reinstate eating.

There is no single acceptable account of why a girl
begins to become anorexic but there is commonly evidence of
considerable social reinforcement for not eating once
serious dieting is under way, since serious weight loss
causes friends and relatives to become increasingly concerned and respond to refusals to eat by attention and
attempts to coax and persuade, and this attention contributes to the maintenance of not eating. Attempts have been
made to make positive reinforcement contingent upon eating
rather than not eating and, to do this, the patient has been
socially isolated and denied pleasures such as radio and
television in order to maximize the rewarding effect of
social contact. It has been arranged that a friendly therapist will eat each meal with the patient and converse with
her when, and only when, she eats a mouthful of food. Once
eating a meal has been established, the reward is made less
immediate by allowing the patient to earn time with the
therapist or friends after the meal has been eaten. She is
also allowed access to television, etc., in the same way.
This kind of procedure has been found to produce important
weight gain in a number of patients. When described in
outline it may appear that the patient is the passive
recipient of reinforcement, unaware of the contingencies
that have been planned, but this is far from the case, as
most patients become involved with the preparation of their
programmes, the negotiation of weight targets, amounts to
be eaten, planning rewards and agreeing to contingencies.

It is clear that reinforcement contingencies can be applied effectively to a wide range of behaviour problems in humans. As long as the contingencies are appropriately rewarding or punishing, and the consequences fairly immediate and consistent, the reinforcement is likely to be effective, but the chances of success will be increased if the person with the problem is involved in the construction and discussion of his own management programme.

In conclusion

Behavioural approaches to change tend to lack appeal when compared to other methods. We would prefer, for example, to think that we are amenable to logic and reason and that if only the facts are made available to us we could change to be in accord with them. Or, in other contexts, we may find the dramatic aspects of psychoanalysis more compelling, with the eccentricities of human behaviour being explained as the result of mysterious and excitingly interesting forces. Certainly, behavioural approaches stand in sharp contrast and seem to inspire all the excitement of Latin conjugations!

On the other hand, while the techniques admittedly tend to apply about as well to animals as to man, their clarity and simplicity arises from sound experimental work and scientific thought, qualities which in any other context would be thought commendable. It is worth while to offer the example of bedwetting as a means of showing how such thinking offers distinct advantages over a more tortuous and complex account.

Psychoanalysts are inclined to regard bedwetting as merely the external sign of some inner turmoil. It has been regarded, for example, as a substitute for sexual gratification or a means by which a child can express aggression and resentment toward others. The behavioural formulation is starkly simple; individuals LEARN to be dry at night and some fail to acquire this skill. If the former view is correct, then simply removing the behaviour (bedwetting) would not cure the inner discontent; if the behavioural view is correct, however, then getting rid of the symptom would be a very useful thing.

Mowrer's (1938) simple device to unlearn bedwetting was in fact highly successful and is very widely used today. It deals directly with the symptom and in most cases bedwetting is eliminated. No evidence exists of any underlying pathological process of the kind postulated by the psychoanalyst.

Naturally, one example of a greater claim to effectiveness does not establish the general superiority of the behavioural approach, yet it does seem that such examples can be multiplied many times over. This is, in fact, what one would expect from a model constructed from painstaking laboratory experimental work and scientific formulations.

It is not, of course, that the approach or the techniques deriving from it, some of which have been briefly reviewed here, are either wildly successful or beyond criticism. There are, indeed, numerous difficulties and shortcomings and, as indicated earlier, one of the most serious of these is the partiality of the purely environmentalist viewpoint and the almost complete neglect of genetic/constitutional influences. Nevertheless, behavioural strategies now occupy a position of high importance for psychologists, and the influence of these strategies in many and diverse areas of application is still growing.

References

Cautela, J.B. (1966)
Treatment of compulsive behavior by covert sensitization. The Psychological Record, 16, 33-41.

Dawkins, R. (1978)
The Selfish Gene. Oxford: Oxford University Press.

Ellis, A. (1962)
Reason and Emotion in Psychotherapy. New York: Kyle Stewart.

Foa, E.B. (1976)
Multiple behaviour techniques in the treatment of transvestism. In H.J. Eysenck, Case Studies in Behaviour Therapy. London: Routledge & Kegan Paul.

Jones, M.C. (1924)
The elimination of children's fears. Journal of Experimental Psychology, 7, 383-90.

Mowrer, O.H. and Mowrer, W. (1938)
Enuresis: a method for its study and treatment. American Journal of Orthopsychiatry, 8, 436-59.

Munroe, R.L. (1955)
School of Psychoanalytic Thought. New York: Dryden Press.

Pavlov, I.P. (1927)
Conditioned Reflexes (Transl. Anrep). London: Oxford University Press.

Rachman, S. (1966)
Sexual fetishism: an experimental analogue. The Psychological Record, 16, 293-296.

Seligman, M.E.P. and Hager, J.L. (1972)
Biological Boundaries of Learning. New York: Appleton-Century-Crofts.

Skinner, B.F. (1953)
Science and Human Behavior. New York: Macmillan.

Vila, J. and Beech, H.R. (1978)
Vulnerability and defensive reactions in relation to the human menstrual cycle. British Journal of Social and Clinical Psychology, 17, 93-100.

Voegtlin, W.L. and Lemere, E. (1942)
The treatment of alcohol addiction. Quarterly Journal of Studies on Alcohol, 2, 717-803.

Watson, J.B. and Rayner, R. (1920)
Conditioned emotional reactions. Journal of Experimental Psychology, 3, 1-14.

Wolpe, J. (1969)
The Practice of Behavior Therapy. New York: Pergamon Press.

Questions

Questions

1. Describe the theoretical underpinnings of systematic desensitization as a treatment strategy to eliminate fear.
2. Drawing upon your personal experience, describe and discuss the incapacitating effect of anxiety on coping with a life problem you have had to face.
3. Describe the process of classical conditioning and how this process can account for the development of abnormal fears.
4. Discuss the differences between individuals in respect of their readiness to develop phobias.
5. To what extent can one argue that man is simply a product of his environmental experiences?
6. What are the implications of classical and operant conditioning for a crime prevention policy?
7. Describe the limitations of using aversive therapy as a means of changing behaviour.
8. What limitations do you perceive in attempting to change behaviour on the basis of experiences created in imagination?
9. Discuss the possible reasons behind the shift from the behavioural to a more 'cognitive' learning approach in dealing with problems of behaviour change.
10. Describe a behaviour modification technique that relies upon 'cognitive' learning.
11. What are the basic differences between 'cognitive' and behavioural strategies where behaviour change is concerned?
12. Describe a form of covert sensitization employed in the aversive control of thoughts.
13. In what sense can the behavioural approach be said to be hedonistic?
14. Responses and consequences are the two basic elements of operant training. Describe and discuss.
15. What are the basic requirements in providing reinforcement in order to secure effective behaviour change?
16. What criticisms of Skinner's approach can be offered?
17. To what extent do you think that we are affected in real life situations by the operation of reinforcement principles?
18. How could one apply an operant approach in a classroom to deal with disruptive class behaviour?
19. What are the main points of difference between the psychoanalytical and behavioural approaches?
20. List some of the common, everyday, psychological difficulties experienced and outline the behavioural strategies that might be useful in overcoming them.

Annotated reading

Rachman, S. (1971) The Effects of Psychotherapy. Oxford: Pergamon Press.
>   An account of the problems associated with psychotherapy and the way in which the behavioural approach deals with issues of treatment and training.

Kanfer, F.H. and Goldstein, A.P. (1975) Helping People Change: A textbook of methods. Oxford: Pergamon Press.
>   An account of practical behavioural approaches to change.

Oakley, D. and Platkin, H. (1979) Brain, Behaviour and Evolution. London: Methuen.
>   Undergraduate level synthesis of disciplines relevant to psychology. How evolutionary perspective can help our understanding of psychological questions.

Walker, S. (1976) Learning and Reinforcement. London: Methuen.
>   Introductory text on key concepts to understanding behavioural approaches to change.

Boddy, A., Martin, F. and Jefferys, M. (eds) (in preparation) The Behavioural Sciences in General Practice. London: Tavistock.
>   Primarily intended for GPs to enable the medical profession to acquire concepts relevant to their work so as to facilitate professional skill and expertise.

13

Counselling and Helping
Barrie Hopson

Counselling today

From a situation in the mid-1960s when 'counselling' was seen by many in education as a transatlantic transplant which hopefully would never 'take', we have today reached the position of being on board a band-wagon; 'counsellors' are everywhere: beauty counsellors, tax counsellors, investment counsellors, even carpet counsellors. There are 'counsellors' in schools, industry, hospitals, the social services. There is marriage counselling, divorce counselling, parent counselling, bereavement counselling, abortion counselling, retirement counselling, redundancy counselling, career counselling, psychosexual counselling, pastoral counselling, student counselling and even disciplinary counselling! Whatever the original purpose for coining the word 'counselling', the coinage has by now certainly been debased. One of the unfortunate consequences of the debasing has been that the word has become mysterious; we cannot always be sure just what 'counselling' involves. One of the results of the mystification of language is that we rely on others to tell us what it is: that is, we assume that we, the uninitiated, cannot know and understand what it is really about. That can be a first step to denying ourselves skills and knowledge we already possess or that we may have the potential to acquire.

It is vital that we 'de-mystify' counselling, and to do that we must look at the concept within the broader context of ways in which people help other people, and we must analyse it in relation to objectives. 'Counselling' is often subscribed to as being 'a good thing', but we must ask the question, 'good for what?'

Ways of helping

'Counselling' is only one form of helping. It is decidedly not the answer to all human difficulties, though it can be extremely productive and significant for some people, sometimes. Counselling is one way of working to help people overcome problems, clarify or achieve personal goals. We can distinguish between six types of helping strategies (Scally and Hopson, 1979).

* Giving advice: offering somebody your opinion of what would be the best course of action based on your view of their situation.

* Giving information: giving a person the information he
  needs in a particular situation (e.g. about legal
  rights, the whereabouts of particular agencies, etc.).
  Lacking information can make one powerless; providing
  it can be enormously helpful.
* Direct action: doing something on behalf of somebody
  else or acting to provide for another's immediate needs;
  for example, providing a meal, lending money, stopping
  a fight, intervening in a crisis.
* Teaching: helping someone to acquire knowledge and
  skills; passing on facts and skills which improve
  somebody's situation.
* Systems change: working to influence and improve systems
  which are causing difficulty for people, that is,
  working on organizational development rather than with
  individuals.
* Counselling: helping someone to explore a problem,
  clarify conflicting issues and discover alternative ways
  of dealing with it, so that they can decide what to do
  about it; that is, helping people to help themselves.

There is no ranking intended in this list. What we do say is
that these strategies make up a helper's 'tool-bag'. Each
one is a 'piece of equipment' which may be useful in particular helping contexts. What a helper is doing is to choose
from his resources whichever approach best fits the
situation at the time.

There are some interesting similarities and differences
between the strategies. Giving advice, information, direct
action, teaching and possibly systems change recognize that
the best answers, outcomes, or solutions rely on the expertise of the helper. The 'expert' offers what he feels is
most useful to the one seeking help. Counselling, on the
other hand, emphasizes that the person with the difficulty
is the one with the resources needed to deal with it. The
counsellor provides the relationship which enables the
clients to search for their own answers. The 'expert' does
not hand out solutions. This does not deny the special
skills of the helper, but does imply that having 'expertise'
does not make a person an 'expert'. We all have expertise.
In counselling, the counsellor is using his expertise to
help to get the clients in touch with their own expertise.
Counselling is the only helping strategy which makes no
assumption that the person's needs are known.

Teaching, systems change, and counselling are only
likely to be effective if the 'helper' has relationship-
making skills. Giving advice, information and direct action
are likely to be MORE effective if he has them. Systems
change is different in that it emphasizes work with groups,
structures, rules and organizations.

The counsellor possibly uses most of the other strategies at some time or other, when they seem more appropriate
than counselling. The other strategies would have an element
of counselling in them if the 'helper' had the necessary

skills. For example, a new student having difficulties making friends at school could involve a counsellor, in addition to using his counselling skills, teaching some relationship-building skills to the student, getting the staff to look at induction provision, making some suggestions to the student, or even taking him to a lunchtime disco session in the school club.

Who are the helpers?

Strictly speaking we are all potential helpers and people to be helped, but in this context it may be useful to distinguish between three groups.

Professional helpers
These are people whose full-time occupation is geared towards helping others in a variety of ways. They have usually, but not always, received specialist training. Social workers, doctors, teachers, school counsellors, nurses, careers officers and health visitors are a few examples. They define their own function in terms of one or more of the helping strategies.

Paraprofessional helpers
These people have a clearly defined helping role but it does not constitute the major part of their job specification or represent the dominant part of their lives, such as marriage guidance counsellors, priests, part-time youth workers, personnel officers and some managers. Probably they have received some short in-service training, often on-the-job.

Helpers in general
People who may not have any specially defined helping role but who, because of their occupational or social position or because of their own commitment, find themselves in situations where they can offer help to others, such as shop stewards, school caretakers, undertakers, social security clerks or solicitors. This group is unlikely to have received special training in helping skills. In addition to these groupings there are a variety of unstructured settings within which helping occurs: the family, friendships, and in the community (Brammer, 1973).

What makes people good helpers?

In some ways it is easier to begin with the qualities that quite clearly do not make for good helping. Loughary and Ripley (1979) people their helpers' rogue's gallery with four types of would-be helpers:

* the 'You think YOU'VE got a problem! Let me tell you about mine!' type;
* the 'Let me tell you what to do' type;
* the 'I understand because I once had the same problem myself' person;
* the 'I'll take charge and deal with it' type.

The first three approaches have been clearly identified as being counter-productive (Carkhuff and Berenson, 1976) while the fourth one certainly deals with a person's problems but prevents the person ever learning skills or concepts to enable him to work through the problem on his own the next time it occurs. The only possible appropriate place for this person is in a crisis intervention. However, even this intervention would need to be followed up with additional counselling help if the needy person were to avoid such crises.

Rogers (1958) came out with clearly testable hypotheses of what constitutes effective helping. He said that helpers must be open and that they should be able to demonstrate UNCONDITIONED POSITIVE REGARD: acceptance of clients as worthwhile regardless of who they are or what they say or do; CONGRUENCE: the helper should use his feelings, his verbal and non-verbal behaviour should be open to the client and be consistent; GENUINENESS: he should be honest, sincere and without façades; EMPATHIC: he should be able to let the client know that he understands his frame of reference and can see the world as he sees it, whilst remaining separate from it. These qualities must be not only possessed but conveyed: that is, the client must experience them.

Truax and Carkhuff (1967) put these hypotheses to the test and found considerable empirical support for what they identified as the 'core facilitative conditions' of effective helping relationships - empathy, respect and positive regard, genuineness, and concreteness - the ability to be specific and immediate to client statements. They differed from Rogers in that whereas he claimed that the facilitative conditions were necessary and sufficient, they only claimed that they were necessary. Carkhuff has gone on to try to demonstrate (Carkhuff and Berenson, 1976) that they are clearly not sufficient, and that the helper needs to be skilled in teaching a variety of life and coping skills to his clients. The other important finding from Truax and Carkhuff was that helpers who do not possess those qualities are not merely ineffective, for they can contribute to people becoming worse than they were prior to helping.

The evidence tends to suggest that the quality of the interpersonal relationship between helper and client is more important than any specific philosophy of helping adhered to by the helper. This has been demonstrated to be the case in counselling, psychotherapy and also teaching (Aspy and Roebuck, 1977). A recent review of the many research studies on this topic would suggest, as one might expect, that things are not quite that simple (Parloff, Waskow, and Wolfe, 1978), but after a reappraisal of the early work of Truax and Carkhuff and a large number of more recent studies, the authors conclude that a relationship between empathy, respect and genuineness with helper effectiveness has been established. They also shed light on a number of other factors which have been discussed periodically as being essential for effective therapists (their focus was therapy, not helping):

* personal psychotherapy has not been demonstrated to be a prerequisite for an effective therapist;
* sex and race are not related to effectiveness;
* the value of therapist experience is highly questionable; that is, someone is not necessarily a better therapist because he is more experienced;
* therapists with emotional problems of their own are likely to be less effective;
* there is some support for the suggestion that helpers are more effective when working with clients who hold values similar to their own.

What they do point out is the importance of the match between helper and client. No one is an effective helper with everyone, although we as yet know little as to how to match helpers with clients to gain the greatest benefits.

Helping and human relationships

Carl Rogers states very clearly that psychotherapy is not a 'special kind of relationship, different in kind from all others which occur in everyday life' (1957). A similar approach has been taken by those theorists looking at the broader concept of helping. Brammer (1973) states that 'helping relationships have much in common with friendships, family interactions, and pastoral contacts. They are all aimed at fulfilling basic human needs, and when reduced to their basic components, look much alike'. This is the approach of Egan in his training programmes for effective interpersonal relating (1975), of Carkhuff and Berenson (1976) who talk of counselling as 'a way of life', of Illich (1977) who is concerned with the de-skilling of the population by increasing armies of specialists, and of Scally and Hopson (1979) who emphasize that counselling 'is merely a set of beliefs, values and behaviours to be found in the community at large'. Considerable stress is placed later in this chapter on the trend towards demystifying helping and counselling.

Models of helping

Any person attempting to help another must have some model in his head, however ill-formed, of the process which he is about to undertake. He will have goals, however hazy, ranging from helping the person to feel better through to helping him to work through an issue for himself. It is essential for helpers to become more aware of the value-roots of their behaviours and the ideological underpinning of their proffered support.

The helper builds his theory through three overlapping stages. First he reflects on his own experience. He becomes aware of his values, needs, communication style, and their impact on others. He reads widely on the experience of other practitioners who have tried to make sense out of their observations by writing down their ideas into a systematic theory ... Finally the helper

forges the first two items together into a unique theory
of his own (Brammer, 1973).

Fortunately, in recent years a number of theorists and
researchers have begun to define models of helping. This can
only assist all helpers to define their own internal models
which will then enable them in turn to evaluate their
personal, philosophical and empirical bases.

CARKHUFF AND ASSOCIATES: Carkhuff took Rogers'
ideas on psychotherapy and expanded on them to helping in
general. He has a three-stage model through which the client
is helped to (i) explore, (ii) understand and (iii) act. He
defines the skills needed by the helper at each stage of the
process (Carkhuff, 1974), and has also developed a system
for selecting and training prospective helpers to do this.
Since the skills he outlines are basically the same skills
which anyone needs to live effectively, he suggests that the
best way of helping people is to teach them directly and
systematically in life, work, learning and relationship-
building skills. He states clearly that 'the essential task
of helping is to bridge the gap between the helpee's skills
level and the helper's skills level' (Carkhuff and Berenson,
1976). For Carkhuff, helping equals teaching, but teaching
people the skills to ensure that they can take more control
over their own lives.

BRAMMER (1973) has produced an integrated, eclectic
developmental model similar to Carkhuff's. He has expanded
Carkhuff's three stages into the eight stages of entry,
classification, structure, relationship, exploration, con-
solidation, planning and termination. He has also identified
seven clusters of skills to promote 'understanding of self
and others'. His list of 46 specific skills is somewhat
daunting to a beginner but a rich source of stimulation for
the more experienced helper.

IVEY AND ASSOCIATES (1971) have developed a highly
systematic model for training helpers under the label
'microcounselling'. Each skill is broken up into its
constituent parts and taught via closed-circuit television,
modelling and practice.

HACKNEY AND NYE (1973) have described a helping
model which they call a 'discrimination' model. It is goal-
centred and action-centred and it stresses skills training.

KAGAN AND ASSOCIATES (1967) have also developed
a microskills approach to counsellor training which is
widely used in the USA. It is called Interpersonal Process
Recall which involves an inquiry session in which helper and
client explore the experience they have had together in the
presence of a mediator.

EGAN (1975) has developed perhaps the next most
influential model of helping in the USA after Carkhuff's
and, indeed, has been highly influenced by Carkhuff's work.
The model begins with a pre-helping phase involving
attending skills, to be followed by Stage I: responding and
self-exploration; Stage II: integrative understanding and

Figure 1

Model of helping
From Loughary and Ripley (1979)

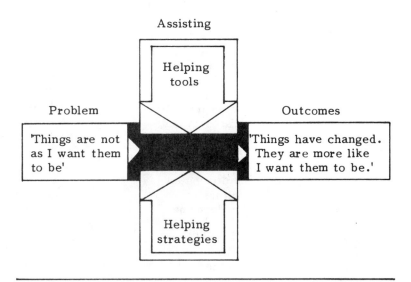

dynamic self-understanding; Stage III: facilitating action and acting. The first goal labelled at each stage is the helper's goal and the second goal is that of the client.

LOUGHARY AND RIPLEY (1979) approach helping from a different viewpoint, which, unlike the previous theorists, is not simply on the continuum beginning with Rogers and Carkhuff. They have used a demystifying approach aimed at the general population with no training other than what can be gleaned from their book. Their model is shown in figure 1.

The helping tools include information, ideas, and skills (such as listening and reflecting dealings). The strategies are the plans for using the tools and the first step is always translating the problem into desired outcomes. Their four positive outcomes of helping are: changes in feeling states, increased understanding, decisions, and implementing decisions. Their approach does move away from the counselling-dominated approach of the other models.

HOPSON AND SCALLY: we reproduce our own model in some detail here, partly because it is the model we know best and it has worked very effectively for us and for the 3,000 teachers and youth workers who have been through our counselling skills training courses (Scally and Hopson, 1979), but also because it attempts to look at all the aspects of helping defined at the beginning of this chapter.

Figure 2 outlines three goal areas for helpers, central to their own personal development. It also defines specific helping outcomes. Helpers can only help people to the levels

Figure 2

Goals of helping

GOALS OF HELPING

SELF-EMPOWERED INDIVIDUALS	PERSONAL DEVELOPMENT OF THE HELPER	HEALTHY SYSTEMS (MICRO, MACRO)	SPECIFIC OUTCOMES

possessing
awareness

self   others   the world

GOALS

commitments outcomes

VALUES

SKILLS
(see figure 3)

INFORMATION

self   others   the world

Increasing self-
awareness and
level and range of
skills

Monitoring own
welfare and
development

Using skills to
assist development
of others

Giving and getting
support

Interacting with,
learning from,
changing and being
being changed by
individuals and
systems

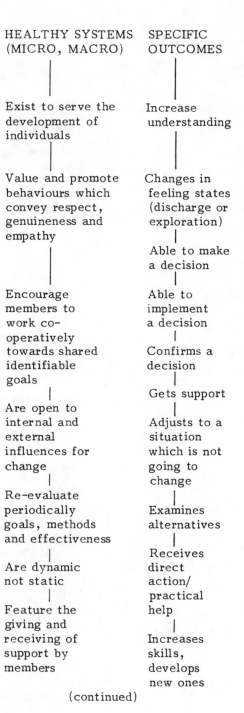

Exist to serve the
development of
individuals

Value and promote
behaviours which
convey respect,
genuineness and
empathy

Encourage
members to
work co-
operatively
towards shared
identifiable
goals

Are open to
internal and
external
influences for
change

Re-evaluate
periodically
goals, methods
and effectiveness

Are dynamic
not static

Feature the
giving and
receiving of
support by
members

Increase
understanding

Changes in
feeling states
(discharge or
exploration)

Able to make
a decision

Able to
implement
a decision

Confirms a
decision

Gets support

Adjusts to a
situation
which is not
going to
change

Examines
alternatives

Receives
direct
action/
practical
help

Increases
skills,
develops
new ones

(continued)

Focus on
individual's
strengths

Receives
information

And builds on
them

Reflects on
acts

Use problem
solving strate-
gies rather than
scapegoating,
blaming or focus-
sing on faults

Use methods which
are consistent
with goals

Encourage power-
sharing and enable
individuals to
pursue their own
direction as a
contribution to
shared goals

Monitor their own
performance in a
continuing cycle of
reflection/action

Allow people
access to those
whose decisions
have a bearing
on their lives

Have effective
and sensitive
lines of
communication

Explore differ-
ences openly and
use compromise,
negotiation and
contracting to
achieve a maxi-
mum of win/win
outcomes for all

Are always open
to alternatives

of their own skills and awareness (Aspy and Roebuck, 1977).
They need to clarify their own social, economic and cultural
values and need to be able to recognize and separate their
own needs and problems from those of their clients. Helpers
see in others reflections of themselves. To know oneself is
to ensure a clarity of distinction between images: to know
where one stops and the other begins. We become less helpful
as the images blur. To ensure that does not happen, we need
constantly to monitor our own development. Self-awareness
is not a stage to be reached and then it is over. It is a
process which can never stop because we are always changing.
By monitoring these changes we simultaneously retain some
control of their direction.

From a greater awareness of who we are, our strengths,
hindrances, values, needs and prejudices, we can be clearer
about skills we wish to develop. The broader the range of
skills we acquire, the larger the population group that we
can help.

As helpers involved in the act of helping we learn
through the process of praxis. We reflect and we act. As we
interact with others, we in turn are affected by them and
are in some way different from before the interaction. As we
attempt to help individuals and influence systems we will
learn, change, and develop from the process of interaction,
just as those individuals and systems will be affected by
us.

Having access to support should be a central concern for
anyone regularly involved in helping. Helpers so often are
not as skilled as they might be at saying 'no' and looking
after themselves.

We would maintain that the ultimate goals of helping are
to enable people to become self-empowered and to make
systems healthier places in which to live, work and play.

Self-empowerment

There are five dimensions of self-empowerment (Hopson and
Scally, 1980a).

* Awareness: without an awareness of ourselves and others
  we are subject to the slings and arrows of our
  upbringing, daily events, social changes and crises.
  Without awareness we can only react, like the pinball in
  the machine that bounces from one thing to another
  without having ever provided the energy for its own
  passage.
* Goals: given awareness we have the potential for taking
  charge of ourselves and our lives. We take charge by
  exploring our values, developing commitments, and by
  specifying goals with outcomes. We learn to live by the
  question: 'what do I want now?' We reflect and then act.
* Values: we subscribe to the definition of values put
  forward by Raths, Harmin and Simon (1964): a value is
  a belief which has been chosen freely from alternatives
  after weighing the consequences of each alternative; it

is prized and cherished, shared publicly and acted upon repeatedly and consistently. The self-empowered person, by our definition, has values which include recognizing the worth of self and others, of being proactive, working for health systems, at home, in employment, in the community and at leisure; helping other people to become more self-empowered.

* Life skills: values are good as far as they go, but it is only by developing skills that we can translate them into action. We may believe that we are responsible for our own destiny, but we require the skills to achieve what we wish for ourselves. In a school setting, for example, we require the skills of goal setting and action-planning, time management, reading, writing and numeracy, study skills, problem-solving skills and how to work in groups. Figure 3 reproduces the list of life skills that we have identified at the Counselling and Career Development Unit (Hopson and Scally, 1980b) as being crucial to personal survival and growth.

* Information: information is the raw material for awareness of self and the surrounding world. It is the fuel for shaping our goals. Information equals power. Without it we are helpless, which is of course why so many people and systems attempt to keep information to themselves. We must realize that information is essential (a concept), that we need to know how to get appropriate information, and from where (a skill).

Healthy systems

Too often counsellors and other helpers have pretended to be value free. Most people now recognize that fiction. Not only is it impossible but it can be dangerous. If we honestly believe that we are capable of being value free, we halt the search for the ways in which our value systems are influencing our behaviour with our clients. If we are encouraging our clients to develop goals, how can we pretend that we do not have them too? Expressing these goals can be the beginning of a contract to work with a client for, like it or not, we each have a concept, however shadowy, for the fully functioning healthy person to which our actions and helping are directed.

As with clients, so too with systems. If we are working towards helping people to become 'better', in whatever way we choose to define that, let us be clear about what changes we are working towards in the systems we try to influence. Figure 2 lists our characteristics of healthy systems. Each of us has his own criteria so let us discover them and bring them into the open. Owning our values is one way of demonstrating our genuineness.

What is counselling?

Having identified six common ways of helping people, counselling will now be focussed on more intensively, which immediately gets us into the quagmire of definition.

Figure 3

Lifeskills: taking charge of yourself and your life

ME

Skills I need to manage and grow

how to read and write

how to achieve basic numeracy

how to find information and resources

how to think and solve problems constructively

how to identify my creative potential
 and develop it

how to manage time effectively

how to make the most of the present

how to discover my interests

how to discover my values and beliefs

how to set and achieve goals

how to take stock of my life

how to discover what makes me do
 the things I do

how to be positive about myself

how to cope and gain from life transitions

how to make effective decisions

how to be proactive

how to manage negative emotions

how to cope with stress

how to achieve and maintain physical
 well-being

how to manage my sexuality

ME AND YOU

Skills I need to relate
 effectively to you

how to communicate effectively

how to make, keep and end a relationship

how to give and get help

how to manage conflict

how to give and receive feedback

ME AND OTHERS

Skills I need to relate
 effectively to others

how to be assertive

how to influence people and systems

how to work in groups

how to express feelings
 constructively

how to build strengths in others

ME AND SPECIFIC SITUATIONS

Skills I need for my education

how to discover the educational options
 open to me

how to choose a course

how to study

SKILLS I NEED AT WORK

how to find a job

how to keep a job

how to change jobs

how to cope with unemployment

how to achieve a balance between my job
 and the rest of my life

how to retire and enjoy it

SKILLS I NEED AT HOME

how to choose a style of living

how to maintain a home

SKILLS I NEED AT LEISURE

how to choose between leisure options

how to maximize my leisure opportunities

how to use my leisure to increase my
 income

SKILLS I NEED IN THE COMMUNITY

how to be a skilled consumer

how to develop and use my political
 awareness

Anyone reviewing the literature to define counselling will quickly suffer from data-overload. Books, articles, even manifestoes, have been written on the question.

In training courses run from the Counselling and Career Development Unit we tend to opt for the parsimonious definition of 'helping people explore problems so that they can decide what to do about them'.

The demystification of counselling

There is nothing inherently mysterious about counselling. It is merely a set of beliefs, values and behaviours to be found in the community at large. The beliefs include one that says individuals benefit and grow from a particular form of relationship and contact. The values recognize the worth and the significance of each individual and regard personal autonomy and self-direction as desirable. The behaviours cover a combination of listening, conveying warmth, asking open questions, encouraging specificity, concreteness and focussing, balancing support and confrontation, and offering strategies which help to clarify objectives and identify action plans. This terminology is more complex than the process needs to be. The words describe what is essentially a 'non-mystical' way in which some people are able to help other people to help themselves (see figure 4).

Training courses can sometimes encourage the mystification. They talk of 'counselling skills' and may, by implication, suggest that such skills are somehow separate from other human activities, are to be conferred upon those who attend courses, and are probably innovatory. In fact, what 'counselling' has done is to crystallize what we know about how warm, trusting relationships develop between people. It recognizes that:

* relationships develop if one has and conveys respect for another, if one is genuine oneself, if one attempts to see things from the other's point of view (empathizes), and if one endeavours not to pass judgement. Those who operate in this way we describe as having 'relationship-building skills';
* if the relationship is established, an individual will be prepared to talk through and explore his thoughts and feelings. What one can do and say which helps that to happen we classify as exploring and clarifying skills (see figure 4);
* through this process an individual becomes clear about difficulties or uncertainties, and can explore options and alternatives, in terms of what he might do to change what he is not happy about;
* given support, an individual is likely to be prepared to, and is capable of, dealing with difficulties or problems he may face more effectively. He can be helped by somebody who can offer objective setting and action planning skills.

Figure 4

_____

The Counselling Process

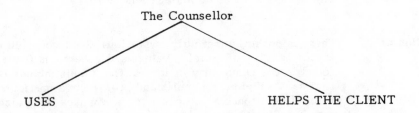

	USES	HELPS THE CLIENT
RELATIONSHIP BUILDING SKILLS	respect genuineness empathy	to feel valued, understood and prepared to trust the counsellor
EXPLORING AND CLARIFYING SKILLS	contracting open questions summarizing focussing reflecting immediacy clarifying concreteness confronting	to talk and explore to understand more about how he feels and why to consider options and examine alternatives to choose an alternative
	objective setting action planning problem-solving strategies	to develop clear objectives to form specific action plans to do, with support, what needs to be done

COUNSELLING IS HELPING PEOPLE TO HELP THEMSELVES

_____

Counselling skills are what people use to help people to
help themselves. They are not skills that are exclusive to
one group or one activity. It is clear that the behaviours,
which we bundle together and identify as skills, are
liberally scattered about us in the community. Counselling
ideology identifies which behaviours are consistent with its
values and its goals, and teaches these as one category of
helping skills.

What may happen, unfortunately, is that the promotion
of counselling as a separate training responsibility can
increase the mystification. An outcome can be that instead
of simply now being people who, compared to the majority,
are extra-sensitive listeners, are particularly good at
making relationships, and are more effective at helping
others to solve problems, they have become 'counsellors' and
licensed to help. A licence becomes a danger if:

* those who have it see themselves as qualitatively
  different from the rest of the population;
* it symbolizes to the non-licensed that they are
  incapable, or inferior, or calls into question valuable
  work they may be doing, but are 'unqualified' to do.

It is important to recognize that labelling people can have
unfortunate side effects. Let us remember that whatever the
nomenclature - counsellor, client or whatever - at a
particular time or place, they are just people. All, at
some time or other, will be able to give help, at other
times will need to seek or receive help. Some are naturally
better fitted to help others; some by training can improve
their helping skills. All, through increased awareness and
skill development, can become more effective helpers than
they are now.

Counselling is not only practised by counsellors. It is
a widespread activity in the community and appears in
several guises. Its constituent skills are described
variously as 'talking it over', 'having a friendly chat',
'being a good friend' or simply 'sharing' with somebody.
These processes almost certainly include some or all of the
skills summarized in figure 4. Often, of course, there are
notable exceptions: for instance, we do not listen well; we
cannot resist giving our advice, or trying to solve problems
for our friends; we find it difficult to drop our façades
and roles. Counselling skills training can help reduce our
unhelpful behaviours and begin to develop these skills in
ourselves, making us more effective counsellors, as well as
simply being a good friend. In almost any work involving
contact with other people, we would estimate there is a
potential counselling component. There is a need for the
particular interpersonal skills categorized here as counselling skills to be understood and used by people at large,
but particularly by all people who have the welfare of
others as part of their occupational roles. Specialist
'counsellors' have an important part to play, but it is not

to replace the valuable work that is done by many who would not claim the title. Having said that, people sometimes think they are counselling, but in fact are doing things very far removed: disciplining, persuading people to conform to a system, etc.

Types of counselling

Developmental versus crisis counselling

Counselling can operate either as a RESPONSE to a situation or as a STIMULUS to help a client develop and grow. In the past, counselling has often been concerned with helping someone with a problem during or after the onset of a crisis point: a widow unable to cope with her grief, the school leaver desperate because he has no idea what job to choose, the pregnant woman with no wish to be pregnant. This is a legitimate function of counselling, but if this is all that counselling is, it can only ever be concerned with making the best of the situation in which one finds oneself. How much more ambitious to help people anticipate future problems, to educate them to recognize the cues of oncoming crisis, and to provide them with skills to take charge of it at the outset instead of running behind in an attempt to catch up! This is counselling as a stimulus to growth: developmental as opposed to crisis counselling. All successful counselling entails growth, but the distinction between the two approaches is that the crisis approach generates growth under pressure, and since this is often limited only to the presenting problem, the client's behavioural and conceptual repertoire may remain little affected by the experience. There will always be a need for crisis counselling in a wide variety of settings, but the exciting prospect of developmental counselling for growth and change has only recently begun to be tackled.

Individual counselling

As counselling was rooted in psychotherapy it is hardly surprising that the primary focus has been on the one-to-one relationship. There are a number of essential elements in the process. The client is to be helped to reach his own decision by himself. This is achieved by establishing a relationship of trust whereby the client feels that the counsellor cares about him, is able to empathize with his problem, and is authentic and genuine in relating to him. The counsellor will enter the relationship as a person in his own right, disclosing relevant information about himself as appropriate, reacting honestly to the client's statements and questions, but at no time imposing his own opinions on the client. His task is to facilitate the client's own abilities and strengths in such a way that the client experiences the satisfaction of having defined and solved his problem for himself. If the client lacks information on special issues, is incapable of generating alternative strategies, or cannot make decisions in a programmatic way, then the counsellor has a function as an educator whose skills are offered to the client. In this way the client is never manipulated. The counsellor is negotiating a contract to use some skills which he, the counsellor, possesses, and which can be passed on to the client if the client wishes to make use of them.

Individual counselling has the advantages over group counselling of providing a safer setting for some people to lower their defences, of developing a strong and trusting relationship with the counsellor, and of allowing the client maximum personal contact with the counsellor.

Group counselling

Group counselling involves one or more counsellors operating with a number of clients in a group session. The group size varies from four to sixteen, with eight to ten being the most usual number. The basic objectives of group and individual counselling are similar. Both seek to help the clients achieve self-direction, integration, self-responsibility, self-acceptance, and an understanding of their motivations and patterns of behaviour. In both cases the counsellor needs the skills and attitudes outlined earlier, and both require a confidential relationship. There are, however, some important differences (Hopson, 1977).

* The group counsellor needs an understanding of group dynamics: communication, decision making, role-playing, sources of power, and perceptual processes in groups.
* The group situation can provide immediate opportunities to try out ways of relating to individuals, and is an excellent way of providing the experience of intimacy with others. The physical proximity of the clients to one another can be emotionally satisfying and supportive. Clients give a first-hand opportunity to test others' perception of themselves.
* Clients not only receive help themselves; they also help other clients. In this way helping skills are generated by a larger group of people than is possible in individual counselling.
* Clients often discover that other people have similar problems, which can at the least be comforting.
* Clients learn to make effective use of other people, not just professionals, as helping agents. They can set up a mutual support group which is less demanding on the counsellor and likely to be a boost to their self-esteem when they discover they can manage to an increasing extent without him.

There are many different kinds of group counselling. Some careers services in higher education offer counsellor-led groups as groundwork preparation for career choices; these small groups give older adolescents an opportunity to discuss the interrelations between their conscious values and preferred life styles and their crystallizing sense of identity. Other groups are provided in schools where young people can discuss with each other and an adult counsellor those relationships with parents and friends which are so important in adolescence. Training groups are held for teaching decision-making skills and assertive skills. There are also groups in which experiences are pooled and mutual help given for the married, for parents, for those bringing up families alone and for those who share a special problem such as having a handicapped child. All these types of groups are usually led by someone who has had training and experience in facilitating them. The word 'facilitating' is used advisedly, for the leader's job is not to conduct a seminar or tutorial, but to establish an atmosphere in which members of the group can explore the feelings around a particular stage of development or condition or critical choice.

Another type of group is not so specifically focussed on an area of common concern but is set up as a sort of laboratory to learn about the underlying dynamics of how people in groups function, whatever the group's focus and purpose may be. These are often referred to as sensitivity training groups (e.g. Cooper and Mangham, 1971; Smith, 1975). Yet a third category of group has more therapeutic goals, being intended to be successive or complementary to, or sometimes in place of, individual psychotherapy. This type of group will not usually have a place in work settings, whereas the other two do have useful applications there. Obvious uses for this type of group occur in induction procedures, in preparation for retirement, in relation to job change arising from promotion, or in relation to redundancy. The second type of group is employed in training for supervisory or management posts, though one hears less about their use in trade unions.

Schools of counselling
Differences in theories of personality, learning and perception are reflected in counselling theory. It is useful to distinguish between five major schools.

1. PSYCHOANALYTIC APPROACHES were historically the first. Psychoanalysis is a personality theory, a philosophical system, and a method of psychotherapy. Concentrating on the past history of a patient, understanding the internal dynamics of the psyche, and the relationship between the client and the therapist are all key concerns for psychoanalysis. Key figures include Freud, Jung, Adler, Sullivan, Horney, Fromm and Erikson.

2. CLIENT-CENTRED APPROACHES are based upon the work of Rogers, originally as a non-directive therapy developed as a reaction against psychoanalysis. Founded on a subjective view of human experiencing, it places more faith in and gives more responsibility to the client in problem solving. The techniques of client-centred counselling have become the basis for most counselling skills training,

following the empirical evaluations by Truax and Carkhuff (1967).

3. BEHAVIOURAL APPROACHES arise from attempts to apply the principles of learning to the resolution of specific behavioural disorders. Results are subject to continual experimentation and refinement. Key figures include Wolpe, Eysenck, Lazarus and Krumboltz.

4. COGNITIVE APPROACHES include 'rational-emotive therapy' (Ellis), 'Transactional analysis' (Berne) and 'reality therapy' (Glasser), along with Meichenbaum's work on cognitive rehearsal and inoculation. All have in common the belief that people's problems are created by how they conceptualize their worlds: change the concepts and feelings will change too.

5. AFFECTIVE APPROACHES include 'Gestalt therapy' (Perls), 'primal therapy' (Janov), 're-evaluation counselling' (Jackins), and 'bioenergetics' (Lowen). These have in common the belief that pain and distress accumulate and have to be discharged in some way before the person can become whole or think clearly again.

There are many other approaches and orientations. The existential-humanistic school is exemplified by May, Maslow, Frankl and Jourard. Encounter approaches have been developed by Schutz, Bindrim and Ichazo, 'psychosynthesis' by Assagioli, 'morita therapy' by Morita, and 'eclectic psychotherapy' by Thorne. In the United Kingdom the biggest influence on counsellor training has been from the client-centred school. Behavioural approaches are becoming more common and, to a lesser extent, transactional analysis, Gestalt therapy and re-evaluation counselling.

Where does counselling take place?

Until recently counselling was assumed to take place in the confines of a counsellor's office. This is changing rapidly. It is now increasingly accepted that effective counselling, as defined in this chapter, can take place on the shop floor, in the school corridor, even on a bus. The process is not made any easier by difficult surroundings, but when people need help, the helpers are not always in a position to choose from where they would like to administer it. Initial contacts are often made in these kinds of environment, and more intensive counselling can always be scheduled for a later date in a more amenable setting.

What are the goals of counselling?

Counselling is a process through which a person attains a higher stage of personal competence. It is always about change. Katz (1969) has said that counselling is concerned not with helping people to make wise decisions but with helping them to make decisions wisely. It has as its goal self-empowerment: that is, the individual's ability to move through the following stages.

* 'I am not happy with things at the moment'
* 'What I would prefer is ...'
* 'What I need to do to achieve that is ...'
* 'I have changed what I can, and have come to terms, for the moment, with what I cannot achieve'.

Counselling has as an ultimate goal the eventual redundancy of the helper, and the activity should discourage dependency and subjection. It promotes situations in which the person's views and feelings are heard, respected and not judged. It builds personal strength, confidence and invites initiative and growth. It develops the individual and encourages control of self and situations. Counselling obviously works for the formation of more capable and effective individuals, through working with people singly or in groups.

In its goals it stands alongside other approaches concerned with personal and human development. All can see how desirable would be the stage when more competent, 'healthier' individuals would live more positively and more humanly. Counselling may share its goals in terms of what it wants for individuals; where it does differ from other approaches is in its method of achieving that. It concentrates on the individual - alone or in a group - and on one form of helping. Some other approaches would work for the same goals but would advocate different methods of achieving them. It is important to explore the inter-relatedness of counselling and other forms of helping as a way of asking, 'If we are clear about what we want for people, are we being as effective as we could be in achieving it?'

Counselling outcomes

This chapter has defined the ultimate outcome of counselling as 'helping people to help themselves'. A natural question to follow might be, 'to help themselves to do what?' There follows a list of counselling outcomes most frequently asked for by clients:

* increased understanding of oneself or a situation;
* achieving a change in the way one is feeling;
* being able to make a decision;
* confirming a decision;
* getting support for a decision;
* being able to change a situation;
* adjusting to a situation that is not going to change;
* the discharge of feelings;
* examining options and choosing one (Scally and Hopson, 1979).

Clients sometimes want other outcomes which are not those of counselling but stem from one or more of the other forms of helping: information, new skills, or practical help.

All of these outcomes have in common the concept of change. All counselling is about change. Given any issue or problem a person always has four possible strategies to deal with it:

* change the situation;
* change oneself to adapt to the situation;
* exit from it;
* develop ways of living with it.

Is counselling the best way of helping people?

In the quest for more autonomous, more self-competent, self-employed individuals the helper is faced with the question, 'If that is my goal, am I working in the most effective way towards achieving it?' As much as one believes in the potential of counselling, there are times when one must ask whether spending time with individuals is the best investment of one's helping time and effort.

Many counsellors say that time spent in this way is incredibly valuable; it emphasizes the importance of each individual, and hence they justify time given to one-to-one counselling. At the other end of the spectrum there are those who charge 'counsellors' with:

* being concerned solely with 'casualties', people in crisis and in difficulty, and not getting involved with organizational questions;
* allowing systems, organizations and structures to continue to operate 'unhealthily', by 'treating' these 'casualties' so effectively.

To reject these charges out-of-hand would be to fail to recognize the elements of truth they contain. One respects tremendously the importance that counselling places on the individual, and this is not an attempt to challenge that. What it may be relevant to establish is that counselling should not be seen as a substitute for 'healthy' systems, which operate in ways which respect individuality, where relationships are genuine and positive, where communication is open and problem-solving and participation are worked at (see figure 2). 'Healthy' systems can be as important to the welfare of the individual as can one-to-one counselling. It is unfortunate therefore that 'administrators' can see personal welfare as being the province of 'counselling types', and the latter are sometimes reluctant to 'contaminate' their work by getting involved in administrational or organizational matters. These attitudes can be very detrimental to all involved systems. The viewpoint presented here is that part of a helper's repertoire of skills in the 'tool-bag' alongside counselling skills should be willingness, and the ability, to work for systems change. Some counsellors obviously do this already in more spontaneous ways; for example, if one finds oneself counselling truants, it may become apparent that some absconding is invited by timetable anomalies (French for remedial groups on Friday afternoons?). The dilemma here is whether one spends time with a series of individual truants or persuades the designers of timetables to establish a more aware approach.

One realizes sometimes also that one may, in counselling, be using one's skills in such a way that individuals accept outcomes which possibly should not be accepted. For example, unemployment specialists in careers services sometimes see themselves as being used by 'the system' to help black youths come to terms with being disadvantaged. Such specialists ask whether this is their role or whether they should in fact be involved politically and actively in working for social and economic change.

Resistance to the idea of becoming more involved in 'systems' and 'power structures' may not simply be based upon a reluctance to take on extra, unattractive work. Some will genuinely feel that this approach is 'political' and therefore somehow tainted and dubious. It is interesting that in the USA during the last five years there has been a significant shift in opinion towards counsellors becoming more ready to accept the need to be involved in influencing systems:

> Their work brings them face to face with the victim of poverty; or racism, sexism, and stigmatization; of political, economic and social systems that allow individuals to feel powerless and helpless; of governing structures that cut off communication and deny the need for responsiveness; of social norms that stifle individuality; of communities that let their members live in isolation from one another. In the face of these realities human service workers have no choice but to blame those victims or to see ways to change the environment (Lewis and Lewis, 1977).

In this country, perhaps a deeper analysis is needed of the 'contexts' in which we work as helpers.

Can counselling be apolitical?

It is very interesting that in his recent book, Carl Rogers (Rogers, 1978) reviewing his own present position vis-à-vis counselling, indicates the revolutionary impact of much of his work as perceived by him in retrospect. Perhaps identifiable as the 'arch-individualist', Rogers signals now that he had not seen the full social impact of the values and the methodology he pioneered. He writes eloquently of his realization that much of his life and work has in fact been political, though previously he had not seen it in those terms. Counselling invites self-empowerment; it invites the individual to become aware and to take more control; it asks 'How would you like things to be?' and 'How will you make them like that?' That process is a very powerful one and has consequences that are likely to involve changing 'status quos'. Clearly processes that are about change, power, and control are 'political' (although not necessarily party political).

From this viewpoint counsellors are involved in politics already. As much as one may like there to be, there can really be no neutral ground. Opting out or not working for change is by definition maintaining the status quo. If the 'status quo' means an organization, systems or relationships which are insensitive, uncaring, manipulative, unjust, divisive, autocratic, or function in any way which damages the potential of the people who are part of them, then one cannot really turn one's back on the task of working for change. 'One is either part of the solution or part of the problem!' We have argued (Scally and Hopson, 1979) that counsellors have much to offer by balancing their one-to-one work with more direct and more skilled involvement in making systems more positive, growthful places in which to live and work.

'o counsel or to teach?

Counselling is a process through which a person attains a higher level of personal competence. Recently, attacks have been made on the counselling approach by such widely differing adversaries as Illich (1973) and Carkhuff (Carkhuff and Berenson, 1976). They, and others, question what effect the existence of counsellors and therapists has had on human development as a whole. They maintain that, however benevolent the counselling relationship is felt to be by those involved, there are forces at work overall which are suspect. They suggest:

* that helpers largely answer their own needs, and consciously or unconsciously perpetuate dependency or inadequacy in clients;
* helping can be 'disabling' rather than 'enabling' because it often encourages dependency.

For counsellors to begin to answer such charges requires a self-analysis of their own objectives, methods and motives. They could begin by asking:

* how much of their counselling is done at the 'crisis' or 'problem' stage in their clients' lives?
* how much investment are they putting into 'prevention' rather than 'cure'?

To help somebody in crisis is an obvious task. It is, however, only one counselling option. If 'prevention' is better than 'cure' then maybe that is where the emphasis ought to be. Perhaps never before has there been more reason for individuals to feel 'in crisis'. Toffler (1970) has identified some likely personal and social consequences of living at a time of incredibly rapid change. Many, like Stonier (1979) are forecasting unparalleled technological developments over the next 30 years which will change our lives, especially our work patterns, dramatically. There are so

many complex forces at work that it is not surprising that
many people are feeling more anxious, unsure, pessimistic,
unable to cope, depersonalized, and helpless. Helpers are at
risk as much as any, but are likely to be faced with ever-
increasing demands on their time and skills. Again, this
requires a reassessment of approaches and priorities, which
could suggest a greater concentration on the development of
personal competence in our systems. We need to develop more
'skilled' (which is not the same as 'informed') individuals
and thereby avert more personal difficulties and crisis. One
view is that this, the developmental, educational, teaching
approach, needs to involve more of those who now spend much
time in one-to-one counselling; not to replace that work but
to give balance to it.

Personal competence and self-empowerment, which are
the 'goals' of counselling, can be understood in many ways.
A recent movement has been to see competence as being
achievable through skill development. 'Life skills' are
becoming as large a band-wagon as counselling has become.

We are producing a series of Lifeskills Teaching
Programmes (Hopson and Scally, 1980b) which cover a range
of more generic personal skills: for example, 'How to be
assertive rather than aggressive', 'How to make, maintain
and end relationships', 'How to manage time effectively',
'How to be positive about oneself', 'How to make effective
transitions', etc. (figure 3). The programmes attempt to
break down the generalization of 'competence' into 'learn-
able' units, with the overall invitation that, by acquiring
these skills, one can 'take charge of oneself and one's
life'. We have the advantage, working in a training unit, of
being able to work directly with teachers and youth workers
on the skills this way. Aspy and Roebuck (1977) have identified that the most effective teachers are those who have,
and demonstrate, a high respect for others, who are genuine,
and display a high degree of empathy with their students.
Many professional counsellors therefore should have the
basic qualities required in teaching, and could make appre-
ciable contributions by being involved in programmes in the
community which encourage 'coping' and 'growth' skills. More
personally skilled individuals could reduce the dependence,
inadequacy and crises which are individually and collectively wasteful, and take up so much counselling time.

**Towards a 'complete
helper'**

The argument here is for the development of more complete
helpers, more 'all-rounders', with a range of skills and
'tool-bags' full of more varied helping equipment. It is
possible to work to increase the level of skill in each
particular helping technique and go for 'broader' rather
than 'higher' skill development. This diagram (figure 5)
could map out for individual helpers how they may want to
plan their own development.

On a graph such as this an effective teacher may be
placed typically along the line marked 'x'. A full-time

counsellor working in a school or workplace may typically be indicated by the line marked 'o'. An organization-change consultant may typically be somewhere along the dotted line.

Figure 5

Helpers' skills levels and possible approaches to increasing them

(What skills do I have and in which direction can I develop?)

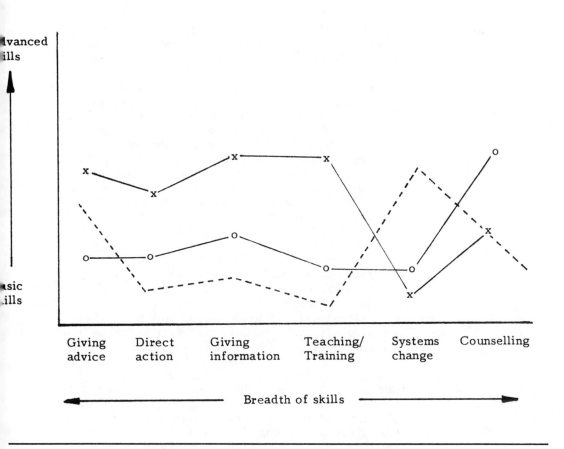

How much one wants to be involved in helping, at whatever level and in whatever form, obviously depends upon many factors. How much one sees helping as part of the roles one fills; how much helping is part of the job one does; how much one wants to be involved as a part-time activity; how much helping is consistent with one's values, politics and personality; all will have a bearing on where an individual may wish to be placed on the graph. One person may decide to specialize in a particular approach and develop sophisticated skills in that field. Another may go for a broader approach by developing skills from across the range. Yet another may at particular times develop new specialisms as a response to particular situations or as part of his own personal career development.

What is advocated here is that basic helping skills can be regarded as essential life skills. These skills can be made available to, and developed very fully in, professional helpers and in those for whom helping is part of their job specification in the workshop, in hospitals, in the social service agencies or in education. They can also be taught to young people in schools and at work.

Counselling in the UK

It is interesting that 'counselling' was a term rarely used in Britain until the mid-1960s. According to Vaughan's analysis (1976),

> three factors gradually tended to focus more attention on this area. One was the emergence throughout this century of a wider band of 'helping' professions, such as the Youth Employment Service, the social work services, and psychotherapy, as well as other 'caring' organizations, such as marriage guidance, and more recently such bodies as the Samaritans and Help the Aged. A second was the development of empirical psychology and sociology, which began to offer specific techniques for the analysis of personal difficulties; and a third was the rapid spread from about the mid-1960s onwards of the concept of counselling as a specific profession derived almost wholly from North America, where it had undergone a long evolution throughout the century from about 1910. Thus today we have a situation comparable in some ways to that of the development of primary education in Britain before the 1870 Act. A new area of specialization seems to be emerging.

It is just because a new area of specialization is developing that people already engaged in, or about to involve themselves in, counselling need to think carefully of where and how they wish to invest their time and resources. Counselling clearly is an important way of helping people, but it is not the only way.

References

Aspy, D. and Roebuck, F. (1977)
Kids Don't Learn from People They Don't Like. Amherst, Mass.: Human Resource Development Press.

Blocher, D. (1966)
> Developmental Counseling (2nd edn). New York: Ronald Press.

Bonnex, J.T. (1965)
> Cells and Societies. Princeton University, NJ: Princeton University Press.

Boy, A.V. and Pine, G.J. (1968)
> The Counselor in the Schools. New York: Houghton Mifflin.

Brammer, L.M. (1973)
> The Helping Relationship. Englewood Cliffs, NJ: Prentice-Hall.

Burnet, F.M. (1971)
> Self-recognition in colonial marine forms and flowering plants. Nature, 232, 230-235.

Carkhuff, R.R. (1969)
> Helping and Human Relations. New York: Holt, Rinehart & Winston.

Carkhuff, R.R. (1974)
> The Art of Helping. Amherst, Mass.: Human Resource Development Press.

Carkhuff, R.R. and Berenson, B.G. (1976)
> Teaching As Treatment. Amherst, Mass.: Human Resource Development Press.

Coombs, A., Avila, D. and Purkey, W. (1971)
> Helping Relationships: Basic concepts for the helping profession. Boston: Allyn & Bacon.

Cooper, C.L. and Mangham, I.L. (eds) (1971)
> T-Groups: A survey of research. Chichester: Wiley.

Corey, G. (1977)
> Theory and Practice of Counselling and Psychotherapy. Monterey, Ca: Brooks/Cole.

Corsini, R. (ed.) (1977)
> Current Psychotherapies (2nd edn). Itasca, Ill.: Peacock Publications.

Egan, G. (1975)
> The Skilled Helper. Monterey, Ca: Brooks/Cole.

Eibl-Eibesfeldt, I. (1971)
> Love and Hate. London: Methuen.

Hackney, H.L. and Nye, S. (1973)
> Counseling Strategies and Objectives. Englewood Cliffs, NJ: Prentice-Hall.

Hoffman, A.M. (1976)
> Paraprofessional effectiveness. Personnel and Guidance Journal, 54, 494-497.

Hopson, B. (1977)
> Techniques and methods of counselling. In A.G. Watts (ed.), Counselling at Work. London: Bedford Square Press.

Hopson, B. and Scally, M. (1980a)
> Lifeskills Teaching: Education for self-empowerment. Maidenhead: McGraw-Hill.

Hopson, B. and Scally, M. (1980b)
> Lifeskills Teaching Programmes No. 1. Leeds: Lifeskills Associates.

Illich, I. (1973)
Tools of Conviviality. London: Calder & Boyars.
Illich, I., Zola, I.K., McKnight, J., Kaplan, J. and Sharken, H. (1977)
The Disabling Professions. London: Marion Boyars.
Ivey, A.E. (1971)
Microcounseling: Innovations in interviewing training. Springfield, Ill.: Thomas.
Jackins, H. (1965)
The Human Side of Human Beings. Seattle: Rational Island Publications.
Kagan, N., Krathwohl, D.R. et al (1967)
Studies in Human Interaction: Interpersonal process recall stimulated by videotape. East Lansing, Mich.: Educational Publication Services, College of Education, Michigan State University.
Katz, M.R. (1969)
Can computers make guidance decisions for students? College Board Review, New York, No. 72.
Kennedy, E. (1977)
On Becoming a Counsellor: A basic guide for non-professional counsellors. Dublin: Gill & Macmillan.
Lewis, J. and Lewis, M. (1977)
Community Counseling: A human services approach. New York: Wiley.
Loughary, J.W. and Ripley, T.M. (1979)
Helping Others Help Themselves. New York: McGraw-Hill.
Maslow, A. (1968)
Toward a Psychology of Being (2nd edn). New York: Van Nostrand.
Mowrer, O.H. (1950)
Learning Theory and Personality Dynamics. New York: Ronald Press.
Newell, P.C. (1977)
How cells communicate. Endeavour, 1, 63-68.
Parloff, M.B., Waskow, I.E. and Wolfe, B. (1978)
Research on therapist variables in relation to process and outcome. In S.L. Garfield and A.E. Bergin (eds), Handbook of Psychotherapy and Behavior Change: An empirical analysis (2nd edn). New York: Wiley.
Pietrofesa, J.L., Hoffman, A., Splete, H.H. and Pinto, D.V. (1978)
Counseling; Theory, research and practice. Chicago: Rand McNally.
Proctor, B. (1979)
The Counselling Shop. London: Deutsch.
Raths, L., Harmin, M. and Simon, S. (1964)
Values and Teaching. Columbus, Ohio: Charles E. Merrill.
Rogers, C.R. (1957)
The necessary and sufficient conditions of therapeutic personality change. Journal of Consulting Psychology, 21, 95-103.

Rogers, C.R. (1958)
  The characteristics of a helping relationship. Personnel
  and Guidance Journal, 37, 6-16.
Rogers, C.R. (1978)
  Carl Rogers on Personal Power. London: Constable.
Scally, M. and Hopson, B. (1979)
  A Model of Helping and Counselling: Indications for
  training. Leeds: Counselling and Careers Development
  Unit, Leeds University.
Sinick, D. (1979)
  Joys of Counseling. Mincie, Indiana: Accelerated
  Development Inc.
Smith, P.B. (1975)
  Controlled studies of the outcome of sensitivity
  training. Psychological Bulletin, 82, 597-622.
Stonier, T. (1979)
  On the Future of Employment. N.U.T. guide to careers
  work. London: National Union of Teachers.
Toffler, A. (1970)
  Future Shock. London: Bodley Head.
Truax, C.B. and Carkhuff, R.R. (1967)
  Toward Effective Counselling and Psychotherapy: Training
  and practice. Chicago: Aldine.
Tyler, L. (1961)
  The Work of the Counselor. New York: Appleton-Century-
  Crofts.
Vaughan, T. (ed.) (1976)
  Concepts of Counselling. London: Bedford Square Press.

Questions

1. Distinguish counselling from other forms of helping.
2. How can counselling and helping be 'demystified'?
3. How large a part do you think counselling does and
   should play in your work?
4. Distinguish between counselling and counselling skills.
5. Who are 'the helpers'?
6. What makes people effective helpers?
7. Compare and contrast two different models of helping.
8. What in your opinion are the legitimate goals of helping
   and why?
9. How useful a concept is 'self-empowerment' in the
   context of helping?
10. What are the advantages and disadvantages of individual
    and group counselling techniques?

Annotated reading

Corey, G. (1977) Theory and Practice of Counseling and
Psychotherapy. Monterey, Ca: Brooks/Cole.
  This contains an excellent review of all the schools of
  counselling described in the chapter. There is an
  accompanying workbook designed for students and tutor
  which gives self-inventories to aid students in
  identifying their own attitudes and beliefs, overviews
  of each major theory of counselling, questions for
  discussion and evaluation, case studies, exercises

designed to sharpen specific counselling skills, out-of-
class projects, group exercises, examples of client
problems, an overview comparision of all models, ethical
issues and problems to consider, and issues basic to the
therapist's personal development.

Corsini, R. (ed.) (1977) Current Psychotherapies (2nd edn).
Itasca, Ill.: Peacock Publications.
An excellent introduction to the main schools of
psychotherapy by leading practitioners who have been
bullied to stick to the same format. Covers
psychoanalysis, Adlerian, client-centred, analytical,
rational-emotive therapy, transactional analysis,
Gestalt, behavioural, reality, encounter, experiential
and eclectic. Contributors include Carl Rogers, Albert
Ellis, William Glasser, Alan Goldstein, Will Schutz and
Rudolf Dreikurs.

Vaughan, T.D. (ed.) (1975) Concepts of Counselling. British
Association for Counselling, London: Bedford Square Press.
A guide to the plethora of definitions of counselling.
Uneven, illuminating, with some useful descriptions of
developments in the UK.

14

Social Behaviour
Michael Argyle

**Introduction: social
behaviour as a skill**

We start by presenting the social skill model of social
behaviour, and an account of sequences of social interaction. This model is very relevant to our later discussion
of social skills and how these can be trained. The chapter
then goes on to discuss the elements of social behaviour,
both verbal and non-verbal, and emphasize the importance and
different functions of non-verbal signals. The receivers of
these signals have to decode them, and do so in terms of
emotions and impressions of personality; we discuss some of
the processes and some of the main errors of person perception. The sender can manipulate the impression he creates
by means of 'self-presentation'. The processes of social
behaviour, and the skills involved, are quite different in
different social situations, and we discuss recent attempts
to analyse these situations in terms of their main features,
such as rules and goals.

We move on to a number of specific social skills.
Research on the processes leading to friendship and love
makes it possible to train and advise people who have difficulty with these relationships. Research on persuasion
shows how people can be trained to be more assertive. And
research on small social groups and leadership of these
groups makes it possible to give an account of the most
successful skills for handling social groups.

Social competence is defined in terms of the successful
attainment of goals, and it can be assessed by a variety of
techniques such as self-rating and observation of role-
played performance. The most successful method of social
skills is role-playing, combined with modelling, coaching,
videotape recorder (VTR) playback, and 'homework'. Results
of follow-up studies with a variety of populations show that
this form of social skills training (SST) is very
successful.

Harré and Secord (1972) have argued persuasively that
much human social behaviour is the result of conscious
planning, often in words, with full regard for the complex
meanings of behaviour and the rules of the situations. This
is an important correction to earlier social psychological
views, which often failed to recognize the complexity of
individual planning and the different meanings which may be
given to stimuli, for example in laboratory experiments.

However, it must be recognized that much social behaviour is not planned in this way: the smaller elements of behaviour and longer automatic sequences are outside conscious awareness, though it is possible to attend, for example, to patterns of gaze, shifts of orientation, or the latent meanings of utterances. The social skills model, in emphasizing the hierarchical structure of social performance, can incorporate both kinds of behaviour.

The social skills model also emphasizes feedback processes. A person driving a car sees at once when it is going in the wrong direction, and takes corrective action with the steering wheel. Social interactors do likewise; if another person is talking too much they interrupt, ask closed questions or no questions, and look less interested in what he has to say. Feedback requires perception, looking at and listening to the other person. Skilled performance requires the ability to take the appropriate corrective action referred to as 'translation' in the model: not everyone knows that open-ended questions make people talk more and closed questions make them talk less. And it depends on a number of two-step sequences of social behaviour whereby certain social acts have reliable effects on another. Let us look at social behaviour as a skilled performance similar to motor skills like driving a car (see figure 1).

Figure 1

The motor skill model (from Argyle, 1969)

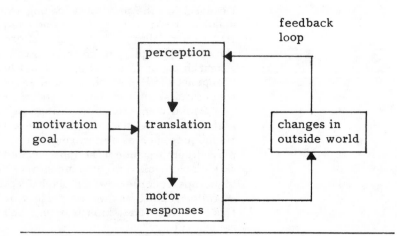

In each case the performer is pursuing certain goals, makes continuous response to feedback, and emits hierarchically-organized motor responses. This model has been heuristically very useful in drawing attention to the importance of feedback, and hence to gaze; it also suggests a number of different ways in which social performances can fail, and suggests the training procedures that may be effective, through analogy with motor skills training (Argyle and Kendon, 1967; Argyle, 1969).

The model emphasizes the motivation, goals and plans of interactors. It is postulated that every interactor is trying to achieve some goal, whether he is aware of it or not. These goals may be, for example, to get another person to like him, to obtain or convey information, to modify the other's emotional state, and so on. Such goals may be linked to more basic motivational systems. Goals have sub-goals; for example, a doctor must diagnose the patient before he can treat him. Patterns of response are directed towards goals and sub-goals, and have a hierarchical structure: large units of behaviour are composed of smaller ones, and at the lowest levels these are habitual and automatic.

The role of reinforcement

This is one of the key processes in social skills sequences. When interactor A does what B wants him to do, B is pleased and sends immediate and spontaneous reinforcements: smile, gaze, approving noises, etc., and modifies A's behaviour, probably by operant conditioning; for example, modifying the content of his utterances. At the same time A is modifying B's behaviour in exactly the same way. These effects appear to be mainly outside the focus of conscious attention, and take place very rapidly. It follows that anyone who gives strong rewards and punishments in the course of interaction will be able to modify the behaviour of others in the desired direction. In addition, the stronger the rewards that A issues, the more strongly other people will be attracted to him.

The role of gaze in social skills

The social skills model suggests that the monitoring of another's reactions is an essential part of social performance. The other's verbal signals are mainly heard, but his non-verbal signals are mainly seen; the exceptions being the non-verbal aspects of speech and touch. It was this implication of the social skills model which directed us towards the study of gaze in social interaction. In dyadic interaction each person looks about 50 per cent of the time, mutual gaze occupies 25 per cent of the time, looking while listening is about twice the level of looking while talking, glances are about three seconds, and mutual glances about one second, with wide variations due to distance, sex combination, and personality (Argyle and Cook, 1976). However, there are several important differences between social behaviour and motor skills.

* Rules: the moves which interactors may make are governed by rules; they must respond properly to what has gone before. Similarly, rules govern the other's responses and can be used to influence his behaviour; for example, questions lead to answers.

* Taking the role of the other: it is important to perceive accurately the reactions of others. It is also
necessary to perceive the perceptions of others; that
is, to take account of their points of view. This
appears to be a cognitive ability which develops with
age (Flavell, 1968), but which may fail to develop
properly. Those who are able to do this have been found
to be more effective at a number of social tasks, and
more altruistic. Meldman (1967) found that psychiatric
patients are more egocentric; that is, talked about
themselves more than controls, and it has been our
experience that socially unskilled patients have great
difficulty in taking the role of the other.
* The independent initiative of the other sequences of
interaction: social situations inevitably contain at
least one other person, who will be pursuing his goals
and using his social skills. How can we analyse the
resulting sequences of behaviour? For a sequence to
constitute an acceptable piece of social behaviour, the
moves must fit together in order. Social psychologists
have not yet discovered all the principles or 'grammar'
underlying these sequences, but some of the principles
are known, and can explain common forms of interaction
failure.

Verbal and non-verbal communication

Verbal communication
There are several different kinds of verbal utterance.

* Egocentric speech: this is directed to the self, is
found in infants and has the effect of directing
behaviour.
* Orders, instructions: these are used to influence the
behaviour of others; they can be gently persuasive or
authoritarian.
* Questions: these are intended to elicit verbal
information; they can be open-ended or closed, personal
or impersonal.
* Information: may be given in response to a question, or
as part of a lecture or during problem-solving
discussion.

(The last three points are the basic classes of utterance.)

* Informal speech: consists of casual chat, jokes, gossip,
and contains little information, but helps to establish
and sustain social relationships.
* Expression of emotions and interpersonal attitudes: this
is a special kind of information; however, this
information is usually conveyed, and is conveyed more
effectively, non-verbally.
* Performative utterances: these include 'illocutions'
where saying the utterance performs something (voting,
judging, naming, etc.), and 'perlocutions', where a goal

is intended but may not be achieved (persuading, intimidating, etc.).
* Social routines: these include standard sequences like thanking, apologizing, greeting, etc.
* Latent messages: are where the more important meaning is made subordinate ('As I was saying to the Prime Minister ...').

There are many category schemes for reducing utterances to a limited number of classes of social acts. One of the best known is that of Bales (1950), who introduced the 12 classes shown in figure 2.

Non-verbal signals accompanying speech

Non-verbal signals play an important part in speech and conversation. They have three main roles:

* completing and elaborating on verbal utterances: utterances are accompanied by vocal emphasis, gestures and facial expressions, which add to the meaning and indicate whether it is a question, intended to be serious or funny, and so on;
* managing synchronizing: this is achieved by head-nods, gaze-shifts, and other signals. For example, to keep the floor a speaker does not look up at the end of an utterance, keeps a hand in mid-gesture, and increases the volume of his speech if the other interrupts;
* sending feedback signals: listeners keep up a continuous, and mainly unwitting, commentary on the speaker's utterances, showing by mouth and eyebrow positions whether they agree, understand, are surprised, and so on (Argyle, 1975).

Other functions of non-verbal communication (NVC)

NVC consists of facial expression, tone of voice, gaze, gestures, postures, physical proximity and appearance. We have already described how NVC is linked with speech; it also functions in several other ways, especially in the communication of emotions and attitudes to other people.

A sender is in a certain state, or possesses some information; this is encoded into a message which is then decoded by a receiver.

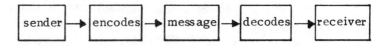

Encoding research is done by putting subjects into some state and studying the NV messages which are emitted. For example, Mehrabian (1972) in a role-playing experiment, asked subjects to address a hat-stand, imagining it to be a person. Male subjects who liked the hat-stand looked at it more, did not have hands on hips and stood closer.

Figure 2

The Bales categories (from Bales, 1950)

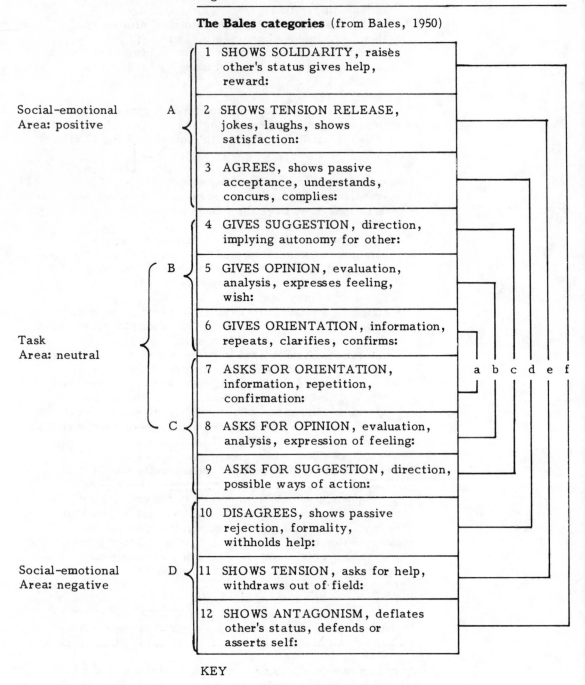

Social-emotional Area: positive — A

1 SHOWS SOLIDARITY, raises other's status gives help, reward:

2 SHOWS TENSION RELEASE, jokes, laughs, shows satisfaction:

3 AGREES, shows passive acceptance, understands, concurs, complies:

Task Area: neutral — B

4 GIVES SUGGESTION, direction, implying autonomy for other:

5 GIVES OPINION, evaluation, analysis, expresses feeling, wish:

6 GIVES ORIENTATION, information, repeats, clarifies, confirms:

C

7 ASKS FOR ORIENTATION, information, repetition, confirmation:

8 ASKS FOR OPINION, evaluation, analysis, expression of feeling:

9 ASKS FOR SUGGESTION, direction, possible ways of action:

Social-emotional Area: negative — D

10 DISAGREES, shows passive rejection, formality, withholds help:

11 SHOWS TENSION, asks for help, withdraws out of field:

12 SHOWS ANTAGONISM, deflates other's status, defends or asserts self:

a b c d e f

KEY

a problems of communication
b problems of evaluation
c problems of control
d problems of decision
e problems of tension reduction
f problems of reintegration

A positive reactions
B attempted answers
C questions
D negative reactions

Non-verbal signals are often 'unconscious': that is, they are outside the focus of attention. A few signals are unconsciously sent and received, like dilated pupils, signifying sexual attraction, but there are a number of other possibilities as shown in table 1.

Table 1

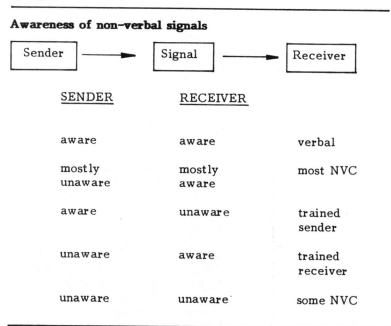

Awareness of non-verbal signals

SENDER	RECEIVER	
aware	aware	verbal
mostly unaware	mostly aware	most NVC
aware	unaware	trained sender
unaware	aware	trained receiver
unaware	unaware	some NVC

Strictly speaking pupil dilation is not communication at all, but only a physiological response. 'Communication' is usually taken to imply some intention to affect another; one criterion is that it makes a difference whether the other person is present and in a position to receive the signal; another is that the signal is repeated, varied or amplified if it has no effect. These criteria are independent of conscious intention to communicate, which is often absent.

* Interpersonal attitudes: interactors indicate how much they like or dislike one another, and whether they think they are more or less important, mainly non-verbally. We have compared verbal and non-verbal signals and found that non-verbal cues like facial expression and tone of voice have far more impact than verbal ones (Argyle et al, 1970).
* Emotional states: anger, depression, anxiety, joy, surprise, fear and disgust/contempt, are also communicated more clearly by non-verbal signals, such as facial expression, tone of voice, posture, gestures and gaze. Interactors may try to conceal their true emotions, but these are often revealed by 'leakage' via cues which are difficult to control.

Person perception

In order to respond effectively to the behaviour of others it is necessary to perceive them correctly. The social skills model emphasizes the importance of perception and feedback; to drive a car one must watch the traffic outside and the instruments inside. Such perception involves selecting certain cues, and being able to interpret them correctly. There is evidence of poor person perception in mental patients and other socially unskilled individuals, while professional social skills performers need to be sensitive to special aspects of other people and their behaviour. For selection interviewers and clinical psychologists the appraisal of others is a central part of the job.

We form impressions of other people all the time, mainly in order to predict their future behaviour, and so that we can deal with them effectively. We categorize others in terms of our favourite cognitive constructs, of which the most widely used are:

* extraversion, sociability;
* agreeableness, likeability;
* emotional stability;
* intelligence;
* assertiveness.

There are, however, wide individual differences in the constructs used, and 'complex' people use a larger number of such dimensions. We have found that the constructs used vary greatly with the situation: for example, work-related constructs are not used in purely social situations. We also found that the constructs used vary with the target group, such as children versus psychologists (Argyle et al, in press).

A number of widespread errors are made in forming impressions of others which should be particularly avoided by those whose job it is to assess people:

* assuming that a person's behaviour is mainly a product of his personality, whereas it may be more a function of the situation he is in: at a noisy party, in church, etc.;
* assuming that his behaviour is due to him rather than his role; for example, as a hospital nurse, as a patient or as a visitor;
* attaching too much importance to physical cues, like beards, clothes, and physical attractiveness;
* being affected by stereotypes about the characteristics of members of certain races, social classes, etc.

During social interaction it is also necessary to perceive the emotional states of others: for example, to tell if they are depressed or angry. There are wide individual differences in the ability to judge emotions correctly (Davitz, 1964). As we have seen, emotions are mainly

conveyed by non-verbal s
sion and tone of voice. T
also based on perception
is in. Lalljee at Oxford
sarily decoded as happy,
regarded as authentic.

Similar consideratio
interpersonal attitudes,
is also mainly based on
mity, gaze and facial e
context to decode thes
be interpreted as a thr
invitation. There are s
pressures towards cogn....
thinks that B likes him more than B on aver_g_
does: if A likes both B and C, he assumes that they both
like each other more than, on average, they do.

It is necessary to perceive the on-going flow of interaction in order to know what is happening and to participate
in it effectively. People seem to agree on the main episodes
and sub-episodes of an encounter, but they may produce
rather different accounts of why those present behaved as
they did. One source of variation, and indeed error, is that
people attribute the causes of others' behaviour to their
personality ('He fell over because he is clumsy'), but their
own behaviour to the situation ('I fell over because it was
slippery'), whereas both factors operate in each case (Jones
and Nisbett, 1972). Interpretations also depend on the ideas
and knowledge an individual possesses: just as an expert on
cars could understand better why a car was behaving in a
peculiar way, so also can an expert on social behaviour
understand why patterns of social behaviour occur.

ituations, their ries and other eatures

We know that people behave very differently in different
situations; in order to predict behaviour, or to advise
people on social skills in specific situations, it is
necessary to analyse the situations in question. This can
be done in terms of a number of fundamental features.

Goals

In all situations there are certain goals which are commonly
obtainable. It is often fairly obvious what these are, but
socially inadequate people may simply not know what parties
are for, for example, or may think that the purpose of a
selection interview is vocational guidance.

We have studied the main goals in a number of common
situations, by asking samples of people to rate the
importance of various goals, and then carrying out factor
analysis. The main goals are usually:

* social acceptance, etc.;
* food, drink and other bodily needs;
* task goals specific to the situation.

We have also studied the relations between goals, within and between persons, in terms of conflict and instrumentality. This makes it possible to study the 'goal structure' of situations. An example is given in figure 3, showing that the only conflict between nurses and patients is between the nurses' concern for the bodily well-being of the patients and of themselves (Argyle Furnham and Graham, in press).

Rules

All situations have rules about what may or may not be done in them. Socially inexperienced people are often ignorant or mistaken about the rules. It would obviously be impossible to play a game without knowing the rules and the same applies to social situations.

We have studied the rules of a number of everyday situations. There appear to be several universal rules; to be polite, be friendly, not embarrass people. There are also rules which are specific to situations, or groups of situations, and these can be interpreted as functional, since they enable situational goals to be met. For example, when seeing the doctor one should be clean and tell the truth; when going to a party one should dress smartly and keep to cheerful topics of conversation.

Special skills

Many social situations require special social skills, as in the case of various kinds of public speaking and interviewing, but also such everyday situations as dates and parties. A person with little experience of a particular situation may find that he lacks the special skills needed for it (cf. Argyle et al, in press).

Figure 3

The goal structure for nurse and patient

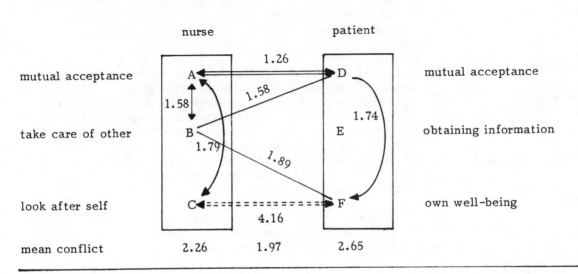

Repertoire of elements

Every situation defines certain moves as relevant. For example, at a seminar it is relevant to show slides, make long speeches, draw on the blackboard, etc. If moves appropriate to a cricket match or a Scottish ball were made, they would be ignored or regarded as totally bizarre. We have found 65-90 main elements used in several situations, like going to the doctor. We have also found that the semiotic structure varies between situations: we found that questions about work and about private life were sharply contrasted in an office situation, but not on a date.

Roles

Every situation has a limited number of roles: for example, a classroom has the roles of teacher, pupil, janitor, and school inspector. These roles carry different degrees of power, and the occupant has goals peculiar to that role.

Cognitive structure

We found that the members of a research group classified each other in terms of the concepts extraverted and enjoyable companion for social occasions, but in terms of dominant, creative and supportive for seminars. There are also concepts related to the task, such as 'amendment', 'straw vote' and 'nem con', for committee meetings.

Environmental setting and pieces

Most situations involve special environmental settings and props. Cricket needs bat, ball, stumps, etc.; a seminar requires a blackboard, slide projector and lecture notes.

How do persons fit into situations, conceived in this way? To begin with, there are certain pervasive aspects of persons, corresponding to the 20 per cent or so of person variance found in P x S (personality and situation) studies. This consists of scores on general dimensions like intelligence, extraversion, neuroticism and so on. In addition, persons have dispositions to behave in certain ways in classes of situations; this corresponds to the 50 per cent or so of the P x S variance in relation to dimensions of situations like formal-informal, and friendly-hostile. Third, there are more specific reactions to particular situations; for example, behaviour in social psychology seminars depends partly on knowledge of social psychology, and attitudes to different schools of thought in it. Taken together these three factors may predict performance in, and also avoidance of, certain situations - because of lack of skill, anxiety, etc. - and this will be the main expectation in such cases.

Friendship

This is one of the most important social relationships: failure in it is a source of great distress, and so it is one of the main areas of social skills training. The conditions under which people come to like one another have been the object of extensive research, and are now well understood.

There are several stages of friendship: (i) coming into contact with the other, through proximity at work or elsewhere; (ii) increasing attachment as a result of reinforcement and discovery of similarity; (iii) increasing self-disclosure and commitment; and sometimes (iv) dissolution of the relationship. Friendship is the dominant relationship for adolescents and the unmarried; friends engage in characteristic activities, such as talking, eating, drinking, joint leisure, but not, usually, working.

Frequency of interaction

The more two people meet, the more polarized their attitudes to one another become, but usually they like one another more. Frequent interaction can come about from living in adjacent rooms or houses, working in the same office, belonging to the same club, and so on. So interaction leads to liking, and liking leads to more interaction. Only certain kinds of interaction lead to liking. In particular, people should be of similar status. Belonging to a co-operative group, especially under crisis conditions, is particularly effective, as Sherif's 'Robbers' cave' experiment (Sherif et al, 1961) and research on inter-racial attitudes have shown.

Reinforcement

The next general principle governing liking is the extent to which one person satisfies the needs of another. This was shown in a study by Jennings of 400 girls in a reformatory (1950). She found that the popular girls helped and protected others, encouraged, cheered them up, made them feel accepted and wanted, controlled their own moods so as not to inflict anxiety or depression on others, were able to establish rapport quickly, won the confidence of a wide variety of other personalities, and were concerned with the feelings and needs of others. The unpopular girls on the other hand were dominating, aggressive, boastful, demanded attention, and tried to get others to do things for them. This pattern has been generally interpreted in terms of the popular girls providing rewards and minimizing costs, while the unpopular girls tried to get rewards for themselves, and incurred costs for others. It is not necessary for the other person to be the actual source of rewards: Lott and Lott (1960) found that children who were given model cars by the experimenter liked the other children in the experiment more, and several studies have shown that people are liked more in a pleasant environmental setting.

Being liked is a powerful reward, so if A likes B, B will usually like A. This is particularly important for those who have a great need to be liked, such as individuals with low self-esteem. It is signalled, as we showed above, primarily by non-verbal signals.

Similarity

People like others who are similar to themselves, in certain respects. They like those with similar attitudes, beliefs and values, who have a similar regional and social class background, who have similar jobs or leisure interests, but they need not have similar personalities. Again there is a cyclical process, since similarity leads to liking and liking leads to similarity, but effects of similarity on liking have been shown experimentally.

Physical attractiveness

Physical attractiveness (p.a.) is an important source of both same-sex and opposite sex liking, especially in the early stages. Walster et al (1966) arranged a 'computer dance' at which couples were paired at random: the best prediction of how much each person liked their partner was the latter's p.a. as rated by the experimenter. Part of the explanation lies in the 'p.a. stereotype'. Dion et al (1972) found that attractive people were believed to have desirable characteristics of many other kinds. However, people do not seek out the most attractive friends and mates, but compromise by seeking those similar to themselves in attractiveness.

Self-disclosure

This is a signal for intimacy, like bodily contact, because it indicates trust in the other. Self-disclosure can be measured on a scale (1-5) with items like:

> What are your favourite forms of erotic play and sexual lovemaking? (scale value 2.56)

> What are the circumstances under which you become depressed and when your feelings are hurt? (3.51)

> What are your hobbies, how do you best like to spend your spare time? (4.98) (Jourard, 1971).

As people get to know each other better, self-disclosure slowly increases, and is reciprocated, up to a limit.

Commitment

This is a state of mind, an intention to stay in a relationship, and abandon others. This involves a degree of dependence on the other person and trusting them not to leave the relationship. The least committed has the more power.

Social skills training

The most common complaint of those who seek social skills training is difficulty in making friends. Some of them say they have never had a friend in their lives. What advice can we offer, on the basis of research on friendship?

* As we showed earlier, social relations are negotiated mainly by non-verbal signals. Clients for social skills training who cannot make friends are usually found to be very inexpressive, in face and voice.
* Rewardingness is most important. The same clients usually appear to be very unrewarding, and are not really interested in other people.
* Frequent interaction with those of similar interests and attitudes can be found in clubs for professional or leisure activities, in political and religious groups, and so on.
* Physical attractiveness is easier to change than is social behaviour.
* Certain social skills may need to be acquired, such as inviting others to suitable social events, and engaging in self-disclosure at the right speed.

The meaning and assessment of social competence

By social competence we mean the ability, the possession of the necessary skills, to produce the desired effects on other people in social situations. These desired effects may be to persuade the others to buy, to learn, to recover from neurosis, to like or admire the actor, and so on. These results are not necessarily in the public interest: skills may be used for social or antisocial purposes. And there is no evidence that social competence is a general factor: a person may be better at one task than another, for example, parties or committees. Social skills training for students and other more or less normal populations has been directed to the skills of dating, making friends and being assertive. SST for mental patients has been aimed at correcting failures of social competence, and also at relieving subjective distress, such as social anxiety.

To find out who needs training, and in what areas, a detailed descriptive assessment is needed. We want to know, for example, which situations a trainee finds difficult: formal situations, conflicts, meeting strangers, etc., and which situations he is inadequate in, even though he does not report them as difficult. And we want to find out what he is doing wrong: failure to produce the right non-verbal signals, low rewardingness, lack of certain social skills, etc.

Social competence is easier to define and agree upon in the case of professional social skills: an effective therapist cures more patients, an effective teacher teaches better, an effective saleswoman sells more. When we look more closely, it is not quite so simple: examination marks may be one index of a teacher's effectiveness, but usually more is meant than just this. A saleswoman should not simply sell a lot of goods, she should make the customers feel they would like to go to that shop again. So a combination of different skills is required and an overall assessment of effectiveness may involve the combination of a number of different measures or ratings. The range of competence is quite large: the best salesmen and saleswomen regularly sell four times as much as some others behind the same counter; some supervisors of working groups produce twice as much output as others, or have 20-25 per cent of the labour turnover and absenteeism rates (Argyle, 1972).

For everyday social skills it is more difficult to give the criteria of success; lack of competence is easier to spot: failure to make friends, or opposite sex friends, quarrelling and failing to sustain co-operative relationships, finding a number of situations difficult or a source of anxiety, and so on.

Methods of social skills training

Role-playing with coaching

This is now the most widely-used method of SST. There are four stages:

* instruction;
* role-playing with other trainees or other role partners for 5-8 minutes;
* feedback and coaching, in the form of oral comments from the trainer;
* repeated role-playing.

A typical laboratory set-up is shown in figure 4. This also shows the use of an ear-microphone, for instruction while role-playing is taking place. In the case of patients, mere practice does no good: there must be coaching as well.

For an individual or group of patients or other trainees a series of topics, skills or situations is chosen, and introduced by means of short scenarios. Role partners are used, who can be briefed to present carefully graded degrees of difficulty.

It is usual for trainers to be generally encouraging, and also rewarding for specific aspects of behaviour, though there is little experimental evidence for the value of such reinforcement. It is common to combine role-playing with modelling and video playback, both of which are discussed below. Follow-up studies have found that role-playing combined with coaching is successful with many kinds of mental patients, and that it is one of the most successful forms of SST for these groups.

Role-playing usually starts with 'modelling', in which a film is shown or a demonstration given of how to perform the skill being taught. The feedback session usually includes videotape playback and most studies have found that this is advantageous (Bailey and Sowder, 1970). While it often makes trainees self-conscious at first, this wears off after the second session. Skills acquired in the laboratory or class must be transferred to the outside world. This is usually achieved by 'homework': trainees are encouraged to try out the new skills several times before the next session. Most trainers take people in groups which provides a source of role partners, but patients may need individual sessions as well for individual problems.

Figure 4

A social skills training laboratory

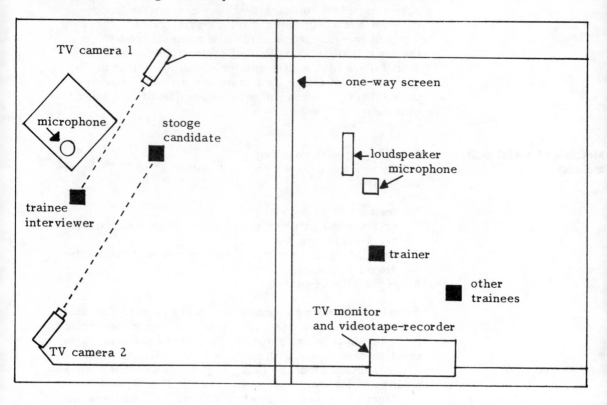

Other methods of training

TRAINING ON THE JOB: this is a widely used traditional method. Some people improve through experience but others do not, and some learn the wrong things. The situation can be improved if there is a trainer who regularly sees the trainee in action, and is able to hold feedback sessions at which errors are pointed out and better skills suggested. In practice this method does not appear to work very well, for example with trainee teachers (see Argyle, 1969).

GROUP METHODS: these, especially T-groups (T standing for training), are intended to enhance sensitivity and social skills. Follow-up studies have consistently found that 30-40 per cent of trainees are improved by group methods, but up to 10 per cent are worse, sometimes needing psychological assistance (e.g. Lieberman et al, 1973). It has been argued that group methods are useful for those who are resistant to being trained.

EDUCATIONAL METHODS: these, such as lectures and films, can increase knowledge, but to master social skills it is necessary to try them out, as is the case with motor skills. Educational methods can be a useful supplement to role-playing methods.

Areas of application of SST

NEUROTIC PATIENTS: role-playing and the more specialized methods described above have been found to be slightly more effective than psychotherapy, desensitization, or other alternative treatments, but not much (Trower et al, 1978). Only one study so far has found really substantial differences; Maxwell (1976), in a study of adults reporting social difficulties and seeking treatment for them, in New Zealand, insisted on homework between training sessions. However, SST does produce more improvement in social skills and reduction of social anxiety. A few patients can be cured by SST alone, but most have other problems as well, and may require other forms of treatment in addition.

PSYCHOTIC PATIENTS: these have been treated in the USA by assertiveness training and other forms of role-playing. Follow-up studies have shown greater improvement in social behaviour than from alternative treatments. The most striking results have been obtained with intensive clinical studies of one to four patients, using a 'multiple baseline' design: one symptom is worked on at a time over a total of 20-30 sessions. It is not clear from these follow-up studies to what extent the general condition of patients has been improved, or how well they have been able to function outside the hospital (Hersen and Bellack, 1976). It has been argued by one practitioner that SST is more suitable than psychotherapy for working-class patients in view of their poor verbal skills (Goldstein, 1973).

Other therapeutic uses of SST

ALCOHOLICS have been given SST to improve their assertiveness, for example in refusing drinks, and to enable them to deal better with situations which they find stressful and make them drink. Similar treatment has been given to drug addicts. In both cases treatment has been fairly successful, though the effects have not always been long-lasting; SST is often included in more comprehensive packages.

DELINQUENTS AND PRISONERS have often been given SST with some success, especially in the case of aggressive and sex offenders. SST can also increase their degree of internal control.

TEACHERS, MANAGERS, DOCTORS, etc.: SST is increasingly being included in the training of those whose work involves dealing with people. The most extensive application so far has been in the training of teachers by 'micro-teaching'. The pupil teacher is instructed in one of the component skills of teaching, such as the use of different kinds of question, explanation or the use of examples; he then teaches 5-6 children for 10-15 minutes, followed by a feedback session and 're-teaching'. Follow-up studies show that this is far more effective than a similar amount of teaching practice, and it is much more effective in eradicating bad habits (Brown, 1975). In addition to role-playing, more elaborate forms of simulation are used, for example to train people for administrative positions.

Training on the job is a valuable addition or alternative, provided that the trainer really does his job.

NORMAL ADULTS: students have received a certain amount of SST, especially in North American universities, and follow-up studies have shown that they can be successfully trained in assertiveness (Rich and Schroeder, 1976), dating behaviour (Curran, 1977), and to reduce anxiety at performing in public (Paul, 1966). Although many normal adults apart from students have social behaviour difficulties, very little training is available unless they seek psychiatric help. It would be very desirable for SST to be more widely available, for example in community centres.

SCHOOLCHILDREN: a number of attempts have been made to introduce SST into schools, though there are no follow-up studies on its effectiveness. However, there have been a number of successful follow-up studies of training schemes for children who are withdrawn and unpopular or aggressive, using the usual role-playing methods (Rinn and Markle, 1979).

Conclusion

In this chapter we have tried to give an account of those aspects of social psychology which are most relevant to the work of teachers, social workers and others, both in understanding the behaviour of their clients and also in helping them with their own performance. We have used various models of social behaviour such as the social skills model and the model of social behaviour as a game. Some of the phenomena described cannot be fully accounted for in terms of these models: for example, the design of sequences of interaction. A number of practical implications are described; in particular, discussion of the skills which have been demonstrated to be the most effective in a number of situations, and the methods of social skills training which have been found to have most impact. It should be emphasized that much of this research is quite new and it is expected that a great deal more will be found out on these topics in the years to come.

References

Argyle, M. (1969)
Social Interaction. London: Methuen.
Argyle, M. (1972)
The Social Psychology of Work. London: Allen Lane and Penguin Books.
Argyle, M. (1975)
Bodily Communication. London: Methuen.
Argyle, M. and Cook, M. (1976)
Gaze and Mutual Gaze. London: Cambridge University Press.
Argyle, M., Furnham, A. and Graham, J.A. (in press)
Social situations. London: Cambridge University Press.
Argyle, M. and Kendon, A. (1967)
The experimental analysis of social performance.

Advances in Experimental Social Psychology, 3, 55-98.

Argyle, M., Salter V., Nicholson, H., Williams, M. and Burgess, P. (1970)
The communication of inferior and superior attitudes by verbal and non-verbal signals. British Journal of Social and Clinical Psychology, 9, 221-231.

Bailey, K.G. and Sowder, W.T. (1970)
Audiotape and videotape self-confrontation in psychotherapy. Psychological Bulletin, 74, 127-137.

Bales, R.F. (1950)
Interaction Process Analysis. Cambridge, Mass.: Addison-Wesley.

Brown, G.A. (1975)
Microteaching. London: Methuen.

Curran, J.P. (1977)
Skills training as an approach to the treatment of heterosexual-social anxiety. Psychological Bulletin, 84, 140-157.

Davitz, J.R. (1964)
The Communication of Emotional Meaning. New York: McGraw-Hill.

Dion, K., Berscheid, E. and Walster, E. (1972)
What is beautiful is good. Journal of Personality and Social Psychology, 24, 285-290.

Flavell, J.H. (1968)
The Development of Role-taking and Communication Skills in Children. New York: Wiley.

Goldstein, A.J. (1973)
Structured Learning Therapy: Toward a psychotherapy for the poor. New York: Academic Press.

Harré, R. and Secord, P. (1972)
The Explanation of Social Behaviour. Oxford: Blackwell.

Hersen, M. and Bellack, A.S. (1976)
Social skills training for chronic psychiatric patients: rationale, research findings, and future directions. Comprehensive Psychiatry, 17, 559-580.

Jennings, H.H. (1950)
Leadership and Isolation. New York: Longmans Green.

Jones, E.E. and Nisbett, R.E. (1972)
The actor and the observer: divergent perceptions of the causes of behavior. In E.E. Jones et al (eds), Attribution: Perceiving the causes of behavior. Morristown, NJ: General Learning Press.

Jourard, S.M. (1971)
Self Disclosure. New York: Wiley Interscience.

Lieberman, M.A., Yalom, I.D. and Miles, M.R. (1973)
Encounter Groups: First facts. New York: Basic Books.

Lott, A.J. and Lott, B.E. (1960)
The formation of positive attitudes towards group members. Journal of Abnormal and Social Psychology, 61, 297-300.

Maxwell, G.M. (1976)
An evolution of social skills training. (Unpublished, University of Otago, Dunedin, New Zealand.)

Mehrabian, A. (1972)
Nonverbal Communication. New York: Aldine-Atherton.
Meldman, M.J. (1967)
Verbal behavior analysis of self-hyperattentionism.
Diseases of the Nervous System, 28, 469–473.
Paul, G.L. (1966)
Insight v. Desensitization in Psychotherapy. Stanford,
Ca: Stanford University Press.
Rich, A.R. and Schroeder, H.E. (1976)
Research issues in assertiveness training. Psychological
Bulletin, 83, 1081-1096.
Rinn, R.C. and Markle, A. (1979)
Modification of social skill deficits in children. In
A.S. Bellack and M. Hersen (eds), Research and Practice
in Social Skills Training. New York: Plenum.
**Sherif, M., Harvey, O.J., White, B.J., Hood, W.R. and
Sherif, C.** (1961)
Intergroup Conflict and Cooperation: The Robbers' Cave
experiment. Norman, Oklahoma: The University of Oklahoma
Book Exchange.
Trower, P., Bryant, B. and Argyle, M. (1978)
Social Skills and Mental Health. London: Methuen.
Walster, E., Aronson, V., Abrahams, D. and Rottmann, L.
(1966)
Importance of physical attractiveness in dating
behavior. Journal of Personality and Social Psychology,
5, 508-516.

Questions

1. Is it useful to look at social behaviour as a kind of skill?
2. What do bad conversationalists do wrong?
3. What information is conveyed by non-verbal communication?
4. In what ways do non-verbal signals supplement verbal ones?
5. How is the perception of other people different from the perception of other physical objects?
6. What information about a social situation would a newcomer to it need to know?
7. Do we like other people primarily because they are rewarding?
8. Why do some people have difficulty in making friends?
9. Can social competence be measured?
10. How can the effectiveness of social skills training be assessed?
11. Is social skills training successful with mental patients?
12. If someone has inadequate social behaviour, what else may he require in addition to SST?
13. What criticisms have been made of experiments in social psychology? What other methods are available?
14. Does social behaviour take the same form in other cultures?

15. Are there fundamental differences between social behaviour in families, work-groups and groups of friends?

Annotated reading

Argyle, M. (1978) The Psychology of Interpersonal Behaviour (3rd edn). Harmondsworth: Penguin.
> Covers the field of the chapter, and related topics at Penguin level.

Argyle, M. and Trower, P. (1979). Person to Person. London: Harper & Row.
> A more popular account of the area covered by the chapter, with numerous coloured illustrations.

Argyle, M. (1975). Bodily Communication. London: Methuen.
> Covers the field of non-verbal communication in more detail, with some illustrations.

Berscheid, E. and Walster, E.H. (1978). Interpersonal Attraction (2nd edn). Reading, Mass.: Addison-Wesley.
> A very readable account of research in this area.

Bower, S.A. and Bower, G.H. (1976). Asserting Yourself. Reading, Mass.: Addison-Wesley.
> An interesting and practical book about assertiveness, with examples and exercises.

Cook, M. (1979). Perceiving Others. London: Methuen.
> A clear account of basic processes in person perception.

Goffman, E. (1956). The Presentation of Self in Everyday Life. Edinburgh: Edinburgh University Press.
> A famous and highly entertaining account of self-presentation.

Trower, P., Bryant, B. and Argyle, M. (1978). Social Skills and Mental Health. London: Methuen.
> An account of social skills training with neurotics, with full details of procedures.

15

Organizational Behaviour
R. Payne

Organizational behaviour is concerned with refining our
knowledge about the behaviour of individuals and groups in
organizations and their role in the growth, development and
decline of organizations. These various outcomes are also
determined by the financial, political and technological
environment in which the organization functions, so
researchers in 'organizational behaviour' also study these
organization-environment relations and their impact on the
behaviour of individuals and groups. It is a multi-
disciplinary enterprise involving economics, politics,
engineering, management science, systems theory, industrial
relations, sociology and psychology.

**What are organizations
like?**

As with men an organization is:

> Like all other organizations
> Like some other organizations
> Like no other organizations.

In your professional work roles you will encounter a unique
organization, like no other organization. In this chapter we
deal with the ways in which organizations are the same as
each other and the ways in which groups of organizations are
similar to each other, but different from other types of
organizations. Apart from its intrinsic interest such information should enable you to appreciate the ways in which
your own organization is unique, and also help you understand something about why it is the way it is.
   We are concerned with work organizations so part of our
definition must be that an organization exists in order to
get work done. They differ in the way they achieve this and
two of the major reasons for the differences are (i) the way
the organization divides its work into different tasks and
(ii) how it co-ordinates those tasks. Most organizations
contain several or many people but according to the present
definition an organization could consist of only one person. Two different silversmiths may divide the different
parts of their work in different ways and co-ordinate the
tasks differently. One might choose to design and make one
complete article at a time. Another might make bowls one

week, handles the next week, assemble them the next week
and then polish and finish them.

They represent two different organizational structures.
Similarly, seven people may work together and agree that
each is capable of doing all the tasks that are required to
get the work done and the co-ordination of these tasks will
be left to the whim of the individuals on a day-to-day
basis. Another seven people might have six people each
doing different tasks with one person left to co-ordinate
the work they do. One thing that is well proven is that once
the work of the organization requires more than just a
handful of people there is a strong preference for dividing
work into different tasks and giving some people (managers)
responsibility for supervising and co-ordinating them.

Henry Mintzberg (1979) describes five main ways in which
organizations achieve co-ordination amongst people doing
different tasks. They are:

*   MUTUAL ADJUSTMENT which relies on informal, day-to-
    day, communication and agreements. Small companies of
    professionals operate in this way, such as architects,
    consulting engineers or small builders;
*   DIRECT SUPERVISION where one person takes the
    responsibility for ensuring that other people satis-
    factorily complete the tasks they have been allocated.
    The typical factory with its hierarchy of charge hands,
    supervisors and managers exemplifies this type of co-
    ordination;
*   STANDARDIZATION OF WORK PROCESSES refers to the
    situation where work has been carefully designed from
    the outset so that the system or technology determines
    what work gets done. As they say in the car industry,
    'The track is the boss'. That is, the operator's work is
    so organized that he can only screw nuts on wheels, or
    only place the front seat in the car, or only spray the
    right side, etc.;
*   STANDARDIZATION OF WORK OUTPUTS achieves co-
    ordination by specifying the nature and quality of the
    completed task. The salesman must take X orders, the
    craftsman make so many articles. How they do it is not
    specified, but what they must achieve is;
*   STANDARDIZATION OF SKILLS is what has produced
    professions. Doctors, lawyers, teachers and engineers
    are replaceable parts. In theory anyone with the correct
    training can be substituted for any other without
    creating major difficulties of co-ordination. This
    substitutability is captured in the colloquialism, 'He's
    a real pro!'

Mintzberg proposes that the major functional parts of more
complex organizations can be divided into five broad categories. At the top of the organization there are people
whose main role is to determine the goals and policies of
the company. These occupy the 'strategic apex'. Below them

are the managers and supervisors who have the responsibility of ensuring that policies and procedures are followed: 'the middle line'. They manage the people who work most directly on the outputs or services of the organization and these Mintzberg describes as the 'operating core'. To the right and left of the middle line, and subordinate to the strategic apex, there are people supporting the main workflow of the organization. There are those in the 'technostructure' whose job is to assist the middle line and the operating core by analysing problems and providing solutions and systems for monitoring and implementing them. They include professional workers such as work study analysts, planning and systems analysts, accountants and personnel analysts. The latter assist this analysing and control process by standardizing skills and rewards. The 'support staff' are not directly connected to the main workflow of the organization but they provide services enabling the rest of the organization to function. They include payroll staff, mailroom, cafeteria, reception, legal advice and research and development. In large organizations any one of these departments may be large enough to have the same five-fold structure so that one gets organizations within organizations.

This very general model is most easily recognized in production organizations but it can also describe the structure of schools, universities or hospitals. In a hospital, however, professionals are the operating core: the doctors, nurses, physiotherapists, occupational therapists and radiologists who provide the treatment and care. Other professionals, such as planners and trainers, are in the technostructure and basic research scientists or laboratory staff are in the support staff. Thus professionals serve different functions within the same organization. Figure 1 presents a conventional tree diagram of a secondary school structure with Mintzberg's concepts overlaid. Note the small technostructure which is provided mainly by the local authority and the inspectorate. They are, strictly speaking, outside the school and this is indicated by a dotted line.

Building on these two sets of concepts and reviewing a large body of literature Mintzberg concludes there are five basic types of organizations. They are theoretical abstractions but some organizations approximate to the pure types and many larger organizations are hybrids of the types or contain examples of more than one pure type within them. Mintzberg continues his fascination with the number five by offering a pentagon model of the pure types. A simplified version appears in figure 2.

The different forms of co-ordination pull the organization towards different structures. The strategic apex pulls the organization structure upwards to centralized decision making and direct supervision. The name for this type is 'simple structure' and some of the organizations that frequently take this form are newer, smaller, autocratic organizations. The technostructure's function is to

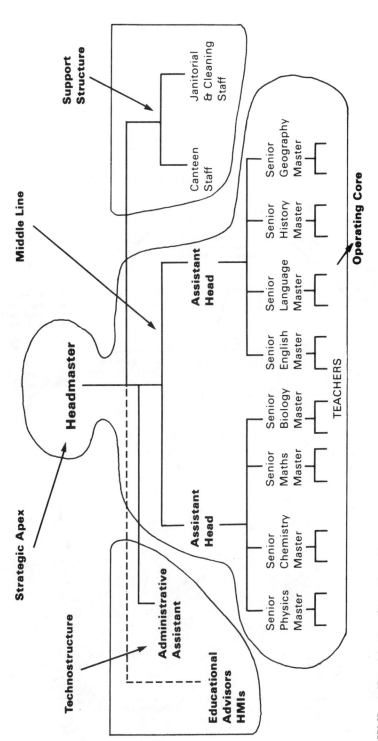

HMIs = Her Majesty's Inspectorates

Figure 1

A tree diagram of a school with Mintzberg's elements of structure superimposed

Figure 2

Mintzberg's Pentagon

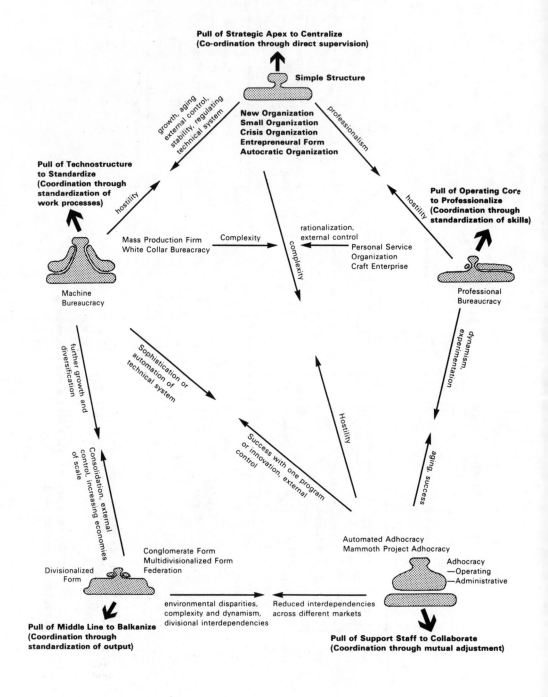

standardize and control the work processes so it pulls in
that direction. Mintzberg mixes two metaphors to describe
the resulting structure as a 'machine bureaucracy'. The
bureaucratic element in the metaphor conveys the written
procedures and documents designed to prescribe and control
the system, and the machine element conveys the rationality,
predictability and reliability of the design that has gone
into it. A car or television assembly line plant are good
examples.

The third pull is that exercised by professionals. They
wish to exercise the skills their training has provided and
argue the case for the quality of what they do within the
discretion of their professionalism. This striving for
autonomy is reflected in the small technostructure that
these 'professional bureaucracies' have (see figure 1 for
the school example). Note they are still bureaucratic.
Despite their professionalism, organizational size leads to
greater complexity which requires records to be kept,
minutes taken, standard procedures followed, and professional standards maintained. Hospitals, universities and
craft organizations tend towards this form because the
services they supply need people with complex skills and
professional training. Since they employ so many professionals it is not surprising that their needs and values
influence the way the organization functions.

The fourth group to bid for influence in the design of
the organization is the middle management. They too wish to
be regarded as professionals and have the responsibility for
their production/workflow units. They achieve this autonomy
only by agreeing to conform to set standards in the production of the output or service: that is, standardization of
outputs. The strategic apex co-ordinates the different units
and supplies financial and technical resources, but each
unit acquires reasonable autonomy to create the 'divisionalized structure'. This is common in conglomerates such as
Imperial Chemical Industries which has separate divisions
dealing with organic chemicals, agriculture, fibres and
plastics. Within each autonomous division, of course, one
may find a different structure: the 'machine bureaucracy' is
prevalent, but if a separate research division exists it may
be a 'professional bureaucracy' or 'adhocracy'.

The support staff represent the final force. Their
preference is to co-ordinate by mutual adjustment and they
are frequently supported in this by the 'operating core'.
This would be the case in the Research Division just mentioned since the operating core would be scientists who are
imbued with values of freedom and innovation. This produces
a structure which Mintzberg calls 'adhocracy'. The title
attempts to convey the fact that there are limited formal
structures and that action and responsibility are defined by
the current problem rather than past precedents or personal
prestige. Large research and development projects sometimes
take this form, as do smaller groups of professionals, such
as advertising organizations. It can also serve the needs of

the automated factory. Since automation itself controls and monitors the workflow process, the executives and their technical staff can concentrate on designing new products and the processes to market, produce and distribute them.

Mintzberg's thesis is that all organizations experience these five forces and that in a search for harmony one of the forces becomes dominant at any particular point in the organization's history. The dominant force pulls towards one of the five configurations. As circumstances change, however, the dominant forces change.

The arrows in figure 2 indicate the main forces acting on each type trying to move it towards another type. The results of these forces are the myriad of organizational forms we actually find in the world.

In summary, the very essence of organization is the co-ordination of activities. There appears to be a limited number of ways in which co-ordination is achievable. They are co-ordination by mutual adjustment, direct supervision, standardization of work procedures, standardization of work outputs and standardization of inputs or skills. If any of these forms of co-ordination dominates in an organization it tends to lead to a structure of a particular type. Thus co-ordination by mutual adjustment tends to produce an 'adhocracy'. Direct supervision leads to 'simple structure', whilst standardization of work processes tends to produce the pure 'machine bureaucracy'. The 'divisionalized structure' arises from a desire to co-ordinate by standardizing the quantity and quality of work outputs, whilst standardizing inputs (skills) results in a 'professional bureaucracy'. These are 'pure' types and most organizations contain elements of more than one. We now consider some of the factors that produce these hybrids.

Why are organizations the way they are?

Because people choose, with more or less awareness, to make them that way. It is only too easy to start talking as if organizations make choices, but it is the men and women in them who determine their nature. This is not to say these decision makers are totally unconstrained. The fundamental purpose of the organization sets contraints, though organizations doing the same things may organize very differently to do them. A basic distinction is whether the organization manufactures things or provides a service. The latter could include providing treatment, providing education, selling goods or doing research. One reason that this is such a basic choice is that the decision to manufacture almost certainly involves the use of energy, tools and technology to a much greater degree than is likely in providing a service. This area of organizational theory has become known as the 'technological imperative' implying that certain forms of technology force certain kinds of organizational structures (see Woodward, 1965).

External influences on structure
The external ones include the market/clients the

organization is trying to serve; the knowledge/technical change that is occurring in the world; the economic situation resulting from changes in the availability of resources such as raw materials and finance; and the political changes resulting from government legislation. Space prevents a separate discussion of these, but together they may be construed as factors which create environmental uncertainty or turbulence (Metcalfe and McQuillan, 1977). To cope successfully with such turbulence requires different structures from those required to survive and develop in a stable and benign environment. One strategy large corporations adopt is to buy out the suppliers or competitors who may be causing uncertainty. This diversification also increases the complexity of the organization so that the divisionalized structure tends to emerge. One of the general principles for dealing with environmental complexity is the 'Law of Requisite Variety' (Ashby, 1956). This states that the variety/complexity inside a system must be sufficient to match the variety/complexity of the environment outside the system. Thus the diversification strategy not only reduces uncertainty but increases intra-organizational variety which also aids in coping with turbulence. Less rich organizations cope by relying much more on their own flexibility and ability to respond to the uncertainty with new strategies and behaviour. One way they achieve this flexibility and responsiveness is by employing a variety of professional, technical and scientific people, each of whom participates intimately in the decision taken within the company. Such organizations have few rules and regulations. This internal diversity, however, creates problems of communication and integration. To achieve co-ordination and integration special groups are sometimes formed to ensure that the necessary communication takes place. These liaison roles (Lawrence and Lorsch, 1967; Chandler and Sayles, 1971) come to demand special skills and qualities of their own.

A structure specially designed to facilitate co-ordination in such situations is the 'matrix structure'. This structure was developed and extensively used by NASA to complete the US lunar programme. Problems of this scale do not come neatly packaged by function or department, so 'project groups' were formed which combined specialists from different functions (e.g. engineering, human factors, physics, finance). The structure is decribed as a matrix because the groups were formed by project and held responsible to the project leader (see table 1), but each member was also responsible to the head of a functional department. It is this dual membership which provides the expert back-up of the function combined with the good communication and involvement of belonging to a project team. These two responses, the liaison group and the matrix structure, are variations of the Mintzberg 'adhocracy'. The existence of these two structures implies that co-ordination by mutual adjustment sometimes needs some structural support if it is to succeed in complex environments.

Table 1
___

The matrix structure

		Functional departments			
		Engineering Head + 7 subs*	Physics Head + 5 subs	Finance Head + 2 subs	Maths Head + 4 subs
	A. leader + 4 members	2		1	1
Project groups	B. leader + 8 members	2	3	1	2
	C. leader + 8 members	1	3	1	3
	D. leader + 6 members	4	1	1	

* A member of a functional department may be a member of more than one project group.
___

Internal influences on structure

If we turn to Mintzberg's pentagon in figure 2 we can see some of the forces within the organization which may influence its structure. These consist of the tensions between the major groups in the organization: the top managers and/or owners, the professionals in the techno-structure and the support structure, and the middle and lower parts of the workflow, the middle line and the operating core (figure 1). Those in the strategic apex want to maintain as much control as they can, but the technocrats, the middle managers and the professionals in the support structure, fight to increase their autonomy and influence. The technocrats wish to consolidate and automate the successes of the creative research staff, but the latter prefer to continue creating new products and processes. The operating core strive to professionalize their skills and provide better products/services to their clients, but the technocrats wish to rationalize and improve what already exists. As Mintzberg says, at any one time there may be harmony amongst these forces, but if the external environment changes the internal environment must respond to it or the organization as a whole will fail. The internal tensions arise again and a new stability emerges through death, amputation, amalgamation or reconciliation.

The professional can now see how he may be caught in any of these cross-fires. The accountant, for example, can find himself attached to the apex, the technostructure, the

operating core or the middle line. In a hospital the nurse
may be in the technostructure, the middle line, the operating core or the support staff. Doctors are trained to
diagnose and treat illnesses, teachers to instruct and educate and each progresses in his profession on the basis of
his ability in these specific skills. Eventually however,
they become managers, administrators and policy makers with
little formal training in these skills. No wonder hierarchical organizations have been accused of promoting people
to the point where they reach their level of incompetence
(Peter, 1969). This only goes to emphasize the flexibility
required of professionals in complex organizations, for the
roles they create extend far beyond those for which the
professional was originally trained. Indeed, roles provide
the link between the broad abstractions so far discussed and
the actual behaviour of people at work.

Roles in organizations

The term 'structure' refers to the pattern of offices or
positions existing in an organization, and to the nature of
the behaviour required of the people filling each of the
offices. It is this dramaturgical aspect of structure, the
definition of the parts to be played, that leads to the use
of 'role' as the central concept. In their work on organizational structure the Aston group (Pugh and Hickson, 1976)
relied heavily on the concept in constructing their major
measures, 'role specialization' and 'role formalization',
and it is important in other concepts such as 'standardization of procedures' (for roles) and 'configuration'
(distribution of roles). A major research project which
utilized the concept contains some useful definitions and
distinctions (Kahn et al, 1964) and these are outlined
below.

ROLE: the activities and patterns of behaviour that should
be performed by the occupant of an office: for example, the
nurse must administer drugs and follow the correct
procedures in so doing.

ROLE-SET: all other office holders who interact with another
office holder, the latter being designated the focal role.
Figure 3 illustrates the role-set of a senior occupational
therapist in a psychiatric day hospital.

ROLE EXPECTATIONS: the attitudes and beliefs that members
of a social system have about what the occupant of any
office ought to do; for example, as well as doing their job,
teachers are expected to be honest, moral, dedicated to
children.

SENT ROLE: the expectations sent to an office holder by
other members of his role-set; for example, a head of a
department presses a scientist for more research, whilst his
colleagues expect him to be a creative theoretician.

RECEIVED ROLE: the role as understood by the occupant based on the expectations sent to him by his role-set, for example, the above-mentioned scientist interprets the message to mean, 'publish as much as you can'.

There may well be a difference between the sent role and the received role. This may be partly due to inadequate information/communication, but can also occur because the receiver, consciously or unconsciously, wishes to see the world in a way which is comfortable and acceptable to him. Cognitive dissonance and perceptual defence are terms used elsewhere in this volume to describe these distorting processes (see p. 146). The disparity may also occur because the role is not clearly specified: small, expanding organizations have often not stopped to clarify who does what and have never written role specifications. Large organizations are sometimes called bureaucracies because they do write rules and specifications for jobs and they are kept in a 'bureau'. The written word is being used here to delineate the role. We can see from the role-set in figure 3, however, that the senior occupational therapist is at the focus of a disparate set of expectations. Even if all expectations are transmitted accurately (low role ambiguity) they are likely to be in conflict. The psychiatrist may want more group work, but the nurses and trainees more individual treatment. Kahn et al defined a number of types of role conflict.

INTER-SENDER CONFLICT: the expectations of two or more role senders are incompatible.

INTER-ROLE CONFLICT: two or more of the roles we occupy are in conflict; for example, manager and trade union representative; worker and father.

INTRA-SENDER CONFLICT: the same role sender has conflicting expectations; for example, increase output and improve quality.

ROLE OVERLOAD: simply means being unable to meet the legitimate expectations of role-senders.

The fact is, of course, that role-senders also develop illegitimate expectations. This is partly because individuals in organizations are not only concerned with meeting the organization's needs; many are more concerned with meeting their own needs. The ambitious manager may develop all sorts of illegitimate ways round the rules to improve the performance of his department so that he gets promotion and leaves the clearing up to somebody else! On the other hand, we as the general public know from bitter personal experience that 'working to rule', the organization's carefully thought out, written down, legalized prescriptions, means inefficiency and frustrations for all. That is,

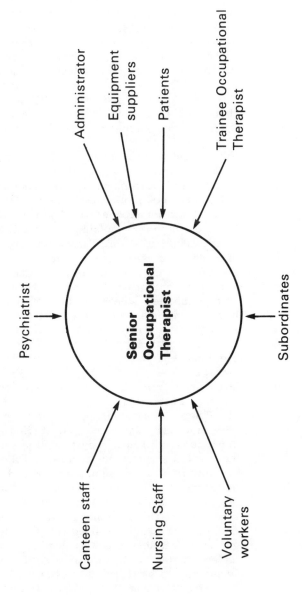

Figure 3

The role set of a senior occupational therapist in a psychiatric day hospital

some bending of the rules is actually highly functional for the organization. The universality of this slip between what is and what is supposed to be has been recognized by the concept of 'the informal organization'. The concept of role enables us to see how and why the slippage occurs. More generally the concepts relating to role enable the occupant of an office to analyse why his role is the way it is, and why it is not the way he expected it to be!

The informal organization

In work organizations role-sets do not occur randomly. They arise from the tasks to be done. In figure 3 we depict one based on the senior occupational therapist. If we were to search for others in the hospital setting we would find them centred on the surgeon's 'firm', on the portering staff, on the accident department, on the administrative office, on the junior doctors and so on. Within each of these role-sets there would be frequent face-to-face interaction and high levels of communication. Relationships between them, however, would be much less clear-cut. In the current jargon they would be 'loosely-coupled' systems (Weick, 1976), whereas within a role-set it would be a 'tightly-coupled' system. It is also obvious that members of one role-set are often members of another. The surgeon's 'firm' will contain some of the junior doctors. The surgeon will be on committees guiding policy-making which will also contain members of the administration. These formally required interactions open up informal communication channels. It is much quicker, and perhaps more revealing, to make a direct informal approach to another department than to work through the formal channels where the information has to go up, along, back, along and then down. It is faster, and perhaps more satisfying, to take the organizational hypotenuse than the organizational right angle. The fact that many people in organizations do prefer them is confirmed by studies of how managers spend their time. About 45 per cent of their time in communication is spent communicating outside the formal chain of authority.

These informal 'grapevines' appear everywhere and are very vigorous. Caplow (1966) studied rumours in war-time conditions and found they travelled surprisingly quickly and were often surprisingly accurate. Davis (1953) studied an organization of 600 people and traced the pattern of various decisions. For one letter from a customer he found that 68 per cent of the executives received the information but only three out of the 14 communications passed through the formal chain of command. Getting things done at all, and certainly getting them done quickly, depends heavily on knowing and understanding the nature of the informal organization. It seems impossible to regulate the behaviour of human beings by fiat and authority alone. Professional, ideological and social interests cross the formally defined boundaries and these reciprocal relationships very quickly begin to twine themselves around the organization's neatly designed trunk and branches. As with vines they provide extra support and bear rich fruits but they sometimes need pruning, or replanting. And if they are accidently uprooted they can leave the ground exposed, as it may be if a consultant recommends and installs a different, perhaps more clearly prescribed structure, but one which breaks up established relationships. An organization risks relying too heavily on the informal system which is why formalization and bureau-cratization are utilized in the first place, but there is danger in trying to eliminate it altogether. Farris (1979) contrasts the formal with the informal as in table 2 and it shows clearly how the informal relies heavily on expecta-tions rather than rules. He quotes several examples of how the formal organization, or at least the managers repre-senting it, can make use of the informal organization to better achieve its purposes; for example, they place new-comers with people at crucial cross-over points in the informal network in order to teach them quickly how the system really works. Effective organizations then allow the formal and informal to work symbiotically: to sustain and support each other. Less effective ones fight a battle for the dominance of one over the other. We can see from Farris' table that the informal is, in fact, very similar to the co-ordination principle of mutual adjustment. As Mintzberg's model indicated, all organizations face the problem of resolving the tensions between the five co-ordinating mechanisms. From the universality of the informal organization it seems that adhocracy is never completely defeated. This incipient victory of adhocracy has an influence on managerial behaviour as we see in the next section.

The nature of managerial work

The difference between what is specified in a job (role) description and what actually happens can also be illus-trated by the study of how managers actually spend their time. The classical description of management is that it involves planning, organizing, co-ordinating and finally controlling systems and people in order to achieve the goals outlined in the plans. A relatively small number of researchers have actually studied what managers do and one of the most influential of these pieces of research has again been done by Henry Mintzberg (1973). In 1975 Mintzberg compared folk-lore to fact. The first element of folk-lore he discussed was that the manager is a reflective, systematic planner.

His own intensive study of five chief executives showed that only one out of 368 verbal contacts was unrelated to a specific issue and could be called general planning. A diary study of 160 British top and middle managers found they worked for a half-hour or more without interruption only once every two days (Stewart, 1967). Mintzberg concludes that not only is a manager's work characterized by brevity, variety and discontinuity but that they actually prefer

Table 2

Some contrasts between formal and informal organizations
From Farris (1979): reprinted with permission.

Element	Organization	
	Formal	Informal
Salient goals	Organization's	Individual's
Structural units	Offices/positions	Individual roles
Basis for communication	Offices formally related	Proximity: physical, professional, task social, formal
Basis for power	Legitimate authority	Capacity to satisfy individuals' needs (often through expert or referent power)
Control mechanisms	Rules	Norms (expectations)
Type of hierarchy	Vertical	Lateral

---

action to reflection. Plans, if they exist, are formulated
and re-formulated in the executive's head; they are not
written down and rationally elaborated.

On the other hand, our folk-lore of the modern super-
hero is that the effective executive has no regular duties
to perform. He sits on the Olympian heights, awaiting the
calls of us lesser mortals. The facts show that he is down
in the valley dealing with the unexpected directly,
encouraging the peasants, negotiating with neighbours, and
even mending the fences.

Executives spend much time meeting important customers,
carrying out regular tours round their organizations, and
officiating at rituals and ceremonies. Much of their time is
spent scanning the environment for information which can
then be passed to their subordinates. This is not 'hard',
easily-available information but 'soft', given in confidence
or as a favour, but which becomes available only as a result
of maintaining regular contact: informal contacts!

A third piece of conventional wisdom is that senior
managers need aggregated information which a formal management information system best provides. Computers have
fostered this view as they seemed to be able to make such
information up-to-date and easily available. The evidence

suggests that managers do not use the information even if it is there. They strongly prefer to rely on meetings and telephone calls. Burns (1954) found managers spent 80 per cent of their time in verbal communication, and Mintzberg 78 per cent. The latter's five managers produced only 25 pieces of mail during the 25 days he investigated them. Only 13 per cent of the mail they received was of specific and immediate use. Managers appear to operate this way because they are future orientated and their active scanning for hints and gossip is felt to be more useful than detailed understanding of the past. Such behaviour puts a heavy premium on their personal ability to store and sort information. It also makes it difficult for them to transfer their personal images and maps to others in the company.

A related piece of folk-lore is that management is a science and a profession. It is true that the technostructure in large organizations uses mathematical modelling and sophisticated planning and control techniques, but these have little influence on senior managers or even on the managers of the specialists running such facilities. All are still reliant on their intuition and judgement. This is because they manage (i) people and (ii) very complex situations: imagine the problems facing the head of a department of management services in a regional hospital authority who manages 70 professional staff ranging from computer specialists, through work study to behavioural science change agents. That it is correct to give people problems priority over situational problems is reflected in Mintzberg's conclusions about the different roles a manager must perform. These appear diagramatically in figure 4.

The titles of the ten roles are precise enough not to require further elaboration. The arrows indicate that the organization gives the manager the authority and status to perform the interpersonal roles, that this requirement leads him to perform the informational roles and that this forces his involvement in the decisional roles. The effective manager is the one who carries out all ten roles but who does so by finding ways to:

* gain control over his time: he tends to be bombarded by others so he must find ways of using these obligations to others to suit his own ends. His only other hope is that people do things for him because of their personal commitment to him. In hierarchical and competitive situations this highly desirable state is often lacking. He may have to be political and devious to achieve his goals;
* some of the time thus gained must be used to determine which issues are really important in the overall picture. This ability has been called the 'helicopter capacity';
* to use the rest of his saved time to ensure that he regularly and systematically shares with colleagues and subordinates his privileged information and how it fits into the images and plans that are guiding his actions.

Figure 4

The ten roles of the manager
Reprinted by permission of Harvard Business Review Exhibit from, 'The Manager's Job: Folklore and fact', by H. Mintzberg (July-August, 1975). Copyright 1975 by the President and Fellows of Harvard College; all rights reserved.

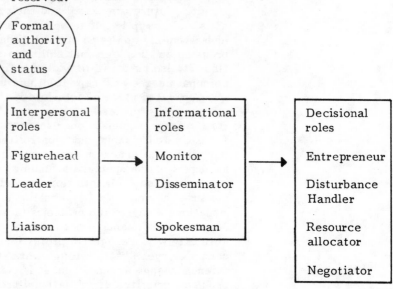

With this amount of preparation the manager has a good chance of sneaking through the interpersonal barrage that makes up his weekly war. This applies to managers and supervisors at all points in the organization: low, middle or high, in the technostructure or the support structure. For these different positions the task changes in quantity rather than quality, and in the severity of the consequences which result from failure.

References

Ashby, W. (1956)
An Introduction to Cybernetics. London: Chapman & Hall.

Burns, T. (1954)
The directions of activity and communication in a departmental and executive group. Human Relations, 7, 73-97.

Caplow, T. (1966)
Rumours in War. In A.H. Rubenstein and C.J. Haberstroth (eds), Some Theories of Organization. Homewood, Ill.: Irwin-Dorsey.

Chandler, M.K. and Sayles, L.R. (1971)
Managing Large Systems. New York: Harper & Row.

Davis, K. (1953)
Management communication and the grapevine. Harvard Business Review, Sept.-Oct., 43-49.

Farris, G.F. (1979)
  The informal organization in strategic decision-making.
  International Studies of Management and Organization, 9,
  131-152.
**Kahn, R.L., Wolfe, D.M., Quinn R.P., Snoek, J.D. and
Rosenthal, R.A.** (1964)
  Organizational Stress. New York: Wiley.
Lawrence, P.R. and Lorsch, J.W. (1967)
  Organization and Environment. Boston: Harvard Business
  School.
Metcalfe, L. and McQuillan, W. (1977)
  Managing turbulence. In P.C. Nystrom and W.H. Starbuck
  (eds), Prescriptive Models of Organization. Amsterdam:
  North-Holland.
Mintzberg, H. (1973)
  The Nature of Managerial Work. New York: Harper & Row.
Mintzberg, H. (1975)
  The manager's job: folklore and fact. Harvard Business
  Review, 53, 49-61.
Mintzberg, H. (1979)
  The Structuring of Organizations. Englewood Cliffs, NJ:
  Prentice-Hall.
Peter, L.F. (1969)
  The Peter Principle. New York: William Morrow.
Pugh, D.S. and Hickson, D.J. (eds) (1976)
  Organizational Structure in its Context. Farnborough:
  Saxon House/Teakfield Press.
Stewart, R. (1967)
  Managers and their Jobs. London: Macmillan.
Woodward, J. (1965)
  Industrial Organization: Theory and practice. Oxford:
  Oxford University Press.

Questions

1. Describe the different ways by which organizations
   attempt to achieve co-ordination. Give examples of
   each.
2. What is a matrix organization? When is it likely to be
   used?
3. What type of organizational structure(s) would you
   expect to find in (i) a medium-sized general hospital;
   (ii) a department store?
4. Illustrate your understanding of the concepts related to
   role-set by analysing the role of student (or any
   suitable variation of that).
5. Compare and contrast the formal versus the informal
   organization. Provide examples from an organization of
   which you are a member.
6. Why do informal organizations develop?
7. Compare and contrast stereotypes about managerial roles
   with what managers actually do.
8. Why might the training of a professional worker fail to
   truly prepare him for a career in a large organization?
9. Which of the main types of organizational structure most
   appeals to you? Why?

10. What factors influence the structural characteristics of organizations? Give examples.

Annotated reading

Mintzberg's ideas are available in his recent book (1979), The Structuring of Organizations. Englewood Cliffs, NJ: Prentice-Hall.

This is a detailed review and synthesis of a mass of literature on organizations. The first chapter describes the five co-ordinating mechanisms and the last describes the five types of structures and the pentagon model.

Child, J. (1977) Organization: A guide to problems and practice (paperback). New York: Harper & Row.

A readable and informed account of the meaning of organizational structure. It discusses the choices managers have when faced with designing an organization around the issues of shaping the jobs/roles people do, having tall or flat chains of command, grouping activities by function, product or some mixture, mechanisms for integrating the divisions so created, and how to control the humans working in the system. Child also discusses how to change organizations and the future forms they may need/choose to adopt.

Handy, C. (1976) Understanding Organizations. Harmondsworth Penguin.

This is an extremely well written and lively book, rich with pertinent examples. The first part introduces basic concepts for understanding organizations: motivation, roles, leadership, power and influence, group processes, structure and politics. The second part applies the concepts to problems such as how to design organizations, how to develop and change them and the working of the various aspects of organizations as systems (budgets, communications, computers, bargaining). The last chapter describes what it is like to be a manager and the dilemmas faced. The book has a very useful third section which is a guide to further study for each of the 12 chapters.

Warr, P.B. (ed) (1978) Psychology at Work (2nd edn). Harmondsworth: Penguin.

This book contains 16 chapters, each written by different authors. It is moderately technical in places, but much of it is quite understandable to the non-psychologist. The chapters cover the following topics: hours of work and the 24-hour cycle, workload and skilled performance, training, the design of machines and systems that optimize human performance, accidents, computers and decision making, selection, interviewing, negotiation and collective bargaining, leadership, attitudes and motives, job redesign and employee participation, work stress, counselling in work settings, how to change organizations and organizational systems as psychological environments.

Some journals which cover these subjects but which aim their content at practitioners and which are widely available in UK: Harvard Business Review, Personnel Review, Personnel Management, Management Today.

16

Institutional Climates
Jim Orford

Introduction

A person's behaviour is influenced by the surrounding
environment, as well as by attributes which the person
brings to that environment, such as personality, abilities
and attitudes; behaviour is a function of person and
environment. Many people either live or work in institutions
of one kind or another. For such people, the institution
constitutes an important part of their environment. For some
people it constitutes almost their total environment. Those
who work in an institutional setting cannot fail to notice
how the institution influences its members, either for good
or ill. Many will have felt frustrated by the values which
the institution seems to embody, or by the practices which
are prevalent within it, feeling that members could be
helped more if things were otherwise, or even that members
are being harmed by the institution. The great importance of
these matters has begun to be recognized in psychology and
there is a growing psychological literature on the organization of institutions and how to change them. The study of
institutions holds wider lessons for social psychology too.
An institution is a social psychological laboratory. The
experiments which take place there are naturally occurring
experiments in the psychology of social interaction, social
roles, inter-group attitudes, conflict and cohesiveness. The
study of institutions is of vital significance for both
theoretical and applied psychology.

Much of the literature on the subject concerns health
care or social service institutions such as mental hospitals
and hostels or homes for children, the elderly, or the
disabled. Although many of the examples upon which this
chapter draws are taken from such institutions, the chapter
attempts to build up a general picture of institutional life
which is equally as relevant, for example, to educational
institutions such as schools and colleges, and to penal institutions such as prisons and detention centres. These different institutions have a great deal in common. Each is a
collection of people, gathered together in a special building or group of buildings. These people are not normally
linked by family ties, but are there because of the special
'needs' (for education, care, treatment, rehabilitation, or
punishment) of inmates, users, or 'clients' (pupils, members, patients, residents). It is the responsibility of

another group of people, the staff, to provide for the clients' needs. This they are in a position to do on account of their special training, skills, or occupation (as teacher, prison officer, warden, doctor or nurse). Usually the institution has been set up by, and is part of, a larger organization which is responsible for managing the institution. Penal institutions in Britain are governed by the complex machinery of the Home Office; hospitals by the Department of Health and its network of Regional, Area and District Authorities, each with a complex system of members, officers and management teams; local authority schools and homes by committees and sub-committees of elected and co-opted representatives, the Authority's officers and the institution's committee of governors or managers; and institutions run by voluntary bodies by their trustees and management committees. Institutions are almost always influenced by people, often a large number of them, who have control over the institution but who are not involved in day-to-day work with the institution's clients. It is more than purely academic to consider some of these defining features of human service institutions. They immediately suggest ways in which an institution differs from a person's own home, and hence they indicate where some problems with institutions are to be expected. The small family home provides the clearest contrast to the large residential institution. People are not gathered together in the former on account of their special needs or their special qualifications: there is no demarcation between staff and clients: and the influence of outside organizations is minimal. It is no wonder that a great deal of thought and effort has been devoted to the goal of making institutions as normal and home-like as possible. Many other comparisons and contrasts between organizations and groups could be made, and there is no absolute definition of an institution.

Ideal types: the total institution and the therapeutic community

It is important to be clear what is meant by a 'total institution' and by the term 'therapeutic community'. They are important ideas which have had much influence but as terms they are liable to be used loosely, and hence may obscure rather than reveal the true facts about institutional climates. In his much-read and often-quoted collection of essays entitled 'Asylums: Essays on the Social Situation of Mental Patients and Other Inmates', Goffman (1961) noted that it is normal in modern society for people to conduct different aspects of their life, for example sleeping, playing and working, in different places, with different people, and under different authorities. Total institutions, in contrast, are places where these barriers between different spheres of life are broken down. All aspects of life are conducted in the same place and, most importantly, under the same single authority. It is quite likely that activities are tightly scheduled by those in authority in accordance with an overall plan. He noted that

many penal and caring institutions were total institutions
in this sense. So were a number of places, with which this
chapter is less concerned, such as army barracks, ships and
monasteries. On the other hand, certain places with which
we are concerned, such as day schools and day hospitals or
centres, would not qualify as total institutions.

It is also important to recognize the variety of climates which exist even within total institutions. In their
book, 'Varieties of Residential Experience', Tizard,
Sinclair and Clarke (1975) point out the danger of general-
izing from studies of single institutions, such as Goffman's
study of an American mental hospital. Used loosely, the
expression 'total institution' can give rise to a misleading
stereotype. There is now ample evidence, some of which is
considered later in this chapter, that institutions vary
greatly, and furthermore that individual institutions can be
changed.

Nevertheless, the harm that institutions may do has
increasingly been recognized. Barton (1959) has gone so far
as to say that the symptoms of institutionalization are so
well marked that they constitute a disease entity which he
called 'institutional neurosis'. He has written:

> Institutional Neurosis is a disease characterized by
> apathy, lack of initiative, loss of interest ...,
> submissiveness, and sometimes no expression of feelings
> of resentment at harsh and unfair orders. There is also
> lack of interest in the future ..., a deterioration in
> personal habits ..., a loss of individuality, and a
> resigned acceptance that things will go on as they are.

The concept of the 'therapeutic community' is an important
one because it represents one type of ideal contrasting
markedly with the most inhumane or least therapeutic institutional climates. The model therapeutic community was the
Henderson Unit at the Belmont Hospital in Surrey. The unit,
described by Maxwell Jones (1952) and studied by Rapoport
(1960), was principally aimed at helping young adult psychiatric patients, many of whom had problems of repeated
antisocial conduct and who were difficult to accommodate
elsewhere. Amongst the ideals of the therapeutic community
are an emphasis on ACTIVE REHABILITATION as opposed to
custodialism; DEMOCRATIZATION, namely that decision making
about the unit's affairs should be shared amongst staff and
patients alike; PERMISSIVENESS: that is, that distressing or
deviant behaviour should be tolerated rather than repressed
in the interests of institutional conformity; COMMUNALISM:
that is, that the climate should be informal without the
development of highly specialized roles, and that relationships should be close but never exclusive; and REALITY
CONFRONTATION: that is, that patients should be continually given interpretations of their behaviour as other
members of the unit see it. It is important to appreciate
that the Henderson model is a very specific one.

Structurally it was a total institution and although its climate was undoubtedly in contrast to that of many large impersonal institutions, in some ways it was rather formal, with a detailed programme of therapeutic and administrative groups, work assignments and other activities. Units are often self-styled 'therapeutic communities', but they are rarely aiming to recreate the type of therapeutic community unit described by Jones and Rapoport.

Structural features of institutions

There are many separate features of institutions which contribute to climate and a number of these are considered in turn.

Size

There is considerable evidence that people prefer, and are more active socially in, small units of organization. One explanation for these findings is based on the idea of 'manning'. Where there are relatively few patients, pupils or residents, there are relatively many tasks and activities for them to undertake. There is much scope for involvement in activity; the setting may be said to be relatively under-manned. In contrast, settings with relatively many individuals may be over-manned, with relatively less opportunity for involvement for all.

This is perhaps why efforts are often made to break up an institution into smaller, more manageable, groups such as classes, houses or year groups in schools, and wards and small units within hospitals. Unfortunately, the overall institution may continue to exercise a strong influence on the smaller units that comprise it. One recent study (reported in Canter and Canter, 1979) found that staff working in institutions for handicapped children adopted more institution-oriented as opposed to child-oriented practices in looking after the children when their unit was part of a larger overall institution. The size of the unit itself was unimportant. Individual units within institutions are rarely fully autonomous but continue to be dependent on the larger institution in many ways. This notion of autonomy is an important one to which this chapter returns.

Location

Location is of both symbolic and concrete significance. The isolated mental hospital symbolizes community attitudes to the mentally ill, for example. Other features of institutions may symbolize a similar relationship between institution and community. Prisons are often located in cities but their isolation is ensured by their high walls and impenetrable, fortress-like entrances; they are in the community, but not of it. It is important to consider what factors are operating to promote closeness of contact between an institution and its local community, and what factors are operating to inhibit it. It is interesting to speculate, for example, on whether a prominent sign

259

announcing that a house is a home for the elderly eases
visiting by members of the community or makes it more
difficult? Certainly many small residential caring units
such as hostels and halfway houses pride themselves on
carrying no such institutional signboard.

Ease of access to community facilities may be crucial
for those who must remain in an institution for a long time.
A lack of interest in, or desire to return to, life outside
are considered by Barton and others to be amongst the main
features of institutionalization, and he lists loss of
contact with the outside world, loss of personal friends,
and loss of prospects outside as three of its main causes.

The issue of location illustrates an important point
about the psychology of social organizations. The point is
that no single variable is independent of others, and
consequently it is almost impossible to impute causal
significance to single features of institutions. In this
case, it is very unlikely that the location of an institution is independent of the philosophy or ideology under
which it operates, or the attitudes of staff who work in it.
A rehabilitation philosophy is likely to be associated with
close community contacts, either because the institution was
located close to the community in the first place, or
because means had been found to overcome an unsatisfactory
location.

Internal design
Large rooms with high ceilings, glossy interior wall paint
in drab colours, no change of decor from one area to
another, lack of personalization by the use of pictures,
photographs and ornaments, lack of privacy, even sometimes
extending to a bathroom and toilet, absence of individual-
ized sleeping accommodation, few personal possessions or
places to keep them, and generally an absence of opportunity
to express individuality; these are amongst the internal
design features of an institution which contribute to an
institutional as opposed to homely atmosphere.

Once again, however, it is important to avoid over-
simple ideas of cause and effect. Two examples from Canter
and Canter's book (1979) on the influence of design in
institutions illustrate this point. One example concerns the
first several years' operation of a purpose-built unit for
disturbed children. A number of features, such as outside
play facilities, were designed by the architect with the
express purpose of reducing institutional climate. Others,
such as doors for bedrooms, were strongly advocated by the
director and were eventually installed. Observation of the
day-to-day life of the unit, however, led to the view that
the overwhelming ideology of the unit, which placed emphasis
on the children's disturbance and on the need for staff
control and surveillance, undermined the use of these design
features. Play facilities were rarely spontaneously used,
bedroom doors were hardly ever closed, and rooms which were
designed for personal use were used as seclusion rooms for

punishment. The second example concerns a purpose-built forensic unit where it was possible to show, by a process of behaviour mapping (a procedure whereby a map of WHO does WHAT and WHERE is produced by observing samples of behaviour in different places at different times), the use to which different spaces were put and the meanings that became attached to them. Certain areas were clearly designated as staff offices, and others as patient lounges. As a result, segregation of staff and patients was the rule rather than the exception.

One small-scale feature of physical layout which is relatively easily manipulated is that of SEATING ARRANGEMENT. The terms 'sociopetal' (meaning encouraging interpersonal relationships) and 'sociofugal' (discouraging relationships) have been used to describe possible seating arrangements in institutions. Seats in the lounge areas of old people's homes and other institutions are often arranged around the edge of the room or in some other sociofugal pattern, such as in rows facing a television set. Sociopetal patterns, on the other hand, have been found to lead to more interaction, more multi-person interaction, and more personal conversations. Once again, it is important to appreciate other, more human, aspects of the environment. It is often found, when attempts have been made to re-arrange furniture in a more sociopetal fashion, that there is a tendency for the seating to revert to its former arrangement. It is as if the institution has a will of its own and is in some way resistant to change. Exploring how this reversion to type comes about, and making a diagnosis of what is to blame, may provide vital insights into the nature of the institution.

It is worth speculating on the function which may be served by furniture arrangement in different types of institution. For example, why is the seating arrangement of pupils in a primary school often very different from, and usually more sociopetal in design than, that to be found in a secondary school? Is this difference accidental, or does it say something about the expected relationship between teacher and pupils, and perhaps thereby about the whole underlying philosophy of education?

Rules, regulations and routines

Studies of institutional practices

Considerable progress has been made in describing the variety which exists within health and social care residential institutions. Similar variety exists within educational establishments, and within penal settings.

Studies have compared hostels and hospitals for mentally handicapped children, and have found the latter to be much more institutional in their handling of the children: routine is more rigid, children are more likely to be treated en bloc, treatment is less personalized, and social distance between staff and children is greater. Wide variation is found in the degree of 'ward restrictiveness' in adult mental hospitals. Similar variation exists in halfway houses for ex-psychiatric patients. On average, hostels are less institutional than mental hospitals, the former having between one-half and two-thirds the number of 'restrictive practices' found in the average hospital ward in one study. However, considerable variation is found in both types of facility and there is an overlap between them. Some of the hostels, whilst being small in size, and designed to provide a link between the large institution and the community, nevertheless retain a number of institutional practices. In one instance a hostel had more institutional practices than the hospital rehabilitation ward from which most of its residents came.

A key idea linking these studies is that of clients' DECISION MAKING freedom. Table 1 provides an indication of some of the major areas of decision making considered in such studies. The list could be expanded greatly to include a large range of day-to-day activities over which most people are able to exercise personal choice. Whether an institution allows this exercise of choice to continue for its clients or whether these decision-making freedoms are curtailed is crucial in determining whether an institution creates a therapeutic climate or institutionalization.

Table 1

A range of decisions which may be allowed or restricted in institutions and which are illustrative of those considered in studies of institutional practices

What time to get up and go to bed
What to wear
What to eat for breakfast and other meals
Planning future meals
Whether to make a drink or snack
Whether to visit the local shops
Whether to go to work
Whether to go to the pictures
How to spend own money
When to have a bath
When to have a haircut
Whether to have medicine
Deciding arrangement of own room
Deciding decoration of own room
Whether to smoke
Whether to play the radio or TV
When to invite friends in
Whether to have a sexual relationship with a friend
Planning decoration or repair of the place
Deciding how to care for or control other members
Deciding policy

Staff autonomy

Reference has already been made, when considering the size
of an institution, to the importance of a unit's autonomy
within the larger institution. Decision-making freedom may
be limited not only for clients but also for those staff who
have the closest dealings with them. The advantages of the
informality which can occur in a truly independent small
unit are illustrated by an incident which occurred at
Woodley House, an American halfway house for the mentally
ill. It concerned a dispute between pro- and anti-television
factions in the house. The former decided to convert part of
the basement of the house for their use, leaving the living
room to the others. A staff member took them in her car to
buy paint and other materials and later the same day the
newly-decorated television room was in use. Such an incident
could not easily occur in that way in a larger and more
formal institution. There are a number of reasons for this,
one being that the staff member at Woodley House was not
limited to a prescribed professional role, and there were no
other members of staff upon whose role territory she was
trespassing.

It is this variable of staff autonomy which Tizard et al
(1975) considered to be one of the strongest influences upon
the quality of staff-client interaction in an institutional
setting. The firmest evidence for this hypothesis is
contained in a chapter of their book written by Barbara
Tizard. It concerns residential nurseries run by voluntary
societies. She observed 13 such units, all of which had been
modernized in recent years to provide 'family group' care.
Mixed age groups of six children each had their own suite of
rooms and their own nurse and assistant nurse to care for
them. Despite this effort at 'de-institutionalizing', marked
differences existed in the degree to which nurses were truly
independent agents. Nurseries were divided by the research
team into three classes on the basis of the amount of unit
autonomy. The first group, it was felt, was in effect run
centrally by the matron:

> Decisions were made on an entirely routine basis or else
> referred to the matron. Each day was strictly time-
> tabled, the matron would make frequent inspections of
> each group, and freedom of the nurse and child was very
> limited. The children were moved through the day 'en
> bloc' ... The nurse had little more autonomy than the
> children, e.g. she would have to ask permission to take
> the children for a walk or to turn on the television
> set. As in hospital each grade of staff wore a special
> uniform, and had separate living quarters, and the
> nurse's behaviour when off duty was governed by quite
> strict rules.

At the other extreme was a group of nurseries which more
closely approximated a normal family setting:

The staff were responsible for shopping, cooking, making excursions with the children and arranging their own day. The children could move freely about the house and garden and the staff rarely referred a decision to the matron. The nurse-in-charge did not wear uniform, and her off-duty time was not subject to rules. Her role, in fact, approximated more closely to that of a foster-mother. Since she could plan her own day and was not under constant surveillance she could treat the children more flexibly.

A third group of nurseries was intermediate in terms of independence. As predicted, the more autonomous staff were observed to spend more time talking to children, and more time playing, reading and giving information to them. Furthermore, children in units with more autonomous staff had higher scores on a test of verbal comprehension. The difficulty of teasing out what is important in complex social situations, such as those that exist in institutions, is illustrated by Barbara Tizard's findings. Autonomy was correlated with having a relatively favourable staff-to-child ratio and hence we cannot be certain that autonomy is the crucial variable.

Nevertheless, an effect of staff hierarchy was noticed which could explain the apparent importance of autonomy. When two staff were present at once, one was always 'in charge'. This had an inhibiting effect on a nurse's behaviour towards children: she would function in a 'notably restricted way, talking much less and using less "informative talk" than the nurse in charge'. This might explain differences between autonomous and less independent units, as staff in the latter type of unit would be much more likely to feel that someone else was in charge whether that person was present or not.

Flexible use of space, time and objects
Inflexible routine is one of the major charges brought against the institution by such writers as Barton and Goffman. Institutional life can be 'normalized' as much as possible by allowing flexible use of different areas of buildings and grounds, by varying time schedules, and by allowing flexible use of objects such as kitchen and laundry equipment, televisions, radios and record players. Residential institutions usually deprive adult inmates of the opportunity to take part in 'complete activity cycles'. Instead of taking part in a complete cycle of shopping for food, preparing it, eating, clearing away and washing up after it, residents may simply be required to eat what others have purchased and prepared, rather like guests in a hotel.

Staff attitudes and behaviour

Ideology
The influence of an institution's ideology or philosophy is

pervasive, although its significance can be missed
altogether by those taken up in the day-to-day activities of
the place. Many examples could be given. The philosophy of
a progressive school such as Summerhill, with its emphasis
on personal development, is distinct from that of a regular
secondary school with its emphasis on academic learning. The
rehabilitation philosophy of Grendon Underwood prison is
distinct from that of most closed penal establishments with
their emphasis on custody. Many institutions have mixed and
competing ideologies. These frequently give rise to conflict
within the institution, the different ideologies often being
represented by different cadres of staff. For example,
educational and child care philosophies compete within
institutions for handicapped children, as do educational and
disciplinary philosophies within institutions for young
delinquents. Important shifts may take place gradually over
time. For example, a general shift from a custodial philosophy to a more therapeutic ideology has occurred in mental
hospitals over the last several decades. Quite recently some
of those working in British prisons have detected a move in
the opposite direction in response to the call for tighter
security.

   Words such as 'open' to describe penal institutions,
'progressive' to describe educational facilities, and
expressions such as 'therapeutic community' to describe an
institution for residential care, all serve as public
announcements of ideology and intended behaviour. However,
it has already been noted that terms such as 'therapeutic
community' are frequently used loosely, and sufficient is
known about the absence of a strong correlation between
attitudes and behaviour to make us doubtful that ideal
philosophies will always be perfectly borne out in
practice.

Staff attitudes

Nevertheless, no one who has worked in an institution for
very long can have failed to notice what appear to be
marked individual differences in staff attitudes. In the
mental hospital setting questionnaires have been devised to
detect staff attitudes of 'custodialism' or 'tradition-
alism'. The matter is by no means simple, however, and
attitudes vary along a number of dimensions. For example,
one study distinguished between 'restrictive control' and
'protective benevolence'. Staff high on restrictive control
tended to be described as 'impatient with others' mistakes'
and 'hardboiled and critical', and not 'sensitive and
understanding' and 'open and honest with me'. Those high on
protective benevolence, on the other hand, were described
as 'stays by himself' and 'reserved and cool', and not 'lets
patients get to know him' and 'talks about a variety of
things'. Staff members high on this attitude scale expressed
attitudes that appeared to suggest kindliness towards
patients and yet they appear to have been seen by the latter
as basically aloof, distant and non-interacting.

A study of hostels for boys on probation also illustrates the complexity of the matter. This study examined the
relationship between failure rate, based on the percentage
of residents leaving as a result of absconding or being re-
convicted, and the attitudes of 16 different wardens. Two
components of attitude were identified, each positively
associated with success: strictness as opposed to permissiveness; and emotional closeness, which included warmth and
willingness to discuss residents' problems with them, versus
emotional distance. However, the two components, each
separately associated with success, were negatively associated with one another. Hence wardens who displayed more
warmth and willingness to discuss problems were also likely
to be over-permissive, whilst those who were relatively
strict tended to be lacking in emotional closeness. The
ideal combination of warmth and firmness was a combination
relatively rarely encountered.

Individual staff attitudes can partly be explained in
terms of individual differences in general attitudes or
personality: members of staff who are more generally authoritarian in personality tend to hold more custodial attitudes. This alone, however, cannot explain differences that
are found between different institutions. Although the correspondence is far from complete, it has been found to be
the case that where the prevailing policy is custodial,
staff subscribe to a custodial view and tend to be generally
authoritarian in personality. This raises the fascinating
question of how such relative uniformity comes about. It can
be presumed that the same three main processes are at work
as those that operate to produce consensus and similarity of
attitude in any social group or organization. The three
processes are (i) selection-in, (ii) selection-out, and
(iii) attitude change. Selection of new staff will most
likely operate in a way that increases uniformity of attitude, both because certain people are more attracted than
others by the prospect of working in a particular institution, and also because certain potential staff members are
thought more suitable by those responsible for the selection
(selection-in). Staff remain in one place for a variable
length of time, and the institution may retain for longer
periods those members whose attitudes are in conformity with
the prevailing ideology (selection-out).

As social psychological experiments on conformity show
so clearly, it is difficult to maintain a non-conformist
position in the face of combined opinion, and the third
process - attitude change - is likely to be a strong
factor.

Staff behaviour and staff-client social distance

Although research leads us to expect none too close a
correspondence between attitudes and behaviour, a number of
studies in institutions suggest that philosophy and attitudes can be conveyed to residents via staff behaviour.
Studies of units for handicapped children, for autistic

children, and for the adult mentally ill, suggest that staff behaviour towards clients is more personal, warmer and less rejecting or critical when management practices are more client-orientated and less institution-orientated. Large differences have also been detected in the amount of time which staff members in charge of hostel units spend in face-to-face contact with their residents. Sharing space and activities together, and spending relatively more time in contact with one another, may be the most important factors in reducing social distance.

Social distance between staff and clients was an important concept in Goffman's and Barton's analyses of institutions. Avoidance, or reduced time in contact, is a fairly universal indication of lack of affection and often of prejudiced and stereotyped attitudes. There are numerous means of preserving social distance including designation of separate spaces, such as staff offices. A clearly designated staff office makes staff and client separation easier, but such a space may be used in a variety of different ways. The door may be kept open, or closed, or even locked with a key only available to staff.

Controversy often surrounds the wearing of staff uniform in institutions. There are arguments for and against, but inevitably the uniform creates or reinforces a distinction and may therefore increase social distance. A movement away from the traditional institutional organization is very frequently accompanied by the abandonment of uniforms where these previously existed. The use of names and titles in addressing different members of a community is another indication of the presence or absence of social distance. Forms of address are known to be good signs of both solidarity and status within social groups. The reciprocal use of first names is a sign of relative intimacy, and the reciprocal use of titles (Mr, Mrs, etc.) a sign of distance. Non-reciprocal forms of address, on the other hand, are indications of a status difference, with the person of higher status almost always using the more familiar form of address (say a first name or nickname) in addressing the person of lower status, and the latter using title and surname towards the former, or even a form of address which clearly indicates the former's superior status (sir, boss, etc.). If forms of address change as people get to know one another better, it is usually the person of higher status who initiates the use of familiar forms of address first.

Hence an examination of a particular institution in terms of designated spaces for staff and others, uniforms and other visual indications of role or rank, and of forms of address, can give useful clues to status divisions and social distance within the institution. However, it is of the utmost importance to keep in mind that social distance, like all of the social psychological features of institutions considered here, is a highly complex matter. It has been suggested, for example, that there are at least two distinct forms of social distance, namely status distance and personal distance. If these aspects of social distance are relatively independent, as has been suggested, it follows that status distance need not necessarily preclude the formation of a personally close relationship.

Institutions as complex systems

The client contribution

Staff may be crucial determinants of climate, particularly senior staff, but so too are the institution's users or clients. The climate in an institution is the product of a bewildering complexity of factors which interact in ways that are far from straightforward. No simple theory which attempts to explain what goes on inside an institution in terms of physical design alone, of the attitudes of senior staff alone, or of management practices alone, can do justice to them. It would be as faulty to ignore the personalities, abilities and disabilities of the users as it would be to ignore the philosophy of the institution or the design of its buildings. This point is forcefully brought home in Miller and Gwynne's (1972) account of homes catering for people with irreversible and severe physical handicaps where the most likely termination of residence is death. They contrasted two ideologies which they believed existed in such institutions: the 'warehousing' philosophy, with its emphasis upon physical care and the dependence of residents; and the 'horticultural' philosophy, with its emphasis on the cultivation of residents' interests and abilities. They stress that each has dangers - the one of dependence and institutionalization, the other of unrealistic expectations being set - and that each is a response to the serious nature of the residents' handicaps.

There are a number of studies of social behaviour on the wards of mental hospitals which prove the point that social climate depends upon the mix of patients who are residing there. A clear instance was provided by Fairweather's (1964) study which is described more fully below. Introducing changes of a progressive nature on a hospital ward increased the level of social interaction generally but significant differences between different patient groups still persisted, with non-psychotic patients interacting most, acute psychotic patients an intermediate amount, and chronic psychotic patients the least. The mix of clients is especially crucial where group influence is considered to be one of the principal media of change (whether the change desired be educational, therapeutic or rehabilitative). Even in the relatively permissive climate of the Henderson therapeutic community, those with particularly socially disruptive personalities cannot be tolerated and, if accidentally admitted, may have to be discharged.

Under circumstances where group influence operates, it is particularly important that the client group exerts its main influence in a manner consistent with the overriding philosophy espoused by staff. This is always in danger of going wrong in secondary schools where the 'adolescent subculture' may exert a countervailing force, and in prisons where the 'inmate code' has to be contended with. In Canadian schools and centres for juvenile delinquents a procedure known as the 'Measurement of Treatment Potential' (MTP) has been in use to assess this aspect of climate. Where clients choose as liked fellow clients the same members as those whose behaviour is approved of by staff, then treatment potential is considered to be high. When there is a mismatch between residents' and staff choices, treatment potential is said to be low.

Climate

Many factors contributing to climate have been considered in this chapter and there are many others which it has not been possible to consider. Repeatedly emphasized has been the complex way in which these factors interact to influence the climate of an institutional unit. 'Climate', a word used here to cover any perceptions of, or feelings about, the institution held by those who use it, work in it or observe it, is not the same thing as success, effectiveness, or productivity. However, the latter are notoriously difficult to define, let alone measure, whereas people's perceptions of atmosphere can be collected and their relationships with features of the institution analysed. A massive programme of research along these lines has been conducted by Moos (1974). He has devised a series of questionnaires to tap the perceptions of members of various types of institutions and organizations. The most thoroughly tested of these scales is the Ward Atmosphere Scale (WAS), which assesses perceptions along the ten dimensions shown in table 2. This list was based upon earlier research by others as well as a great deal of preliminary work of Moos' own. He claims that dimensions 1-3 (the relationship dimensions) and 8-10 (the system maintenance and system change dimensions) are equally relevant across a wide range of institutions including schools, universities, hospitals and penal institutions. Dimensions 4-7 (the personal development dimensions), on the other hand, need modification depending upon the setting.

Amongst the many findings from research based upon the WAS and similar scales are the following. First, when staff and patient perceptions are compared in hospital treatment settings, average staff scores are regularly found to be higher on all dimensions except Order and Organization (no difference between staff and patients), and Staff Control (patients scoring higher than staff). Second, when scores are correlated with size of unit and with staff-to-patient ratio, it has been found that Support and Spontaneity are both lower and Staff Control is higher where patient numbers are greater and staff-to-patient ratios are poorer (MTP has also been found to correlate with smallness of size and favourability of staff to pupil ratios). Third, where patients have greater 'adult status' (access to bedrooms, television, unrestricted smoking, less institutional admission procedure, etc.), Spontaneity, Autonomy, Personal

Table 2

The 10 dimensions measured by Moos' Ward Atmosphere Scale

RELATIONSHIP DIMENSIONS

1. INVOLVEMENT measures how active and energetic patients are in the day-to-day social functioning of the ward. Attitudes such as pride in the ward, feelings of group spirit, and general enthusiasm are also assessed.

2. SUPPORT measures how helpful and supportive patients are towards other patients, how well the staff understand patient needs and are willing to help and encourage patients, and how encouraging and considerate doctors are towards patients.

3. SPONTANEITY measures the extent to which the environment encourages patients to act openly and to express freely their feelings towards other patients and staff.

PERSONAL DEVELOPMENT DIMENSIONS

4. AUTONOMY assesses how self-sufficient and independent patients are encouraged to be in their personal affairs and in their relationships with staff, and how much responsibility and self-direction patients are encouraged to exercise.

5. PRACTICAL ORIENTATION assesses the extent to which the patient's environment orients him towards preparing himself for release from the hospital and for the future.

6. PERSONAL PROBLEM ORIENTATION measures the extent to which patients are encoura to be concerned with their feelings and problems and to seek to understand them through openly talking to other patients and staff about themselves and their past.

7. ANGER AND AGGRESSION measures the extent to which a patient is allowed and encouraged to argue with patients and staff, and to become openly angry.

SYSTEM MAINTENANCE AND SYSTEM CHANGE DIMENSIONS

8. ORDER AND ORGANIZATION measures the importance of order on the ward; also measu organization in terms of patients (do they follow a regular schedule? Do they have carefully planned activities?) and staff (do they keep appointments? Do they help patients follow schedules?)

9. PROGRAMME CLARITY measures the extent to which the patient knows what to expect in the day-to-day routine of his ward and how explicit the ward rules and procedures are.

10. STAFF CONTROL measures the necessity for the staff to restrict patients: that is, the strictness of rules, schedules and regulations, and measures taken to keep patients under effective control.

Problem Orientation, and Anger and Aggression are all higher and Staff Control is lower. Fourth, all scales correlate positively with ratings of general satisfaction with the ward and with ratings of liking for staff, with the exception of Staff Control which correlates negatively with both.

Changing institutions

A knowledge of the factors discussed in this chapter should enable those involved in policy, planning and management to generate ideas for constructive change, and those in relatively junior positions to try and bring about change in their practice within the prevailing limits of autonomy. However, major changes may require innovations or interventions from outside and it is these that are now discussed in the remainder of this chapter.

Innovative programmes

One of the best documented programmes of institutional change in the mental health care system is the work reported in a series of publications by Fairweather and his colleagues. The first report (Fairweather, 1964) described dramatic differences in patient social behaviour between an experimental 'small group' ward and a physically identical 'traditional' ward in a mental hospital. In the traditional ward, staff members made final decisions on all important matters. By contrast, on the small group ward it was the responsibility of a group of patients to orient new fellow patients to the ward, to carry out work assignments, to assess patient progress, and to recommend privileges and even final discharge. The total experiment lasted for six months, and staff switched wards halfway through. Social activity was at a much higher level on the small group ward, and the climate in the daily ward meeting was quite different with more silence and staff control on the traditional ward, and more lively discussion, less staff talk, and many more patient remarks directed towards fellow patients on the small group ward. Nursing and other staff evaluated their experience on the small group ward more highly, and patients spent significantly fewer days in hospital.

In a further report, Fairweather et al (1969) compared the community adjustment of ex-patients who moved together as a group from a small group ward in the hospital to a small hostel unit in the community (the 'lodge'), and others who moved out of the hospital in the normal way. The results were quite dramatic, with the lodge group surviving much better in the community in terms of the prevention of readmission to hospital, the amount of time in work (much of which was organized by the ex-patient group as a consortium), and residents' morale and self-esteem. This is a particularly good example of the setting-up from scratch of a new small institution designed to avoid many of the most disagreeable features of large institutions.

Changes in the philosophies and modes of practice in institutions mostly take place over a period of years as a result of the slow diffusion of new ideas. A third report by Fairweather et al (1974) was concerned with this process.

Having established the value of the lodge programme, they set out to sell the idea to mental hospitals throughout the USA. They were concerned to know the influence of a number of variables upon the diffusion process, and consequently adopted a rigorous experimental approach. First, they varied the degree of effort required on the part of the hospital contacted in order to accept the initial approach offered. Of 255 hospitals contacted, one-third were merely offered a brochure describing the lodge programme (70 per cent accepted but only 5 per cent finally adopted the lodge programme), one-third were offered a two-hour workshop about the programme (80 per cent accepted and 12 per cent finally adopted), and one-third were offered help with setting up a demonstration small group ward in the hospital for a minimum of 90 days (only 25 per cent accepted but 11 per cent finally adopted the lodge). A second variable was the position in the hospital hierarchy of the person contacted with the initial approach offer. One-fifth of initial contacts were made to hospital superintendents and one-fifth to each of the four professions, psychiatry, psychology, social work and nursing. This variable turned out to be relatively unimportant: contacts were just as likely to result in the adoption of the lodge programme when they were made to people in nursing as to superintendents or those in psychiatry.

Much more important than the status of the person who initiates an idea is, according to Fairweather et al, a high level of involvement across disciplines, professions, and social status levels within the institution. When change did occur there was most likely to exist a multi-disciplinary group which spearheaded the change, led by a person who continuously pushed for change and attempted to keep the group organized and its morale high. The disciplinary group to which this person belonged was of little importance. Nor was change related to financial resources. The need for perseverance is stressed. The need to keep pushing for change despite 'meetings that came to naught, letters that stimulated nothing, telephone calls unreturned, and promises unkept' is a necessary ingredient of institutional change.

Action research

Fairweather's studies concerned the setting-up of new facilities or units. If, on the other hand, constructive change is to be brought about in existing institutions and their units, the total climate of the institution, and particularly the autonomy of the individual staff members, are limiting factors. A number of schemes have been described for providing helpful intervention from outside in the form of a person or team who act as catalysts or change agents. Several of these involve the process known as Action Research. For example, Towell and Harries (1979) have described a number of changes brought about at Fulbourne psychiatric hospital in Cambridgeshire with the help of a specially appointed 'social research adviser'.

The process begins when the interventionist(s) is invited to a particular unit to advise or help. It is stressed that the initiative should come from the unit and not from the interventionist, although it is clearly necessary for the latter to advertise the service being offered, and Moos (1974), for example, has argued that feeding back research data on social climate can itself initiate a change process. After the initial approach there follows a period during which the action researcher gets to know the unit, usually by interviewing as many members as possible individually, by attending unit meetings, and by spending time in the unit observing. Then follow the stages which give 'action research' its name. With the help of the action researcher, members of the unit (usually the staff group collectively) decide upon a piece of research which can be quickly mounted and carried through and which is relevant to the matter in hand. The results of this research are then used to help decide what changes are necessary. The action researcher remains involved during these phases and subsequently as attempts are made to implement changes and to make them permanent.

For example, one of the Fulbourne projects concerned a long-stay ward which had adopted an 'open door', no-staff-uniforms policy and which was designated as suitable for trainee nurses to gain 'rehabilitation experience'. The staff, however, felt 'forgotten' at the back of the hospital, felt that scope for patient improvement was not often realized, and that they were unable to provide the rehabilitation experience intended. The social research adviser helped the staff devise a simple interview schedule which focussed on such matters as how patients passed their time, friendships amongst patients, and feelings patients had about staff and their work. Each member of staff was responsible for carrying out certain interviews and for writing them up and presenting them to the group. All reports were read by all members of staff and discussed at a special meeting. The group reached a consensus that patients were insular, took little initiative, expected to be led by staff, had no idea of 'self-help', saw little treatment function for the nurses, saw little purposeful nurse-patient interaction, and had only negative feelings, if any, towards fellow patients.

Although there were no immediate or dramatic changes, a slow development over a period of 18 months was reported in the direction of a much increased 'counselling approach to care'. The research interview was incorporated into routine care. This itself involved the setting-up of a special contact between individual nurse and individual patient, a factor which is mentioned in other projects described by Towell and Harries and by many other writers who have described constructive changes in institutions. At first the social research adviser took a leading role in groups in helping to understand the material gathered in interviews. This role was later taken over by the ward

doctor and later still by a senior member of the nursing staf
At this point the social research adviser withdrew. Later on
patients read back interview reports and there were many
other signs of reduced staff and patient distance. Over the
three-year period during which these changes came about, the
number of patients resettled outside the hospital increased
from two in the first year to eight in the second and eleven
in the third.

It is stressed by those who have described 'action
research' and schemes like it, such as 'administrative
consultation' and the type of social systems change faci-
litated by a consultant described by Maxwell Jones (1976),
that staff of a unit must be fully involved and identified
with any change that is attempted. It is relatively easy to
bring about acceptance of change on an attitudinal level,
largely through talking, but to produce a behavioural commitment to change is something else. Those who have written
of the 'action research' process talk of the importance of
'ownership' of the research activity. The aim is to get the
unit's members fully involved and to make them feel the
research is theirs.

Resistance to change
We should expect such complex social systems, whose mode
of operation must have been arrived at because it serves
certain needs or produces certain pay-offs for those involved, to be resistant to change. Particularly should we
expect it to be resistant to change when this threatens to
involve change in status and role relationships. Unfortunately, it is just such changes for which we so frequently
search. The themes of decision-making autonomy and social
power have been constant ones throughout this chapter; they
lie at the heart of what is wrong with many of the worst
institutions. Maxwell Jones (1976) believes it is almost
always the required task of the social systems facilitator
to 'flatten' the authority hierarchy, and to support lower
status members in taking the risks involved in expressing
their feelings and opinions, whilst at the same time supporting higher status members in the belief that they can
change in the direction of relinquishing some of their
authority.

As in most earlier sections of this chapter, examples of
attempts to change institutions or parts of institutions
have been taken from the mental health field. Nevertheless,
the processes and problems involved can be recognized by
those whose main concern is with other types of institution
such as the educational and penal. In particular, those who
have in any way, large or small, attempted to change such
institutions can recognize the problem of resistance to
change. Nothing illustrates better the need to add to our
understanding of how institutions work. In the process of
finding out more on this topic we learn more of man in a
social context, which is part of the central core of the
study of psychology.

References

Barton, R. (1959; 3rd edn, 1976)
Institutional Neurosis. Bristol: Wright.

Canter, D. and Canter, S. (eds) (1979)
Designing for Therapeutic Environments: A review of research. Chichester: Wiley.

Fairweather, G.W. (ed.) (1964)
Social Psychology in Treating Mental Illness. New York: Wiley.

Fairweather, G.W., Sanders, D.H., Cressler, D.L. and Maynard, H. (1969)
Community Life for the Mentally Ill: An alternative to institutional care. Chicago: Aldine.

Fairweather, G.W., Sanders, D.H. and Tornatsky, L.G. (1974)
Creating Change in Mental Health Organizations. New York: Pergamon.

Goffman, E. (1961)
Asylums: Essays on the social situation of mental patients and other inmates. New York: Anchor Books, Doubleday.

Jones, Maxwell (1952)
Social Psychiatry: A study of therapeutic communities. London: Tavistock (published as The Therapeutic Community, New York: Basic Books: 1953).

Jones, Maxwell (1976)
Maturation of the Therapeutic Community: An organic approach to health and mental health. New York: Human Sciences Press.

Miller, E.J. and Gwynne, G.V. (1972)
In Life Apart: A pilot study of residential institutions for the physically handicapped and the young chronic sick. London: Tavistock.

Moos, R.H. (1974)
Evaluating Treatment Environments: A social ecological approach. New York: Wiley.

Rapoport, R.M. (1960)
Community as Doctor: New perspectives on a therapeutic community. London: Tavistock.

Tizard, J., Sinclair, I. and Clarke, R.V.G. (eds) (1975)
Varieties of Residential Experience. London: Routledge & Kegan Paul.

Towell, D. and Harries, C. (1979)
Innovations in Patient Care. London: Croom Helm.

Questions

1. Give two different definitions of 'institution' and give examples of places which fit both definitions, which fit one but not the other, and which fit neither.
2. What do you understand by the term 'total institution'? Why is it thought that they may do harm?
3. What principles are embodied in a proper Therapeutic Community? Is it possible in your view to say when these have been achieved, and when not?

4. What structural features contribute to the climate of an institution, and why?
5. How can the internal design of an institutional unit be changed to bring about change in the behaviour of those who live or work in it?
6. Write an essay on decision-making in institutions.
7. Give some evidence for the importance of staff autonomy in institutions and speculate on why this should be an important factor.
8. Discuss the proposition that the most important thing to change in an institution is staff attitudes.
9. In what ways might social distance between staff and residents of an institution be detected?
10. Are staff more important than the users or residents in determining the climate of an institution?
11. What formal and informal methods would you use to assess the climate or atmosphere of an institution?
12. Describe and comment on Fairweather's work in changing institutions and creating new ones.
13. What do you understand by the expression 'action research'?
14. What important principles should be kept in mind when trying to change an institution in some way?
15. Is the concept of 'institutional climate' a useful one in your view?
16. The only sensible thing to do with institutions is to abolish them altogether. Discuss.

Annotated reading

Barton, R. (1959; 3rd edn, 1976) Institutional Neurosis. Bristol: Wright.
> This is now a classic, describing institutionalization as a state analogous to a disease. It is written from a medical perspective but is brief, easy to read, describes the effects of institutionalization within a hospital setting, but forcefully makes the point that the state can arise in any institutional setting.

Fairweather, G.W., Sanders, D.H., Cressler, D.L. and Maynard, H. (1969) Community Life for the Mentally Ill: An alternative to institutional care. Chicago: Aldine.
> The main part of this book describes the story of a group of mental hospital patients who left the hospital together and set up home in a 'lodge', living and working productively together. Elsewhere in the book research findings are reported. Those who enjoy reading about research findings may also wish to read Fairweather, G. W. (ed.) (1964), 'Social Psychology in Treating Mental Illness', New York: Wiley.

Goffman, E. (1961) Asylums: Essays on the social situation of mental patients and other inmates. New York: Anchor Books, Doubleday & Co.
> Another classic, in which a sociologist describes the events and processes he saw in a large American mental

hospital. The book is full of telling sociological insights, but it is important when reading 'Asylums' to have in one's mind the knowledge that not all institutions, not even all mental hospitals, are alike and that there are important differences amongst them.

Jones, Maxwell (1952) Social Psychiatry: A study of therapeutic communities. London: Tavistock. (Published as 'The Therapeutic Community', New York: Basic Books, 1953).
Again a classic. The original description of the concept of the Therapeutic Community. Revolutionary in its time and still very well worth reading to understand the basic ideas behind the concept.

King, R.D., Raynes, N.V. and Tizard, J. (1971) Patterns of Residential Care: Sociological studies in institutions for handicapped children. London: Routledge & Kegan Paul.
This book is detailed and has quite a high research content. It is especially useful for the definitions and criteria for assessing institutional practices. Because of this it has been an influential book upon which later research has been based.

King's Fund (undated). Living in Hospital: The social needs of people in long-term care. London: Research Publications Limited.
This is an easy to digest pamphlet designed to be read by people who work in institutions. It poses a number of very detailed questions which the reader should ask himself about the environment created in his own institution for those who reside there.

Miller, E.J. and Gwynne, G.V. (1972) A Life Apart: A pilot study of residential institutions for the physically handicapped and the young chronic sick. London: Tavistock.
This is an account of a study of several homes and hospital units for a very disadvantaged group, most of whom would never leave the institutions in which they were resident. It describes several places in considerable detail and in the course of so doing raises many of the issues with which the present chapter on institutional climates is concerned.

Otto, S. and Orford, J. (1978) Not Quite Like Home: Small hostels for alcoholics and others. Chichester: Wiley.
This book is in two parts. The first reviews work on institutions and on small hostels for the mentally ill, offenders, and people with drinking problems in particular. The second part describes in detail a research study of two particular hostels for problem drinkers. It covers a great deal of important ground but is probably not such an easy read as some of the other books suggested.

Tizard, J., Sinclair, I. and Clarke, R.V.G. (eds) (1975) Varieties of Residential Experience. London: Routledge & Kegan Paul.

This book is an important collection of chapters written by different authors describing a variety of studies of residential institutions of one kind or another, mostly for children or adolescents. Particularly important are the first chapter in which the editors criticize the simplicity of Goffman's approach in 'Asylums', and the chapter by Barbara Tizard in which she shows how residential nurseries can be run in very different ways.

Towell, D. and Harries, C. (1979) Innovations in Patient Care. London: Croom Helm.

These authors describe how changes were brought about in the running of a mental hospital. Particularly inspiring in my view is chapter 2 which describes how significant change was brought about in an acute psychiatric ward and on a long-stay ward.

Rutter, M., Maughan, B., Mortimore, P. and Ouston, J. (1979) Fifteen Thousand Hours: Secondary schools and their effects on children. London: Open Books.

Here is a recent account of a detailed research project concerning the organization of a number of London secondary schools and their effect on the pupils' achievement and behaviour. The research is detailed and painstaking and the book is probably not an easy read, but for those who find statistics heavy going it contains some valuable passages about differences in school organization.

Walter, J.A. (1978) Sent Away: A study of young offenders in care. Farnborough, Hants.: Teakfield.

Walter's book describes his detailed observations and results of interviews at one Scottish List D school (the equivalent of the English Community Home or, as it used to be called, Approved School). It is a racy, easy to read account, concentrating particularly on the overall ideology or philosophy of the school and its effect upon staff and boys.

17

Ageing and Social Problems
Peter G. Coleman

What is it to be old?

The study of ageing and problems associated with it are now recognized as important. This is not surprising, for older people have become the major clients of the health and social services. They also have a lot of free time at their disposal. If there is to be an expansion in adult education and opportunities for creative leisure activities, the benefits should go especially to retired people.

What is surprising is that it has taken so long for the social sciences to pay attention to ageing and old age. So many young professionals are called on to devote their attention to the needs of people at the other end of the life span, yet they are likely to have received little in the way of stimulating material about the distinctive psychological features of old age.

Professional people do nevertheless have to be introduced to the subject of ageing, and it is interesting to note how that introduction has come to take on certain standard forms over the last ten years. There are two very popular, almost obligatory it seems, ways to begin talking or writing about ageing. The first way is to present the demographic data about the increasing numbers of elderly people in the population; the second way is to discuss the negative attitudes people have about working with the elderly.

The common introduction to ageing

In important respects old age as we know it today is a relatively modern phenomenon. Though there may have been individual societies in the past where a comparably large part of the population was old, it is clear that there has been a dramatic change in developed countries since the turn of the century. At that time in Britain those over the age of 65 constituted one in 20 of the population; today they constitute one in seven.

In recent years much more use is being made of the statistic 'over the age of 75', since it has become clear that this is the group in the population which makes the largest demands on the health and social services. This has highlighted the worrying news for service planners in a time of economic constraints that, while the total number of those over 65 will not increase very much in the coming

years, the population of those over 75 has already passed 5
per cent of the total population and will reach 6 per cent
by the end of the 1980s.

However, expressing concern simply at the number of
elderly people in the population is misleading. Why after
all should it be a problem that 15 per cent rather than,
say, 10 per cent or 5 per cent of the population is over the
age of 65, or that 6 per cent rather than 4 per cent or 2
per cent is over the age of 75? A lot of the issues have to
do with economics. The state must find the means to continue
paying adequate and perhaps even improved pensions, and to
provide welfare services to larger numbers of people.

Yet perhaps the more fundamental issues are the
availability and willingness of people, whether relatives,
neighbours, professionals or volunteers, to give assistance
to large numbers of disabled people in the population. For
ageing, as any introduction to the subject makes abundantly
clear, is associated with an increasing likelihood of
developing chronic disability.

Global estimates of disability in daily living (in getting around the house and providing for oneself) indicate
that the need for assistance is present in 15-20 per cent of
the age group 65-74, rising to 35-40 per cent in the 75-84
age group and over 60 per cent in those above 85. If one
adds on the number of people living in institutions (hospitals and old people's homes), which is about 4-5 per cent
of the total elderly population, one can conclude that about
30 per cent, or nearly one in three, of all people over the
age of 65 are disabled and in need of help.

A typical introduction to ageing then goes on to present
further numerical data on the social position of the
elderly. Almost one-third of people over 65 have been found
to live alone and large numbers are lonely. Many live in
poor housing, lack basic amenities and so on.

The need for a life span perspective
Large numbers of elderly people, large numbers of disabled
elderly people, and large numbers of elderly people live in
deprived circumstances; such is a typical introduction to
old age. But there are vitally important perspectives missing. No wonder indeed that we should be concerned with
attitudes, with finding enough people prepared to work with
the elderly, enough geriatricians, enough nurses, enough
social workers and so on, when the only image we present
of old age is a negative one. If the only perspective we
emphasize is one of endless problems, often insoluble
because of irremediable physical and mental deterioration,
we cannot expect many people to have the courage to become
involved.

Old people are people like the rest of us. What is
special about them is not that they may be mentally
deteriorated, disabled or isolated. The majority, after all,
are none of these things and many people reach the end of

their lives without suffering any disadvantages. What is special about old people is that they have lived a long time. They have had all the kinds of experience we have had and many, many more. They are moving towards the end of life it is true, but it is every bit as important how one ends one's life as how one begins it.

The perspective on ageing that is needed is one which takes into account the whole life span. The discovery any student of old age has to make is not only that old people have a long life history behind them but that their present lives, their needs and wishes, cannot be understood without an appreciation of that life history.

If we really talk to old people all this will become evident. But how often do we do this? A most eloquent testimony of our neglect is a poem (88 lines long) that was found in the hospital locker of a geriatric patient. (It can be found in full, quoted in the preface of the recent Open University Text, Carver, V. and Liddiard, P. (1978), 'An Ageing Population', Hodder & Stoughton.)

> What do you see nurses
>   What do you see?
> Are you thinking
>   When you are looking at me
> A crabbit old woman
>   Not very wise,
> Uncertain of habit
>   With far-away eyes
> ....
> Then open your eyes nurse,
>   You're not looking at me.

The writer emphasizes the continuity between her identity as an old person and her identities at previous stages in the life cycle. She is still the small child of ten with a large family around her, still the 16 year old full of hopes and expectations, still the bride she was at 20 and the young woman of 30 with her children growing up fast. At 40 her children are leaving home, and she and her husband are on their own again. But then there are grandchildren for her to take an interest in. Years pass and she has lost her husband and must learn to live alone. She is all of these people. But the nurse does not see them.

Psychological changes with age

It is only proper to admit at the outset that the main activity of psychologists interested in ageing, with some exceptions, has not been of a life span perspective. Their work has mainly been concerned with trying to establish what psychological changes, usually changes of deterioration, occur with advancing age, with understanding the bases of such changes and finding ways of compensating for them. These are obviously important questions.

Cognitive deterioration

It would be wishful thinking to deny that there is any
deterioration with age. Physical ageing is a fact which is
easy to observe, though it may occur at different rates in
different people. Performance in everyday tasks in which we
have to use our cognitive ability to register things we see
or hear, remember them and think about them also deteriorates. Absent-mindedness is one of the most common complaints
of older people in everyday life.

In more recent cross-sectional studies of the performance of different age groups on experimental tasks, psychologists have tried their best to control for obvious factors
which might produce differences in their own right, like
education, illness, sensory impairment and willingness to
carry out the tasks in question. Of course, certain question
marks remain over differences in attitude and perceived
role: for instance, whether older people see the purpose of
such tasks in the same way as younger people. Nevertheless,
certain conclusions can be drawn about the abilities which
seem to change the most as one grows older. In the first
place, older people take much longer to carry out tasks and
this is not only because their limb movements are slower. In
tasks in which they have to divide their attention ('try to
do two things at once'), decline with age is very marked and
is already evident in those over 30. Ability to remember
things we have seen or heard declines, as does the ability
to hold associations in mind.

However, in some older people decline is not evident at
all. Particular experiences, for example particular occupational backgrounds, may develop certain abilities in an
individual to such an extent that they remain well developed
throughout old age. Retired telephone operators who have no
difficulty in dividing attention between a number of messages are a case in point. The prominence of so many older
people in public life where they reap the fruit of years of
experience in political dealings is also an obvious illustration. Moreover, it seems to be true that in some old
people deterioration does not, in fact, occur. There are
studies which indicate that the cognitive ability of a
sizeable minority of elderly people, perhaps as many as one
in ten, cannot be distinguished from that of younger
people.

This, then, is evidence that age itself is not the
important thing. Indeed it seems better to view age simply
as a vector along which to measure the things that happen
to people. Some things that happen with age are universal.
They occur at different times, but they are unavoidable.
These things we can, if we like, describe as 'age' changes.
But a lot of the things we associate with old age are not
due to ageing processes and are not universal. There is a
great variation in the extent to which people are hit by
physical and social losses as they grow old. Some people
are fortunate, some people are unfortunate.

From the point of view of cognitive ability, the most
unlucky are those people who suffer from the various forms

of dementia or brain diseases which lead to a progressive
deterioration in mental functioning. But health is by no
means the only extrinsic factor influencing mental state in
old age. A lot of research has been done recently on the
psychological effects of such brain-washing treatments as
isolation and sensory deprivation. Disorientation and
confusion are common results. Yet we are often slow to
recognize that old people may be living in circumstances
where by any ordinary standards they are extremely isolated
and deprived of stimulation. No one calls to see them, to
engage them, to remind them of their names, roles and
relationships. Disorientation in time and space, and confusion about identity and relationship with others, can be
a natural result. From our own experience we know how time
can lose meaning after one has been ill in bed for a day or
two, away from the normal daily routine.

Other social and psychological factors play a role too.
Motivation to recover or maintain abilities is obviously a
crucial factor, and a number of studies have shown that
amount of education remains one of the major factors in
cognitive ability and performance throughout life.

Personality and life style
Scientific work on personality and style of life in old age
does not match the amount that has been done on cognitive
functioning. The evidence we do have, however, relates both
to change and stability.

One clear finding from research is that introversion or
interiority increases with age. This means that as people
grow old they become more preoccupied with their own selves,
their own thoughts and feelings and less with the outside
world. This change is only relative, of course, but it is
evident both from responses to questionnaires and also from
projective tests, where people are asked to describe or
react to stimuli they are presented with, such as pictures
of family and social situations.

The term disengagement has been used to describe such
a change in orientation; a decreased concern with interacting with others and being involved in the outside world
and an increased satisfaction with one's own world of
memories and immediate surroundings. However, critics have
been quick to point out the dangers of exaggerating the
extent to which disengagement is a 'natural' development in
old age. Most of the decreased interaction and involvement
of older people is forced upon them by undesired physical
and social changes: disability, bereavement, loss of occupational roles and so on. Moreover, there is also clear evidence that old people are happier when there is a good deal
of continuity between their past and present activities.

Indeed, in contrast to any change in personality that
may occur, the stability that people show in their characteristics and style of life over a period of time is far
more striking. Longitudinal studies show that people continue to enjoy the same interests and activities. When
striking negative changes occur in a person's interests or

familiar mode of activities, or ways of coping with life in
old age, for no obvious reason, this is often a sign of
psychiatric illness, especially depression.

Some of the most valuable studies on personality in old
age are, in fact, those which have shown how important it
is to take into reckoning a person's life style, for instance in explaining why people react differently to changes
and losses such as retirement, bereavement and living alone,
or a move to a residential home. Any research finding about
old people usually has to be qualified by a reference to
life style. This is mentioned again when talking about
adjustment to relocation.

Growth and development

Though deterioration has been the main perspective of
psychological research on ageing up to now, it is not the
only one. Certainly in literature old age has been treated
much more generously. The works of Nobel prize winners, such
as Patrick White ('The Eye of the Storm', 1973), Saul Bellow
('Mr Sammler's Planet', 1969) and Ernest Hemingway ('The
Old Man and the Sea', 1952), present vivid and compelling
pictures of old age that, like King Lear, have to do with
deterioration and change but also with growth in understanding and the values of existence.

Indeed, a characteristic theme in literature is of old
age as a time of questioning; of one's own achievements, of
the meaning of one's life, of the values one lived by and of
what is of lasting value. It is as if an old person, freed
from the strait-jacket of society, suffering losses in his
ability to function and in his social position - perhaps
indeed precisely because of them - is, somehow, let free to
question life. Psychologists have only begun tentatively to
approach these issues, but there is a lot in writers like
Jung to consider.

**Adaptation to loss
in old age**

From what has already been said it should be clear that old
age is a time of great inequality. It is a time when losses
occur, loss of physical and mental abilities, loss of people
who were close to one, loss of roles and loss of activities.
These losses are not inevitable; they do not occur in the
same degree to everyone; but adapting to loss is a characteristic feature of old age.

Attitudes to health and well-being

Severe disability is one of the major losses of old age and
its central importance in shaping the rest of an individual's life is one of the most common findings to emerge
from investigations on social aspects of ageing. People who
are disabled have more problems in maintaining their desired
styles of life and are more dissatisfied than people who are
not disabled. This is not surprising.

What is more surprising, or at least not logically to be
expected, is the fact that, in general, levels of well-being

do not decline with age. This is despite the fact that the incidence and severity of disability tend to increase with age and have a great influence on well-being. The key to understanding this comes from studies on subjective health.

The clear evidence from both longitudinal and cross-sectional studies is that whereas objective health and physical functioning of elderly people tend to deteriorate with age, the same is not true in regard to how they feel about their health. The most likely explanation has to do with expectations. People expect to become somewhat more disabled with old age. If they do, they accept it. But if their physical functioning remains stable they may in fact experience this as a bonus and feel better as a result. Only if their health deteriorates beyond the expected norm are they likely to feel badly about it.

This argument applies strictly only to feeling well, but it has a wider implication for well-being generally and for reactions to other losses in old age. Expectation is a very important aspect of reaction to loss. It is what people expect and what people find normal that determines how they react to things and how satisfied they feel with their situation. This kind of consideration also leads one to reflect how different things could be if old people's expectations changed. This is in fact not so unlikely. Future generations of elderly people may be far less accepting of lower standards of health and also, for instance, of income. They may expect things to be a good deal better for them. And if things are not going to be better they are going to be less happy as a result.

Adjustment to relocation

Another misfortune often following from disability is that people can find themselves being obliged to move, sometimes quite unexpectedly and against their will, to different environments, particularly institutional settings, where they often have to remain for the rest of their lives. Though this is usually done to them 'for their own good' (they are judged incapable of looking after themselves in their own homes), the end result may be much worse than leaving them alone: for instance, further deterioration and loss of interest in life.

There has been growing realization of the extent to which environmental changes can contribute to physical illness and psychiatric disorders. Even where it is voluntarily undertaken and has otherwise favourable effects, there are indications that rehousing can undermine a person's health. There is also a great deal of variation between individuals in their reactions, so it is important to discover which factors might predict the ability to adjust easily to new surroundings.

Among psychological factors cognitive ability is clearly crucial. There appear to be two major reasons why cognitively impaired old people react worse to relocation. In the first place, their lack of ability to anticipate and prepare means that they experience more stress on making the move. Second, because of their poor short-term memory and orientation abilities it may take them a long while to understand their new surroundings.

Personality is important too. We are not sufficiently sensitive to the fact that the institutional environments we provide may be fine for one kind of elderly person but not for another. American studies have shown the importance, for instance, of rebellious and aggressive traits, as opposed to passive and compliant ones, in predicting survival and lack of deterioration after relocation to institutional settings. Vital as well, of course, are attitudinal factors concerned with what the move means to the person, whether he wants to go, and how he sees his own future in the new setting.

Self-esteem and its sources: the lynchpin of adjustment?

Disability and environmental change have been picked out for consideration as two of the negative changes associated with old age. There are others, of course. Bereavement requires a major adjustment which seems to follow certain definite stages. Grieving is a normal, healthy part of the process, and the support and understanding of those around in allowing the bereaved person to express himself may be very important to it. Loss of occupational role with retirement is another big change. Indeed, adjustment to it is often thought of in the same terms as adjustment to the old age role itself. Most people make good adaptations, but not all, and retirement can be a major precipitating factor in the onset of late life depression.

Then again, a very significant loss for many people as they grow older is that of income: they must adapt to making do with less. There has been almost no psychological investigation of this kind of adaptation. From what one can see it would seem that a lot of old people positively take pride in stretching their money. This, of course, may also have a lot to do with their experience of deprivation in the past.

Naturally, in all these adaptations much depends on the characteristics of the individual person involved, and one is led to ask whether there are any general ways in which one can conceptualize how a person adapts to the various losses and changes that occur with old age. Some authors talk in terms of the individual possessing particular qualities: for instance, 'coping ability'. But the most valuable index of adjustment in old age is that of self-esteem.

Maintenance of positive attitudes to oneself seems to be one of the key issues in old age. An especially important component of self-image is a sense of being in control of one's own life. Development in childhood and adulthood is associated with an increasing sense of effectiveness and of impact on the external world. In old age this sense may well be taken away.

Intrinsic to this conception of self-identity is the notion that it must have roots outside itself. Therefore, if an individual is to maintain his self-esteem he has a continuing need of sources from which he can define an acceptable image of himself to himself. For some people these sources can exist in past relationships and achievements or in an inner conviction about the kind of person one is, but in the main they depend on the present external circumstances of their lives; their roles in the family, in relation to other people, in work and in other activities.

When these circumstances change, as they often do in old age, a person may have to find alternative sources to maintain a positive view of himself. Here again it is vital to understand a person's life history. A person whose sense of self has been based on one particular kind of source, for instance relationships with members of his close family, is going to suffer especially if he loses such family contacts through death.

One way to investigate sources of self-esteem is to ask people directly what makes them say that they feel useful or feel useless, for instance. Not surprisingly, lack of infirmity and contact with other people including the family emerge as the major sources of self-esteem. Especially in disabled people, being able to do things for oneself, and in particular to get around, appear to be key factors; also being a source of help and encouragement to others is very important.

In this context it is worth putting in a good word for residential care and other types of grouped housing schemes. In a previous part of this section it was noted that a move to an institutional setting can be damaging for certain types of individual, but a good institutional setting can also be of great benefit to certain people. This is possible when sources of self-esteem are likely to be strengthened rather than weakened by the move.

For instance, some people could be said to be 'living independently in the community'. But in reality they may be extremely isolated and totally dependent on the services being brought to them. Once they have moved to a genuine communal setting the burden of infirmity and consciousness of being alone can be diminished. Precisely because they are better able to cope for themselves in the new environment and to be of importance to others, they may gain a new lease of life.

Helping old people

Not all the loss and trauma of old age can be countered from an individual's own resources. The modern welfare state provides a range of services for the elderly; housing, health and social services. These are, of course, limited, subject to decisions about what level of services the country can 'afford'. We do not know what a perfect service for the elderly would be like, but we certainly do know that what we provide at present falls a long way short of it.

However, the achievement of the present level of services needs to be respected if we are to develop further, and it is important that people in the various caring professions who carry out these services remember their responsiblities. One of the real dangers is taking the operation of a service for granted and applying it automatically or mindlessly. The people on the receiving end then cease to be considered as individuals.

A key element, it seems to me, in any work with elderly people is the individual assessment, and it is here that the psychological perspective has a vital role. We need a good assessment not only of people's physical condition and capabilities and of their social situations, but also of their individual needs, their abilities and interests, which should include a good picture of how they used to be.

Besides helping in assessment, psychology can also play a role in the actual provision of therapeutic interventions both to old people themselves and to those around them. Applied psychology should be able to show the best way: for example, to help recover abilities that seem to be lost or to mend social relationships that have become tense.

Maintenance of interests, activities and functioning

One of the most tragic images we have of old age is that of an old person with shoulders sunk, sitting collapsed in a chair, totally uninvolved in the world around. In a previous section the question of 'disengagement' in old age was raised, and let us repeat the point made there that, although some decline in activity may be an intrinsic part of growing old, most of such decline is the result of physical disability and environmental trauma.

When there is a dramatic decline in a person's activities for no obvious reason, we need to alert ourselves to the possibility that the person may be depressed. Loss of well-established habits and activities and lack of interest or anxiety about trying to regain them may be symptoms of the kind of depression which will respond to treatment, even though the person may not admit to having depressed feelings. But, of course, there also has to be some activity and interests for the person to go back to. Particularly if someone is disabled there may be few possibilities open to him and the person is then likely to decline again. It is also quite clear that prolonged inactivity has deleterious effects both on physical and psychological functioning. Skills that are not exercised tend to atrophy.

In recent years a lot of new initiatives have been taken in geriatric hospitals in providing opportunities for patients to engage in different types of activity, arts and crafts, music discussion and so on. Generally, staff report improvements in elderly people who do take part in such activities, which can be seen in their personal appearance, in their physical and mental functioning and in their contact with others.

An even greater challenge is offered by people who are mentally deteriorated. In the first place it is very important to distinguish elderly people who really have irretrievable brain disease from those who only appear to have because they are depressed. Indeed, it may be symptomatic of someone's depression that he thinks his brain is rotting. It may be no easy matter to distinguish this, because it is difficult to motivate someone who is depressed actually to demonstrate his abilities. With the right treatment and support depressed people can be encouraged to regain their old abilities.

However, elderly people who clearly are deteriorating mentally should not be abandoned to their fate. Tests have shown that such people, given encouragement and help, can still acquire and retain new information and maintain skills. But the effort needed from outside is great. A good example is the use of so-called 'reality orientation', where people around the elderly person, either informally throughout the day or in concentrated formal classes, systematically try to help remind the person of time, place and season, of names of people, of objects, and of activities and so on.

Psychologists have a lot to do applying findings from the study of learning and memory to help old people. The trouble at present is that such people are often left alone, and this only exacerbates their condition. Dementia is a progressive illness, but what happens between its onset and death is important. If in the future we find medical means of slowing down its progress, it will become an even more urgent matter to find means as well to allow people to maintain their optimum potentialities in the time that remains left to them.

Family relationships

Another vital issue is the relationship between disabled elderly people and their families. Many more of such people are supported by their families than live in institutions for the elderly. For instance, in the case of severe dementia, there are four to five times as many suffering from such a condition living in the community as live in residential homes or hospitals. Yet often families who are doing the caring get pitifully little in the way of support services.

If they become overburdened by the stress of their involvement, both they and their elderly relatives suffer. The old person's mental condition may well be aggravated by tired and irritable relatives, and if there is a breakdown in care and there is no alternative but to take the old person into an institution, the family members are likely to suffer greatly from feelings of guilt. They often want to care for a relative until that person dies, but need help in carrying it out.

It is an important principle to accept that work with families is an integral part of work with elderly people. Family ties after all usually form a substantial part of an individual's identity. If those ties are damaged, so is the person's identity. The physical and mental deterioration that affects many people as they grow older and their

ensuing state of dependency can put a strain on many
relationships. Men, for instance, usually do not expect to
outlive their wives. They can encounter great problems if
they find instead that they have to spend their old age
looking after a physically or mentally deteriorated wife,
especially if in the past it was their wives who ran the
household. Children too often find difficulty in taking over
responsibility for ailing parents.

The actual symptoms, particularly of mental disturbance
in old age, can be very disturbing. In some forms of dementia (probably dependent on the part of the brain that has
been affected) the behavioural changes that can occur, cari-
caturing the person's old personality, increasing aggression
or leading to a loss in standards of cleanliness, can be
very painful for relatives to bear. It may be difficult for
them to accept that the patient is not simply being difficult or unreasonable.

Families need counselling about the nature of the
illness and, in the case of dementia, of its progressive
nature, and preferably, too, promise of continued practical
support. Group meetings held for relatives of different
patients by doctors, social workers or other professionals
can also be useful in allowing relatives to share common
experiences and problems. Groups for the bereaved, particularly husbands or wives, can also play their part. The
last years of their lives may have revolved around the care
of a sick spouse and they must now find new meaning in
life.

The future

In discussing ageing and social problems it may seem strange
to end with a note about the future. But from what has been
said it should be obvious that great improvements need to
take place, both in society's provision for the elderly and
in the attitudes of each and every one of us to the elderly
people we live among.

For most people old age is not a particularly unhappy
time, though for some it is. In part that may be, as we
have suggested, because old people have low expectations.
They quietly accept a society that treats them meanly and
as somehow less important. In the future that may all
change. We may see new generations of elderly people,
foreshadowed in today's Grey Panthers in America, who will
mobilize their potential power as a numerically important
part of the electorate and pressurize society to give them a
better deal.

On the other hand, old people may continue to remain
on the sidelines. They may refuse to see their own material
and other interests as being of central importance to
society, in which case the rest of the population must see
they are not forgotten.

The most important changes indeed are the attitudinal
ones. We must recognize that old people are ourselves. They
are our future selves. There is a continuity in life both

between their past and present and between our present and future.

Old people remain the same people they were. Indeed, if we really want to know about a person's needs and wants and how they could be satisfied, the best introduction would be to let them tell us about their life history. Whatever new steps are taken in the future must follow on from this and make sense in relation to it.

Better provision would follow from such a recognition. If we really respected people's individuality we would provide them with choice about the circumstances and activities with which they end their days, not just enforce certain standard solutions. In short, we must allow people to grow old in ways that suit them, perhaps to explore new avenues of development in order to make the most of the years that remain. Also, when we consider those who need our help, who suffer in old age and perhaps are dependent upon us, we should not forget these wider perspectives.

References

Birren, J.E. and Schaie, K.W. (eds) (1977)
  Handbook of the Psychology of Ageing. London: Van Nostrand Reinhold.
Brearley, C.P. (1975)
  Social Work, Ageing and Society. London: Routledge & Kegan Paul.
Bromley, D.B. (1974)
  The Psychology of Human Ageing (2nd edn). Harmondsworth: Penguin.
Carver, V. and Liddiard, P. (eds) (1978)
  An Ageing Population (Open University text). Sevenoaks: Hodder & Stoughton.
Chown, S.M. (ed.) (1972)
  Human Ageing. Harmondsworth: Penguin.
Dibner, A.S. (1975)
  The psychology of normal aging. In M.G. Spencer and C.J. Dorr (eds), Understanding Aging: A multi-disciplinary approach. New York: Appleton-Century-Crofts.
Gray, B. and Isaacs, B. (1979)
  Care of the Elderly Mentally Infirm. London: Tavistock.
Kastenbaum, R. (1979)
  Growing Old - Years of Fulfilment. London: Harper & Row.
Kimmel, D.C. (1974)
  Adulthood and Ageing. An interdisciplinary developmental view. Chichester: Wiley.
Miller, E. (1977)
  Abnormal Ageing. The psychology of senile and presenile dementia. Chichester: Wiley.
Neugarten, B. and associates (1964)
  Personality in Middle and Later Life. New York: Atherton Press.

Questions

1. Discuss the view that old people do not differ from young people except in the number of years they have lived.
2. Should the study of the psychology of ageing be part of developmental psychology or a separate field of study altogether?
3. 'Deterioration in function is the main psychological characteristic of old age.' Do you agree?
4. What factors influence mental performance in old age? What evidence do we have on their relative importance?
5. Is there more truth in 'disengagement' theory as a sociological or psychological theory of ageing changes?
6. What explanations are there for the decline in activities that some people show as they grow older?
7. How important is a knowledge of life style or personality type to understanding how people react to change and stress in old age?
8. Are the changes we observe in old people's behaviour related more to the physical and social losses they incur or more to intrinsic processes of ageing?
9. Do old people show genuine developmental changes as well as changes of deterioration?
10. Analyse the relationship between well-being and health in old age with particular regard to increasing occurrence of disease and disability.
11. Which psychological factors predict the success or failure of re-location to new forms of housing (e.g. old people's home, sheltered housing)? What are the implications for practice of professional people involved?
12. Discuss the role of 'expectations' in adaptation to loss in old age.
13. Write an essay on self-esteem and sources of self-esteem in old age. How is self-esteem nourished, and how is it threatened?
14. Under what circumstances is a move to a residential home or other institutional environment likely to be successful/unsuccessful?
15. Has the psychologist a role to play in community welfare services for the elderly; for example, in primary medical care or social services agencies?
16. What behavioural and other psychological techniques are there available to help people to recover interests and customary activities that they may have lost in old age?
17. Which psychological factors are related to the onset of and recovery from depression?
18. Do any therapies exist that might be helpful to people suffering from mental impairment in old age?
19. Discuss the problems that can arise in a family as a result of the disabilities of old age and the relevance of a psychological perspective in helping to resolve them.
20. 'Social and psychological factors are more responsible

for mental deterioation in old age than are physical disorders of the brain.' Discuss.

21. What methods can we use in studying psychological changes with age? What are their respective strengths and weaknesses?

22. 'The psychology of ageing cannot be considered in isolation from the medical or sociological study of ageing.' Do you agree?

23. 'Too many of our views on the psychology of ageing are restricted by the limits of our own society.' Discuss the value of a cross-cultural approach to the psychology of ageing.

24. Which psychological research and theories are of value in the design of long-stay environments for the elderly?

25. It has been said that both doctors and social workers are dominated by a 'disease' model which they use excessively in 'labelling' old people's behaviour. How can a psychological perspective help towards a better understanding?

26. 'The problems of old age are more a function of society's attitude to ageing than of ageing itself.' Do you agree?

27. 'Old age, far from being the least important, is the most important period of life. It is the last opportunity an individual has to achieve identity and self-fulfilment and develop a sense of integrity.' Discuss this view and its implications for the way we treat elderly people.

Annotated reading

Kastenbaum, R. (1979) Growing Old - Years of Fulfilment. London: Harper & Row.

> A short introduction to the subject written by an American psychologist. He presents a balanced approach to old age, giving due weight to positive perspectives. The book is also attractively illustrated.

Bromley, D.B. (1974) The Psychology of Human Ageing (2nd edn). Harmondsworth: Penguin.

> A much longer book written by a British psychologist. It gives a very thorough coverage of subjects such as changes in performance and cognitive skills with age, and is good on the methodological issues involved in doing research on ageing.

Carver, V. and Liddiard, P. (eds) (1978) An Ageing Population (Open University Text). Sevenoaks: Hodder & Stoughton.

> A collection of readings prepared for the Open University course. The papers have been drawn from a variety of sources to provide a multidisciplinary perspective on the needs and circumstances of the elderly.

Brearley, C.P. (1975) Social Work, Ageing and Society. London: Routledge & Kegan Paul.

A book written for social workers, bringing together a wide range of material from medicine, psychology and sociology.

Gray, B. and Isaacs, B. (1979) Care of the Elderly Mentally Infirm. London: Tavistock.

A more specialized book on the elderly mentally infirm also intended for social workers, written jointly by a geriatrician and a social worker.

18

Dying and Bereavement
A. T. Carr

Demographic trends

If you had been born at the beginning of this century, your life expectancy at birth would have been 44 years if you were male or 48 years if you were female. If you were born today, your initial life expectancy would be 70 years or 76 years respectively. These figures reflect an ageing of the population that has occurred in all western industrial societies over the past 80 years. Although we all will die, most of us will do so at a relatively advanced age. Although we all will be bereaved, most of us will not suffer this until we are young adults or until we are in our middle years.

The fatal conditions of the present day, once hidden by the mass diseases, are those associated with longevity. In 1978, almost 590,000 people died in England and Wales and 85 per cent of these deaths were attributable to only three categories of illness: diseases of the circulatory system (heart and blood circulation), neoplasms (cancer) and diseases of the respiratory system (OPCS, 1979). Also, more than two people in every three now die in institutions of one form or another.

In the absence of any radical changes of events, the vast majority of us will die aged 65 years or over, in an institution of some sort and as a result of a disease of our circulatory system, respiratory system, or of cancer. This underlines an important feature of dying and death at the present time: they have become unfamiliar events that take place in unfamiliar surroundings, watched over by unfamiliar people. We all know that we will die and that we may be bereaved, yet we have very little relevant experience upon which to develop our construing or anticipation of these events and states.

Telling

The majority of fatally ill people realize, at some point, that they will not recover, even if they have not been informed of the nature of their illness. However, it would appear that only about half of all fatally ill people appreciate their condition before significant changes in health force the conclusion 'I am dying'. This is almost certainly an under-estimate: there will be some people who know that they will not recover but who do not communicate this.

Although about one-half of terminally ill people appear to appreciate the seriousness of their illness, this awareness is usually achieved independently, informally and indirectly. No more than 15 per cent of terminally ill cancer patients are told of their prognosis either by their general practitioner or by a hospital doctor (Cartwright et al, 1973). This contrasts markedly with the experiences of their close relatives. Almost 90 per cent of the close relatives of terminally ill patients are aware that the patient's illness is terminal and most of them are informed of this by a general practitioner or by a hospital doctor. There are several implications of these data, the two most obvious being that fatally ill people and their principal carers often do not share the same information about the illness, and that doctors usually are unwilling to tell patients when they have a disease that will kill them. Perhaps the most serious consequence is that one or more of the familial participants has to cope with the demands of this most stressful period without adequate support.

It is remarkable how little emphasis is placed upon the wishes of the patient. Most people, including doctors, whether they are young or old, ill or well, say they would want to know if they had a fatal illness or that they are glad they do know. Several studies have examined this issue and the results are consistent in showing that more than 70 per cent of all the samples used say they would want to be informed if they had a terminal disease. It is clear that most people say they would want to be informed of the seriousness of their illness, most doctors say that they would want to be told and yet the majority of fatally ill patients are not told. Also, the existence of a real threat to life does not reduce the very high proportion of people who want to know if they have a fatal illness.

In general, learning that one has a fatal illness is followed by a period of disquiet, even grief, although the emotional response may be concealed from others. It is worth noting that some patients do not 'hear' or at least appear not to remember, what they have been told regarding their prognosis. Although it has been proposed that the defence mechanism of denial is a ubiquitous response to learning of a fatal prognosis (Kubler-Ross, 1969), there are other more mundane possibilities. The first is the use of terminology that may have very precise meanings for a professional but which may mean nothing, or something very different, to the patient. To inform a patient of 'malignant lymphoma' or 'secondary metastases' may not constitute communication. Even when the words that are used are understood reasonably well, they may not convey what was intended. For some individuals, the knowledge of their impending death will be extremely distressing; in such cases the person may be quite unable to accept what is plain to everybody else. They may become distraught as their bodies show increasing signs of impending death while they continue to deny that they are dying. Such extreme responses, as a terminal illness progresses, correspond to denial as elucidated by Kubler-Ross (1969). However, it would be inappropriate to regard as denial a person's failure to comprehend or to recall initial statements of his prognosis. Quite apart from the communication problems mentioned above, if a person has no prior suspicions that his condition may be terminal it is probable that he will be unable to accept a fatal diagnosis. It is not that he REFUSES to accept such information, but he is UNABLE to accept it. It demands a radical revision of a person's view of the world and such a major psychological adjustment takes time. Initially, such news is not disbelieved, but on the other hand, it cannot be fitted into a person's perception of the world: it cannot be accommodated. The revised view of the world will need to be tested, amended and confirmed in the light of further information. The person will seek such information in what people say, how they behave and how his body feels. It is only when the revised view of the world 'fits', in the sense that it is not violated by new observations or new information, that the person is able fully to accommodate the 'truths' that have been offered. An individual who has prior suspicions about the seriousness of his illness has already constructed, at least in part, a view of his world that includes himself as a dying person.

Our aim must be to maintain dignity, to alleviate suffering and to help the person live as fully as possible for as long as he is able: he should be told what he is prepared to hear at a time when he is prepared to listen. The same principle might be kept in mind when dealing with relatives. There are indications that those who are told with care show improved family relationships, less tension and less desperation during their terminal illnesses than those who are not (Gerle et al, 1960). Helping a person towards fuller awareness of and adjustment to a fatal prognosis is the beginning of a communication process which is itself an integral part of caring for the terminally ill.

Terminality and dying

The two words terminality and dying are being used to draw a distinction that can have important implications for the way in which fatally ill people are managed and treated. The main implication is that of regarding someone as terminally ill, but nevertheless living and with some valuable life remaining, rather than regarding him as dying with all the negative attitudes this provokes. Once an illness has been diagnosed as terminal we need to regard the patient as living and possibly living more intensely than the rest of us, until he clearly is dying. Terminality, then, begins when a terminal diagnosis is made but dying starts later, usually when death is much closer and when the person is prepared to relinquish his biological life in the absence of valuable, functional life.

Sources of distress

Effective and appropriate care of the fatally ill requires an awareness of potential sources of distress so that distress can be anticipated and thus be avoided or alleviated. Of course, distress is not confined to the patient: effective care and support for those who are close to the patient is merited not only on humanitarian grounds, but also because of the exacerbation of the patient's suffering that can result from the distress of relatives and friends. Table 1 summarizes some of the most common sources of distress for the patient and those who are close to him.

The listing contained in table 1 is by no means exhaustive, but it illustrates a number of points. First, given some capacity for empathy on the part of the survivor(s) there is little that the terminally ill person must endure that the survivor can avoid. This commonality of the sources of distress argues strongly for the need to attend to the welfare of survivors before they become bereaved. Second, it is clear that almost all the potential sources of distress are psychological in nature. Even some of the physical symptoms such as incontinence or smells are distressing because of our values and expectations. Also, pain itself is an experience that is subject to psychological factors rather than a sensation that is elicited by an appropriate stimulus.

Although we cannot examine in detail the physical distress of terminal illness, our discussion would be incomplete without a summary of this. Cartwright et al (1973) and Ward (1974) identified retrospectively the physical symptoms experienced by their samples of terminal cancer patients, 215 and 264 individuals respectively. These data are summarized in table 2.

It is striking that the rank order of symptoms is the same for both samples and a significant proportion of patients in each sample experienced each of the symptoms listed. Other common physical symptoms were breathing difficulties, 52 per cent; coughing, 48 per cent (Ward); and sleeplessness, 17 per cent (Cartwright et al).

Distress and coping

An examination of tables 1 and 2 points to a number of psychological processes that predispose people to react with depression and anxiety during a terminal illness. Current approaches to depression emphasize the role of loss and helplessness as aetiological factors. Loss refers to the real or imagined loss of a valued object, role, activity, relationship, etc. The individual relevance of the concept of loss lies in the individual differences of our value systems. For example, a person who highly values physical abilities, physical appearance, etc., is likely to be more at risk for depression as a result of physical debility, tiredness and deterioration in appearance, than someone for whom such attributes are low in his hierarchy of values.

Helplessness describes a state that is characterized by an awareness that one's behaviour is unrelated to the events

Table 1

Common sources of distress

Fatally ill person (P)	Those who love P
Awareness of impending death	Awareness of impending bereavement
Anticipation of loss	Anticipation of loss
Physical sequelae of disease process, e.g. tumours, lesions, nausea, incontinence, breathlessness, unpleasant smells	Empathic concern, aversion, etc.
Frustration and help-lessness as disease progresses	Frustration and help-lessness as disease progresses
Uncertainty about the future welfare of the family	Uncertainty about the future welfare of the family
Anticipation of pain	
Empathic concern	Caring for P, night-sitting, tiredness, etc.
Changes in roles with family, friends, etc.	Changes in roles with family, friends, etc
Changes in abilities as illness progresses	Empathic concern
Changes in appearance as illness progresses	Empathic concern, aversion, etc.
Uncertainties about dying	Empathic concern
Dying	Empathic concern
	Discovery of death, directly or indirectly
	Practicalities, funeral, etc.
	Grief
	Role changes
	Reconstruction of life

Table 2

Symptoms suffered by terminal cancer patients

Symptom	Per cent in sample of Cartwright et al	Per cent in sample of Ward
Pain	87	62
Anorexia	76	61
Vomiting	54	38
Urinary incontinence	38	28
Faecal incontinence	37	20
Bedsores	24	13

which impinge upon oneself. When a person is subjected to aversive events whose occurrence, intensity, duration, etc., is quite independent of behaviour, a characteristic state may ensue. This state, which occurs in the majority of subjects tested, is known as learned helplessness. There are individual differences in susceptibility to learned helplessness, but the more aversive the events and the more frequently they are experienced as independent of behaviour the more likely it is to develop. It is a generalized state characterized by apathy, dysphoric mood, psychomotor retardation (that is, slowness in thought and action), and feelings of hopelessness. Many clinical depressions are explained most fully in terms of the development of helplessness and there is evidence that sudden death is not an uncommon consequence of learned helplessness in laboratory animals. There can be little doubt about the relevance and importance of helplessness to our consideration of the welfare of the terminally ill.

Let us now return to the sources of distress summarized in tables 1 and 2. It is clear that some of these are intrinsically uncontrollable and others duplicate the procedures that are used in experimental work to induce helplessness in that they are aversive, uncontrollable and repeated: for instance, urinary incontinence and vomiting. Furthermore, many patients undergo physical investigations and treatments that they do not understand, that they find unpleasant or painful and about which they feel they have little choice other than to accept them passively. It is not surprising to find that depression is commonly encountered in the terminally ill. A significant minority of fatally ill people and their next-of-kin become moderately or severely depressed (about one in five people in each group). Those most at risk are adolescents, young parents with dependents, those who have many physical symptoms and those who experience lengthy hospitalization.

The reciprocal interaction of physical and psychological processes must not be overlooked. We have already considered the depressive role of repeated, unpleasant physical symptoms. However, the interaction also proceeds in the other direction: adverse emotional states such as depression and anxiety augment pain and other physical discomforts. The essential point is that pain is not a simple response to an appropriate physical stimulus such as tissue damage: it is an experience that is compounded of the stimulation and the person's response to that stimulation. The motivational and emotional state of the person acts, as it were, to colour the sensation and to produce the experience we call pain. Without such 'colouring' and evaluation the sensation may be perceived but not experienced as painful.

It is the experience of most who work in terminal care that the relief of anxiety or depression through appropriate support, communication and practical help reduces the pain of patients and, not insignificantly, reduces the need for medication. The point is not that attention to the psychological state of the patient removes the need for relevant medication but that it reduces the dosages that may be required to bring relief. There are many obvious advantages that derive from this, not the least of which is the ability to alleviate pain without resorting to medications that render the patient confused, drowsy or comatose.

Anxiety arises when a future event is appraised as threatening. This appraisal is the evaluation of an event in terms of its harmful implications for the individual, harm being the extent to which continued physical and psychological functioning is endangered. Threat appraisal is a highly subjective process that depends upon the subjective likelihood of an event - that is, how probable the person feels the event to be - and the degree of harm that will result, this again being subjectively assessed. So a terminally ill person is anxious to the extent that the events that he anticipates are both likely and harmful in his own terms: if they are not perceived as likely or harmful then they will not provoke anxiety.

Anxiety is an essentially adaptive emotion, in that it motivates us to initiate behaviours that prevent the anticipated harm being realized. To the extent that a person accepts that he is dying and is unable to reduce or eliminate the harmful consequences of this process, he is liable to remain anxious. An inspection of tables 1 and 2 reminds us that there are many potential types of harm that the fatally ill person is motivated, by anxiety, to alleviate. It is reassuring to note that the intense panic that is such a common feature of clinical anxiety states occurs rarely in terminal illness except, perhaps, in those who continue to deny the imminence of death as the end

approaches and those for whom breathing is difficult.
However, moderate anxiety is by no means uncommon in the
terminally ill. This is not only an extra burden of suffering for the person but it also exacerbates other
discomforts including pain.

There are few systematic reports of anxiety in terminal
illness but from the data that do exist it is clear that
moderate anxiety is experienced by between one-quarter and
one-half of patients. The anxiety may be readily discerned
in those people who are able to verbalize their fears, and
who are given the opportunity to do so, but it may be less
obvious in those who communicate less well verbally. However, the physiological and behavioural concomitants of
anxiety are good indicators of the presence of unspoken
fear. Often it is difficult to distinguish between physiological signs of anxiety such as gastric upset, nausea,
diarrhoea, muscular pains, etc., and symptoms of the disease
process or side effects of treatment. Nevertheless, the
possibility that a patient might be persistently anxious
should not be overlooked.

Given the subjective nature of threat appraisal, the
causes of an individual's anxiety can be surprisingly idiosyncratic, but there are a few consistencies that may provide some clues. Younger adults expect to be distressed by
pain and parting from the people they love, whereas the
elderly fear becoming dependent and losing control of bowel
and bladder functioning. Hinton (1972) reports that almost
two-thirds of his patients who died aged 50 years or less
were clearly anxious but this was true of only one-third of
those aged 60 years and over. There is a clear and understandable trend for young parents of dependent children to
be more anxious than other groups. Perhaps it is not insig-
nificant that younger patients also tend to experience more
physical discomfort during their terminal illnesses.

According to Hinton (1963), anxiety is more common in
people with a lengthy terminal illness. He found more than
50 per cent of those who had been ill for more than one year
to be clearly anxious, but only 20 per cent of those who had
been ill for less than three months showed similar levels of
anxiety. Although anxiety levels fluctuate during a
patient's terminal illness, there is no general trend for
anxiety to increase as the person draws closer to death.
Some people become more apprehensive as their illnesses
progress, but others become more calm during the last stages
of their lives.

Some specific experiences of illness may be potent
sources of anxiety. Prior episodes of intolerable pain can
provoke great anxiety when they are recalled or when their
return is anticipated. Difficulties in breathing are commonly associated with anxiety and a tendency to panic. Also,
in the context of a mortal illness there are a number of
sources of distress that are intrinsically uncontrollable
and uncertain, such as the final process of dying, death and
the nature of the world in which one's dependent survivors

will be living. When anticipated harm remains and the person perceives it as beyond his ability to influence, he becomes liable to the state of helplessness. If this is severe he may become depressed, as we have discussed: if less severe, then he may exhibit the resignation that has been termed 'acceptance' (Kubler-Ross, 1969). If he persists in his attempts to control and influence events that are beyond his reach he is likely to remain anxious and even to become more anxious as he approaches death.

For the fatally ill child under five or six years of age, anxiety takes the form of separation anxiety, loneliness and fears of being abandoned. The young child does not appear to fear death and its implications, but his fears are aroused by those aspects of illness and hospitalization which elicit fear in most ill children who require hospital treatment.

Between the ages of six and ten or eleven years, separation fears persist, but the child is increasingly prone to anxiety over painful treatments and bodily intrusions. Such fears of mutilation and physical harm are intensified in the absence of familiar, trusted adults. Some children in this age group, because of differing prior experiences or more advanced cognitive development, are also aware of the cessation of awareness and bodily functioning consequent upon death.

Although there is some dispute as to whether the child under ten years of age is aware of his impending death at a conceptual level, there is little doubt that many young children perceive that their illness is no ordinary illness. This is a frequent clinical observation and there is a good deal of evidence that it is so whether or not the diagnosis is discussed with the child (Spinetta, 1974). Of course there are many cues that may indicate to the child that something very serious and threatening is happening, quite apart from his numerous tests, treatments and visits to hospital. Most children are finely tuned to detect meaningful and subtle signs in the verbal and non-verbal behaviour of adults: the things that are not talked about, tone of voice, eye contact, posture, etc. Also, there are many cues that the child would find it hard to overlook: whispered conversations, unusually frequent and intense bodily contact, unusual generosity and freedom of choice with regard to presents and treats, and so on.

Parents and others usually begin to grieve for the fatally ill child soon after they accept the prognosis. Their ability to cope with this grief is an important determinant of their effectiveness in supporting the child. Since familiar adults and siblings are likely to be the child's greatest potential source of comfort and reassurance, it is important that time and attention is devoted to these significant others for the sake of the child's welfare. There are indications of a high incidence of psychological difficulties in family members, particularly siblings, during the terminal illness of a child. Clearly

parents, who are themselves struggling with their own
emotions, may have difficulty sustaining the other children in the family, let alone in providing comfort and
reassurance to the one who is ill.

Adolescents and some younger children will be aware of
the finality of death. Although dependent upon adults in a
functional sense, they may perceive themselves as having
important roles to play in the welfare of others and thus be
subject to fears for the well-being of their survivors in
much the same way as adults with dependents. The very young
child may endure a terminal illness with striking calmness
and acceptance of his lot, provided that his separation
fears are allayed, but once he is past the age of six or
seven years he becomes prone to a wide range of fears that
exceed those of his 'normally ill' counterpart with severe,
chronic, but non-fatal illness. Although children may be
reluctant to express their fears, or may express them
unclearly and indirectly, they should be anticipated in all
aspects of care.

We have examined the range of potential sources of
distress in terminal illness and the most common types of
distress that result from these. Pain, anxiety and depression are sufficiently frequent and severe to merit attention
when services are being planned and delivered. However, a
majority of fatally ill people do not become severely
anxious, deeply depressed or suffer from unrelieved pain.
This does not minimize the awful suffering of the large
minority or the pressing need for improvements in care to
which this suffering testifies. It indicates only that, with
whatever help they receive, most people who endure a terminal illness cope reasonably well, keeping their levels of
distress within limits that are acceptable to themselves and
to those who care for them.

The responses of people who are faced with impending
death show sufficient uniformity to enable observers to
write of stages, phases and patterns of coping (e.g. Kubler-
Ross, 1969; Falek and Britton, 1974). Quite apart from
doubts about the uniformity and progressive nature of stages
of coping in terminal illness (e.g. Schulz and Aderman,
1974), it cannot be assumed that any particular individual
NEEDS to negotiate these stages in order to cope most
effectively with his impending death. The emotional responses and their dependent behaviours are indicators of the
difficulties, and triumphs, experienced by people in their
attempts to cope. The absence of a specific emotion does not
mean that the person has omitted a necessary stage of the
'normal' coping pattern and that this omission detracts from
his adjustment. Provided we do not equate typical with ideal
or necessary, an awareness of the emotional stages or phases
that are commonly encountered in terminal patients can help
us to understand the problems they face, to provide the
types of help and support that might be beneficial and to
improve our ability to cope with the emotions that their
behaviours arouse in relatives and in ourselves.

However, there are a number of general points that can be made about a stage model of terminal illness. The responses delineated, including denial, anger, bargaining, depression and acceptance (Kubler-Ross, 1969), are not specific to people who are facing death; they have been observed in many other stressful situations that involve loss and uncontrollable harm, such as bereavement, amputation and imprisonment. The generality evidenced by these observations does not confirm the progression of the stage model: it highlights the normality of disbelief, anger, sadness, etc., in the face of irretrievable and severe loss.

Often it is difficult to decide which stage or phase a person is in. Without reasonable certainty in the identification of stages, the predictive value of a stage model is severely impaired. This predictive aspect of the model is also reduced if the stages are not ubiquitous and if they are not successive. Clinical observation suggests that the emotion displayed by a person is responsive to many internal and external events. Perhaps all that can be said with any certainty is that some responses, when they occur, are likely to predominate earlier in a terminal illness, for example denial, and some are more likely to appear later, for example depression and acceptance.

We must take care not to lose sight of the individual in anticipating responses to a terminal illness. The fatally ill person brings with him his own particular view of himself, his family, his future, doctors, death, etc. The importance of individual differences during the terminal phase of life is well illustrated by the work of Kastenbaum and Weisman (1972). They found that their patients could be divided into two broad groups, both of which were aware of the imminence of death but which differed markedly in their behavioural styles. One group gradually withdrew from their usual activities and social contacts, remaining inactive until their final illness. The other group was characterized by involvement: patients in this group remained busily engaged in everyday activities until death occurred as an interruption in their living.

Dying

The relationship between a patient's reactions to a terminal illness and his dying is not only that these are the psychological context within which the final process occurs, but also there are increasing indications that they influence the timing of death (see Achterberg and Lawlis, 1977). Whereas blood chemistries reflect on-going or current disease status, psychological factors are predictive of subsequent disease status and longevity. Poorer prognosis and shorter survival occurs in patients who, typically, show great dependence upon others, who deny the severity of their conditions, who have a history of poor social relationships and who do not have access to, or do not utilize, supportive social relationships during their illnesses. These patients tend to become more withdrawn, pessimistic and depressed as their illness progresses. Longer survival is associated with patients who maintain good personal and social relationships in the context of an existing network of such relationships. They can be assertive without hostility, asking for and receiving much medical and emotional support. They may be concerned about dying alone and seek to deter others from withdrawing from them without their needs being met. These patients also experience less pain, or at least complain less about pain and discomfort.

Dying is a process rather than an event that occurs at one point in time. This final process that constitutes the transition from life to death is usually of short duration, a matter of hours or days. For the vast majority of people it is not dramatic. Most people, both ill and well, express a desire to die peacefully or to die in their sleep. There is little doubt that this wish is fulfilled in most cases. Although there are a few people for whom pain or breathlessness may increase near the end, most slip knowingly or unawares into the unconsciousness that continues until their dying is finished.

After a terminal illness lasting some months, most patients are tired and wearied by their experiences. During his last days, apart from having his needs tended, a patient may wish to be alone or to avoid news and problems of the 'outside world'. He may well become less talkative and prefer shorter visits. Communication tends to shift increasingly towards the non-verbal. In terms of interaction he may want little more than somebody to sit with him in silence, perhaps holding his hand. It is clear from those who wish to talk briefly in their last hours of life that there is an experience of 'distance' from life. As Saunders (1978) so aptly puts it, 'They were not frightened nor unwilling to go, for by then they were too far away to want to come back. They were conscious of leaving weakness and exhaustion rather than life and its activities. They rarely had any pain but felt intensely weary. They wanted to say good-bye to those they loved but were not torn with longing to stay with them'.

Euthanasia

Euthanasia, meaning a gentle and easy death and the act of bringing this about, has been a source of discussion and controversy for many years. The level of current interest is evidenced by the large number of recent publications on the topic in the professional literature and the increasing support of the public for such organizations as the Voluntary Euthanasia Society in the UK and the Euthanasia Education Council in the USA.

The public support for euthanasia is probably based upon an expectation that death will come as a result of a lengthy illness, an illness that may well be prolonged unduly by the application of current medical knowledge and techniques. It is based upon fears of the physical and psychological

incompetence, dependence, indignity and pain that may result
from a chronic or terminal illness. Even those professionals
who oppose euthanasia on ethical, religious or practical
grounds readily concede that such fears are not unjustified
for many people. We have already examined the potential
distress of terminal illness but, for many people, support
for euthanasia is prompted by thoughts of an unwanted,
useless existence where biological life is maintained
artificially and against their wishes in a hospital, nursing
home or geriatric ward. Sadly, such thoughts are all too
often reinforced by cases that Saunders (1977) rightly
describes as 'truly horrendous'. As a society we cannot
escape the reality that far too many elderly people end
their days in loneliness, isolation and degradation. Even
when the physical care provided is good, the psychological
distress can be great. The prima facie case for euthanasia
appears to be strong.

The many logical, philosophical and ethical arguments
relating to the legalization of voluntary euthanasia, both
active and passive, have been well stated several times
(e.g. Rachels, 1975; Foot, 1978), and space precludes their
consideration here. However, these arguments frequently take
little account of relevant practical and psychological
issues. In drawing up the necessary guidelines for the
legalization of voluntary euthanasia there are major problems in guarding against error and potential abuse, both by
relatives and professionals. Nevertheless, many of these
problems could be surmounted by the use and recognition of
the Living Will. This document, as distributed by the Euthanasia Educational Council, is signed and witnessed when the
person is in good health. Its aim is to avoid an existence
in dependence, deterioration, indignity and hopeless pain.

Doctors spend their lives preserving the lives of others
and alleviating their suffering. It can be argued that, in
recent years, the pendulum has swung too far in the direction of the maintenance of life at the expense of the relief
of distress, but the activities of doctors make demands upon
their energies and their personal time that few other professions would tolerate. This degree of commitment is consistent with, and continually reinforces, a value system
that places a very high priority upon the preservation of
life and actions that serve this end. For an individual in
whom such values relate closely to his self-concept, the
active termination of a patient's life may be damaging to
his self-regard and to his concept of his own worth as a
person. Although there is little difference between active
and passive euthanasia on moral and logical grounds, for an
individual doctor the difference may be vast and unbridge-
able in terms of his own psychology. It would be quite
unjustifiable to place such men in a position where society
expected them to implement active euthanasia.

From the patient's point of view, the availability of
euthanasia has a wider potential than the avoidance of
further suffering. People who are given control over

aversive and painful stimulation, by having the facility to terminate, reduce or avoid it in some way, are better able to cope with the experience. Even though the available control is rarely exercised, the aversive stimulation is better tolerated and provokes less distress. Provided that the patient is quite sure that his life can be terminated when he wishes, and only when he wishes, he is likely to cope better with the effects of his illness or condition and to be less distressed by them.

To allow a patient to die in order to release him from hopelessness and irreducible suffering, while continuing to treat his current distress, is thoroughly compatible with the humanitarian principle of care. Whether or not one wishes to describe this as passive, voluntary euthanasia is a matter of personal choice. There are grounds for a more widespread recognition of this compatibility and for more weight to be given to the wishes of patients and their families. Of course, the same grounds demand that more effort, time and resources should be devoted to improving the quality of care that is offered. All such improvements weaken the case for regarding death as a desirable release from suffering, as a release that is needed so frequently that its use should be regularized. In the long term, and certainly in the shorter term, there are likely to be some people for whom death is the preferred option. It is a problem that will become more acute as our society continues to age and as the life-preserving techniques of medicine continue to develop.

Bereavement

Bereavement is a state characterized by loss. The main focus of interest is upon the loss occasioned by the death of a significant person but people are bereaved by other losses such as loss of role, loss of status, separation and amputation. The state of loss serves as the stimulus for the bereavement response, a response that is manifested culturally and individually. The cultural response constitutes mourning and is a pattern of behaviour that is learned from and supported by one's immediate culture as appropriate following bereavement. Grief is the individual response and is the main area of concern for researchers and clinicians alike. In that grief typically follows a reasonably consistent course over time, ending ultimately in its resolution, it can be regarded as an individual process that occurs in response to individual loss.

The nature of grief

Although the major features of grief are known to most of us either intuitively or through personal experience, the chief findings of the many descriptive studies can be summarized broadly as follows:

* grief is a complex but stereotyped response pattern that includes such physical and psychological 'symptoms' as

withdrawal, fatigue, sleep disturbance, anxiety and loss
of appetite;
* it is elicited by a rather well-defined stimulus
situation, namely the real or imagined loss of a valued
object or role, and it is resolved when new object
relations are established;
* it is a ubiquitous phenomenon among human beings and
appears in other social species, especially higher
primates;
* it is an extremely stressful response both physically
nd psychologically, but grief-related behaviour is
ften antithetical to the establishment of new object
elations and hence to the alleviation of the stress.
or example, fatigue and withdrawal make it much more
ifficult for the bereaved person to develop new roles
nd new personal relationships in place of those lost
rough bereavement.

mplexity and stress of grief is readily appreciated
e number and nature of its components are consi-
Hinton's (1972) description of grief adumbrates the
mmonly observed characteristics: shock, denial,
, depression, guilt, anger and a wide variety of
signs of anxiety. Other components include searching
ur, suicidal thoughts, idealization of the lost per-
nic, a heightened vulnerability to physical illness
sychological disorders.
nature of grief as a process is emphasized by the
ion of stages by many observers and authors.
there is a sequential character to the process it
incorrect to anticipate an orderly progression
he stages in all people. As with the notion of
dying that was discussed earlier, the component
of the various stages overlap and merge into one
Also, there are frequent 'regressions' to earlier
gain, it is better to think in terms of components,
hich will predominate earlier in the process and
t will predominate later. In general, three stages
have been delineated and labelled according to
n: perhaps the best descriptive labels are shock,
nd recovery.
ally there may be a period of numbness and detach-
ending, to some extent, on the unexpectedness of
of the death. During this immediate response the
nay appear stoical and calm. Normal routines may be
ned especially where domestic or other factors
str ture the situation. Alternatively, the person may
ap r dazed and quite unable to comprehend the reality of
the news; he may be unresponsive to his environment and in
need of care and support during this period. Whatever the
specific initial reaction in a particular instance, it can
last from a few minutes to two weeks or so, with the stoical
reaction being the more likely to persist longer. The
bereaved person is less able than the terminally ill to deny

successfully the reality of the situation: sooner or later, and in many different ways, powerful and pointed signs of the reality of loss occur, such as the empty place at table, the empty bed or chair, the funeral or the silent house when friends and relatives depart. As with the news of terminal diagnosis, people need time to assimilate and to accommodate to a new state of the world. Whether the period of shock and disbelief is long or short, a sense of unreality or even disbelief is likely to return periodically for several months.

As awareness of the loss develops the person may express anger at himself, at staff or at God for not preventing the death. Whether or not anger is present, the phase of acute grieving or despair is the most painful. Lindemann (1944), in his pioneering study of bereavement, observed the following 'symptoms' as common to all individuals suffering acute grief: somatic distress lasting between 20 minutes and one hour at a time, feelings of tightness in the throat, choking with shortness of breath, muscular weakness and intense subjective distress described as tension or psychological pain. This specific response, which appears to be unique to bereavement, occurs against a background of stress, anxiety and sadness or depression, together with the somatic concomitants of these emotions.

Behaviourally, the grieving person may be unable to maintain goal-directed activity, appearing disorganized and unable to make plans. He may be restless, moving about in an aimless fashion and constantly searching for something to do. He may find himself going, unwittingly, to the places where the dead person might be found if he were alive. A preoccupation with the lost person creates a perceptual set that leads to misinterpretations of ambiguous sights and sounds as indicative of his being alive. Some grieving people report seeing the dead person with a clarity that goes beyond illusion and misperception. Such experiences can occur long after the phase of acute grieving is past. Obviously, the physical and psychological demands of this period are heavy and it is not surprising that irritability is common, especially when the person is eating and sleeping poorly. Anger, frustration and resentment may be directed at friends and neighbours irrespective of merit. Such feelings may also be directed against the dead person for abandoning the survivor.

The intense anguish of the despair phase can be unremitting, rising to peaks of distress with thoughts of the loved one who has died. Most bereaved people seem unable to prevent themselves from thinking and talking about the one who has died even though this usually exacerbates their distress. Whether this is conceptualized as 'grief-work' or as repeated exposure leading to habituation, it appears to be necessary to recovery from grief. A reduction in the frequency and intensity of periods of peak distress may be the first sign that the process of recovery is beginning.

Although estimates vary, the acute despair phase of grief typically lasts for three to ten weeks.

The process of recovery from grief is a process of reconstruction. Although some aspects of the person's private and public 'self' may survive bereavement relatively unchanged, it is necessary to develop new roles, new behaviours and new relationships with others. Whatever else may or may not be changed by bereavement, the survivor must live without one important and potentially crucial personal relationship that had existed previously: the loss of this relationship is the loss of the psychological and practical advantages, and disadvantages, that it conferred. Socially, the survivor is now a widow or a widower rather than one of a married couple: he is now a boy without a father, or she is now a mother without a child, etc. Apart from the direct, personal impact of such changes, they also influence the way survivors are viewed and treated socially. The bereaved person has to develop a new private and public self that enables him to live in a changed world.

Although a reduction in the frequency and intensity of periods of extreme distress may herald the process of recovery, it cannot begin in earnest until the person has periods in which he is not overwhelmed with despair nor preoccupied with thoughts of the one who has died. Many bereaved people recall with clarity the moment when they realized that they had not been preoccupied with their loss: when, for a brief period at least, their thoughts had been directed elsewhere and their emotions had been less negative, even positive. These moments of 'spontaneous forgetting', together with improvements in sleeping and appetite, provide the person with some opportunity to reconstrue and to reconstruct himself and his future. With less exhaustion and a lightening of mood, decisions and actions become more feasible and the person can begin the active process of reviving previous relationships and activities, perhaps in a modified form, and of developing new ones. This period of active readjustment may never be complete, especially in the elderly, but it usually lasts for between six and 18 months after the phase of acute grief and despair.

Determinants of grief

Strictly speaking, it is inaccurate to talk of determinants of grief for the available data do not allow us to identify the causative factors that lead to variations in the response to bereavement. However, it makes intuitive sense to talk of determinants and is in keeping with other literature on the topic. Parkes (1972) groups the factors of potential importance according to their temporal relationship to the event of death, that is, antecedent, concurrent and subsequent determinants. Among antecedent factors, the most influential appear to be life stresses prior to bereavement, relationship with the deceased and mode of death. On the whole, an atypical grief response with associated psychological problems is more likely when bereavement occurs as one of a series of life crises, when the death is sudden, unanticipated and untimely, and when the relationship with the deceased had been one of strong attachment, reliance or ambivalence.

A number of demographic variables (concurrent) relate to the nature of grief. In particular, being young, female and married to the deceased increases the likelihood of problems arising after bereavement. Of course, these factors are not unrelated to such antecedent factors as strong attachment, reliance and untimely death. Other concurrent factors with adverse implications are susceptibility to grief, as evidenced by previous episodes of depression, an inability to express emotions, lower socio-economic status and the absence of a genuine religious faith.

The presence of religious faith might be placed more appropriately with subsequent determinants, for its role is likely to be one of supporting the bereaved person during the stressful period of grief. Also, someone with an active belief system probably will be associated with a supportive social group, and there is little doubt that a network of supportive social relationships is the most advantageous of the subsequent determinants. Other subsequent factors that have positive implications are the absence of secondary stresses during the period of grief and the development of new life opportunities at work and in interpersonal relationships, for instance. Again, these are more probable when a good network of supportive social relationships exists. It is worth recalling our earlier conclusion about the value of such relationships in a person's adjustment to impending death.

Among the wide range of factors that have implications for a person's reaction to bereavement, there is most controversy about the importance of anticipatory grief. As the term implies, this refers to grief that occurs in anticipation of an expected death, particularly the death of a child or a spouse. Overall, it can be concluded that younger widows experience more intense grief, with associated problems, than those aged 46 years or over. Sudden death exacerbates the severity of the grief response for young widows but not for the middle-aged or the elderly. For the latter two groups there appears to be a small effect in the opposite direction: that is, some symptoms of grief, especially irritability, are greater after a prolonged illness prior to death. It should be noted that the potentially beneficial effects of anticipatory grief are not confined to conjugal bereavement but also mitigate the response to other losses, such as that of a child. Also, it seems possible that there is an optimum period for the anticipation of death, perhaps up to six months, after which the lengthy duration of illness may increase stress and exhaustion and increase the likelihood of adverse reactions in subsequent grief.

Illness and death after bereavement

There are clear data that reveal an elevated mortality risk after bereavement. At all ages, bereaved persons experience a higher risk of dying than married people of corresponding sex and age. The increase in risk is greater for bereaved males than females, and for both sexes, the increase is greater at younger ages.

The elevated risk of death is concentrated particularly in the first six months after bereavement especially for widowers, with a further rise in the second year for widows. The predominant causes of death are coronary thrombosis and other arterio-sclerotic or degenerative heart diseases. Most of these causes can be seen as a result of continued stress and a lack of self-care. In general, when the data from replicated studies in the UK and the USA are taken together, the risk of dying is at least doubled for widows and widowers at all ages for a great variety of diseases.

Having briefly examined the possible psychological and physical consequences of bereavement, and having considered relevant predictive factors, it is important to remember that we are talking only of probabilities. A person may be at great risk of problems following bereavement, in the statistical sense, and yet survive the experience well. Another person with only favourable indicators may suffer badly and experience severe physical or psychological problems.

The vast majority of bereaved people, with a little help from their friends, cope well with the experience and reconstruct lives that are worth while in their own terms. There are no persuasive grounds for considering the provision of professional services for the bereaved. The most useful strategy is to maintain some form of non-intrusive follow-up after bereavement with ready access to an informal support group if this should be necessary. The bereaved need somebody who will listen when they want to talk, somebody who will not try to push them into things before they are ready: somebody who will support them emotionally and practically when appropriate and just by showing that they care. This demands an informal response rather than a professional one. However, professional care and concern should not end with the death of a patient: the newly bereaved person still has a long way to go and every effort should be made to ensure that they will have access to whatever social support may be needed.

References

Achterberg, J. and Lawlis, G.F. (1977)
Psychological factors and blood chemistries as disease outcome predictors for cancer patients. Multivariate Experimental Clinical Research, 3, 107-122.

Cartwright, A., Hockey, L. and Anderson, J.L. (1973)
Life Before Death. London: Routledge & Kegan Paul.

Falek, A. and Britton, S. (1974)
Phases in coping: the hypothesis and its implications.
Social Biology, 21, 1-7.

Foot, P. (1978)
Euthanasia. In E. McMullin (ed.), Death and Decision.
Boulder, Colo.: Westview Press.

Gerle, B., Lunden, G. and Sandblow, P. (1960)
The patient with inoperable cancer from the psychiatric
and social standpoints. Cancer, 13, 1206-1211.

Hinton, J.M. (1963)
The physical and mental distress of the dying. Quarterly
Journal of Medicine, 32, 1-21.

Hinton, J.M. (1972)
Dying. Harmondsworth: Penguin.

Kastenbaum, R. and Weisman, A.D. (1972)
The psychological autopsy as a research procedure in
gerontology. In D.P. Kent, R. Kastenbaum and S.
Sherwood (eds), Research Planning and Action for the
Elderly. New York: Behavioral Publications.

Kubler-Ross, E. (1969)
On Death and Dying. London: Tavistock.

Lindemann, E. (1944)
Symptomatology and management of acute grief. American
Journal of Psychiatry, 101, 141-148.

Office of Population Censuses and Surveys (1979)
Mortality Statistics. London: HMSO.

Parkes, C.M. (1972)
Bereavement. London: Tavistock.

Rachels, J. (1975)
Active and passive euthanasia. New England Journal of
Medicine, 292, 78-80.

Saunders, C. (1977)
Dying they live. In H. Feifel (ed.), New Meanings of
Death. New York: McGraw-Hill.

Saunders, C. (1978)
Care of the dying. In V. Carver and P. Liddiard (eds),
An Ageing Population. Sevenoaks: The Open University.

Schulz, R. and Aderman, D. (1974)
Clinical research and the stages of dying. Omega, 5,
137-143.

Spinetta, J.J. (1974)
The dying child's awareness of death. Psychological
Bulletin, 81, 256-260.

Ward, A.W.M. (1974)
Telling the patient. Journal of the Royal College of
General Practitioners, 24, 465-468.

Questions

1. How has the pattern of dying changed in the UK since the
   turn of the century? What has caused these changes and
   what are their consequences?
2. Who should be informed of a patient's fatal prognosis?
   Give reasons for your answer.
3. Summarize the most common sources of distress of the

terminally ill and their families: what are the implications of these?

4. Why do terminally ill people become depressed and how large a problem is this?

5. How common is anxiety in terminal illness and why does it arise?

6. What psychological problems might arise for a fatally ill six-year-old child and his family? What steps could be taken to mitigate these problems?

7. Why should there be growing public support for the legalization of voluntary euthanasia and why is this not reflected in professional attitudes?

8. What is the bereavement response and what causes it?

9. What factors are important in influencing the nature of grief?

10. Construct a stereotypic, but detailed, character sketch of the person most likely to cope badly with a terminal illness: do the same for the person most likely to cope well. Justify your answer.

11. How would you respond to a 40-year-old dentist, with two children, who is suffering with terminal cancer, when he asks you 'what will it be like?' What points would you hope to cover in this and subsequent conversations and why do you consider these important?

Annotated reading

General

Kastenbaum, R.J. (1977) Death, Society and Human Experience. St Louis, Mo.: Mosby.

> Written by a psychologist, but for a general readership, this book provides broad coverage of the psychological and social aspects of death at a level that is readily understood, without being unduly simplistic. Relevant data are cited together with many illustrative examples. A good deal of space is given to concepts of death, from childhood to old age, and there are sections on bereavement and suicide. A few exercises for students are also included.

Terminal illness and dying

Hinton, J. (1972) Dying. Harmondsworth: Penguin.

> This is an eminently readable book by a psychiatrist with much practical experience of caring for the terminally ill and the dying. This experience enables Hinton to write with some authority on practical considerations and to place research findings in perspective. Relevant data are cited appropriately throughout the text and the book contains a good deal of useful information. The best sections are upon dying and the care of the dying and there is a concluding section on bereavement.

Doyle, D. (ed.) (1979) Terminal Care. Edinburgh: Churchill-Livingstone.

> This is a collection of papers arising from a multi-disciplinary conference. Accordingly, it provides useful reading for a wide range of health-care professionals including nurses, social workers and ministers of religion. In addition to examining the roles of different professions there are chapters on grief, domiciliary care and primary care.

Euthanasia

Glover, J. (1977) Causing Death and Saving Lives. Harmondsworth: Penguin.

> This is a clear and concise consideration of the ethical and practical problems associated with most aspects of taking life, from abortion to euthanasia. For those who want a brief but careful consideration of euthanasia and those who are seeking to place euthanasia in a wider context, this is a most valuable book.

Russell, R.O. (1977) Freedom to Die. New York: Human Sciences Press.

> Although the author examines arguments for and against the legalization of voluntary euthanasia, the tone of the volume is clearly in favour of this. The value of the book lies in its uncomplicated style, broad coverage and extensive appendices. In addition to examining the relevant arguments, the author traces the development of public awareness of euthanasia and attempts that have been made to promote the practice. The appendices include an example of the Living Will and various legislative proposals and bills that have been proposed in the UK and USA.

Bereavement

Parkes, C.M. (1972) Bereavement. London: Tavistock.

> This volume appeared in Pelican Books in 1975 and, although it is now beginning to age, it is probably the best single source of information on bereavement. The reader is taken progressively through the response to bereavement in its many manifestations and is provided with a clear account of grief, the factors that influence this and the nature of recovery. Illustrative examples and research findings are used throughout the text and the book concludes with a substantial section on helping the bereaved.

Smith, K. (1978) Helping the Bereaved. London: Duckworth.

> This is a short and unpretentious book aimed at a general readership. It is valuable for its reliance on the statements of bereaved people to convey powerfully the experience of grief and the range of emotions and events that commonly occur. The examples help one more accurately to empathize with the bereaved.

19

Psychopathology
D. A. Shapiro

'Psychopathology', literally defined, is the study of
disease of the mind. Our society entrusts most of the care
of individuals whose behaviour and experience are problematic or distressing to medical specialists (psychiatrists). Being medically trained, psychiatrists see their
work as requiring diagnosis and treatment of 'patients'.
Psychologists, on the other hand, have sought alternative
means of understanding abnormal behaviour, and the aim of
this chapter is to outline the progress that has been made
in this direction.

<table>
<tr><td>

**The varieties of
psychopathology**

</td><td>

A good way to appreciate the great variety of problems we
are concerned with is to examine the system of classifi-
cation used by psychiatrists, summarized in table 1. Readers
requiring more detailed descriptions of these should consult
a psychiatric textbook. In the NEUROSES, the personality and
perception of reality are fundamentally intact, although
emotional disturbances of one kind or another, usually
involving ANXIETY or its presumed effects, can make life
very difficult for the individual. The PSYCHOSES, on the
other hand, are characterized by gross impairments in per-
ception, memory, thinking and language functions, and the
individual is fundamentally disorganized, rather than merely
emotionally disturbed. However, there is no clear-cut brain
disease, and so the disorder cannot be explained in purely
biomedical terms. The layman's conception of 'madness' is
based on the symptoms of schizophrenia, including delusions
(unshakeable, false beliefs), hallucinations (such as hear-
ing 'voices') and thought disorder (manifested in 'garbled'
speech). The third category of table 1, PERSONALITY
DISORDERS, comprises deeply ingrained, motivational and
social maladjustments. Table 1 also includes ORGANIC
SYNDROMES, which are behaviour disorders associated with
identified brain disease. Not included in the table are the
important group of PSYCHOSOMATIC illnesses. These are
characterized by physical symptoms whose origins are in part
psychological (emotional). They include asthma, high blood
pressure, gastric and duodenal ulcers. More generally,
psychological stress is increasingly implicated in many
physical illnesses.

</td></tr>
</table>

Table 1

Major category	Neuroses (milder disturbances)				
Illustrative syndromes	Anxiety state	Obsessive-compulsive disorders	Phobias	Conversion reactions	Neurotic depression
Characteristic symptoms	Palpitation, tires easily, breathlessness, nervousness anxiety	Intrusive thoughts, urges to acts or rituals	Irrational fears of specific objects or situations	Physical symptoms, lacking organic cause	Hopelessness dejection

Major category	Psychoses (severe Non-organic disturbances		Personality disorders (antisocial disturbances)	Organic syndromes		
Illustrative syndromes	Affective disorders	Schizophrenia	Psychopathic personality	Alcoholism and drug dependence	Epilepsy	Severe mental handicap
Characteristic symptoms	Disturbances of mood, energy and activity patterns	Reality distortion, social withdrawal, disorganization of thought, perception and emotion	Lack of conscience	Physical or psychological dependence	Increased susceptibility to convulsions	Extremely low intelligence, social impairments

The medical model of psychopathology

Before describing psychological approaches to behaviour disorder, it is necessary to examine critically the predominant medical approach. This makes three major assumptions, which are considered in turn.

The diagnostic system

The first assumption of the medical model is that the various kinds of abnormal behaviour can be classified, by DIAGNOSIS, into SYNDROMES, or constellations of SYMPTOMS regularly occurring together. This diagnostic system has already been summarized in table 1. It has a number of disadvantages. First, some disorders appear to cut across the boundaries of the system. Thus an individual whose severe anxiety is associated with fears of delusional intensity may defy classification as 'neurotic' or 'psychotic'. Second, scientific studies of the ability of psychiatrists to agree on the diagnosis of individuals have suggested that the process is rather unreliable, with agreement ranging from about 50 per cent to 80 per cent depending upon the circumstances (Beck et al, 1962). Third, research also suggests that the diagnosis given to an individual may bear little relationship to the symptoms the individual has (Zigler and Philips, 1961). Fourth, the diagnosis of psychiatric disorder is much more subjective and reflective of cultural attitudes than is the diagnosis of physical illness; one culture's schizophrenic might be another's shaman; similar acts of violence might be deemed heroic in battle but psychopathic in peacetime. Careful comparisons of American and British psychiatrists have shown that the two groups use different diagnostic criteria and hence classify patients differently.

Despite these limitations, the psychiatric classification persists. This is largely because no better descriptive system has been developed, whilst improvements have been obtained in the usefulness of the system by refining it in the light of earlier criticisms. For example, agreement between psychiatrists has been improved by standardization of the questions asked in diagnostic interviews and the use of standard decision-rules for assigning diagnoses to constellations of symptoms. But it is still necessary to bear in mind that the diagnostic system is not infallible and the 'labels' it gives individuals should not be uncritically accepted.

Physiological basis of psychopathology

The second assumption of the medical model is that the symptoms reflect an underlying disease process, physiological in nature like those involved in all illnesses, causing the symptoms. Three kinds of evidence are offered in support of this. First, the influence of hereditary factors has been assessed by examining the rates of disorder among the relatives of sufferers. To the extent that a disorder is heritable, its origins are considered biological in nature. For example, comparison between the dizygotic (non-identical) and monozygotic (identical) twins of sufferers suggests that there is some hereditary involvement in schizophrenia, anxiety-related disorders, depression and antisocial disorders, with the evidence strongest in the case of schizophrenia (Gottesman and Shields, 1973). Studies of children adopted at birth also suggest that the offspring of schizophrenic parents are more liable to suffer from schizophrenia than other adopted children, despite having no contact with the biological parent. On the other hand, the evidence also shows that hereditary factors alone cannot fully account for schizophrenia or any other psychological disorder. Even amongst the identical twins of schizophrenics, many do not develop the disorder. Both hereditary and environmental influences are important.

The second line of evidence for a 'disease' basis of psychopathology concerns the biochemistry of the brain. This is a vastly complex subject, and one whose present methods of investigation are almost certainly too crude to give other than an approximate picture of what is going on. Over the years, a succession of biochemical factors have been suggested as causes for different forms of psychopathology. Unfortunately, the evidence is not conclusive, as biochemical factors found in sufferers may be consequences rather than causes. Hospital diets, activity patterns or characteristic emotional responses may influence the brain biochemistry of disordered individuals.

Despite these problems, there are some promising lines of biochemical research. For example, it has been suggested that schizophrenia may be caused by excess activity of dopamine, one of the neurotransmitters (substances with which neurons stimulate one another: see Snyder et al, 1974). This suggestion is supported by the similarity in molecular structure between dopamine and the phenothiazine drugs which are used to alleviate schizophrenia, suggesting that these drugs block the reception of dopamine by taking its place at receptors which normally receive it. These drugs also cause side effects resembling the symptoms of Parkinson's disease, which is associated with dopamine deficiency. Although this and other evidence supports the dopamine theory of schizophrenia, some research has failed to support it, and so the theory has yet to be universally accepted. In sum, biochemical evidence is suggestive, and consistent with presumed physiological origins of psychopathology, but it is not conclusive, nor can such evidence make a psychological explanation redundant. It is best seen as an important part of our understanding of psychopathology, whose causal significance varies from disorder to disorder.

The third line of evidence for the physiological basis of psychopathology concerns disorders with clear organic causes. Disease or damage to the brain can result in severe disturbance of behaviour. A classic example of this is 'general paresis of the insane', whose widespread physical and mental impairments were discovered in the last century to be due to the syphilis spirochete. This discovery encouraged medical scientists to seek clear-cut organic causes for other psychological abnormalities. A large number of ORGANIC BRAIN SYNDROMES have been established, in which widespread cognitive and emotional deficits are associated with damage to the brain by disease, infection, or injury. EPILEPSY, in which the individual is unusually susceptible to seizures or convulsions, is associated with abnormal patterns of brain activity measured by the electroencephalogram (EEG) even between seizures. Many individuals with severe MENTAL HANDICAP (Clarke and Clarke, 1974), who attain very low scores on tests of general intelligence and show minimal adaptation to social requirements and expectations, suffer from clear-cut organic pathology, often accompanied by severe physical abnormalities.

On the other hand, all of these disorders are affected by the person's individuality, experience and environment. For example, similar brain injuries result in very different symptoms in different individuals. Those suffering from epileptic seizures can make use of their past experience to avoid circumstances (including diet and environmental stimuli) which tend to trigger their convulsions. Most mentally handicapped people do not have clearly identifiable organic illnesses. Even amongst those who do, the environment can make a big difference to the person's ability to learn the skills of everyday living. Psychologists have found that special training can help mentally handicapped people who might otherwise appear incapable of learning.

Medical treatment of psychopathology

The third assumption of the medical model concerns how psychopathology should be managed. Physical treatments are offered in hospitals and clinics to persons designated 'patients'. It is beyond our present scope to describe the extensive evidence supporting the effectiveness of drugs and electro-convulsive therapy (ECT), the major physical treatments currently employed. However, there are several reasons why psychologists are often inclined to question the support this evidence gives to the medical model. First, individuals differ in their responsiveness to physical treatments, and nobody really understands why some individuals are not helped. Second, the fact that abnormal behaviour can be controlled by physical means does not prove that its origins are physical. Third, the physical treatments often lack a convincing scientific rationale to explain their effects.

The medical model: conclusions

In sum, the medical model gains some support from the evidence, but is sufficiently defective and incomplete to warrant the development of alternative and complementary approaches. Although the diagnostic system is of some value, it must be used with caution. Although hereditary influences, biochemical abnormalities and organic pathology have a part to play in our understanding of psychopathology, they cannot explain its origins without reference to environmental and psychological factors. The apparent efficacy of physical treatment does not establish the physical origins of what they treat. The remainder of this chapter is concerned with five alternative approaches developed by psychologists and social scientists, and assesses their contribution with respect to some of the most important kinds of psychopathology. The evidence presented is, of necessity, very selective, and a full appreciation of these approaches can only follow more extensive study. It should also be borne in mind that the present emphasis on origins of disorder entails a relative neglect of research on treatment.

The statistical model

The statistical model identifies individuals whose behaviour or reported experience is sufficiently unusual to warrant attention on that basis alone. Abnormal individuals are those who greatly differ from the average with respect to some attribute (such as intelligence or amount of subjective anxiety experienced). For example, according to Eysenck (1960), people who score highly on dimensions known as 'neuroticism' (very readily roused to emotion) and 'introversion' (quick in learning conditioned responses and associations) are likely to show what the psychiatrist calls 'anxiety neurosis'. Although this approach is commendably objective, it is not very helpful alone. Not all unusual behaviour is regarded as pathological. Exceptionally gifted people are an obvious case in point. Some statistically abnormal behaviours are obviously more relevant to psychopathology than are others, and we need more than a statistical theory to tell us which to consider, and why. But the model is of value for its suggestion that 'normal' and 'abnormal' behaviour may differ only in degree, in contrast to the medical model's implication of a sharp division between them.

The psychodynamic model

The psychodynamic model is very difficult to summarize, based as it is on theories developed early in the century by Freud, and revised and elaborated by him and subsequent workers within a broad tradition (Ellenberger, 1970). Like the medical model, it seeks an underlying cause for psychopathology, but this is a psychological cause, namely, unconscious conflicts arising from childhood experiences. Freudians have developed a general theory of personality from their study of psychopathology. Freud viewed the personality as comprising the conscious EGO, the unconscious ID (source of primitive impulses) and partly conscious, partly unconscious SUPER-EGO (conscience). The ego is held to protect itself from threat by several defence mechanisms. These are a commonplace feature of everyone's adjustment, but are used in an exaggerated or excessively rigid manner by neurotic individuals, and are overstretched to the point of collapse in the case of psychotic individuals.

For example, neurotic anxiety is learned by a child punished for being impulsive, whereupon the conflict between wanting something and fearing the consequences of that desire is driven from consciousness (this is an example of the defence mechanism known as REPRESSION). According to this theory, pervasive anxiety is due to fear of the person's ever-present id impulses, and phobic objects, such as insects or animals, are seen as symbolic representations of objects of the repressed id impulses. Dynamic theory views depression as a reaction to loss in individuals who are excessively dependent upon other people for the maintenance of self-esteem. The loss may be actual (as in bereavement) or symbolic (as in the misinterpretation of a rejection as a total loss of love). The depressed person expresses a child-like need for approval and affection to restore self-esteem. In psychotic disorders such as schizophrenia, the collapse of the defence mechanisms leads to the predominance of primitive 'primary process' thinking.

Despite its considerable impact upon the ways in which we understand human motivation and psychopathology, psychodynamic theory has remained controversial. Most of the evidence in its favour comes from clinical case material, as recounted by practising psychoanalysts, whose work is based on the belief that unconscious conflicts must be brought to the surface for the patient to recover from the symptoms they have engendered. Whilst this method often yields compelling material which is difficult to explain in other terms (Malan, 1979), it is open to criticism as insufficiently objective to yield scientific evidence. It is all too easy for the psychoanalyst unwittingly to influence the material produced by his patient, and the essential distinction between observations and the investigator's interpretations of them is difficult to sustain in the psychoanalytic consulting-room. The abstract and complex formulations of psychodynamic theory are difficult to prove or disprove by the clear-cut scientific methods favoured by psychologists, and the patients studied, whether in Freud's Vienna or present-day London or New York, are somewhat unrepresentative.

There is some scientific evidence which is broadly consistent with psychodynamic theory; for example, the defects in thinking found in schizophrenia are compatible with the dynamic concept of ego impairment, and loss events of the kind implicated by dynamic theory are associated with the onset of depression. Although psychologists hostile to dynamic theory can explain these findings in other terms, there is little doubt that the theory has been fruitful, contributing to psychology such essential concepts as unconscious conflict and defence mechanism.

The learning model

The learning model views psychopathology as arising from faulty learning in early life, and conceptualizes this process in terms of principles of learning drawn from laboratory studies of animals and humans. The most basic principles are those of Pavlovian or 'classical' conditioning (in which two stimuli are presented together until the response to one stimulus is also evoked by the other), and 'operant' conditioning (whereby behaviour with favourable consequences becomes more frequent). According to proponents of the learning model, the symptoms of psychopathology are nothing more than faulty habits acquired through these two types of learning. The 'underlying pathology' posited by the medical and psychodynamic models is dismissed as unfounded myth.

For example, it is suggested that phobias are acquired by a two-stage learning process; first, fear is aroused in

Psychopathology

response to a previously neutral stimulus when this stimulus occurs in conjunction with an unpleasant stimulus; then the person learns to avoid the situation evoking the fear, because behaviour taking the person away from the situation is rewarded by a reduction in fear. Another learning theory is that schizophrenic patients receive more attention and other rewards from other people, such as hospital staff, when they behave in 'crazy' ways, thereby increasing the frequency of this behaviour. Again, depressed people are seen as failing to exercise sufficient skill and effort to 'earn' rewards from situations and from other people; a vicious circle develops and activity reduces still further in the absence of such rewards.

In general, the learning model provides a powerful set of principles governing the acquisition of problem behaviour. But it has severe limitations. For example, the fact that fears and phobias can be established by processes of conditioning in the laboratory does not prove that this is how they come about naturally. The theory cannot readily explain how people acquire behaviours which lead to such distress (it is hardly 'rewarding' to suffer the agonies of depression or anxiety, and learning theorists acknowledge their difficulty over this fact by referring to it as the 'neurotic paradox'). Recently, learning theorists have examined the important process of imitative learning or modelling, whereby the behaviour of observers is influenced by another's actions and their consequences. Fear and aggression can be aroused in this way, with obvious implications for the transmission of psychopathology from one person (such as a parent) to another. But human thinking is considered by many psychologists too complex to be understood in terms of these relatively simple learning theories. Hence the development of the cognitive approach, to which we now turn.

The cognitive model

The cognitive model focusses upon thinking processes and their possible dysfunctions. 'Neurotic' problems are seen as due to relatively minor errors in reasoning processes, whilst 'psychotic' disorders are held to reflect profound disturbances in cognitive function and organization.

For example, it is well known that depressed people hold negative attitudes towards themselves, their experiences and their future. According to cognitive theory, these attitudes give rise to the feelings of depression (Beck, 1967). Although an episode of depression may be triggered by external events, it is the person's perception of the event which makes it set off depressed feelings. Experiments in which negative beliefs about the self are induced in non-depressed subjects have shown that a depressed mood does indeed follow. But whether similar processes account for the more severe and lasting depressive feelings of clinical patients is another matter, although the promising results of 'cognitive therapy', in which the attitudes of depressed patients are modified directly, may be taken as indirect evidence for the theory.

Cognitive theory also embraces people's beliefs about the causation of events (known as ATTRIBUTIONS). For example, it has been suggested that the attributions one makes concerning unpleasant experiences will determine the impact of those experiences upon one's subsequent beliefs about oneself; thus, if a woman is rejected by a man, this is much more damaging to her self-esteem if she believes that the main cause of the event is her own inadequacy, than if she attributes the event to the man's own passing mood. An attributional approach suggests that failure experiences are most damaging if the individual attributes them to wide-ranging and enduring factors within himself. Consistent with this, depressed people have been found to attribute bad outcomes to wide-ranging and enduring factors within themselves, whilst they attribute good outcomes to changeable factors outside their control.

Psychologists have devoted considerable efforts to precise descriptions of the cognitive deficits of schizophrenic patients through controlled laboratory experiments. For example, schizophrenics have difficulty performing tasks requiring selective attention to relevant information and the exclusion from attention of irrelevant information. Schizophrenics are highly distractable. This may help to explain how irrelevant features of a situation acquire disproportionate importance and become interpreted as part of their delusional systems of false beliefs, or how speech is disorganized by the shifting of attention to irrelevant thoughts and mental images which other people manage to ignore.

The cognitive approach is of great interest because it combines the systematic and objective methods of experimental psychology with a thoroughgoing interest in an important aspect of human mentality. It is a very active 'growth area' of current research, and shows considerable promise. It is perhaps too soon to evaluate many of its specific theories, however, and it does carry the risk of neglecting other aspects of human behaviour.

The socio-cultural model

The final model to be considered attributes psychopathology to social and cultural factors. It focusses upon malfunctioning of the social or cultural group rather than of an individual within that group.

In terms of the socio-cultural model schizophrenia, for example, has been considered both in relation to the quality of family life and to larger socio-economic forces. Within the family, behaviour labelled schizophrenic is seen as a response to self-contradictory emotional demands ('double binds') from other family members, notably parents, to which no sane response is possible. Although graphic accounts have been offered of such patterns in the family life of schizophrenic patients, there is no evidence that these are peculiar to such families. If anything, the research evidence suggests that abnormalities of communication within the families of schizophrenics arise in response to the behaviour of the patient, rather than causing the disorder. Looking beyond the family, the higher incidence of schizophrenia amongst the lowest socio-economic class, especially in inner city areas, is attributed to the multiple deprivations suffered by this group. Episodes of schizophrenia are triggered by stressful life events, some of which are more common, or less offset by social and material supports, amongst lower-class people. On the other hand, cause and effect could be the other way round, with persons developing schizophrenia 'drifting' into poverty-ridden areas of the city. Indeed, schizophrenic patients tend to achieve a lower socio-economic status than did their parents.

The socio-cultural approach is of undoubted value as a critical challenge to orthodox views, and has generated useful research into social and cultural factors in psychopathology. Its proponents have also made valuable contributions by bringing a greater humanistic respect for the personal predicament of troubled individuals, and to the development of 'therapeutic communities' and family therapy as alternatives to individually-centred treatments. However, many of its propositions concerning cause-effect relationships have not stood the test of empirical research.

The psychology of illness

It is well known that certain physical illnesses are related to psychological factors. These 'psychosomatic disorders' include ulcerative colitis, bronchial asthma and hypertension. It is not so widely appreciated, however, that psychological factors may be involved in ANY physical illness. This is because the physiological changes associated with stress (for instance, the release of the 'stress hormones' such as adrenalin) can suppress immune responses and so increase the individual's susceptibility to many diseases, ranging from the common cold to cancer (Rogers et al, 1979). Many aspects of a person's life have been implicated in ill-health, presumably because of their effects on such physiological mechanisms. These include physical stresses such as noise, highly demanding and/or repetitive jobs (whether physical or mental), catastrophic life events (such as accidents, illness or bereavement) and major emotional difficulties (such as marital discord).

However, for physical illness as for psychopathology, the cause-effect relationship is not simple. Some individuals are more constitutionally stress-prone than others, it appears. Some people live in congenial and supportive surroundings, enabling them to withstand pressures which might otherwise lead to illness. Most of the events implicated in psychological distress and ill-health are in part the results of the individual's own state and behaviour. For example, marital conflict may reflect prior strains felt by the individuals involved. Furthermore, the impact of a stressful event or circumstance depends on the individual's appraisal of it. For example, noise is less distressing if we know we can silence it should it become unbearable. Thus consideration of psychological factors in ill-health demonstrates clearly the interaction between features of individuals and of their surroundings. For physical illness as for psychopathology, we must realize that there are many interacting causes rather than imagine that any one factor is alone responsible for the problem at issue.

Conclusions

Each of the approaches surveyed has contributed to our understanding of psychopathology. The evidence presented for each can only illustrate the massive amounts of research which have been carried out. Nonetheless, several clear themes emerge which have profound implications for our present and future knowledge of psychopathology.

First, the system of classification is inadequate, and research shows that different people within the same broad diagnostic group (such as schizophrenia) behave very differently; it therefore follows that different causes may be found for the difficulties experienced by these sub-groups of people.

Second, the different approaches could profitably be integrated rather more than they have been in the past. For example, elements of the medical, statistical, socio-cultural and cognitive approaches have been combined in recent work on schizophrenia, in which the vulnerability of an individual to the disorder is seen as reflecting both heredity and environment; this vulnerability determines whether or not a person experiences schizophrenia when he faces stresses which are too much for him to cope with (Zubin and Spring, 1977). The fact that psychopathology generally has multiple causes lends particular urgency to the need to construct broad theories incorporating the facts which were hitherto regarded as supporting one or another of the competing approaches.

Third, the different approaches have more in common than is often acknowledged. In relation to schizophrenia, for example, the breakdown of ego functioning described by psychodynamic theory resembles the inability to process information identified by cognitive theory.

Fourth, the limitations of existing models have encouraged the growth of alternative approaches. For example, the 'transactional' approach emphasizes the importance of the individual's active part in bringing about apparently external stressful events and pressures (Cox, 1978). This approach views the individual as neither a passive victim of circumstances, nor as irrevocably programmed from birth to respond in a particular way. Person and environment are seen as in continuous interaction, so that one-way cause-effect analysis is inappropriate. For example, harassed executives and mothers of small children bring some of the stress they suffer upon themselves as they respond sharply to colleagues or children and thus contribute to a climate of irritation or conflict. Research using this approach has only recently begun, but it holds considerable hope for the future. Finally, what can this psychological study of psychopathology offer the professional? There are as yet no certain answers to such simple questions as 'What causes schizophrenia?' or 'Why does Mrs Jones stay indoors all the time?' If and when such answers become available, they will not be simple. They will involve many interacting factors. Meanwhile, the psychological approach teaches us a healthy respect for the complexity of the human predicament, and is a valuable corrective to any tendency to offer simplistic or unsympathetic explanations of human distress. Furthermore, professionals will often find it illuminating to apply some of the approaches outlined here to help understand distressed individuals they encounter in their daily work.

References

Beck, A.T. (1967)
Depression: Clinical, experimental and theoretical aspects. New York: Harper & Row.

Beck, A.T., Ward, C.H., Mendleson, M., Mock, J.E. and Erlbaugh, J. (1962)
Reliability of psychiatric diagnosis II: a study of consistency of clinical judgements and ratings. American Journal of Psychiatry, 119, 351-357.

Clarke, A.M. and Clarke, A.D.B. (1974)
Mental Deficiency: The changing outlook (3rd edn). London: Methuen.

Cox, T. (1978)
Stress. London: Macmillan.

Ellenberger, H.F. (1970)
The Discovery of the Unconscious. London: Allen Lane/ Penguin.

Eysenck, H.J. (1960)
The Structure of Human Personality. London: Methuen.

Gottesman, I.I. and Shields, J. (1973)
Genetic theorising and schizophrenia. British Journal of Psychiatry, 122, 15-30.

Malan, D.H. (1979)
Individual Psychotherapy and the Science of Psychodynamics. London: Tavistock.

Rogers, M.P., Dubey, D. and Reich, P. (1979)
The influence of the psyche and the brain on immunity and disease susceptibility: a critical review. Psychosomatic Medicine, 41, 147-164.

Snyder, S.H., Banerjee, S.P., Yamamura, H.I. and Greenberg, D. (1974)
Drugs, neurotransmitters and schizophrenia. Science, 184, 1243-1253.

Zigler, E. and Philips, L. (1961)
Psychiatric diagnosis and symptomalogy. Journal of Abnormal and Social Psychology, 63, 69-75.

Zubin, J. and Spring, B. (1977)
Vulnerability - a new view of schizophrenia. Journal of
Abnormal Psychology, 86, 103-126.

Questions

1. Outline the psychiatric system of classification.
2. What problems are raised by the diagnostic system used by psychiatrists? Can it be improved?
3. What can the study of twins tell us about psychopathology?
4. Outline the evidence for a biochemical basis for schizophrenia.
5. Give an example of psychopathology with a known organic cause, and explain what this cause is. Do environmental factors play any part in the disorder you have described?
6. How useful is the medical model of psychopathology? Does it have any disadvantages?
7. Outline the statistical approach to psychopathology, indicating its value and limitations.
8. What are defence mechanisms, and how are they involved in psychopathology?
9. Compare and contrast the explanations of phobias offered by psychodynamic and learning theories.
10. What is wrong with psychoanalysis as a scientific method of investigating psychopathology?
11. Outline some differences between neurotic and psychotic disorders.
12. How might you recognize depression in a client or pupil you encountered in the course of your professional work?
13. Is psychopathology simply behaviour which has been learned because it produces rewards?
14. What is the importance of self-esteem in psychopathology?
15. How can family life affect well-being and psychopathology?
16. Which of the models of psychopathology do you prefer? Give your reasons.
17. How can psychological factors affect susceptibility to physical illness?
18. 'The child is father to the man'. Does this statement gain support from psychological research into psychopathology?
19. Sometimes people confuse 'mental illness' and 'mental handicap'. How would you explain the difference to a colleague or student?
20. Which forms of psychopathology would be particularly disabling to a person employed in your profession, and why?

Annotated reading

Davison, G.C. and Neale, J.M. (1977) Abnormal Psychology: An experimental clinical approach (2nd edn). Chichester: Wiley.

> The chapter can provide no more than an introduction to psychopathology. This is the best of the textbooks available: it is readable, comprehensive and, in general, accurate. It is useful in teaching, and has been drawn upon extensively for drafting the chapter. If you want to follow up any aspect of the chapter in more detail, look up the topic in the Index of this book.

Hilgard, E.R., Atkinson, R.L. and Atkinson, R.C. (1979) Introduction to Psychology (7th edn). New York: Harcourt Brace Jovanovich (chapters 14, 15 and 16).

> Intermediate in length between the present chapter and the Davison and Neale book, this group of chapters gives a good general account. Chapter 14 reviews conflict and stress in terms of both experimental and psychoanalytic work; chapter 15 gives a good outline of much of the ground covered in this chapter; and chapter 16 discusses methods of treatment.

Spielberger, C. (1979) Understanding Stress and Anxiety. New York: Harper & Row.

> A very readable and well-illustrated introduction to experimental and clinical work on stress and anxiety, recommended for the student wishing to look further into these aspects.

Seligman, M.E.P. (1975) Helplessness: On depression, development and death. New York: Freeman.

> Seligman presents his theory of learned helplessness in a very stimulating and engaging book. Although the theory was based on laboratory studies with animals, Seligman has injected a great deal of 'human interest' into this account. Students who are especially interested in the theory of depression should note, however, that Seligman's ideas have moved on since the book was written to incorporate attributional concepts.

Stafford-Clark, D. and Smith, A.C. (1979) Psychiatry for Students (5th edn). London: Allen & Unwin.

> The present chapter does not attempt to do full justice to psychiatry. This is the most readable of the general textbooks on psychiatry, written for students rather than for practitioners. It is a good source for more details of psychiatric symptoms, disorders and treatments.

Inechen, B. (1979) Mental Illness. London: Longman.

> This reviews the field from a sociological viewpoint, and covers a good deal of research on social factors in psychopathology.

Bannister, D. and Fransella, F. (1971) Inquiring Man.
Harmondsworth: Penguin.
   A persuasive account of George Kelly's personal
   construct approach to psychology and psychopathology,
   written by two of its leading exponents.

20

Interviewing
Russell P. Wicks

If there is one universally applied technique to be found
in behavioural research it is 'interviewing'. If there is
one technique basic to all professional practice it is the
interaction between people that is called 'interviewing'. It
is the nature of this interaction between people which is
the concern of this chapter. It is to be hoped that what
is said can be applied not simply to 'the interview' in
'an interview situation' but to all purposive contacts
between individuals, the critical feature, it is claimed,
being the purposive nature of the encounter. The participants bring hopes, fears, expectations, misconceptions and
many other cognitions to the situation most times in the
hope that their wishes will be met, fears reduced and so on.
Customarily this view is found in the characterization of an
interview as a 'conversation with a purpose'. So it is, but
ALL those participating in an interview have their purposes
and not simply, for example, the interviewer. In the complex
transactions of getting and giving information we observe
effort aimed at achieving purposes. Thus the psychologist
testing a client by means of, say, the Wechsler Adult
Intelligence Scale is conducting an interview as defined.
The purpose from one point of view is to help the client in
some way, from the other to be helped. In the exchange of
information each has purposes and expectations that they
hope will be met. Each may be optimizing their strategies
towards fulfilling these purposes. Roles will be assumed
constraining and shaping behaviour. If participants in
interviews can become more skilful and aware of the processes involved there is some hope of raising levels of
satisfaction. It is, therefore, the aim of this chapter to
examine such interview processes with this goal in mind. For
this purpose a simple model of an interview will be described (see figure 1) and for illustrative purposes reference made to three particular interview situations;
occupational counselling, job interviews and research
interviewing.

Initiation

The view that it is the purposive nature of the interview that is crucial leads us to consider the motives of the
participants. An individual approaching a counselling

Figure 1

Model of an interview

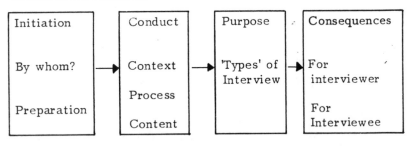

situation may be motivated by a complex of needs and voluntary or compulsory attendance may be crucial in structuring
these needs. Whether these needs are shared and whether they
can be fulfilled is another matter. It may well be the case
that some frequently voiced criticisms of interviews arise,
in part, from a failure to make explicit the needs and
expectations of the parties involved. Nowhere is this more
important than in those situations with a high level of
emotional involvement. Two people may look back on an
interview as a total failure because each had different
expectations which unfortunately were not fulfilled. We all,
interviewers and interviewees, bring hopes and fears to the
task. Just as Orne (1962) draws our attention to the 'demand
characteristics' of the experimental situation as a result
of which subjects perform as they believe they are expected
so to do, so participants in interviews will seek a role
that they perceive as being appropriate. Not always,
unfortunately, do they choose correctly.

In analysing an interview it follows, therefore, that
attention to preliminaries and preparation is vital. Many
writers on interviewing stress the physical preparations
needed, literally setting the scene. Here, 'cognitive' scene
setting is judged to be more important; for example, in
employment interviewing paying attention to providing
information about the organization, or providing an adequate
job description. Considering the contribution of application
forms and references, together with other 'scene setting'
activities, will go a long way towards minimizing the cognitive gap that may occur. Furthermore, such preparations
are in fact part of the information exchange that lies at
the heart of an interview. In general, preparation from the
interviewer's point of view means careful planning of all
aspects of the situation. Briefing oneself, rehearsing the
interview, anticipating needs; all contribute to an
efficiently managed, worth-while encounter.

Recently, increasing attention has been given to preparation on the part of the interviewee, especially for
those about to be interviewed for a job. For example, a
great deal of work stemming from careers work with young
people has resulted in programmes aimed at developing 'life

skills'. There is clear evidence that all can profit from paying attention to the activities and skills involved in job seeking. The material included in such programmes varies widely but may cover:

* where to get job information;
* work experience;
* how to reply to advertisements;
* how to become more self-aware;
* how to be interviewed.

The techniques employed range from self-instructional material to the use of video-recording of role-play situations. In general, however, the emphasis is on providing guidelines, improving social skills, self-presentation and making people more aware of the processes of social interaction.

Conduct

Context

What effect on the behaviour of the participants in an interview might the following environments have: a police station; a doctor's surgery; a street corner; a psychology laboratory? Clearly the effect can be dramatic. We have the clearest evidence here for the importance of the frame of reference, role expectations and construal of the situation upon behaviour in an interview. Indeed, the subtlety of the rules of the 'games' played out in different contexts is such that we spend our lives refining and editing our private rule books. Within each context there may be a range of indicators signalling to us how to behave, how to address people, what to say and what not to say, an obvious example being dress, particularly a uniform which may be anything from a pin-stripe suit to a white coat. What is the experience of people who customarily wear a 'uniform' when they discard it? What might people say to a priest in mufti that they would not say if he donned his clerical garb? Thus our perception of the interview context is an essential part of the scene setting previously discussed. Most interviewers, being aware of this, go to some trouble to ensure that the physical setting signals what they wish it to: they dress in a particular style, arrange the seats appropriately, adjust the lighting, ensure that interruptions do or do not occur. They try to ensure that the interview is conducted in a 'good mannered' way.

A further aspect is that participants bring substantial resources to the task: their background knowledge, and skills expectations. Whilst these resources may bring benefits to an interview, they sometimes create problems. Such difficulties have been extensively investigated by Rosenthal (1969) and his co-workers in studies of the characteristics of 'volunteers' in research and studies of the expectations of subjects in experiments, as well as the experimenters. Avoiding bias and error arising from these factors is a major concern of investigators; thus one should be aware that volunteers for survey research tend to be better educated, if male score higher on IQ tests, and are better adjusted than non-volunteers. Such factors should be taken into account in evaluating data. Similarly, the survey interviewer asked to find a sample of five people, even though certain characteristics of the sample are specified, may unwittingly choose those they feel it would be 'nice' to interview.

Process

A great deal of what we know about interpersonal communication has been learnt by systematic study of interviews, especially the face-to-face two-person encounter. What is offered here, however, is a general communication model which may be used to analyse an interview (see figure 2). The utility of this model as a tool for examining inter-personal behaviour rests upon the conceptualization of communication as a system; the model is dynamic because it has independent parts with provision for feedback.

Figure 2

A communication model

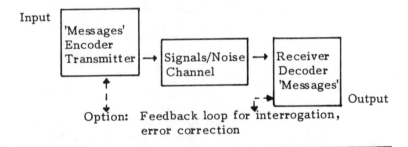

Option: Feedback loop for interrogation, error correction

Such a model could stand for many communication systems; radio or television tranmission, a nervous system or, in this case, an interview. A useful procedure arising from the 'system' model is that we can examine its integrity. In other words, we can see what happens when one part of the system is distorted or eliminated. Examples of this approach are given in the exercises included in the teaching material for this volume.

In this model, 'message' is taken to stand for that which we wish to transmit. Embedded in this is the difficult problem of meaning and an obvious use of the model is to compare inputs and outputs according to some criterion of meaningfulness. Such a comparison is the basis of an often hilarious game in which the distortion occurring when a 'message' is passed along a line of people by word of mouth is examined. Bartlett (1972) showed in his method of serial reproduction the simplifications and intrusions which occur in this process.

Within the interview, 'meaning' arises at a number of levels. First, at the level of verbal content. What was the question and what is the answer? Much has been written about asking the right sort of question in an interview, whether to use direct or indirect questions, the appropriate form of words, and the dangers of certain questions such as leading or multiple forms. Skilful interviewers do not seem to be constrained by rigid rules but show flexibility, constantly probing and following up interesting leads. They tend to ask: 'Tell me', 'When was that?', 'How was that?', 'What did you do?' and perhaps the most difficult question of all, 'Why?'

Second, the question of meaning arises at the level of recording the interview material. What gets lost or distorted when an interviewer distils a reply into notes or makes a decision? Third, a consideration arising especially in the research interview is: what has happened to the original meaning when a response is coded, probably into a pre-determined category, and is lumped together with others when the study is reported?

However, the verbal content of the message is only a small part of the signal. Many researchers assert that the non-verbal component of a signal is of greater importance. Argyle (1973, 1975) in particular has drawn our attention to the role of non-verbal communication factors such as:

* bodily movements: body language: gestures;
* facial expression;
* eye movements and eye contact;
* personal space: proximity.

The socially skilled performer is simultaneously transmitting signals using all these components together with verbal material whilst reacting to similar signals constituting feedback from their partner.

Utilizing and decoding this complex of information involves us in consideration of interpersonal perception, a key area in the analysis of interviewing. How we form judgements about other people is at the heart of interview decisions: the substantial literature on this topic, for example Cook (1979), suggests that the information we use includes:

* a person's actions;
* the situation in which the person is observed;
* appearance - including facial expression, physique, speech characteristics and dress style;
* non-verbal cues mentioned previously.

The powerful influence of some cues is seen most clearly in the study of stereotypes. Picking up one piece of information and building often unwarranted assumptions upon it is the classic error in judging others. Reacting to a regional accent, to hair colour, to ethnic origin or any other isolated item is all too common. Such a reaction, especially to irrelevant information, is usually dubbed the 'halo effect'. Since the judge or interviewer is striving for cognitive consistency, information is often interpreted in such a way that it fits this single judgement. Thus favourable material or even attributions will be ascribed to a liked person. Contrariwise, undue weight may be given to negative indications in the case of dislike. Clearly, interviewers must be constantly on their guard against introducing bias of this kind. Awareness of their prejudices and the sorts of errors we make in judging others will help.

It is the process component of interviewing which has received most attention in the training of interviewers. Such training commonly takes the form of general social skills training together with exercises directed at the specialization of the interviewer; for example, obtaining clinically relevant material in the hospital setting. Just how effective training may be is not easy to assess. Largely this is so because published studies of interview training tend to use different criteria, thus making comparisons difficult. The benefits to the trainee probably come from receiving informed feedback in role-playing or group tasks about their performance together with enhanced self-awareness.

Content

The point has been made that the absence of a shared common aim or lack of a clear plan in an interview leads to many difficulties. Specifically, criticisms in terms of interview decisions tend to the view that they may leave much to be desired. It is claimed, for example, that the research literature points overwhelmingly in this direction. Without wishing to dismiss the many studies leading to this conclusion, it must be pointed out that they cover a wide range of interview outcomes made by many interviewers at different levels of experience and training with their decisions based on imprecise criteria. The message of these studies seems to be that all concerned with interviews should be aware of the shortcomings and take steps to overcome them. Apart from errors arising from factors already mentioned in describing context and process aspects at an interview, the principal source is often the lack of a clear plan for an interview; in other words, content must be tailored to the particular aim in mind, each interview requiring careful planning with preparation related to a desired outcome. By way of illustration let us consider the content of interviews within the three professional contexts of counselling, job interviews and research interviewing.

Counselling: occupational guidance
What is the aim of an occupational guidance procedure? At one time the approach was modelled upon the notion of talent matching. Specify the job, specify the man and attempt to

match the two. On the job side of the equation, techniques of task analysis, job description and content specification were developed whilst evidence of congruent relevant behaviour was sought from the interviewee. It is no coincidence that the heyday of this approach coincided with the early boom in psychological test production. Aptitude tests, occupational interest guides, and tests of specific skills were all produced to aid the matching. Today, with the application of computer-based matching procedures, the approach is enjoying a revival. The role of the interview in this model was largely to establish the congruence of job and applicant profiles by comparison through discussion. From this approach evolved the contemporary developmental model, with an emphasis on career decision making as a process over time, starting in the early years with educational counselling, proceeding to occupational counselling and then to career development counselling, with perhaps counselling for retirement in later years. Thus there may be many interviews within this model each with a specific aim, the sum aimed at the overall development of the individual. Among the sub-goals of this process we can recognize the following:

* self-appraisal: equipping the client to achieve realistic self-assessment;
* self-perception: providing frames of reference, categories of occupationally significant behaviours;
* job perception: acquiring the skills required to assess the world of work in terms of job content, values, roles and life style;
* reality testing: matching aspirations and goals with opportunities within one's limitations;
* setting goals and objectives: specifying attainable goals and precise objectives;
* hypothesis generation: helping the client to generate occupational 'theories';
* interaction of the person and the job environment: examining the complexities of the person/work situation interaction;
* sharing information: providing the client with educational and occupational information, and providing the counsellor with perceptions of the client;
* task setting: translating immediate goals into discrete tasks, such as finding an address, seeking information, reading a pamphlet, etc.

The task of the interviewer/counsellor therefore becomes that of achieving these goals at the appropriate time and in a manner which meets the client's needs. Flexibility, wide background knowledge and the ability to relate to the client are clearly prerequisites on the part of the counsellor. Similar goals are shared by modern staff appraisal schemes and staff development procedures.

Job interviews

Being interviewed for a job, for promotion or for annual
assessment is probably the most commonly experienced form
of interview. It has certainly attracted a substantial body
of folk-lore, myth, jokes and hard-luck stories. That this
is so is, in itself, of considerable psychological significance. The job interview comes in many varieties, not least
the panel interview. Here especially the crucial importance
of planning an interview is seen. The justifiable criticism
of such encounters is frequently due first to poor interviewing skills on the part of the individual board members,
and second to the lack of an agreed role for each.

Whilst not normally included under the heading of
interviews, such behavioural observation techniques as role-
playing by candidates, group discussions, problem-solving
exercises and others raise the same problems previously
mentioned of reliable and valid judgements about other
people.

Two examples of interview plans used in job interviews
will be presented here: one is a general approach commonly
employed, namely, the biography; the second a well-known
technique called the Seven-Point Plan.

THE BIOGRAPHY: the majority of job interviews employ this
approach, often, however, in an undisciplined fashion,
hunting and pecking at a person's history. However, a simple
structure which can be readily shared consists of establishing landmarks within relevant areas; commonly times of
change such as leaving school. Bearing in mind the selectivity of recall, in itself an important indicator within an
interview, and that the recent past may be more accessible,
one should not expect uniform coverage of a life history.
This raises the problem of breadth and depth within the
interview in relation to the relevance of the information.
Too often an interviewer will spend time on an irrelevant
area, missing the opportunity to explore a significant point
in detail.

However, a plan such as that shown in figure 3 provides
a secure frame of reference for interviewer and interviewee.
Not least, the interviewee can be assembling information and
anticipating questions; the task is not unlike talking
through a curriculum vitae. A final benefit of this approach
is that it enables the interviewer to check dates, spot gaps
in the account and draw out the inter-relationships between

Figure 3

	Education	Interests	Home	Work
The past Landmarks The present	Dates			

events. This approach is underpinned by application forms and curricula vitae, which are customarily set out in biographical order.

THE SEVEN-POINT PLAN: probably the best known of all assessment and interview formats, the plan was originally developed by Alec Rodger within the framework of the talent matching approach to occupational guidance. It was intended to apply to both candidates and jobs, to obtain relevant information about people and by asking the same questions of a job to facilitate matching.

The plan was rapidly adopted for job interviewing and has undoubtedly been highly influential insofar as it provides the unskilled interviewer with a robust, easily understood framework within which to work. Over the years, a number of modifications have been suggested to the original plan. Similarly based schemes have been published, but what is essentially the original is presented here (Rodger, 1974).

1. Physical characteristics:
   Physical abilities of occupational importance.
   State of health. Vision, hearing. Appearance. Speech.
2. Attainments (and previous experience):
   Educational background, achievements. Occupational and professional training. Experience. How well has this person done? Personal achievements in any area: sports, pursuits, etc.
3. General ability:
   Especially general intelligence and cognitive skills - words, numbers, relationships.
4. Special aptitudes:
   Particularly occupationally applicable talents - scientific, mechanical, mathematical, practical, literary, artistic, social skills.
5. Interests:
   Often the core information: type of interests, how they are pursued, to what effect. Intellectual, practical, physical, social and artistic interests may be occupationally significant.
6. Personality:
   What is this person like? Especially in terms of self-perception. Social relationships, behaviour indicative of self-reliance, dependability.
7. Circumstances:
   The context of the person's life insofar as it affects his aspirations. Family circumstances, financial background, current problems.

The first six points apply particularly to the study of jobs. What physical characteristics, what attainments and so on are required for this job? It should be added that Rodger emphasized the importance of paying attention to individual likes and dislikes, to difficulties or distastes mentioned by people, and to the individual's strengths and weaknesses when applying the plan; in particular, stressing the importance of negative information in making selection decisions and the noting of danger signs.

Finally, in considering job interviews it should be noted that advice and preparation for interviewees is widely available in relation to the job interview. Social skills training, and self-presentation courses are examples.

Research interviews

The place of the interview in social research is central. Its contribution ranges from preliminary information gathering to a place as the principal research tool. Clearly it takes many forms but the main dimension along which it varies is that of being unstructured/structured, from free to semi to structured. Here, the highly structured form typically found in market research and surveys will be considered, the characteristics of the unstructured form being similar to counselling interviews. For the structured approach a unique feature is the use of an interview schedule: in effect, a carefully prepared script meticulously adhered to by the interviewer. A great deal of thought is put into preparing the schedule in order that question form and content, question order, response mode, use of response aids and other factors can be taken into account.

Customarily these factors are checked by conducting pilot studies. Another feature of research interviewing is the attention paid to teaching interviewers how to present a particular schedule, together with supervision of their work in the field. Finally, since it is often the case that large numbers of respondents are involved, it is usual to design the schedules with data analysis in mind. For example, the coding of responses by interviewers for data entry.

As an example of research interviewing the approach of the Government Social Survey is now described. The Social Survey began work dealing with wartime problems of the 1940s. It is now a Division of the Office of Population Censuses and Surveys carrying out a wide range of studies of social and economic interest for public departments. A detailed description of the practices and procedures it employs is to be found in the handbook for interviewers (Atkinson, 1971).

Steps in producing such surveys include:

* identifying research question: decide on form and content of survey, consider costs;
* draft proposals: content of schedule, sampling of respondents;
* pilot stage: explore degree of structure appropriate, such as free to highly. Coding of replies. Analyse pilot material;
* brief and train interviewers: careful training including practice on schedule. How to contact the public.

Identifying the person to be interviewed (e.g. by age, sex, role). Putting over the purpose of the survey; problem of refusals or non-co-operation. Conducting the interview: defining the roles of interviewer and informant;

* timetable: prepare addresses, number of interviewees, target dates;

* carry out field survey: interviewers adhere to research officers' instructions on each question. Comprehend the purpose of each question: (i) factual information; (ii) expression of opinion; (iii) attitude measures.

Deploy response modes without distortion: open questions with free response, closed/forward choice questions with pre-coded or scaled responses. Interviewers practise use of response aids: prompt cards for scaled responses, self-completion scales, repertory grids, examples of products in market research.

Interviewers pay particular attention to prompting and probing. Guard against distortion in recording data: both precoded and open response items are susceptible;

* coding: check schedules and categorize response;
* computing: produce tables, analyse data;
* conclusion: write report.

Purpose

At this stage in the discussion of our model of an interview it must be clear that so many varieties exist as to demand careful consideration of each in terms of purpose. The variety of purposes has been mentioned, and also that the approach may vary from structured to unstructured according to purpose. Thus a number of recognizable forms of interview have emerged to meet particular needs. Examples include:

* non-directive counselling, client-centred therapy;
* psychotherapeutic encounters of many kinds;
* depth interviews emphasizing motivational factors;
* group interviews involving a number of respondents in a discussion group type format;
* psychological testing, especially individual tests such as WAIS (Wechsler Adult Intelligence Scale);
* problem-solving interviews such as individual role-playing for a variety of purposes.

Consequences

Accepting the purposive nature of the interview implies that outcomes are important for all concerned and that their nature depends on the situation, and not least how the situation is perceived. For the interviewer, this will involve achieving the particular aims which have been identified together with maintenance of professional competence; for example, in the research interview maintaining the validity, reliability and precision of data with errors eliminated as far as possible.

For the interviewee or respondent one might ask: what do they get out of the experience? All too often what might be called the public relations aspect of interviewing is ignored. Symptoms of this include fears on the part of correspondents regarding the confidentiality of data, or that in some way they are being threatened. Such considerations appear to bring us full circle, for if attention is paid to the initiation stage of the proceedings by way of setting the scene such alarms can be reduced. Nevertheless, the sometimes necessary use of subterfuge in research needs to be handled with great care, a minimum requirement being the provision of an adequate explanation after the event on an account of the research.

References

Argyle, M. (1973)
Social Interaction. London: Tavistock.
Argyle, M. (1975)
Bodily Communication. London: Methuen.
Atkinson, J. (1971)
A Handbook for Interviewers (2nd edn). London: HMSO.
Bartlett, F.C. (1932)
Remembering. Cambridge: Cambridge University Press.
Cook, M. (1979)
Perceiving Others. London: Methuen.
Orne, M.T. (1962)
On the social psychology of the psychological experiment. American Psychologist, 17, 776-783.
Rodger, A. (1974)
Seven Point Plan. London: NFER.
Rosenthal, R. and Rosnow, R.L. (1969)
The volunteer subject. In R. Rosenthal and R.L. Rosnow (eds), Artifact in Behavioral Research. New York: Academic Press.

Questions

1. 'The interview is a wide-band procedure with low fidelity'. Discuss.
2. Assess the contribution of the study of social skills to the improvement of job selection interviewing.
3. 'Interviewing is the most commonly used selection tool'. Why do you think this is and what else are its strengths and weaknesses?
4. What future do you see for the interview?
5. Discuss the significance of role expectations for the conduct of an interview.
6. Write an account of the function of non-verbal communication in the interview.
7. Critically assess the form of an interview in a counselling situation with which you are familiar.
8. What are the advantages and disadvantages of using a scheme such as the Seven Point Plan for job interviewing?

9. Identify common sources of error in research interviewing. How might these be eliminated?
10. Choose a particular type of interview and design an appropriate interviewer training course.

Annotated reading

Anstey, E. (1976) An Introduction to Selection Interviewing. London: HMSO.

Originally prepared for staff training in the Civil Service, this practical guide is useful for the advice it gives on general preparation for selection interviewing as well as the conduct of interviews.

Bingham, W.V. and Moore, B.V. (1959) How to Interview (4th edn). New York: Harper & Row.

A classic work. An early attempt to offer general guidance for those engaged in selection, survey interviews and counselling. Rather general in its approach.

Cannel, C.F. and Kahn, R.L. (1968) Interviewing. In G. Lindzey and E. Aronson (eds), The Handbook of Social Psychology, Volume II: Research methods (2nd edn). London: Addison-Wesley.

A systematic account of the research interview. Tends towards a theoretical presentation, problems of reliability and validity and measurement using interview data being examples. Includes discussion of interview technique, question form and the training of interviewers.

Cross, C.P. (1974) Interviewing and Communication in Social Work. London: Routledge & Kegan Paul.

A useful guide to the 'helping' interview. Represents the movement towards enhancing social skills of all involved in such encounters.

Sidney, E. and Brown, M. (1973) The skills of Interviewing. London: Tavistock.

Aimed at managers, especially personnel staff. A generally acclaimed book, based on the extensive experience of the authors, it offers a very practical guide to the selection interview.

Sidney, E., Brown, M. and Argyle, M. (1973) Skills with People. London: Hutchinson.

A guide for managers. Concerns itself with a wide range of topics: communication in general, social skills, interviews, meetings and committees, interpersonal skills and training in social skills.

Ungerson, B. (ed.) (1975) Recruitment Handbook (2nd edn).
London: Gower Press.
Very useful guide to the context of job interviewing,
preparing job specifications, advertising, references;
all the supporting activities of selection are covered.

Index